T0328845

The Big End of Town

BIG BUSINESS AND CORPORATE LEADERSHIP IN TWENTIETH-CENTURY AUSTRALIA

Never before has a book been published which provides such a comprehensive study of Australian corporate leadership over the past 100 years. *The Big End of Town* is the first proper national business history of twentieth-century Australia. This book traces the evolution of large business enterprises in Australia, from the giants of the nineteenth century — such as Dalgety, CSR and BHP — to the contemporary leaders in News Corporation and Qantas. It delves into why the market leaders became the major players, examines what was crucial to their success, and their roles in leading the Australian economy. By investigating their evolution, this book provides a useful evaluation of the factors that have led to their competitive success and provides an essential guide for all businesses in Australia and beyond.

Grant Fleming is a senior lecturer in the School of Finance at the Australian National University and Vice-President, Wilshire Australia. David Merrett is an associate professor in the Department of Management at the University of Melbourne, and recently edited *Business Institutions and Behaviour in Australia*. Simon Ville is Professor of Economics at the University of Wollongong. He is the author of several books including *The Rural Entrepreneurs* and *The Development of Modern Business*.

'Nothing even remotely like it has been published in Australia. It will be widely quoted for many years to come.'
Geoffrey Blainey

'There is nothing like it available. The volume is in the tradition of others that deal with the major industrial nations around the world.'
Mira Wilkins, Florida International University

The Big End of Town

Big Business and Corporate Leadership in Twentieth-Century Australia

GRANT FLEMING, DAVID MERRETT
AND SIMON VILLE

CAMBRIDGE
UNIVERSITY PRESS

CAMBRIDGE UNIVERSITY PRESS
Cambridge, New York, Melbourne, Madrid, Cape Town, Singapore,
São Paulo, Delhi, Dubai, Tokyo

Cambridge University Press
The Edinburgh Building, Cambridge CB2 8RU, UK

Published in the United States of America by Cambridge University Press, New York

www.cambridge.org
Information on this title: www.cambridge.org/9780521689908

First published 2004

A catalogue record for this publication is available from the British Library

National Library of Australia Cataloguing in Publication data
Fleming, Grant A., 1964— .
   The big end of town: big business and corporate leadership
   in twentieth-century Australia.
   Bibliography.
   Includes index.
   ISBN 0 521 83311 6.
   1. Big business — Australia — History. 2. Corporations —
   Australia — History. I. Ville, Simon P. II. Merrett,
   David, 1944—   . III. Title.
338.740994

ISBN 978-0-521-83311-0 Hardback
ISBN 978-0-521-68990-8 Paperback

Transferred to digital printing 2010

Contents

Preface

Australia s leading corporations today are household names — Telstra, Qantas, BHP-Billiton, AMP, Commonwealth Bank — to name but a few. They have contributed to and had influence over our economic progress throughout the twentieth century, and their broad spread of shareholders helps to keep them in the public consciousness. Few Australians, however, would know much about how our leading corporations came into being or which firms were our corporate leaders 100 or even 50 years ago. The history of Australian enterprise has not been well served by academic scholarship (the exceptions are few), which has focused largely upon the evolution of the broad macroeconomy. We lack the rich tradition of business history scholarship available in nations such as the United Kingdom or the United States.

This book begins the process of redressing these omissions. It brings to light our corporate leaders and analyses the course of their progress over the twentieth century, locating their experience within the broader Australian economy and the comparative experience of enterprise in other developed nations. We are less concerned with the operational detail of these firms and more with their broad and long-run strategic directions. In particular, we focus upon the common (or unique) features of their corporate strategies and structures. In which directions did they develop? What methods and resources were deployed? What organisational form did these firms take? And how were they governed? We do not seek to provide a comprehensive story of one or all of our companies, but rather to present a broad, representational picture by drawing upon wide-ranging evidence relating to many relevant firms. Thus, we see this work as an important grounding for business history in Australia in the years to come, providing a base on which students and scholars may build to pursue new or more focused issues, and to evaluate critically our broad conclusions.

In completion of this project we acknowledge financial support from the Australian Research Council. Valuable academic feedback was received from three anonymous referees, participants at the Corporate Leadership in Australia conference at Wollongong in September 2002, and, in particular, paper discussants Professors Paul Robertson and Gordon Boyce. Earlier drafts of particular chapters were also presented at conferences of the Economic History Society of Australia and New Zealand in Sydney (1999) and Kalgoorlie (2001). The Faculty of Commerce at the University of Wollongong provided facilities and funding towards the organisation of the corporate leadership conference, with Sonya McKay conscientiously administering the event. We are grateful to Andrew Parnell, Helen Bridge, Paola Crinnion, and Janne Skinner for research assistance.

The story of Australia's corporate leaders is dynamic: after all, corporate leaders come and go, although their time in the spotlight will vary. As we write at the beginning of a new century, many of the firms most prominent in our study are experiencing new challenges — Pacific Dunlop has been fundamentally restructured as Ansell; BHP has merged with international mining and metallurgy company Billiton; CSR has demerged its heavy materials from its building products and sugar businesses; Australian Gas Light Company is enduring increased competition from the deregulation of its traditional energy markets; Coles Myer and General Motors-Holden's are struggling to maintain domestic market share; National Australia Bank, Foster's and Lend Lease are faltering in their internationalisation; Burns Philp, Mt Isa Mines and AMP are at critical stages in re-evaluating their corporate strategies and past decisions; and Ansett has collapsed. The twenty-first century will bring a new generation of corporate leaders to Australia. We hope that through this book we might understand something of their evolution and place in the wider scope of Australian business history.

This book is supported by a website, which contains valuable additional information including updates on particular corporate leaders where their circumstances have changed subsequent to the book's publication. In addition, the website will support what is referred to as Appendix C in the text. This is the full companies database containing the names and asset size of all of the top 100 companies in each of the six benchmark years studied. Space constraints and the ability to update this list where necessary account for its location on a website. Follow the links from <http://www.cambridge.edu.au>.

Grant Fleming
David Merrett
Simon Ville
June 2003

CHAPTER 1

Introduction

Large corporations are dominating institutions in Australia, their influence pervading economic development, social structures and political relationships. Whether they provide the cost efficiencies and overseas contacts to drive economic growth and increased wealth or, alternatively, are bureaucratic leviathans that use their power to extract rents from the rest of society, is a question of sustained interest and discussion. While our principal corporations today are well known, we are far less familiar with their early development and predecessors. By investigating their evolution over the course of the twentieth century we intend to uncover a much closer understanding of Australia's leading corporations, particularly the bases of their success and their role in our modern economy and society.

It is surprising how little we know about the growth of big business in Australia. Economic historiography has focused primarily upon the broad macroeconomic changes of the economy and the role of government in those changes.[1] Little attention has been paid to analysing the evolution of business enterprises and their contribution to the nation's economic development. Recent research in business history, however, indicates that Australians are slowly discovering the similarities and differences between domestic and overseas corporate development.[2] However, at this stage there is no comprehensive identification and investigation of Australian corporate leaders – that is, our major business enterprises – in the twentieth century. We propose to fill this gap in our nation's knowledge.

A study of the distinctiveness of Australia's corporate leaders not only extends the boundaries of our understanding of business history, but serves an important public good role in disseminating the lessons from corporate practice of the twentieth century. Firms rarely possess an extensive corporate memory or recognise the importance it might play in future decision-making. The issues addressed in this book relate to how we should view the performance of Australian corporate leaders in a longer (and wider) historical context than that often undertaken in company histories or contemporary analyses of strategy. While one accepts that business challenges may change markedly over generations, the threads linking past and future performance are so strong that it is worthwhile stopping to contemplate the history, nature and form of our domestic corporate structures.

There is no doubt that the beginning of such a large, firm-oriented business history poses methodological challenges. Such studies involve a complex set of decisions about which firms to analyse, what time periods to cover, the extent to which one draws upon earlier work for industry or time series data, the definition of concepts, the interpretative framework used for analysing patterns of development, and so forth.

In order to set the scene for our analysis, some words on the existing literature and our method are appropriate here. Therefore, this chapter has four goals: to review briefly the international literature on corporate leaders, and relate this research to the Australian context; to discuss some definitional issues; to present our model used to study firms' strategic growth paths; and to introduce the major information sources used in the study.

Studies in corporate leadership

Studies of the evolution of large-scale enterprise overseas provide direction for understanding the foundations of business success. Using extensive empirical evidence, Chandler argued that firms which undertook a three-pronged investment in production, marketing and management, could build up corporate capabilities from which to sustain a competitive advantage over long periods of time.[3] Production technologies yielding new processes and products captured greater efficiencies and new markets. Forward vertical integration into marketing improved feedback mechanisms and fostered product loyalty. Administrative structures managed by tiers of professional managers evolved in response to changing strategies to avoid bureaucratic diseconomies and to improve decision-making. In a dynamic analysis, Chandler indicates how economies of scale strategies and centralised management structures emerged in the late nineteenth century, to be replaced by economies of scope and multidivisional forms from the interwar period. He went on to assert that these successful corporations provided the competitive structure and resources appropriate for the rapid development of the United States economy.

Chandler's interpretation of the rise of big business in the United States and the efficiency gains associated with large-scale operations, at least up to the 1960s, has almost universal acceptance.[4] However, Chandler and many other writers clearly demonstrated that the United States model of 'managerial capitalism' did not provide a comprehensive explanation of the rise of big business in most of the other industrialised economies. His comparative study of the United States, Britain and Germany led him to develop a typology for each, 'competitive managerial capitalism', 'personal capitalism' and 'cooperative managerial capitalism', respectively, that reflected profound differences in the nature of the competitive process, the boundaries of the firm, and the role of the state across countries.[5]

The expansion of country-based studies more recently has extended the contextualised picture as researchers have identified unique features of national experience that have overstepped the bounds of the existing typologies.[6] Further, Chandler's claims regarding the superiority of the United States model of 'competitive managerial capitalism', particularly its role in the ascendancy of the United States to dominance of the global economy by mid-century at the expense of Britain, has sparked a vigorous, if inconclusive, debate.[7]

No comparable studies have been undertaken for Australia. It would not be surprising to find elements of both the British and United States typologies of personal capitalism and competitive managerial capitalism in Australian corporate development, given the pervasive local influence of both nations. However, Australian firms have also responded to a unique combination of elements in the local operating environment. These have included a strong comparative advantage towards the output of primary industries, substantial inflows of foreign direct investment, wide distances between highly urbanised metropolitan markets, the distance from major trading partners, the influential role of the state in operating many large businesses in communications and energy, and in providing protection to domestic firms against foreign competitors, the lack of an anti-trust policy, and an immature local capital market. Taken together, these have resulted in a distinctive business culture. Australia has shared some of these environmental features with other nations, such as high levels of inward foreign investment for Canada, the small population size in the Netherlands, or the active role of government in Britain, allowing comparisons to be drawn with work being undertaken there and elsewhere.[8] However, Australia's combination of environmental triggers has been unique, and therefore we expect to find distinctive results.

While grounding our work in an international tradition of studying the growth of big business, our approach will differ from most of the previous literature in several important respects. Most previous writers have concentrated upon manufacturing; we will analyse leading firms from all sectors of the economy.[9] Manufacturing in Australia has been less significant than in many other advanced nations, particularly before World War Two, and therefore the picture would be substantially incomplete if pastoralism, mining and the service industries were to be excluded from an analysis of large-scale enterprise. Emphasis upon the contribution of multinational enterprises will be a further distinguishing feature of this study, in light of their preponderance within the Australian economy.

The study is primarily concerned with competition in the private sector, but broad comparisons will be drawn with publicly-owned companies in light of the importance of the government sector in Australia. While Chandler's ideas have motivated many business historians, the work of a range of management theorists will also be used widely. Porter, for example, has described how firms achieve and sustain competitive advantages through such strategies as cost leadership, product differentiation and market segmentation.[10] Analysing formal inter-firm relationships between foreign parents and local subsidiaries and among joint venture partners will also be a significant part of our story and reflects the growing emphasis on such alliances in recent theoretical work.[11]

Definitional issues in sample selection

There are many criteria for measuring the relative size of firms in order to identify our largest enterprises. These include assets, output, sales, paid-up and market value of capital, or labour force, but none provide an unambiguous measure of size. Enumeration by workforce size can be misleading for cross-industry comparisons where different capital–labour requirements exist; output or sales figures are only helpful where they can distinguish value added. Equity capitalisation represents aggregate ownership claims on the company and is most accurate where it gives market rather than book values. However, exogenous factors driving equity markets can introduce an element of volatility that would not be reflected in other measures such as assets, sales or workforce numbers. Furthermore, this indicator is inappropriate for firms whose shares are not listed or are rarely traded. Asset measurement is not without its shortcomings. It relies upon consistent accounting and disclosure practices on balance sheets, and in some sectors, notably finance, it can produce an inflated picture of size through loan policies that have made the company asset rich.[12] While capitalisation and assets are the preferred forms of measurement, the relationship between the two is not always uniform.[13]

Historical measurements of changes in firm size encounter significant data collection problems. Since detailed data for many firms are not extant, summary published data, usually annual financial reports, must be used. Before 1945 this rarely included information on company workforces or value added in production. Most scholars, therefore, have used capitalisation or assets data. Hannah and Wardley each used equity market values together with debentures for Britain.[14] Schmitz used equity market values in comparing nations but substituted assets where data was not extant.[15] Chandler used assets for German and United States companies while Fruin has provided a range of assets, capital values and sales data for Japanese firms.[16]

The use of different methodologies means that figures on absolute firm size must be analysed circumspectly, although the broad parameters for comparison remain valid. In analysing Australian firms, asset size has been adopted as the unit of measurement, being the most readily available data across the time period under consideration. Incorporation of businesses became increasingly common from the late nineteenth century. Company law required the publication of a balance sheet and a profit and loss account. The asset approach has enabled the inclusion, where possible, of those firms whose shares were unquoted or rarely traded. The accuracy of share capitalisation as a form of measurement of firm size, especially in the early years, is compromised by the belated development of Australian stock markets and many firms' heavy reliance upon bank debt.

Australia has always attracted a good deal of inward foreign investment. This has taken the form of both 'free-standing' companies – those who earned revenues from business activities in Australia but had no operational counterpart in the country of ownership, principally in Britain – and, more recently, local subsidiaries of 'classic' foreign-owned and operated multinationals.[17] While frequently not quoted on the Australian stock exchange, these firms were often among the largest in the country. Therefore, in contrast to studies of some of the larger and more self-contained economies, assets of free-standing companies and subsidiaries of multinationals will be included where they can be identified. Measurement and data problems arise from their inclusion. The assets of free-standing firms could be taken to approximate their 'size' in Australia, as that was the locus of their business activities. Greater problems arise in singling out the Australian assets of subsidiaries of multinational enterprises, particularly where such data resides in the firm archives rather than the public domain. For example, there is no record of the assets employed by either Lever Brothers Limited (Australia) or the Shell Company of Australia in the range of sources used to generate our lists before 1964. However, the capital employed by Lever Brothers and Shell would have placed them at number 26 and 40 respectively in the list of the 100 largest companies in 1930.[18]

Identifying and analysing Australian corporate leaders

In order to determine the changes in the population of the largest firms occurring through the twentieth century, six years have been investigated, each about a generation apart: 1910, 1930, 1952, 1964, 1986 and 1997. For each benchmark year we determine the composition of the top 100 firms by total assets. The years 1930 and 1952 had previously been analysed in an unpublished thesis. That data provided an initial comparator against which to work: where discrepancies emerged it was possible to re-check the sources.[19] The inclusion of 1910 has extended the study of big business back close to its earliest years, while carrying the investigation forward to 1997 permits an observation of the impact of the rapid growth in the relative importance of services in the economy and brings the analysis up close towards the present day. The full data set, known as Appendix C, can be found on the book's web page, as indicated in the preface.

Because of the asset rich nature of financial institutions, which inflates their apparent importance, a separate list of the leading 25 firms in this sector has been developed for each benchmark year. Cross-sectional comparisons between firms are facilitated by categorising them according to the Australian Standard Industrial Classification (ASIC) (and newly revised ANZSIC) system, notwithstanding several shortcomings of this methodology.[20] These dates track the profound changes in the structure of the Australian economy as it became industrialised and allow comparisons with similar studies for other countries using proximate years, including the global comparisons of Schmitz for 1912 and 1937, and the country studies of Chandler for the United States, Britain and Germany, Taylor and Baskerville for Canada, Levy-Leboyer for France, Fruin for Japan and Hannah and Wardley for Britain. We add more recent years than most of these studies to link with contemporary work in strategic management and applied corporate finance.[21] Chapter 2 will analyse our big business lists for Australia and provide a comparison with the experience of a range of other nations.

Determining the strategic direction of corporations requires a dynamic economic model that can incorporate economic, political and social influences on strategy formation. We use the term model in the sense that we attempt to analyse the development of Australian firms in a rigorous way – not with the elaborate use of mathematical or statistical techniques, but with the use of consistent assumptions relating to the rational behaviour of firms and their managers.[22] The model in Figure 1.1 is used to analyse observations with clearly defined growth paths that a firm can undertake. It draws upon the economics of strategy to provide a consistent approach to examining the strategic choices faced by Australian corporate leaders. This is not to suggest that non-economic factors are not used in our analysis – indeed, variables to be entered into such a model may be technological, legal, cultural, political and psychological. Nevertheless, we believe that on the whole opportunities for gain will not be left unexploited, even if the nature of that arbitrage might involve the complex motivations associated with self-interest, ethical considerations and altruistic outcomes. In order to provide a focused analysis of the strategic growth of Australia's leading corporations, in Chapter 3 we condense

Figure 1.1: Model for determining growth paths of corporations

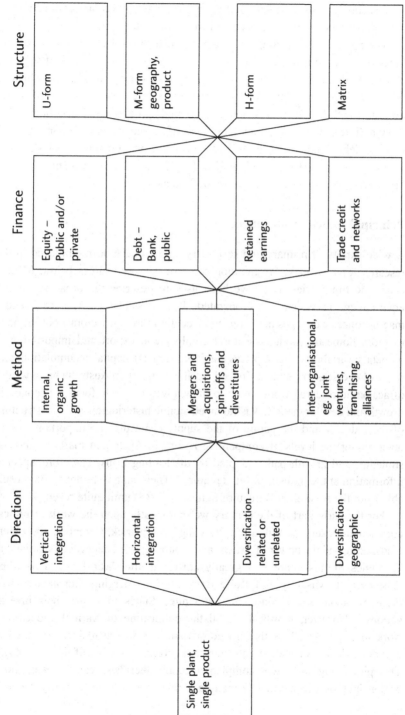

our benchmark lists to isolate those firms that have played a sustained role in the corporate economy; in other words our 'corporate leaders'.

The process of collecting and ordering the data can be seen as our attempt to reconstruct the firms' analyses of their environment and choice of strategic options. In doing so, we draw from contemporary strategy and business history literature. Figure 1.1 sets out the firms' strategic choices in terms of direction of growth (vertical, horizontal, diversified and geographical), methods of growth (internal, merger, interfirm), use of resources in achieving growth (equity, debt, retained earnings and networks), and organisational structure (U-form, M-form, H-form and matrix).[23] In chapters 4 to 7 we analyse each of these strategic options for our corporate leaders.

Principal information sources

A wide variety of primary and secondary sources have been employed in the research for this book. We mention some of the key sources below. Macroeconomic time series data have been used to describe the broader external environment in which firms operated. It is possible to map the broader macroeconomic changes in the twentieth century through sectoral contributions to gross domestic product, sectoral employment, export and import trends, monetary variables (wages, prices and interest rates), capital accumulation, and flows of overseas investment. Indeed, business history in Australia has a wealth of academic research from which to draw, given the early focus on economic growth and development in Australian economic historiography.[24] The structure of the industry and the nature of the supply chain play an important role in determining the levels of competitive rivalry in Australian markets, and the strategies and growth paths adopted by the leading firms. Therefore, specific information at the industry level is required. These data were not readily available from the Australian Bureau of Statistics (ABS) until quite recently.

For the early part of the century we rely mostly upon the work of radical commentators such as Wilkinson, Rawlings, Fitzpatrick, Campbell and others who denounced the power of 'trusts' and monopolies.[25] The level of scholarship in studies of this genre was greatly advanced after World War Two when Wheelwright, Miskelly and Rolfe drew on the emerging radical academic literature about big business in the United States to frame their investigations.[26] However, it was not until the publication of Karmel and Brunt's work in the early 1960s that a rigorous analysis was available, grounded in economic theory, of market concentration across all sectors of the economy.[27] This pioneering work was complemented by Sheridan's careful estimations of concentration levels in 109 manufacturing industries in the early 1960s.[28]

The important role of multinationals is particularly traced in regular government publications.[29]

For firm-specific information, such as asset data, growth strategies, and firm profitability, we have drawn upon a range of contemporary investment, government and business reports, and company sources. The sources of information about firms' assets used to identify the firms to be analysed varied between different benchmark years. *The Australasian Insurance and Banking Record*, published annually from 1877, was used for the years preceding World War One and provides summary balance sheet data of firms listed on the Australian or London stock exchange. By the interwar period, data was taken from the *Jobson's Investment Digest of Australia and New Zealand*, ('Jobson's') an annual publication compiled by Alex Jobson from 1920 and including, 'a summary of all Australian company reports published … up to the latest moment'.[30]

In the period following World War Two Jobson's became less comprehensive and was replaced by the more complete coverage of the *Official Melbourne Stock Exchange Record*. This source was supplemented by reference to an occasional publication known as the *Delfin Digest of the Top Companies in Australia, New Zealand and South East Asia*, which ranked companies according to various criteria including shareholder funds, paid-up capital, assets, profits and employees. These sources have been compared with each other where overlap exists and additional information about the nature of individual firms has been obtained from a miscellany of supplementary references.[31] The sources capture firms complying with the disclosure requirements of Australian company laws and stock exchanges. Foreign firms operating in Australia are included in these lists, although none of the sources indicate clearly the basis on which these firms have been selected.

The quality of the data in the 1910 and 1930 lists is the most problematic. The key issue in 1910 is the limited amount of information extant. Many large firms were still trading as partnerships or had registered as private companies. Others were in the process of converting to public company status. In order to counter this truncation problem, the timeframe for data collection of asset values has been extended to 1915, as long as the company existed in the same form at 1910. There remain one or two unresolved individual cases that are mostly small outliers, although David Jones, the Sydney retailer, for whom no financial records can be found would probably have been in the top 50. The crux of the problem regarding the 1930 list, as indicated above, is that our records do not capture all of the many foreign firms that entered Australia in the 1920s.[32]

Closer to the present, information on companies both local and foreign becomes more extensive, but its interpretation is more difficult because of the increasing numbers of complex business organisations involving holding companies, subsidiaries and joint venture arrangements. Consolidated accounts were rare before the 1950s. Rudimentary adjustments have been made to asset values of the parent in those circumstances where consolidation seemed appropriate to avoid double counting.[33]

The earliest time series of profits of public companies categorised by industry and published in *Jobson's Investment Digest of Australia and New Zealand* from 1919 to 1938, gives only net profit, dividend payment, and the sum of paid-up capital and shareholders' funds. The lack of more detailed information reflects the limited disclosure required of companies under the current company legislation and the listing requirements of the stock exchanges. The Commonwealth Bank of Australia's series of company profits that began in the late 1930s became much more useful for our purposes from the early 1960s, when it began to reveal both tax and depreciation data.

Company strategies have been identified in many cases through reports in *Wild Cat Monthly*, J. B. Were and other investment and broker reports, supplemented with material from the business press and company publications, histories, web pages and archives. *Huntley's Delisted Companies Report* provides information on restructures, mergers and acquisitions dating back to 1929, while Reserve Bank of Australia data covers takeovers and takeover bids for more recent years. Cross-sectional comparisons between companies, domestically and internationally, have drawn upon evidence from business research organisations such as Fortune and Forbes, together with national (Bureau of Industry Economics, Department of Industry, Trade and Commerce) and supranational government agencies (United Nations, World Bank).

Conclusion

In summary, therefore, our aim in this study is to uncover the identity and investigate the nature and national contribution of our largest and most enduring firms, our corporate leaders. We will pursue this by reference to the methodology and major sources foreshadowed above, beginning with a comparative assessment of Australian big business in an international context, before focusing more closely upon the strategies and structures of our corporate leaders in subsequent chapters, and finishing with a broad overview of their role and importance within the context of the national economy.

CHAPTER 2

The Development of Large-scale Enterprise in Australia

Research about the rise of large-scale enterprise has concentrated on the world's leading industrial economies, particularly the United States, Britain, Germany, France and Japan.[1] By way of contrast, this study discusses the evolution of large business enterprises in an economy at the 'periphery' of the world's economic system rather than at the 'centre'. The drivers of the emergence of big business in Australia were fundamentally the same as those operating in many other mature and later starting industrial economies. However, it will be argued that the nature of the Australian economy, and particularly its economic relationship with the rest of the world, had a powerful impact on the timing of the emergence of big business and its subsequent character. These local issues will be explored before turning to an examination of the characteristics of top 100 non-financial and 25 financial firms operating in Australia at various dates from 1910 up to 1997. This chapter deals with aggregate data and trend movements rather than the identification and histories of individual firms. The rise of firms within industries is considered in Chapter 3.

Drivers of big business in Australia

The large-scale industrial firms that emerged in the United States and Europe in the later part of the nineteenth century were powerful agents of economic change. Utilising new technologies in communication and production, they transformed existing industries and created new ones through research and development-related diversification, and widened markets from local to regional to national and, in many cases, international.[2] The size of the market at any point in time and its subsequent expansion, either domestically or internationally, set a limit on the size and growth of firms operating within those markets. The scale and pattern of big business in Australia reflects the unique national environment in which it operated. While the new technologies that unleashed the second industrial revolution and spawned its handmaidens, big business, in the Northern Hemisphere wrought similar changes within Australia, big business tended to operate on a smaller scale and in a broader set of activities than was the case in the larger and more open industrial economies. Big business in Australia dominated the local economy to an unusual degree while being relatively small when compared to firms from the same industries in other countries.

A number of factors impacted on the size and sectoral location of big business. The first was the size of the local market and the relatively low levels of internationalisation of Australian firms. The size of the market had two dimensions, as a place to sell and a place to buy. With respect to the latter, Australia was not well endowed, either absolutely or relatively, with capital, skilled managers and workers or technology. Secondly, Australia's comparative advantage lay in resource-based industries that occupied an unusually large role in the economy. Mining, increasingly capital-intensive, produced an impressive array of large enterprises. However, farming remained the province of small business. Thirdly, the government's role in the economy had two important consequences for the development of big business. Many transport, communications and power utilities industries became government monopolies, locking out private operators until the 1990s. Moreover, the trade barriers that rose from the 1920s until the 1970s stimulated the growth of manufacturing that accelerated the rise of big business. Fourth, these trade barriers attracted foreign direct investment by overseas firms that became very important players in manufacturing and service industries. These arguments will be considered in more detail below.

The growth of firms located in Australia was limited by the size of the domestic market and the ability of firms to find markets abroad. Across the century under consideration, Australia's population rose from four to 20 million. Despite an impressive growth rate, Australia had less than a third of one per cent of the world's population at the end of the 1990s. Its economy generated only 1.3 per cent of world GDP. By comparison, the high-income group of countries that were homes to big business, of which Australia was a part, collectively comprised 15 per cent of the world's population and produced 79 per cent of world GDP.[3] Australia's domestic market could never provide a base for the largest firms in the world. Throughout the twentieth century, her population, while among the wealthiest in the world, was smaller than Canada's and slightly larger than a range of mid-size European countries.[4]

Moreover, Australian firms did not avail themselves of wider international markets to any great extent. The country's ratio of exports to GDP fell from an average of 25 per cent in the years 1899–1914 to 18 per cent in the years 1918–39, and 17 per cent from 1946 until 1989.[5] Indeed, it was the farming and mining industries, rather than manufacturing or services, that generated the bulk of exports throughout the twentieth century. As late as 1980, more than a half of Australia's exports were still unprocessed primary products and less than a quarter were manufactured goods, many of which were semi-processed raw materials.[6] In addition, Australian firms were slow to undertake foreign direct investment. From the 1950s until 1980, the estimated stock of outward foreign direct investment was only 1.5 per cent of GDP. This figure rose sharply, partly inflated by definitional changes, to nearly 12 per cent by the mid-1990s.[7] Those firms that went abroad before the 1970s largely confined themselves to the much smaller nearby markets of New Zealand and Melanesia.[8] This limited scale and geographic span of outward foreign direct investment was in marked contrast to the experience of other small industrial economies.[9]

The resources of savings, managerial talent, skilled labour and technology, all of which were necessary conditions for the emergence and growth of big business, were constrained to a degree compared with the leading industrial economies. Australia's savings rate was not markedly different from that of the United Sates and Canada.[10] However, the absolute amounts available for investment were limited by comparison, and the immaturity of local securities and corporate debt markets before the 1980s forced Australian firms, hardly any of whom were listed on foreign stock exchanges, to rely heavily on internal sources of funds to finance growth.[11]

Australian workers received high wages throughout the century, not necessarily because they were highly productive. Labour market outcomes were heavily influenced by the actions of governments. Tariff protection of urban manufacturers allowed those workers who increasingly became unionised to bargain for higher wages than otherwise would have been the case. Moreover, government wage tribunals put a floor under the wage level from early in the century with the creation of the 'basic' or living wage, which was a bedrock of the social security system until the 1970s.[12]

This high wage workforce in manufacturing was not highly trained in technical areas that were crucial to competitiveness in the science-based industries of the second industrial revolution.[13] Firms' spending on research and development was well below that of leading industrial nations.[14] All in all, the combination of natural and man-made resources available to Australian entrepreneurs throughout the twentieth century did not provide an environment that would favour the rise of big business on a scale that would match those in better-endowed economies of the United States, Europe or Japan.

The size and character of Australia's largest firms were further shaped by the nature of the country's resources. Geology and geography conferred upon Australia a comparative advantage in a number of farm products, wool, meat, grains, sugar and dairy products, and minerals. Agricultural and pastoral production was undertaken on some 250 000 farms in the 25 years after World War Two, more than two-thirds of which were family operations. Those farmers that hired non-family labour averaged less than three employees.[15] It was only in mining that large-scale, capital-intensive production techniques necessitated the rise of big business.

The nature and pace of Australian economic development were powerfully affected by the state that itself monopolised the provision of many services, notably in transport and communications, and acted as a regulator of most industries.[16] It was the government that invested in, and managed, the key land transport and communications infrastructure, the railways, mail, telegraph and telephone. It later became a major provider of air transport and telecommunications. For most of the century, government-owned businesses, including many banks, were among the largest enterprises in Australia, as shown in Appendix A.

A comparison of the top three government business enterprises and private firms is shown in Table 2.1. In 1910, the Victorian Railways' assets were nearly six times those of the largest private firm. It was not until 1964 that the largest private sector firm, BHP, came in second behind the post office, run by the federal Department of the Postmaster-General. The dominance of the public sector business enterprises was finally overturned only in the 1990s. This outcome reflected a combination of the dramatic growth of global private firms, such as News Corporation and the resource companies, BHP and Conzinc Riotinto Australia, and the downsizing of the public sector utilities. The largest government-owned enterprise, Telstra, was partly privatised by this date.[17]

While the provision of these government services was an important enabling factor in the rise of big business by widening the size of the domestic market and facilitating linkages with overseas markets, many commentators have emphasised the growing operational inefficiencies and sluggish innovation in these activities from the 1920s onwards. Governments also became the most important suppliers of electricity from the 1920s for domestic and industrial consumption. Many of these businesses were corporatised and partially or fully privatised in the 1980s and 1990s as part of a process that became known as 'microeconomic reform'.[18] In nearly all these cases, what had been statewide monopolies were broken down into a number of smaller regional providers, or there was a separation of energy generation and distribution businesses.

The impact of state ownership was twofold. It closed off an avenue for the rise of privately owned big business through most of the twentieth century. Second, the efficiencies of these public sector businesses had a direct bearing on the costs of business customers. While private businesses sometimes were the beneficiaries of special deals from the state – for example, the provision of electricity to Alcoa's aluminium smelter plant at Portland[19] – it is difficult to escape the conclusion that inefficient government monopolies imposed costs on downstream users. The relative lack of efficiency and dynamic responsiveness

Table 2.1: Three largest government and private businesses, 1910–97

1910	$m	1930	$m	1952	$m	1964	$m	1986	$b	1997	$b
VRail	92	NSWR	266	PMG	436	PMG	1289	*BHP*	16.5	*News*	54.5
PMG	28	VRail	163	SECV	294	*BHP*	780	Telecom	14.5	*BHP*	37.1
Dalgety	16	PMG	107	VRail	166	SECV	772	*CRA*	8.6	Telstra	26.5
Br Tob	10	CSR	30	*BHP*	122	NSWR	669	*News*	8.4	*Rio T*	25.6
CSR	9	*Dalgety*	22	*CSR*	97	*Shell*	558	SECV	8.3	Q Rail	6.5
		Br Tob	19	*CZC*	80	*CSR*	272	ECNSW	6.6	QPowerT	6.3

Note: Private sector firms presented in italics.

Sources: 1910–52: Auditor-General's Reports for state and Commonwealth governments, 1964: *Delfin Digest*, 1986 and 1997: *Business Review Weekly*; Various issues of: *Australasian Insurance and Banking Record*; *Jobson's Investment Digest*; *Official Melbourne Stock Exchange Record*; *Delfin Digest*; *Business Review Weekly* 6.11.1986, pp. 89–116, and 16.11.1998, pp. 108–60.

from the key 'related and supporting industries'[20] placed further constraints on the potential scale of Australian firms in a global economy.

Australian governments intervened in the economy throughout the century using a variety of industry or sectoral specific taxes and subsidies. Trade barriers, in the form of tariffs and, for shorter periods, import quotas and foreign exchange controls, sheltered the domestic market from foreign competition. Protection stimulated the growth of manufacturing, and its relative importance in the economy, from the 1920s until the 1970s. Locally based firms had privileged access to markets for both consumer and producer goods compared with foreign competitors exporting into the country. In many respects, Australia's industrialisation was largely a state-sponsored process of import substitution that attracted many foreign firms to undertake foreign direct investment.

However, foreign firms entered the local market for many reasons other than the existence of trade barriers. The sectoral distribution of foreign firms in the top 100 non-financial businesses is shown in Table 2.2. Foreign firms were a very important component of the top 100. There are reasons to believe that the numbers shown in Table 2.2, particularly those in manufacturing, are an under-estimate, a point that will be discussed below. This caveat notwithstanding, their contribution averaged a quarter of all firms and 28 per cent of assets across the six time periods, ranging from a maximum of 31 per cent of all firms and 49 per cent of all assets in 1910 to a minimum of 9 per cent of firms and 12 per cent of assets in 1952. In all years from 1910 to 1964, the share of assets of foreign firms exceeded their share of the number of firms, a situation that was reversed in 1986 and 1997.

Multinationals entered the Australian market to exploit its resource base. Agriculture was an important host up to 1930, while the mining industry continued to attract large foreign firms over the longer term. Most of the inward movement of firms was to supply the local market. Service firms, including financial firms that will be discussed below, were far more numerous than manufacturers before 1964. Roughly a half of all multinationals in the top 100 operated in the wholesale and retail trades in 1910 and 1930, with another 20 per cent in utilities and transport. Manufacturing multinationals accounted for only a small part of the introduction of large foreign firms into Australia until 1964. From that time until 1997, the number of manufacturing firms dominated those in other sectors. Firms in agriculture, utilities and transport drop out of the list in 1930 and 1952 respectively. The numbers in the whole-sale and retail trades fall continually until 1986 before recovering in 1997. In that year, there are new foreign firms in the list from the transport and communication sectors.

The issue of foreign firms in manufacturing deserves fuller consideration. Trade barriers and high transport costs encouraged foreign manufacturing firms

Table 2.2: Foreign ownership of top 100 companies by sector, 1910–97

	Number	Assets %	A	B	C	D	F	G	H
1910	31	49	7	1	2	3	15	3	–
1930	20	25	4	–	2	3	10	1	–
1952	9	12	–	2	–	1	6	–	–
1964	36	41	–	3	29	–	4	–	–
1986	24	16	–	4	19	–	1	–	–
1997	30	22	–	2	19	–	7	1	1

A   Agriculture, Forestry, Fishing and Hunting
B   Mining
C   Manufacturing
D   Electricity, Gas and Water
E   Construction
F   Wholesale and Retail Trade
G   Transport and Storage
H   Communication
I   Finance, Insurance, Real Estate and Business Services
J   Public Administration and Defence
K   Community Services
L   Entertainment, Recreation, Restaurants, Hotels and Personal Services

Note: For all years prior to 1964, foreign companies were identified by place of registration. From 1964 forwards, identification was on the basis of majority ownership of shares in foreign hands. For a full description of ASIC classifications see pp. 237–8. There were no foreign-owned companies in categories I–L for this period.

Source: Various issues of: *Australasian Insurance and Banking Record*; *Jobson's Investment Digest*; *Official Melbourne Stock Exchange Record*; *Delfin Digest*; *Business Review Weekly* 6.11.1986, pp. 89–116, and 16.11.1998, pp. 108–60.

to come to Australia from before the turn of the century. This process was accelerated by the rising tariffs after World War One, with another 84 firms identified as having entered in the 1920s.[21] Fewer firms were willing or able to enter Australia during the following decade and a half of depression and war. The influx of multinationals recommenced in the 1950s. By the early 1960s, unofficial estimates put the number of companies at 208 from the United States alone, more than a half of which had arrived after 1950.[22] Official statistics indicated that the number of Australian manufacturing firms with equity interest owned overseas was 872 in 1966 and 980 in 1971. By this later date, foreign firms with more than 50 per cent of equity in their local subsidiary accounted for 22 per cent of the total value of manufacturing production, while all firms with overseas equity generated 26 per cent.[23] By 1986–87, the respective percentages for value added in manufacturing had risen to 31 and 33.[24]

Foreign manufacturing firms were concentrated in those capital-intensive, science-based industries that provided fertile ground for big business in the advanced industrial economies. As shown in Table 2.3, nearly one-half of the 980 multinationals operating in Australian manufacturing in 1971 were located in the chemical and the industrial machinery, equipment and household equipment industries, with another quarter in food, drink and tobacco, fabricated

Table 2.3: Foreign direct investment in Australian manufacturing by industry, 1971

Industry	Firms	% total firms	Share of output by foreign-owned factories (%)
Food, drink, tobacco	85	8.7	23.0
Textile	44	4.5	13.5
Clothing, footwear	20	2.0	4.2
Wood, wood products	14	1.4	
– sawmills			4.7
– furniture			2.9
Paper, printing	52	5.3	10.7
Chemical, petroleum	189	19.3	64.7
– industrial chemicals			58.7
– pharmaceuticals			75.1
– oils, mineral			79.5
Glass, clay	35	3.6	9.4
Basic metals	37	3.8	
Fabricated structural	93	9.5	
– non-ferrous rolling			62.4
Transport equipment	60	6.1	
– motor vehicle			88.3
– agricultural equipment			32.0
Other industrial	299	30.5	
– plant, equipment, machinery			19.3
– electrical machinery			36.0
– wireless and amplifying			39.3
Leather, rubber	52	5.3	
– rubber			22.3
Other			7.7
Total	980	100	22.2

Source: Department of Trade and Industry, *Directory of Overseas Investment*, Tables 1 & 2, pp. 5–6.

structural metal products, principally aluminium, and transport equipment. Foreign firms generated more than a half of total output in the tobacco, industrial chemicals, pharmaceuticals, petroleum, aluminium and motor vehicle industries. The dominance of multinationals in so many of the key industries that spawned and supported big business overseas limited the opportunities available to local firms who were late starters. Moreover, the restricted export franchise placed on many foreign subsidiaries by their parents limited these firms to the small local market.[25]

The pattern of big business in Australia

The number of firms that became part of 'big business' in Australia, their size, and their distribution across industrial sectors was grounded in the structure and growth of the Australian economy. Data in Table 2.4 shows the broad shift in the composition of economic activity and the number of firms located in each industry category. Before World War One, agriculture and mining contributed 29 per cent of GDP at factor cost, manufacturing 14 per cent, wholesale and retail trades 16 per cent, and construction 10 per cent. Big business was disproportionately located in mining, manufacturing, the wholesale and retail trades, transport and utilities.

As the relative importance of agriculture and mining in the economy declined over the longer period to the mid-1960s, the number of big businesses located there fell significantly. The number of utilities in the list fell heavily after 1928–29 as public ownership became the norm in electricity production and distribution.[26] Town gas, on the other hand, became a state enterprise only in Victoria and Western Australia.[27]

Manufacturing's share of GDP more than doubled from 1913–14 to 1962–63. Over that timeframe, the number of the top 100 non-financial firms coming from manufacturing rose from 30 to 71. The number of top 100 firms from the wholesale and retail trades fell from around 30 in the first half of the century to 18 in 1962–63, despite that industry's share of GDP remaining roughly constant.

The next 25 years saw a dramatic change in the structure of the economy due in large part to the mineral discoveries of the 1960s, reductions in trade barriers in the 1970s, and financial deregulation in the 1980s. Agriculture and manufacturing's share of GDP fell sharply, although the latter still provided 50 of the top 100 firms in 1986. Mining's share of output rose to 5 per cent, while 18 of the largest firms were located in that industry. The remaining third of the largest firms came from the service sector. The number of firms in the distributive trades fell sharply, with that decline more than offset by new large firms in construction, transport, communication, and real estate and business services.

Table 2.4: Share of GDP at factor cost and number of firms in top 100 by industry, 1913–14 to 1989–90

Industry	1913–14 Share	1913–14 No.	1928–29 Share	1928–29 No.	1950–51 Share	1950–51 No.	1962–63 Share	1962–63 No.	1989–90 Share	1989–90 No.
Agriculture	23.6	9	21.4	6	29.0	1	12.9	–	4.3	2
Mining	5.2	13	1.9	5	2.1	9	1.5	5	4.7	18
Manufacturing	13.5	30	16.9	39	23.7	55	28.3	71	16.3	50
Electricity, Gas and Water	–	9	–	10	1.5	3	3.4	2	3.3	1
Construction	9.6	–	8.3	–	6.3	–	7.8	2	8.2	6
Wholesale and Retail Trade	16.4	28	17.7	31	14.7	27	14.6	18	14.9	7
Transport	–	11	–	5	6.3	4	7.9	2	8.4	6
Communication	–	–	–	–	4.2	–	7.2	–	–	5
Finance, Insurance etc.	1.7	–	2.1	–	2.2	–	3.2	–	12.5	5
Public Administration and Defence	4.0	–	4.8	–	3.2	–	3.8	–	4.0	–
Community Services	–	–	–	4	–	1	–	–	12.7	–
Entertainment	–	–	–	–	–	–	–	–	4.2	–
Unallocated	26.0	100	26.9	100	6.8	100	9.4	100	6.5	100

Notes: Major definitional changes affect continuity of industry classification.
Data for firm numbers for years 1910, 1930, 1952, 1964 and 1986.

Source: Boehm, *Economic Development*, Table 1.2, pp. 8–9; Appendix C.

Lists of the largest 100 non-financial and 25 financial services firms at our benchmark dates between 1910 and 1997 are shown in Appendices B and C of the book. As explained in Chapter 1, firms were ranked on asset size rather than other indicators. This measure makes the financial services firms much larger, relative to those non-financial firms, than would be the case if other measures such as market value or the number of employees had been used. It is for this reason that the two lists have been kept separate.

A number of salient features of the data will be discussed in more detail below. First, large-scale enterprise was never a phenomenon associated only with the rapid industrialisation of the Australian economy from the 1920s onwards. Large firms, exhibiting a separation of ownership and control, and being run by hierarchies of salaried managers, were evident in the resource-based industries, distributive trades and financial services, as well as in manufacturing, from before World War One. The 1930, 1952 and 1964 lists confirm the subsequent ascendancy of manufacturing as the centre of large-scale non-financial firms. However, the last third of the century saw a resurgence of firms from the resources and service sectors at the expense of manufacturing. Financial services firms in the top 25 were overwhelmingly deposit-taking institutions such as banks across the whole of the century, despite some shift towards non-bank financial institutions from the 1960s onwards. Foreign ownership of these financial firms waned and then waxed, reflecting changing government attitudes to foreign ownership of licensed banks in the mid-1980s.

Non-financial firms

The sectoral composition of the top 100 non-financial firms at each observation point from 1910 until 1997 is shown in Table 2.5. Manufacturing is the most important contributor of big business at each of the six observations, with its lowest share being 30 in 1910 and its highest 71 in 1964. In 1910, 70 of the largest 100 non-financial firms came from elsewhere in the economy. The resources sector, agriculture and mining, provided 22. Privately owned utilities and transport firms contributed another 20, while there were 28 firms from the retail and wholesale trades, the most prominent of which serviced the pastoral industry. By 1964, the contribution of the non-manufacturing sectors had declined to only 29, with disappearances occurring across the board. However, the 1980s and 1990s saw a dramatic reversal of fortune as manufacturing's contribution fell 25 percentage points with more than half of the top 100 firms coming, once again, from the resources and service sectors.

Another perspective on the relative importance of non-financial firms within the top 100 is to compare the sectoral distribution of firms with the sectoral share of assets. This measure is shown in Table 2.6. Of the 47 observations,

Table 2.5: Sectoral distribution of top 100 firms, 1910–97

Date	A	B	C	D	E	F	G	H	I	K	L
1910	9	13	30	9	–	28	11	–	–	–	–
1930	6	5	39	10	–	31	5	–	–	–	4
1952	1	9	55	3	–	27	4	–	–	–	1
1964	–	5	71	2	2	18	2	–	–	–	–
1986	2	18	51	1	6	7	5	5	5	–	–
1997	–	14	49	1	3	14	4	5	1	1	8

Note: ASIC classifications listed in Table 2.2 and detailed on pp. 237–8.

Sources: Various issues of: *Australasian Insurance and Banking Record*; *Jobson's Investment Digest*; *Official Melbourne Stock Exchange Record*; *Delfin Digest*; *Business Review Weekly* 6.11.1986, pp. 89–116, and 16.11.1998, pp. 108–60.

21 show that the number of firms exceeds the share of assets, in 12 they are equally matched, and in 14 cases an industry's share of assets exceeds its share of firms. This measure suggests that the wholesale and retail trade was more important in 1910 than the number of firms from that category indicates, as those firms employed 40 per cent of all assets of the top 100. On the other hand, at the same date the share of assets employed by manufacturing firms (25) was significantly less than their number in the top 100 (30). From that date until 1964, manufacturing's share of assets rose faster than its share of firms. In most industries there were variations from enumeration to enumeration as shares of firms and assets differed. The differences were greatest in 1986 and 1997.

Table 2.6: Asset intensity of top 100 firms by industry, 1910–97

Date	A	B	C	D	E	F	G	H	I	K	L
1910	+1	–2	–5	–4	–	+12	–2	–	–	–	–
1930	–1	–1	+1	+3	–	–1	0	–	–	–	–1
1952	0	+2	+3	+1	–	–3	–2	–	–	–	0
1964	0	0	0	–1	–1	+1	–1	–	–	–	–
1986	–1	–5	+5	0	–3	0	–1	+3	+3	–	–
1997	0	+11	–14	0	–2	–7	+1	+18	0	0	–5

Note: ASIC classifications listed in Table 2.2 and detailed on pp. 237–8.

Sources: Various issues of: *Australasian Insurance and Banking Record*; *Jobson's Investment Digest*; *Official Melbourne Stock Exchange Record*; *Delfin Digest*; *Business Review Weekly* 6.11.1986, pp. 89–116, and 16.11.1998, pp. 108–60.

Communication's share of assets, including media, exceeded its number of firms by 21 percentage points. Mining experienced large swings but had a cumulative increase in its asset intensity of 6 percentage points. On the other hand, both manufacturing and the wholesale and retail trades, experienced falls of 9 and 7 percentage points when comparing the share of assets with the number of firms from those sectors.

These changes in the sectoral distribution of the number of firms are shown in more detail in Table 2.7. In 1910, the top 100 are spread across six industry groups, as discussed above. Between 1910 and 1930, 17 of the firms present in the 1910 list were replaced by a similar number of new entrants. There were significant losses among agriculture, mining and transport. The additional firms were located in manufacturing, utilities, wholesale and retail trades, and entertainment. The turnover rate between 1930 and 1952 rose to 20. Mining and manufacturing were the only industries that experienced an increase in their numbers, with losses across all the other industries. Manufacturing's growth dominated the transition between 1952 and 1964 by providing 16 of the 18 new additions. Six other industry groups lost ground. The period from 1964 to 1986, the longest of the postwar intervals between enumerations, saw the largest number of entries and exits as 33 places were gained or lost. Two-thirds of the decline came from manufacturing, with most of the balance coming from the distributive trades. The resources, especially mining, and the service sectors experienced strong growth. The rate of turnover of places reduced to 16 in the

Table 2.7: Changes in number of top 100 firms by industry, sub-periods 1910–97

Date	A	B	C	D	E	F	G	H	I	K	L
1910	9	13	30	9	–	28	11	–	–	–	–
1910–30	(3)	(8)	9	1	–	3	(6)	–	–	–	4
1930–52	(5)	4	16	(7)	–	(4)	(1)	–	–	–	(3)
1952–64	(1)	(4)	16	(1)	2	(9)	(2)	–	–	–	(1)
1964–86	2	13	(20)	(1)	4	(11)	3	5	5	–	–
1986–97	(2)	(4)	(2)	–	(3)	7	(1)	0	(4)	1	8
1997	–	16	46	1	3	14	4	6	2	1	7
Cumulative	(9)	(3)	16	(8)	3	(13)	(7)	6	1	1	7

Notes: Negative movement shown in parentheses. Rows for each time interval sum to zero. ASIC classifications listed in Table 2.2 and detailed on pp. 237–8.

Source: Various issues of: *Australasian Insurance and Banking Record*; *Jobson's Investment Digest*; *Official Melbourne Stock Exchange Record*; *Delfin Digest*; *Business Review Weekly* 6.11.1986, pp. 89–116, and 16.11.1998, pp. 108–60.

decade between 1986 and 1997. Resources and manufacturing numbers experienced modest losses, while the service industries showed mixed results with nearly all of the gains being in distribution and entertainment.

The distribution of the top 10 firms is shown in Table 2.8. The data shows that the largest firms came from a narrower range of industries than the top 100. Manufacturing was the only sector that contributed firms to the top 10 at every enumeration. Furthermore, it accounted for more than a half of the top 10 firms in 1952, 1964 and 1986. Mining and the wholesale and retail trades were the next most represented sectors, appearing in five of the six lists. Their greatest contributions were at opposite ends of the time scale. The wholesale and retail trades were particularly important in the first half of the century but fell away thereafter, largely as a result of the declining influence of the pastoral service firms. Mining's most important contribution was in 1997, when it had three in the top 10. Four other sectors were represented only once, and communications appeared twice. Three sectors – construction, community service and entertainment – had no firms large enough to reach the top 10.

Financial firms

Financial services firms, most notably banks, have played a major role in the Australian economy over the period of European settlement. As financial intermediaries, the banks and non-bank institutions, such as life offices, insurers, finance companies, merchant banks, building societies and credit unions, have managed net flows of about 20 per cent of GDP between savers and borrowers on average over the past 100 years.[28] Moreover, banks' deposits and paper

Table 2.8: Distribution of top 10 non-financial firms by sector, 1910–97

Date	A	B	C	D	E	F	G	H	I	K	L
1910	1	1	2	–	–	6	–	–	–	–	–
1930	–	–	4	2	–	4	–	–	–	–	–
1952	–	1	7	–	–	2	–	–	–	–	–
1964	–	1	8	–	–	1	–	–	–	–	–
1986	–	1	6	–	–	1	–	1	1	–	–
1997	–	3	4	–	–	–	1	2	–	–	–

Note: ASIC classifications listed in Table 2.2 and detailed on pp. 237–8.

Source: Various issues of: *Australasian Insurance and Banking Record*; *Jobson's Investment Digest*; *Official Melbourne Stock Exchange Record*; *Delfin Digest*; *Business Review Weekly* 6.11.1986, pp. 89–116, and 16.11.1998, pp. 108–60.

currency, an exclusive private bank activity until the Queensland government issued notes in the 1890s and the Commonwealth government took over the note issue in 1910, were key elements in the money supply. The ratio of assets of all financial institutions to GDP and the money supply to GDP rose very sharply in the second half of the nineteenth century as the number and range of financial institutions expanded. Thereafter, the ratios fluctuated but remained well above pre-1900 levels.[29]

The financial system was dominated by the banks, both trading and savings, over nearly all of the period. The trading banks were privately owned, with the exception of the Commonwealth Bank of Australia established in 1912, and a few minor state banks. A number were British in origin. On the other hand, nearly all of the savings banks were state-owned, with the exception of a few trustee savings banks in Tasmania, before the trading banks were allowed to open savings bank subsidiaries in the 1950s.

Lists of the top 25 financial institutions and their assets at each date from 1910 until 1997 are presented in Appendix B. A summary of that data is shown in Table 2.9. Banks were the most important institutions both in terms of

Table 2.9: Top 25 financial institutions by type, asset share and ownership, 1910–97

	1910	1930	1952	1964	1986	1997
Private banks	16	10	9	7	8	12
% assets	67.3	47.1	46.0	42.4	53.1	72.7
Foreign	4	3	2	2	2	6
Government banks	5	5	7	5	7	–
% assets	18.4	32.1	34.7	28.2	26.3	–
Life offices	4	8	9	6	3	6
% assets	14.3	20.4	19.3	23.7	11.5	18.7
Foreign	–	–	–	–	–	2
Other nbfi	–	2	–	7	8	7
% assets	–	0.3	–	5.7	9.1	8.6
Foreign	–	–	–	1	–	1
Foreign total	4	3	2	3	2	9
Foreign % of total assets	22	16	15	14	2	11

Note: Private banks include the Hobart and Launceston Savings Banks in 1930.
nbfi = non-bank financial institutions.

Sources: *Australasian Insurance & Banking Record*; Butlin, *Australian Monetary System*; Gray, *Life Insurance*; Butlin, Hall & White, *Australian Banking and Monetary Statistics*, pp. 98–101 & Tables 54(ii), 56(ii), 57(ii), 58(ii) & 59(ii); *Australian Banking and Monetary Statistics*, Table 70, p. 503; Block (ed.), *Delfin Digest 1964*, pp. 102–5 & 108–11; *Business Review Weekly*, 20 November 1987; *Business Review Weekly*, 16 November 1998.

numbers and asset share. The number of banks fell irregularly over time. They numbered 21 in 1910, 15 in 1930, 16 in 1952, 12 in 1964, 15 in 1986, and 12 in 1997. There were more private than government banks, although the number of these publicly owned institutions was unusually high compared with many other advanced economies. Government bank numbers remained between five and seven between 1910 and 1986, before being reduced to zero by privatisations in the 1990s. Bank assets, both private and government, averaged 78 per cent of the assets of all financial institutions across the six observations. The biggest fluctuations were across the last three observations, reflecting the cross currents of, on the one hand, the positive impact of deregulation on the size of bank balance sheets, as against the growth of super-annuation funds and other financial markets on the other.

Levels of foreign ownership were much lower among financial service firms than in the rest of the economy as shown earlier in Table 2.2 (p. 17). The number of foreign-owned financial firms fell from four to two between 1910 and 1952, where it remained, with the exception of 1964, until 1986. A liberalisation of the restrictions on foreign ownership, culminating in the granting of banking licences to overseas banks in 1985, saw a sharp increase in their number by 1997. The share of assets employed by foreign institutions fell from a high of 22 per cent in 1910 to only 2 per cent in 1986. This decline was due in large part to the restrictions on foreign entry noted above, and the transfer of domicile of the Australian and New Zealand Bank from Britain to Australia in 1976. The influx of foreign banks following deregulation in the late 1980s and 1990s lifted the share of foreign-owned assets in the financial sector back to 11 per cent.

Australian top firms in an international perspective

How do the largest firms in Australia rank compared with those in other countries? This question has a number of dimensions. First, have the largest Australian firms been in the same broad sectors as those in other countries for which similar studies have been undertaken? Following Chandler, nearly all research on big business in other economies has focused on manufacturing activity. This study traces firms from the resource, service and financial services industries, making direct comparisons difficult. Within manufacturing, have the largest Australian firms been clustered in those same capital-intensive and science-based industries as elsewhere? Many of the arguments pursued above would suggest that the character of Australian economic development, particularly its comparative advantage in resource-based activities and government policies, would have given a unique shape to the sectoral structure of its largest firms. Second, how important were these largest firms in the context of their local economy, both absolutely and comparatively? Did the small size of the domestic market and low rates of internationalisation shrink Australia's largest firms *pari passu*? Third, how large were Australian firms relative to those in other economies, both in the bigger and more mature industrial countries such as the United States, Britain, Germany and Japan, and in a number of smaller economies?

Studies of big business in other nations have emphasised that most of the largest industrial firms were to be found in a narrow range of industries, namely, food, beverages and tobacco, textiles, chemicals, petroleum, metals, machinery, and transport equipment. It was these industries that were most affected by the technological and market imperatives that were driving the growth of scale in manufacturing industry.

Data in Table 2.10 suggests that Australia's largest industrial firms had a sectoral distribution unlike that of the four leading industrial economies. In many respects this was not surprising. As argued above, the cost disadvantages associated with the small-scale Australian market and the nature of its factor markets meant that large sections of Australian manufacturing were not internationally competitive.[30] The high levels of protection offered against imports encouraged local production by both domestic and foreign firms in a range of industries that yielded lower returns from economies of scale or scope.

Table 2.10 shows that no less than two-thirds of the Australian manufacturing firms from the top 100 were located in the capital-intensive and science-based consumer and producer good sectors. However, firms in the United States, Japan and Germany were clustered in the producer goods sectors to a far higher extent. Only Britain had a comparable bias towards consumer goods. Australia, like Japan, increased its reliance on producer goods industries over time. What marks Australia as different from the others is the greater concentration of firms from the miscellaneous category that included less technologically complex activities such as clay, concrete, paper and leather products.

Big business dominated the Australian economy to a greater extent than appears to have been the case in other leading economies. Direct comparisons are unavailable from the data sets being used, as Australian firms are from all non-financial sectors while only manufacturing firms have been included for the rest. This caveat notwithstanding, the data presented in Table 2.11, following Schmitz's approach of comparing the size of the leading 25 firms with the level of national income, suggest that Australia's top firms had an above average weight within the economy. Although there were some fluctuations from year to year, the general trend in all four countries was for the relative weight of the largest 25 firms to increase over time. Australia had either the highest, in 1910, or second highest ratio, trailing Britain, at each observation date.

Table 2.10: Share of consumer and producer goods in manufacturing output, selected countries, 1910–97

	Consumer goods	Producer goods	Miscellaneous
United States			
1917	21	65	14
1930	20	63	17
1948	20	67	13
1973	14	61	25
1988	12	64	24
Japan			
1918	42	41	17
1930	47	38	15
1954	30	58	12
1973	15	66	19
1987	13	66	21
Germany			
1913	21	69	10
1929	27	61	12
1953	24	65	11
1973	17	68	15
Britain			
1919	45	47	8
1930	44	40	16
1948	38	47	15
1973	24	53	23
Australia			
1910	57	27	17
1930	36	31	33
1952	35	40	25
1964	21	54	25
1986	18	66	16
1997	30	46	24

Note: Covers top 200 manufacturing firms for each nation and manufacturers among top 100 for Australia.

Sources: Schmitz, *Big Business*, p. 36; Fruin, *Japanese Enterprise System*, p. 164; Chandler and Hikino, 'Large industrial enterprise', p. 40.

Table 2.11: Ratio of assets of leading 25 firms to GDP, selected countries, 1910–85

	1910–18		1930–38		1948–53		1985	
	US$m	% GDP	US$m	% GDP	US$m	% GDP	US$m	% GDP
USA	7 934	10	17 714	19	28 840	11	620 500	15
Japan	616	10	1 227	17	2 397	15	221 210	16
Germany	1 131	9	3 778	10	3 310	9	114 075	17
Britain	1 399	11	7 662	28	7 480	18	216 463	45
Australia	290	19	702	21	1 269	16	85 433	38

Notes: Book asset values are used for all countries, except for Britain where market capitalisation has been used for all dates before 1985. For all countries other than Australia, these are assets of the 25 largest industrial firms. The 1985 data for countries other than Australia are the assets of the top 25 industrial firms ranked by sales. The column dates for Australia are 1910, 1930, 1952 and 1986. The dates for the other countries are: USA 1917, 1930, 1948, 1985; Japan 1918, 1930, 1954, 1985; Germany 1913, 1938, 1953, 1985; Britain 1912, 1937, 1948, 1985. All figures are in US$m.

Sources: Schmitz, *Big Business*, p. 34; Chandler, *Scale and Scope*, pp. 638–732; Fruin, *Japanese Enterprise System*, pp. 329–59; 'Fortune 500', *Fortune International*, 29 April 1985, p. 154; 'The international 500', *Fortune International*, 19 August 1985, pp. 159–65.

An alternative measure of the importance of large-scale enterprise to the Australian economy is to examine the size distribution within the largest firms. A comparison of the ratio of the aggregate asset value of the bottom five firms to the top five indicates the gap between the smallest and largest – the higher the ratio, the more modest the rate of descent from the giants to the pygmies. In 1910 the ratio for the top 100 Australian firms was 0.039. This was well below the ratios in both Japan and Britain. The figure for the top 100 industrial firms in Japan in 1918 was 0.065. While the relative size of the fiftieth British firm to the first ranked by market value in 1904–05 was 0.052.[31]

By 1930 the Australian ratio had risen to 0.094, indicating a marked lessening in the inequality between the largest and smallest. The comparable figures for Japanese industrials in 1930 also rose to 0.086, and Britain's remained little changed at 0.049 in 1934–35. From this peak, Australia's ratio fell away to 0.074 in 1952 and 0.068 in 1964. However, from that date forward, the biggest Australian firms' assets grew much faster than those of the ninety-sixth through to one hundredth firms, driving the ratio down to 0.034 in 1986 and 0.024 in 1997. This shift was in stark contrast with the Japanese and British experience. The ratio in Japan rose to 0.114 in 1954, and remained high at 0.079 in 1973 and 0.081 in 1986, whereas in Britain the ratio had risen sharply to 0.063 in 1985. The explosive increase in the size of the very largest Australian firms in the 1980s and 1990s reflects the rise of 'global' firms such as News Corporation, BHP and Conzinc Riotinto Australia and the corporatisation or privatisation of former public utilities in telecommunications and air travel, Telstra and Qantas.

This growth of large firms within a small economy resulted in very high levels of seller concentration in many markets. Radical writers and pamphleteers had denounced the rise of monopoly in the Australian economy from early in the century.[32] Oligopolies and regional monopolies were evident in sugar refining, brewing, shipping, banking and wool broking, even before World War One.[33] A pioneering study by Karmel and Brunt, noted that in 1959 over the previous 25 years, 'Big Business and positions of market dominance have gone hand in hand. The one has served to reinforce the other.'[34] They observed that of the 20 largest listed manufacturing firms, 19 were monopolists in their leading product markets or operated in an industry where the first eight firms accounted for at least a half of employment. Their research identified similarly high levels of concentration in retailing, mining and financial services.[35] Subsequent data prepared by the Australian Bureau of Statistics confirms the continuance of high levels of seller concentration in many parts of manufacturing.[36] In the last 30 years of the twentieth century, giants from the resources and media industries eclipsed manufacturing firms in size.

If Australia's largest firms occupied an unusually prominent place in the economy and particular industries, were they large by international standards? It is to be expected that they would be of a markedly smaller size. Australia stood apart from the industrial economies of the Northern Hemisphere in terms of absolute size, as well as its structure. Its population and domestic markets were only a fraction the size of those of the leading economies. For example, the largest company in the first four of the years analysed was Dalgety (1910), CSR (1930), and BHP (1952 and 1964). In each case the leading firm was at least 20 per cent larger than its nearest domestic rival but compared poorly with dominant firms in other nations. Thus, Dalgety's £8m of assets in 1910 puts it well down the list of the world's top 100 industrial firms for 1912 at 62nd, and the second largest firm, British Tobacco (Australia), would only just have got in the list at 99.[37] CSR's assets in 1930 would not have brought it close to the top 50 industrials globally for 1937 and it was only one-sixtieth the size of America's top industrial company of 1930, US Steel. By 1952 Australia's BHP possessed little more than a thirtieth of the assets that America's Standard Oil (New Jersey) had boasted four years earlier.[38]

The diminutive nature of Australian corporations is likewise reflected in a comparison with the top 25 corporations in the United States: the aggregate assets of the Australian firms representing only 3.0, 3.6, and 4.0 per cent of their United States counterparts for the years 1910/17, 1930, and 1948/52. Differences of similar magnitudes were carried over into the 1980s, as Australia's largest firm, BHP once again, ranked 94th by sales in the list of the 500 largest international firms, and would have come in at 76th in the United States firm list.[39]

The issue of comparative size can be brought into sharper focus by measuring firms within the same industries on a population-adjusted basis. Table 2.12 shows the asset size of the largest Australian and United States firms in similar industries. In 1930, the United States firms' assets exceed those of their Australian peers in every category. However, the population of the United States was some 19 times larger than Australia's at this time. On a per capita basis, only the United States firms in paper, chemicals, basic metals and transport equipment were larger than their counterparts. By the early 1950s, Australian firms were catching up in both absolute and per capita measures. Australia's largest sugar refiner now had more assets than the American Sugar Refining Company. The United States population was roughly 16 times larger than Australia's in 1952. Multiplying the assets of Australian firms by this number, all the local firms were bigger than the United States firms, once adjustments were made for the size of the market.

The most important difference between the two economies was the number of large firms within particular industries, rather than the absolute difference in

Table 2.12: Comparison of Australia's and the United States' largest manufacturing firms by industry, selected years

	Aus 1930	Assets $m	US 1930	Assets $m	Aus 1952	Assets $m	US 1948	Assets $m
Sugar	CSR	30	AmSR	32	CSR	98	AmSR	42
Tobacco	Br Tob	20	AmTob	49	Br Tob	50	AmTob	214
Brewing	Tooth	14	–		Tooth	30	An-Bus	27
Paper	APM	4	IPP	179	APM	72	IP	101
Chemical	CFC	3	DuPont	135	ICIANZ	58	DuPont	370
Glass	AGM	2	Pitts	22	ACI	40	Pitts.	71
Basic metals	BHP	18	US Steel	522	BHP	122	US Steel	789
Transport	Holden	4	GMC	287	GMH	50	GMC	921
Rubber	Dunlop	12	Goodyear	50	Dunlop	38	Goodyear	132

Note: All figures are in A$m.

Source: Australian firms: Various issues of: *Australasian Insurance and Banking Record*; *Jobson's Investment Digest*; *Official Melbourne Stock Exchange Record*; *Delfin Digest*; *Business Review Weekly* 6.11.1986, pp. 89–116, and 16.11.1998, pp. 108–60. US firms from Chandler, *Scale and Scope*, Appendix A.2 and A.3, pp. 644–57.

size. While Australian industries were highly concentrated with monopolists or duopolists, the United States market was large enough, and augmented by exports and offshore production by multinationals, to support a larger number of sizeable competitors. Leading Australian firms increasingly came to be of sufficient size to require Chandler's three-pronged investments in production, distribution and management. It is unlikely that the Australian market was large enough for more than one firm in any manufacturing industry to capture fully the economies of scale and scope available to multiple firms in the larger markets. Lack of rivalry in many local markets undermined the incentives for Australian firms to augment their capabilities.

A similar picture emerges when comparing the assets of Australian banks with those of leading British and Canadian banks from the 1930s to the 1990s. The results are shown in Table 2.13. In the mid-1930s, Australian banks were

Table 2.13: Assets of leading Australian, British and Canadian banks, 1936–95

	1936	1969	1995
Australia			
National/NAB	44	1 878	98
BNSW/Westpac	89	3 808	80
Bank A'sia/ANZ	60	3 805	75
UBA	44	–	–
ES&A	39	–	–
CBA	29	1 262	–
CBCS	54	836	–
Britain			
Barclays	485	15 137	262
Westminster	411	10 642	261
Lloyds TSB	543	6 692	229
Midland	569	7 796	–
National Provincial	403	–	–
Canada			
Royal Bank Canada	194	9 599	132
CIBC	150	8 629	128
Bank Montreal	180	7 579	110
Novia Scotia	57	5 377	106
Toronto Dominion	31	4 918	77

Note: 1936 data A£m; 1969 in US$m and 1995 in US$b.

Source: *Bank and Insurance Shares Year Book 1937* (London, n.d.); *The Banker*, June 1970, and July 1996.

far smaller than the big British clearing banks and smaller again than the biggest Canadian banks. This broad ranking is repeated in 1969 and 1995. The gap closed over time. In 1936, the Bank of New South Wales was 16 per cent the size of Barclays and 46 per cent the size of the Royal Bank of Canada. It was a quarter the size of Barclays in 1969 and 40 per cent the size of the Royal Bank of Canada. National Australia Bank, now Australia's largest bank, was 37 per cent the size of Barclays and 74 per cent of the size of the Royal Bank of Canada. Adjusting for the differences in the populations of these countries, the Australian banks had more assets per capita than their British counterparts at every date and their Canadian peers in 1995.

The conclusion that emerges from the data is that the population and income levels of the local market largely determined the size of Australian banks. The failure of Australian banks to take their business offshore (by opening branches as distinct from offering services through correspondent banks) to the same extent as the Canadian banks in particular, tied them to a small domestic base and a presence in New Zealand.

Australian banking in particular, and the financial services industry in general, was characterised by high levels of seller concentration. A series of mergers between banks from 1917 to 1931 reduced the numbers to seven big private banks that increasingly operated as a collusive oligopoly. Government regulation of banking from 1941 until deregulation in the 1980s, ended price competition and dampened product innovation. Like manufacturing, banking lacked the spur of competition, at least until the 1980s, to augment their capabilities.

A comparison of the largest Australian firms in the mid-1990s with those from economies of comparable levels of development and populations highlights the constraints faced in creating and sustaining big business in this country.[40] The data in Table 2.14 shows the number of firms, the size of their assets measured in billions of US dollars, and their sectoral distributions from Australia, Canada, the Netherlands, Sweden and Switzerland. Together, these five small economies sustained 75 of the top 500 international firms selected by *Forbes*.[41] In terms of population, Australia with 18 million was well short of Canada's 29 million, but roughly the same size as the Netherlands and twice that of Sweden and Switzerland. In terms of the number of firms per capita, and average assets per firm and per capita, Australia trailed on almost every measure. Australia and Sweden each had 12 firms in the list, trailing behind Canada, Switzerland and Sweden with 16, 17 and 18, respectively. Australia had fewer firms per head of population than any country other than Canada. The Netherlands and Sweden had double the number, and Switzerland, treble. The average size of the Australian firms, in terms of assets, was significantly smaller than every other country, with the exception of Sweden. However, a comparison of the average size of non-financial firms places Australia firmly at the bottom of the list. On a per capita basis, the assets of all Australian firms and those of firms in the non-financial sectors fell well behind these other countries.

Table 2.14: Firms in *Forbes* 'Foreign 500' by country and industry, 1995

	Australia	Canada	Netherlands	Sweden	Switzerland
Population	**18m**	**29m**	**15m**	**9m**	**7m**
Finance	NAB 99	RBC 132	ING 247	Skandia 27	CSH 359
	ANZ 76	CIBC 128	ABN 341	Svenska 72	UBS 336
	Westpac 71	BNS 106	Fortis 161	SkEnB 66	Swiss 257
	Comm 63	BM 110	Aegon 94		Zurich 83
		TDB 77			W'thur 71
					Baloise 31
					Swiss Re 32
Sub-total	[4] $309	[5] $553	[4] $843	[3] $165	[7] $1169
Airline	Qantas 6		KLM 10		Swissair 9
Media	News 21	Thomson 10	Reed 9		
Retail	Coles 5	G. Weston 4	Ahold 6		
	W'worths 2		Vendex 3		
Telecom		BCE 28			
Utilities		TC PL 8			
Construction				Skanska 6	
Sub-total	[4] $34	[4] $50	[4] $28	[1] $6	[1] $9
Forest	Amcor 5		KNP-BT 6	SCA-S 10	
				Stora 9	
Energy	BHP 22	Imp Oil 9	Shell 118		
Metals	RTZ 16	Alcan 10	R. Hoog. 5		
		Noranda 9			
Food, etc.		Seagram 21	Unilever 30		Nestlé 39
			Heineken 6		
Multi-indy	Pac-Dun 5	Imasco 41			Al-Lo. 5
		Can Pac 12			Cie F R 9
Chemicals			Akzo Nob.12	Astra 7	Ciba 26
			DSM 6		Sandoz 18
					Roche 31
Engineering		Bombard. 5	Philips 33	ABB 32	ABB 32
		Schlumb. 9		Volvo 21	Sulzer 6
				Electr. 13	
				Ericsson 14	
				SKF 6	

continued next page

Table 2.14: Continued

	Australia	Canada	Netherlands	Sweden	Switzerland
Building materials					Holderb. 13
Sub-total	[4] $48	[7] $107	[9] $225	[8] $112	[9] $179
Total assets	$391	$710	$1096	$283	$1357
Total firms	12	16	18	12	17
Firm/m. pop	0.7	0.6	1.2	1.3	2.4
Av asset	$32.6	$44.4	$60.9	$23.6	$79.8
Av asset non-financial	$10.3	$14.3	$18.1	$13.1	$19.9
Assets/popn	$21 722	$24 483	$73 067	$31 444	$193 857
Non-fin/popn	$4 556	$5 414	$16 867	$13 111	$26 857

Notes: Firms selected into *Forbes* 'Foreign 500' on basis of sales revenue. All financial data are in US$bn, except assets to population ratios in final two rows.

Source: Davis (ed.), *Forbes Top Companies*, pp. 169–90.

Not only were Australian firms generally smaller than their counterparts from other countries, but their distribution across sectors suggests important differences in the industrial structure and international competitiveness of these economies. Australia's 12 firms were split evenly in number across the finance, services and manufacturing sectors, in marked contrast to the others. Australia was seriously underweight in manufacturing, and overweight in the financial sector and other service industries. Only Switzerland had a greater concentration of its firms in financial services.

Australia's largest financial firms, all banks, were far smaller than the leading firms in Canada, and especially the Netherlands and Switzerland. In the service sector, Australia had only one clear winner, as News Corporation was more than twice the size of Canada's Thomson and the Netherlands' Reed-Elsevier publishing groups. Both KLM and Swissair eclipsed Qantas, government-owned for most of its history. Australia's retailing duopolists, Coles Myer and Woolworths, were no larger than the two leading firms from the Netherlands.

The contrasts within manufacturing provide the starkest evidence of Australia's status as an 'outlier'. Three of its four firms – Amcor, BHP and Conzinc Riotinto Australia – were resource-based, while the fourth, Pacific Dunlop, was a widely diversified manufacturer operating in predominantly low technology businesses including food, clothing, tyres, cables and surgical gloves.[42] Amcor, a paper and packaging company, was smaller than its Dutch and Swedish counterparts. BHP and Conzinc Riotinto Australia were minnows compared to Royal Dutch Shell. Pacific Dunlop's asset size was easily eclipsed by the Canadian duo of Imasco and Canadian Pacific, and Switzerland's Cie Financière Richemont. Australia had no firms large enough in the beverage or food processing industries or the chemical and engineering sectors, the heartland of the second industrial revolution, to make the Forbes' list, while the four other countries possessed 20. These included global leaders such as Seagram, Unilever, Nestlé, Akzo-Nobel NV, Philips, ABB Group, Volvo, Ericsson, Electrolux Group, Roche, and the Swiss building materials firm, Holderbank Financière Glarus, all of whom were among the world's largest 100 transnationals.[43]

High survival rates among firms could be indicative of their ability to exploit organisational capabilities as a source of competitive advantage or of a lack of competitive pressure in markets with few firms. It was probably some combination of the two. Whatever the reason, the ability to survive within the cohort of leading firms is especially impressive, given the rapid and volatile rates of economic and political change, which have been a feature of the twentieth century.

Data in Table 2.15 show that a significant number of the top firms in any one list do not survive to the next. Turnover rates measure the loss of companies from the list through relative decline or being acquired by a firm not in the list. Using Chandler's data, turnover rates for American, British and German firms have been calculated at between 1.0 and 1.8 per cent per annum. On average, one or two firms drop out and are replaced each year. Among the top 200 Japanese firms, average turnover rates were higher, varying from 2.9 per cent per annum in 1918–30, to 1.7 per cent in 1930–54 and 1954–73.

The data suggest that the turnover rates tended to decline, with the exception of Britain, up to around the middle of the century. Another study of the United States data over a longer timeframe supports the view that the turnover rates fell until around 1950, then remained roughly stable before rising sharply between 1977 and 1986.[44] Declining and then more stable turnover rates among industrial firms can be attributed to a number of factors: the entrenchment of first mover advantages; a reduction in the rate of technological change that would create new demands; growing professionalism of managers who seek the 'preservation of the firm qua organisation'; and, the adoption of diversification strategies that provided firms with a hedge against changes in demand.[45]

It would seem reasonable to suppose that this same set of generic factors would be at work in Australia, where turnover rates were consistently higher than the other nations in Table 2.15 except Japan in 1918–30. However, the data sets do not allow an exact comparison, since the Australian data include firms from a wider set of industries. The major drivers of turnover rates among the

Table 2.15: Turnover rates within top firms, selected countries, 1913–97

Country	Period	Percentage	Percentage p.a.
Germany	1913–29	29	1.8
	1929–53	31	1.3
Britain	1919–30	11	1.0
	1930–48	21	1.2
United States	1917–30	18	1.4
	1930–48	24	1.3
Japan	1918–30	35	2.9
	1930–54	41	1.7
	1954–73	32	1.7
Australia	1910–30	45	2.3
	1930–52	48	2.2
	1952–64	33	2.8
	1964–86	55	2.5
	1986–97	55	5.0

Note: Figures for Japan, USA, Germany and Britain refer to 200 largest industrial firms, for the latter three they include only food, chemical and machinery industries. Turnover measures the number of companies from the top 200 (Australia 100) at each enumeration not appearing in the next. Disappearance reflects liquidation, a decline in asset value or acquisition by a non-listed firm.

Sources: Schmitz, *Big Business*, p. 34; Chandler, *Scale and Scope*, pp. 638–732; Fruin, *Japanese Enterprise System*, pp. 329–59; 'Fortune 500', *Fortune International*, 29 April 1985, p. 154; 'The international 500', *Fortune International*, August 19 1985, pp. 159–65.

top 100 Australian firms are changing demand patterns across the economy as a whole rather than factors that would impact upon the stability of leadership within industries. The point is made in Table 2.4 on p. 20. Australia's economy underwent profound change in its structure over the long term, with the relative importance of industries waxing and waning.

It is difficult to offer a meaningful interpretation of turnover rates among Australian manufacturing firms as the numbers altered significantly between observations, rising from 30 in 1910 to 71 in 1964 and falling back to 46 in 1997. Government policy, particularly towards manufacturing, played a large part in the structural transformation of the economy. Removing the protective apparatus of trade barriers and subsidies, changing the rules with respect to the ownership of media and communications businesses, legalising gambling, privatising government businesses and outlawing restrictive trade practices from the 1980s onwards, all contributed to sharply increased turnover rates at the end of the century, as some firms shrank and new ones came forward. The process was accelerated by a wave of acquisitions in the late 1980s that resulted in many of the top 100 firms acquiring one another.

Conclusion

This chapter has dealt with the general rather than the particular. It has sought to place the phenomena of the emergence of large firms in Australia in a wider comparative context. The combination of forces that gave rise to the development of big business in many other modern industrialised countries from the late nineteenth and early twentieth centuries also operated in Australia. The broad principle was the same, the details differed. Whereas the largest firms were generally found in manufacturing activity abroad, Australian business people created very large organisations in the resources and service sectors of the economy. Our list of those top 100 and top 25 non-financial and financial firms at various dates is presented in Appendices B and C.

Entrepreneurs and managers responded to the opportunities presented within an economy that was unusually rich in natural resources and whose wealthy population exhibited a high demand for business and consumption services. Large firms emerged in all those parts of the economy where there were economies of scale and scope to be exploited. Large firms tended to dominate the markets they served. However, Australia's largest firms tended to be smaller in absolute terms than their counterparts in similar industries based in the world's biggest economies. The position is not so clear cut when the firm size is adjusted for population.

The following chapters take on a new direction. The book moves away from a review of broad issues to focus on individual firms. By what means did these firms come to be and remain as corporate leaders?

CHAPTER 3

Identifying the Corporate Leaders

In Chapter 2 we used a range of time series and cross-sectional data on the economy and firms to present a broad picture of the growth of big business in the Australian economy, and drew parallels with the experience of other nations. We were able to identify in which sectors our largest firms have been located, how this changed over the course of the twentieth century, and who these firms were. This provides the basis for a closer investigation of some of these firms in this and subsequent chapters. Therefore, in this chapter, we will develop the concept of a *corporate leader*, a firm that is distinguished by more than just its size. We design a methodology for identifying corporate leaders in Australia, and then examine who these firms actually were. Reducing the number of firms analysed from 354 to around 78 enables us in chapters 4 to 7 to investigate more closely the pattern of their development using the methodological schema outlined in Chapter 1, notably the methods, resources, directions, and structure of development. From this, we seek to identify if any common patterns existed. In Chapter 8 we then assess what sort of role corporate leaders have played in the evolution of individual industries, the business sector, and the economy as a whole.

Prime movers and challengers

The notion of the first or prime mover examines the existence of firms that have played a dominant role in developing a new industry or transforming an existing one. Successful prime movers stand to benefit from being first, but will soon face challengers seeking to share in these gains. Where a first mover is able to resist such challenges to retain its dominant position it is said to possess first mover advantages. As Grant has noted, 'The idea of first-mover advantage is that the initial occupant of a strategic position or niche gains access to resources and capabilities that a follower cannot match'.[1] The first mover is able to sustain its leadership of the industry by erecting barriers to entry or, at least, establishing forms of competitive advantage over new entrants.

There is a broad conceptual literature on the nature and extent of first mover advantages. The benefits can be divided into the initial pre-emption of scarce resources, such as particular materials and skilled labour, by the first mover, and its subsequent attempts to pursue corporate strategies and develop capabilities as an organisation that is designed to perpetuate that initial dominance.[2] Porter has described how firms sustain competitive advantage through such strategies as cost leadership, product differentiation, and market segmentation.[3] The first mover can use the profits of the initial monopoly period to extend its knowledge advantage over other firms and introduce a range of enduring firm competences. Such competences might include a workforce specifically trained for that industry and an organisational structure oriented to the type of product being manufactured. Mueller has linked first mover advantages with the 'path dependency' principle to show why it is often difficult to catch up, irrespective of the strategies of the first mover.[4] He cites a series of demand related, inertial advantages benefiting the first mover, including uncertainty over the new competing product, habit formation and switching costs. On the supply side, the challenger faces compacted set-up costs and greater difficulties raising finance through the capital market, where investors need to be convinced of the challenger's ability to overcome these hurdles and wrest market share from the first mover. While the theoretical literature largely deals with the efficiency properties of individual firms, applied and historical studies additionally draw attention to the predatory actions of first movers in erecting entry barriers, and to the vagaries of public policy.[5]

There are also disadvantages of being first, which may lead to rapid dissipation of the initial leadership in some cases. Late entrants may free-ride on the development costs incurred by the pioneer, commencing production after a significant reduction in costs has occurred. First movers in rapidly evolving industries are particularly vulnerable to supersession by new entrants who can orient their set-up costs to a changing infrastructure. Technological, resource or market shifts may make it expensive for the pioneer to refocus and write off sunk costs, but easy for the challenger to get started. Where several of these shifts occur simultaneously, sometimes known as a punctuated equilibrium, the first mover's dominance is particularly vulnerable.

First mover inertia, born of a firm's uncontested dominance, can also weaken its ability to respond to challenges when they do ultimately occur. In addition, much depends upon the strength of the challengers. Empirical research suggests that successful challengers are rarely new firms attempting to mimic the success of the first mover. Most successful challengers are either the product of mergers that yield synergies from among competing firms in the industry, or they are existing firms diversifying from other sectors or geographical areas, bringing with them established organisational capabilities.[6]

The ability of first movers to establish sustainable advantages is thus highly contingent; the magnitude of advantage varies over product categories, geographic areas, time periods, the degree of initial leadership, and the respective competences of first mover and challenger. Leiberman and Montgomery have expressed concern that, 'as a focus for empirical research, the concept of first mover advantage may be too general and definitionally elusive to be useful'.[7] However, it is only through empirical investigations that we can more accurately understand the sources and broader consequences of corporate leadership. Historical studies of United States business have provided us with the most extensive evidence of how firms can convert first mover status into sustained corporate leadership.

Chandler argued that environmental changes occurring in the United States economy in the nineteenth century created new opportunities in many industries, particularly the introduction of fast, regular railway and telegraph services, bringing with them wider markets and easier access to raw materials.[8] He suggests that first movers, particularly in capital-intensive industries, were able to sustain their leadership by making the three-pronged set of core investments in production, marketing, and management, as outlined in Chapter 1. The effect of these investments was to build up corporate competences by developing low-cost production technologies, marketing facilities that supported complex products, and management teams capable of providing strategic direction for the firm. He cites firms such as Du Pont, General Electric, Goodyear, Remington, Singer, Heinz, NCR, American Telephone and Telegraph Company, Standard Oil, and Alcoa as examples. Consistent with this perspective was the experience of Ford, whose failure to invest in a modern management team prepared it poorly for adaptation to the changing vehicle market after World War One and the successful challenge by General Motors.[9]

The fate of some United States prime movers fits less comfortably with Chandler's hypothesis. Standard Oil's break-up in 1911–12 was due at least in part to public policies: the rise of United States competition policy and the British government's support of Anglo-Persian. American Telephone and Telegraph Company extended their leadership in communications not by improving their operational efficiency but through predatory policies against new entrants. This included collusion with telegraph companies, the acquisition of telephone manufacturers, and using its capital market connections, especially J. P. Morgan, to deny financial support to other companies. In addition, follower companies had to pay more for their telephone service franchises as their real value became more apparent.[10]

First movers in Britain less often followed the three-pronged investment strategy. There were many reasons for this: firms faced a different operating environment, particularly a more heterogeneous market less suited to mass production, along with a tradition of personal management and inter-firm cooperation that contrasted with the internalised professional management structures of United States corporations. Finally, corporate leaders in Britain were more often located in industries less suited to mass production methods, such as shipping and shipbuilding. Nonetheless, there emerged in Britain many firms, either prime movers or challengers, that provided leadership in key industries. These included Cadbury's, Lever Brothers, Cunard, Harland & Wolff, Coates, Imperial Tobacco, Imperial Chemical Industries and Pilkington.

Corporate leaders

Therefore, both first movers and challengers can attain a position of dominance in an industry. As Golder and Tellis have noted, 'The logic of success is not to be first to enter the market, but to strive for leadership by scanning opportunities, building on strengths, and committing resources to serve consumers effectively'.[11] Resource-based theories of the firm that examine the development of a firm's organisational capabilities over time and its interaction with its environment, help us to understand how certain firms become *corporate leaders* of their industry.[12] Organisational capabilities refer to a firm's capacity to undertake particular functions or activities. Where such capabilities are durable and can be renewed in response to environmental change, they provide firms with powerful and sustaining competitive advantages.[13] To be a corporate leader, therefore, also implies a sense of permanence that goes beyond an initiating role quickly followed by exit, or a challenge that does not endure.

Using the broader concept of corporate leader facilitates empirical analysis. It is often difficult to clearly identify the prime mover in an industry, and indeed some of the firms cited as British corporate leaders above were not the first to initiate their industry or a particular product within it, especially in cases of industries that have survived many centuries and experienced incremental innovations over long periods, such as in shipping and shipbuilding. Many of the firms mentioned above could be perceived in a dual role as both first mover and challenger.

As we noted earlier, successful challengers are often firms diversifying geographically or sectorally: Lever Brothers and Nestlé are examples of European first movers who became challengers in the United States market. Many United States first movers proved to be strong challengers in the European market. Corporate leadership may be beneficent or selfish. Its leadership may benefit other companies and the economy more broadly, for example, by initiating or increasing the demand for a product or introducing growth-inducing innovations that transform the industry's performance. This is the form of leadership Chandler has in mind in linking United States prime mover corporations with the broader story of national economic expansion.

An alternative version is the leader that uses its power to stifle change and maintain its dominance: like the poisonous upas tree in whose shadow no other shrub may grow.[14] The example above of American Telephone and Telegraph Company is an apposite one. Either way, the firm may draw upon its organisational capabilities and is a leader in the sense of keeping ahead of the pack, but its impact on the development of the industry and the broader macroeconomy will differ.

Therefore, our main unit of analysis is the firm as corporate leader. We refer to the organisation rather than individuals, although the abilities of particular business leaders within the company will help drive success, especially in personally managed enterprises. One can extend analysis from the level of the firm to that of the industry and, indeed, the nation: leadership can reside at each of these levels. Corporate strategy and capabilities build leadership at the firm level. Product life cycle theory helps us understand the changing fortunes of individual industries as they follow a distinct pattern of change over time. The national environment impacts on leadership at the country level.

These levels do not act independently of one another; a conducive environment and the explosion of new industries enabled United States firms to build leadership advantages in their own industries. A recent international study of seven industries follows through these interactions of leadership at different levels and attempts to establish whether leadership resides more commonly at one of these levels.[15] It finds no clear pattern. In chemicals, for example, there has been long-term stable leadership at the firm level, while in computers there was relatively stable leadership, until recently, at the national level (United States), but regular turnover among leaders at the firm level. The study also confirms that the locus of leadership is sometimes at intermediate levels, such as clustering of firms and entrepreneurs or the development of partnerships between firms and universities or official bodies. While our main focus concerns firm leadership in Australia, the rise and fall of industries and the international competitiveness of our corporate economy are also interwoven into the story.

Corporate leadership in Australia

In the remainder of this chapter we seek to delve more closely into the corporate leader concept and apply it to Australian experience. The starting point is to design a methodology to identify Australia's corporate leaders, and then examine some of their key features. In Chapter 2 we identified Australia's largest 100 non-financial companies and 25 largest financial companies at different periods of the twentieth century. In the remainder of this chapter we seek to narrow, occasionally extend, this list to identify the true corporate leaders.

Methodology

Identifying corporate leaders is not an easy task. Golder and Tellis have criticised most management writers for reliance upon single informant, retro-spective self-reporting of only surviving firms. Instead, they advocate historical analysis by use of contemporary books and periodicals to glean more accurate, objective, corroborated and comprehensive information about the key firms in an industry.[16] Business historians have sought to identify corporate leaders in many countries, mostly by the use of benchmark cross-sectional data to identify the leading 100 or 200 firms in specified years as we did for Australia in Chapter 2.[17] From this, Chandler, who was a pioneer of this methodology, and other writers, used case study material, sector by sector, from some of these firms to contextualise, and deduce general observations.

Chandler concentrated upon a 60-year period (1880s to the 1940s) during which, he believed, the first mover firms continued to dominate most of America's leading industries.[18] We study the longer period of the twentieth century, and seek to understand the extent to which the identity of corporate leaders changes over this time. To identify Australian corporate leaders we have extended and refined Chandler's methodology by making more extensive use of our top companies series; adding the financial sector to our analysis; and bolstering this with further comparative data and qualitative evidence, which typified leaders and may help us to identify additional firms with a claim to leadership.[19]

Our starting point, therefore, is to analyse the top companies data presented in Chapter 2 more closely. Among these lists we expect to find most of our corporate leaders. We use a matrix of criteria to identify these firms. *Size* is a natural starting point: it provides firms with the power and influence to lead an industry or group of industries. Additionally, our leader needs to have played a sustained role over time in order to build up its organisational capabilities and to have an economic and business impact. On this basis, a company that has been in the top 100 during at least half of the benchmarked years (three of six) has a stronger case for being a corporate leader than one that is very high up the top 100 list but which exits after one enumeration. It also means the company that survived in the list for at least three spot years had been prominent for more than 30 years and endured through at least one of the major

environmental shocks that characterised the twentieth century, notably two
World Wars, depression, and rapid postwar economic growth. Thus, *staying
power* is an important additional leadership criterion on both corporate strategy
and environmental grounds.

There are additional relevant criteria for corporate leadership for which less
quantitative evidence survives. They particularly include a firm's market share,
its expansion into a national organisation, its innovativeness, and the broader
influence of its leading figureheads. Information on some of these criteria is
difficult to obtain; the personality of figureheads being particularly subjective.
The availability of information varies for each company, although extant
material on leading Australian companies is comparatively good.[20] Developing
this matrix of benchmarks enables us to decide if some additional firms will be
added that were not in our top 100 or did not appear three times. It also helps
us to assess the leaders in the financial sector, which, for the methodological
reasons discussed in Chapter 2, were excluded from the original top 100
rankings, but are included in our analysis here.

Results

Table 3.1 lists our corporate leaders. Before discussing these firms in more
detail it should be remembered that, contrary to the implicit assumption of the
first mover–challenger literature, at any one time there was more than one
leader in some of the nation's key industries and none of significance in others.
In addition, in a longitudinal study over the course of a century, leaders may
come and go. Using economy-wide criteria may lead us to find a clustering of
qualifying firms in several industries. By so doing, this tells us something about
leadership at the industry and nation level, as well as at the firm level. Indeed,
our study seeks to address questions about the Australian corporate economy as
a whole, as well as individual firm behaviour.

Most Australian firms did not survive long in the top 100, confirming
the relatively high rates of turnover indicated in Table 2.15. In total, only
63 companies survived for at least three enumerations from a total number
of 354 companies aggregating over the six benchmark years. This provides
our '*top 100 corporate leaders*'. To these we add the five dominant finance
companies from the top 25 finance companies list. Ten other firms justify
inclusion by dint of alternative factors such as their market share, geographic
growth, innovation, dominant personalities, or being a former nationalised
industry or large private company whose asset data could not be obtained
accurately for a sustained period. In total this gives us 78 as our '*full list of
corporate leaders*'.[21]

Table 3.1: Profile of Australian corporate leaders

Company	Sector	ASIC	Longevity	Rankings
BHP	Metallic minerals	B11	1910–97 (6)	12, 4, 1, 1, 1, 2
British Tobacco (Aust)/Amatil	Tobacco, beverages	C21–22	1910–97 (6)	2, 3, 7, 17, 43, 6
CSR	Food	C21–22	1910–97 (6)	3, 1, 2, 3, 5, 9
Dunlop Australia	Leather, rubber, plastic	C34	1910–97 (6)	59, 11, 12, 31, 24, 16
Australian Gas Light Company	Utilities	D36	1910–97 (6)	11, 5, 21, 35, 39, 32
Burns Philp	Wholesale	F46–47	1910–97 (6)	30, 14, 19, 24, 52, 41
North Broken Hill	Metallic minerals	B11	1930–97 (5)	32, 24, 45, 28, 18
Tooth	Brewing	C21–22	1910–86 (5)	20, 6, 18, 37, 55
Herald & Weekly Times	Paper, printing, publishing, media	C26	1910–86 (5)	70, 51, 58, 67, 67
Australian Paper Manufrs/Amcor	Paper, printing, publishing	C26	1930–97 (5)	54, 4, 19, 23, 10
General Motors-Holden's	Transport equipment	C32	1930–97 (5)	45, 8, 4, 45, 53
David Jones	Retail	F48	1930–97 (5)	42, 40, 29, 37, 84
Adelaide Steamship Company	Sea transport	G53	1910–86 (5)	32, 27, 76, 97, 32
Howard Smith	Sea transport	G53	1910–52, 86–97 (5)	26, 24, 44, 56, 49
Conzinc Riotinto Australia	Metallic minerals	B11	1952–97 (4)	3, 10, 2, 4
Mount Isa Mines	Metallic minerals	B11	1952–97 (4)	17, 11, 4, 13
Carlton & United Breweries	Brewing	C21–22	1910–64 (4)	19, 23, 20, 27
Henry Jones	Food	C21–22	1910–64 (4)	45, 41, 39, 77
Tooheys	Brewing	C21–22	1910–64 (4)	49, 39, 65, 88
Nestlé Company Australia	Food	C21–22	1930–64, 97 (4)	18, 29, 74, 62
James Hardie	Glass, clay, non-metallic	C28	1952–97 (4)	62, 75, 27, 48
AGM/ACI	Glass, clay, non-metallic	C28	1930–86 (4)	53, 10, 15, 15

continued next page

Table 3.1: Continued

Company	Sector	ASIC	Longevity	Rankings
Amalgamated Wireless Australasia	Industrial machinery, household appliances	C33	1930–86 (4)	79, 68, 89, 84
Email	Industrial machinery, household appliances	C33	1952–97 (4)	26, 60, 77, 58
AMLF	Pastoral agent	F46–47	1910–64 (4)	6, 16, 27, 73
Australian Estates	Pastoral agent	F46–47	1910–64 (4)	7, 21, 33, 49
Woolworths	Retail	F48	1952–97 (4)	28, 12, 29, 20
Coles (Myer)	Retail	F48	1952–97 (4)	30, 18, 7, 11
Kauri Timber	Primary	A3	1910–52 (3)	34, 87, 36
Mount Lyell	Metallic minerals	B11	1910–52 (3)	9, 30, 42
Western Mining Corporation	Metallic minerals	B11	1952, 86–97 (3)	66, 26, 7
Broken Hill South	Metallic minerals	B11	1930–64 (3)	36, 23, 53
Swan	Brewing	C21–22	1910–52 (3)	63, 67, 46
Unilever Australia	Food	C21–22	1964–97 (3)	70, 83, 98
News Corporation	Paper, printing, publishing, media	C26	1964–97 (3)	82, 3, 1,
Australian Newsprint	Paper, printing, publishing	C26	1952–64, 97 (3)	41, 85, 81
Fairfax	Paper, printing, publishing, media	C26	1964–97 (3)	46, 44, 46
ICIANZ	Chemical, petroleum, coal	C27	1952–86 (3)	5, 5, 20
Shell Australia	Chemical, petroleum, coal	C27	1964–97 (3)	2, 6, 14
BP Australia	Chemical, petroleum, coal	C27	1964–97 (3)	9, 17, 35
Mobil Oil Australia	Chemical, petroleum, coal	C27	1964–97 (3)	7, 34, 36
Boral	Chemical, petroleum, coal	C27	1964–97 (3)	25, 22, 15
Commonwealth Industrial Gases	Chemical, petroleum, coal	C27	1952–86 (3)	50, 78, 64
Esso Australia	Chemical, petroleum, coal	C27	1964–97 (3)	38, 70, 28
Ampol Petroleum	Chemical, petroleum, coal	C27	1952–86 (3)	49, 8, 40

Company	Industry	Code	Years	Values
Humes	Glass, clay, non-metallic	C28	1952–86 (3)	53, 66, 66
Alcoa of Australia	Basic metal products	C29	1964–97 (3)	23, 9, 33
Comalco Industries	Basic metal products	C29	1964–97 (3)	28, 10, 23
Ford Australia	Transport equipment	C32	1964–97 (3)	16, 49, 56
Clyde Industries	Industrial machinery, household appliances	C33	1952–86 (3)	59, 55, 99
Kodak Australia	Industrial machinery, household appliances	C33	1910, 64–86 (3)	97, 71, 91
South Australian Gas Company	Utilities	D36	1910–30, 64 (3)	53, 33, 86
Lend Lease	Construction	E41	1964–97 (3)	54, 36, 12
Dalgety	Pastoral agent	F46–47	1910–52 (3)	1, 2, 6
Elders	Pastoral agent	F46–47	1910–52 (3)	10, 10, 9
NZLMA	Pastoral agent	F46–47	1910–52 (3)	4, 8, 16
Goldsbrough Mort	Pastoral agent	F46–47	1910–52 (3)	8, 7, 22
Winchcombe Carson	Pastoral agent	F46–47	1910–52 (3)	85, 82, 74
Robert Reid	Wholesale	F46–47	1910–52 (3)	25, 46, 61
Myer	Retail	F48	1930–64 (3)	15, 14, 13
Farmer	Retail	F48	1910–52 (3)	46, 48, 98
Huddart Parker	Sea transport	G53	1910–52 (3)	24, 34, 56
Ansett	Air transport	G54	1952–64, 97 (3)	83, 30, 19
NZ&A Land Co	Primary	A1	1910–30 (2)	5, 19
Brambles	Land transport	G51	1986–97 (2)	38, 24
Publishing & Broadcasting Ltd	Paper, printing, publishing, media	H56	1964, 97 (2)	98, –, 25
Hooker, LJ	Construction	E41	1964–86 (2)	47, 46
Repco	Transport equipment	C32	1952–64 (2)	73, 52
Rothmans of Pall Mall (Australia)	Tobacco	C21–22	1964–86 (2)	64, 78
Goodman Fielder	Food	C21–22	1986–97 (2)	25, 37

continued next page

Table 3.1: Continued

Company	Sector	ASIC	Longevity	Rankings
Petersville	Food	C21–22	1930, 1986 (2)	90, 69
Metal Manufacturers	Fabricated metal	C31	1964–86 (2)	26, 76
Qantas	Air transport	G54	1997 (1)	5
National Australia Bank	Banking			
Australian and New Zealand Bank	Banking			
Commonwealth Bank	Banking			
BNSW/Westpac	Banking			
AMP	Life office			

Sources: *Australasian Insurance & Banking Record*; Butlin, *Australian Monetary System*; Gray, *Life Insurance*; Butlin, Hall & White, *Australian Banking and Monetary Statistics*, pp. 98–101 & Tables 54(ii), 56(ii), 57(ii), 58 (ii) & 59(ii); *Australian Banking and Monetary Statistics*, Table 70, p. 503; Block (ed.), *Delfin Digest 1964*, pp. 102–5 & 108–11; *Business Review Weekly*, 20 November 1987; *Business Review Weekly*, 16 November 1998; Various issues of: *Australasian Insurance and Banking Record*; *Jobson's Investment Digest*; *Official Melbourne Stock Exchange Record*; *Delfin Digest*; *Business Review Weekly* 6.11.1986, pp. 89–116, and 16.11.1998, pp. 108–60.

Notes:

Dunlop – various name changes including to Pacific Dunlop in 1986.

CRA – formed in 1962 from merger of Consolidated Zinc Corporation and Rio Tinto Mining Company.

CSR – changed name from Colonial Sugar Refining Company Ltd to CSR Ltd in 1973.

APM – name changed to Amcor in 1986.

British Tobacco – renamed Allied Manufacturing and Trading Industries Ltd in 1973, AMATIL in 1988 and Coca-Cola Amatil in 1989.

AGM – name changed to Australian Consolidated Industries in 1939.

Coles Myer – 1985 merger.

Position and longevity in the top 100

Of the 63 *top 100 corporate leaders*, 28 continued through four periods, 14 to a fifth period. Only six companies remained in the top 100 throughout the six spot years, notably BHP, CSR, Dunlop, Burns Philp, British Tobacco/Amatil and Australian Gas Light Company, providing the clearest examples of sustained corporate leadership. These figures suggest a fairly consistent attrition rate of around half the companies falling out with each additional period. Overwhelmingly, firms remained in the top 100 for consecutive benchmark years before falling out, rather than making intermittent appearances. Can longevity be correlated with ranking in the top 100; that is, did the longest survivors tend to be found highest up the lists? Four of the six firms that survived all six periods, indeed, remained in the top 50 throughout, Burns Philp, slipping just below to 52nd on one occasion and Dunlop once to 59th. Their average position was 16th. This average ranking falls away for firms who survived for exactly five periods to 39th, and is then not appreciably different from those in the top 100 for exactly four periods (36th) and three periods only (39th). These are all above the 50th percentile ranking, indicating that the longer surviving companies also tended to be larger than the median for the top 100, thus reaffirming their status as leaders.

What has been the ultimate fate of our corporate leaders? Focusing on our *top 100 corporate leaders*, 33 remained in the top 100 in 1997 but only seven of these were at or above their highest ranking. Of those companies that had disappeared from the top 100 before the final ranking in 1997, 21 (70 per cent)

Figure 3.1: Longevity of top 100 corporate leaders

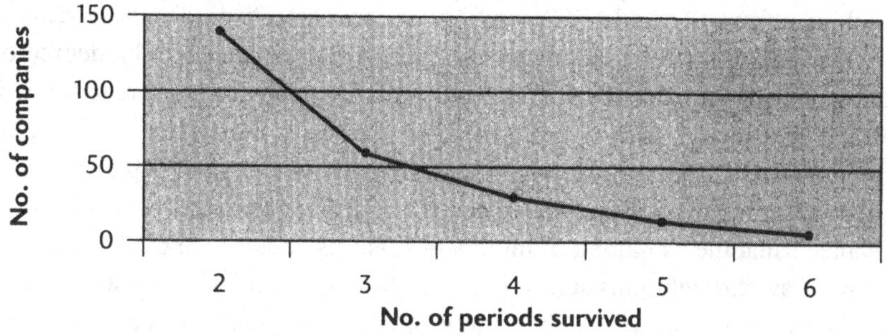

Note: Total number of firms surviving to each period.

Sources: Various issues of: *Australasian Insurance and Banking Record*; *Jobson's Investment Digest*; *Official Melbourne Stock Exchange Record*; *Delfin Digest*; *Business Review Weekly* 6.11.1986, pp. 89–116, and 16.11.1998, pp. 108–60.

had been involved in a merger or acquisition and nine (30 per cent) simply fell to a lower ranking. This is consistent with the consecutive rather than inter-mittent appearance of most firms noted above. Of the additional 15 companies that make the *full list of corporate leaders*, only six had dropped out by 1997 or, in the case of financial institutions, declined from their leading positions.

Thus, most disappearances from the corporate leadership list were due to mergers and of these, two-thirds (14 of 21) had fallen to their lowest ranking in their final benchmark year in the top 100. Moreover, most acquisitions came from other companies in the top 100.

These results indicate some important conclusions. First, it confirms the existence of an active market in takeover among corporate leaders, although mostly in the second half of the century; second, the success of several chal-lenger firms is evident; and third there has been a continuity of corporate leadership and its accompanying assets and resources, if in a modified form and changed name.

The influx of multinationals

As we saw in Chapter 2, foreign multinationals are an important part of the big business story in Australia. We can see in Table 3.2 the importance of foreign-owned and registered companies among our corporate leaders. They accounted on average for nearly 25 per cent of corporate leaders at each benchmark, a figure similar to that in the top 100 lists analysed in Chapter 2. The place of registration measurement used before 1964 understates their role, since locally registered multinationals would not be identified as foreign. This was especially significant for 1930 and 1952 with the establishment of local subsidiaries in the interwar period. If we were to define these companies as foreign, the figures would rise from 13 and 14 to 21 and 24 per cent respectively for these years.

Our data for 1964 is more precise in providing evidence of the degree of foreign ownership, thus 18 of 55 (33 per cent) corporate leaders were more than 50 per cent foreign owned, or 20 of 55 (36 per cent) were at least 20 per cent foreign owned. That most foreign ownership was in excess of 50 per cent also suggests strong ownership links to controlling parent multinationals. We saw in Chapter 1 that the weighting of multinationals was understated by the data in a second way, through omission of evidence from companies whose asset value in Australia is unknown or difficult to separate from its parent's accounts. It is possible that this is a less important consideration for our smaller elite group of corporate leaders; their enduring features often required them to establish a local subsidiary, thereby yielding information on asset values.

The foreign corporate leaders were generally larger than the average cor-porate leader, except in 1986 and 1997. This reflected the greater scale of most

Table 3.2: Foreign ownership of top 100 corporate leaders by sector, 1910–97

	Number of corporate leaders (%)	Assets as % of corporate leaders total	Average number of spot years as ratio of corporate leaders total	A	B	C	F
1910	8 (28)	53	0.87	1	–	1	6
1930	5 (13)	20	0.79	1	–	–	4
1952	7 (14)	16	0.87	–	1	–	6
1964	18 (33)	40	0.89	–	2	14	2
1986	11 (23)	16	0.82	–	–	11	–
1997	11 (27)	23	0.96	–	1	10	–

Note: Prior to 1964, foreign companies were identified by place of registration. From 1964 forwards, identification was on the basis of majority ownership of shares in foreign hands.

A   Agriculture, Forestry, Fishing and Hunting
B   Mining
C   Manufacturing
F   Wholesale and Retail Trade

For a full description of ASIC classifications see pp. 237–8.

Sources: Various issues of: *Australasian Insurance and Banking Record; Jobson's Investment Digest; Official Melbourne Stock Exchange Record; Delfin Digest; Business Review Weekly* 6.11.1986, pp. 89–116, and 16.11.1998, pp. 108–60.

incoming multinationals arriving from the much larger British and United States economies. However, only three of the 14 firms enduring through five or more spot years could be considered a foreign multinational or closely tied to one, notably Dunlop, British Tobacco/Amatil, and General Motors-Holden's. Multinationals, instead, were common among corporate leaders enduring for just three enumerations. Table 3.2 shows that, for each spot year, the average lifespan as a corporate leader was less for the multinationals than the cohort as a whole, constituting a ratio of 0.79 to 0.96. The reason for this lack of long-term survival is related to their sectoral distribution: most multinationals were concentrated either in rural agency and land ownership in the first half of the century or manufacturing in the second half. With the exception of Dunlop and British Tobacco/Amatil, therefore, none showed the versatility needed to adapt to the changing Australian macroeconomy.

The addition of the five financial firms, who were predominantly Australian, dilutes the importance of multinationals. The primary value of multinational corporate leaders lies perhaps less in their aggregation but more in their importance to the growth of a few specific industries of strategic importance for Australia. Foreign pastoral agents such as Dalgety, New Zealand Loan & Mercantile Agency, and Australian Mercantile Loan & Finance Company provided vital commercial services to the wool industry as the staple of early Australian economic growth. Oil refining (Shell, BP, Mobil, Esso), automobile manufacture (Ford, General Motors-Holden's), and food processing (Nestlé, Unilever) constituted new scientific-based industries drawing upon imported technology.

Sectoral distribution

The sectoral distribution of corporate leaders is shown in Table 3.3. It reveals a similar pattern to the top 100 lists in Chapter 2 (tables 2.5 to 2.7), being dominated by particular manufacturing products (food/drink, paper/publishing, petrol, building materials, engineering), service industries (wholesale/retail trade, transport, finance, and utilities), and resource industries (mining and primary). The main change over time is the rising incidence of manufacturing firms, the declining importance of most existing services, and the cyclical changes in mining.

Table 3.3 also compares the sectoral distribution of *top 100 corporate leaders* with national accounts figures for investment and production. Our figures show that in the two earliest spot years, 1910 and 1930, new leaders were mostly spread across manufacturing, wholesale/retail, mining and transport. The largest share was 40 per cent from manufacturing, despite that sector's much smaller 16 per cent share of national income. By 1952 and 1964, the

Table 3.3: Sectoral distribution of top 100 corporate leaders

	Total companies		1910–30 Companies*			1952–64 Companies*		
	No.	%	No.	%	% invest-ment	No.	%	% invest-ment
A–Primary	2	2.6	1	2.7	24.0	0	0.0	
B–Mining	7	9.0	4	10.8	3.6	3	11.5	5.3
C–Manufacturing	39	50.0	15	40.5	16.0	19	73.1	55.4
D–Utilities	2	2.6	2	5.4		0	0.0	
E–Construction	2	2.6	0	0.0		1	3.8	
F–Wholesale, Retail	14	17.9	12	32.4	18.8	2	7.7	19.3
G–Transport/Storage	6	7.7	3	8.1		1	3.8	
H–Communication	1	1.3	0	0.0		0	0.0	
I–Finance, Property, Business Services	5	6.4	0	0.0		0	0.0	
J–Public Administration	0	0.0	0	0.0		0	0.0	
K–Community Services	0	0.0	0	0.0		0	0.0	
L–Leisure	0	0.0	0	0.0		0	0.0	
Number	78	100.0	37	100.0		26	100.0	

Notes. *Covers corporate leaders that first entered top 100 in 1910–30 or 1952–64 and remained for at least 3 spot years.

1910–30 National income is calculated on averages for the period using Gross Domestic Product by Industry.

1952–64 National income is calculated on average for the period using New Fixed Capital Expenditure by Private Enterprises.

Source: W. Vamplew (ed.) *Australians. Historical Statistics*, pp. 133, 144.

share of new leaders deriving from manufacturing had risen to a dominant 73 per cent, still ahead of a national income share of the sector of 55 per cent. The lagged growth of manufacturing economy-wide, compared with its import-ance among new corporate leaders, suggests, perhaps, that these dominant firms played a positive role in pulling the Australian economy away from its traditional primary industry orientation to develop a more diversified manu-facturing base.

In the early twentieth century, corporate leaders were mostly pastoral agents and more general wholesalers, miners, shipowners, utilities, together with a significant number of food and alcohol producers. Six of the top 10 non-financial companies in 1910 were pastoral agents whose growth was closely related to the major expansion in wool output and export from the middle of the nineteenth century. They provided finance, marketing and business services to the farming community. It continued to be a heavily represented industry up to mid-century despite relative decline; the same six firms remained in the top 33 by 1952. In 1962–63 the four major players merged to form two new entities, which in turn were absorbed by industrial conglomerates over the last few decades. Interspersed with the pastoral agents was the New Zealand and Australian Land Company, a land-owning and pastoral company that had pioneered land investment by British investors in the previous century. It fell away more quickly than the agents, exiting the top 100 before 1952 due to its greater concentration of investment risks on specific properties and areas, and its more limited scope for related diversification.

Mining companies, with their capital intensive needs, were strongly represented throughout the century, with two firms in the top 20 in 1910 (BHP, Mt Lyell) and five in 1997 (BHP, North Broken Hill, Conzinc Riotinto Australia, Mount Isa Mines and Western Mining Corporation). BHP was Australia's largest top 100 company for three of our benchmark years (1952–86) and remained in the top dozen companies throughout the century. North Broken Hill appeared in all years between 1930 and 1997 and Conzinc Riotinto Australia and its constituent companies for 1952–97, the latter being in the top 10 throughout. The firms' longevity owed much to the abundant mineral resources of Australia, and the resulting opportunities to expand into metal production and build up sustainable competitive advantages in international commodity markets.

Shipowners Adelaide Steamship Company, Howard Smith and Huddart Parker stood in the top 40 in 1910, reflecting the strong demand for coastal shipping in the context of poor inland transport. Their relative positions declined through the twentieth century as domestic communications infrastructure developed. Huddart Parker, with its strong emphasis on coasting, was particularly affected, from being the top-ranked shipowner in 1910, it fell out of the top 100 first after 1952. Although 'cabotage' laws sheltered Australian owners from foreign competition in coasting, improved inland transport (road and air) and the strength of government carrier, Australian National Line, along with private carriers such as BHP, damaged Huddart Parker, which was acquired by Boral in 1961. Adelaide Steamship Company and Howard Smith diversified in order to remain in the top 100 in the postwar period. In wholesale trading, Burns Philp (30) and Robert Reid (25) were highly ranked in 1910. Reid dropped out after 1952 but Burns Philp, expanding its South Seas empire, remained in the 100 list throughout the century.

Regional utility companies flourished in the early twentieth century to supply the growing urban centres with services such as gas and electricity. These included Melbourne Electricity Supply and Adelaide Electricity Supply.

From the 1920s, electricity generation and distribution was mostly placed under government control and ownership, with the establishment of a series of state commissions, but gas remained in private hands. Australian Gas Light Company, supplying gas to the large Sydney market, was the dominant utility corporation. South Australian Gas Company, supplying the Adelaide and South Australian market, also featured in the top 100. Commonwealth Industrial Gases was formed in 1935 as the amalgamation of several companies producing and distributing industrial and medical gases.

Among manufacturers, it was the consumer-oriented areas of food, tobacco and brewing that generated sufficient demand to produce large companies at the beginning of the century. They contributed four companies to the top 20 in 1910 and three in 1997, of whom only CSR survived throughout the century, the others falling victim to a long process of mergers and acquisitions in these sectors. CSR ranked in the top 10 in each of the years for which lists have been prepared, and was in the top three from 1910 to 1964. Brewers Tooth, Tooheys, Swan and Castlemaine were all in the top 100 in 1910 and remained there until at least 1952. British Tobacco and jam producer Henry Jones survived in the top 100 from 1910 until 1964, the former then diversifying into snack foods and soft drinks. Multinational food company Nestlé joined the top 100 in 1930, although Unilever did not enter until 1964, possibly due to lack of asset information.

By mid-century more manufacturers appeared among our corporate leaders. Producers of industrial machinery and household appliances exploited technological developments and rising real incomes, notably Email, Amalgamated Wireless Australasia and Clyde Industries. The population and property booms of the 1950s and 1960s contributed to the ascendancy of materials producers James Hardie, Australian Consolidated Industries, and Alcoa, along with construction and property management firms Lend Lease and L. J. Hooker, and the fabricated metal products of Metal Manufacturers.

The rise of the popular automobile generated many new leaders, particularly multinationals exploiting tariff protection, including vehicle makers Ford and General Motors-Holden's; the latter appearing in every benchmark year since 1930 with a lowest ranking of 52. Oil refiners Shell, Esso, BP and Mobil expanded their Australian operations in response to the motoring boom. Each entered the top 100 in our 1964 list and has remained there in a fairly consistent order relative to each other, and competing with domestic rival Ampol. Components manufacturing has been dominated by Repco, which entered the top 100 in 1952. Imperial Chemical Industries of Australia and New Zealand was formed in 1928 from among the Australian and New Zealand based companies that constituted the formation of Imperial Chemical Industries in Britain two years earlier, although it did not enter the top 100 until 1952.

Mid-century emergent corporate leaders in the service industries included retailers David Jones and Myer, who entered the top 100 in 1930, and the rapidly growing chains of Woolworths and Coles, both entering the top 30 by 1952. Publishers News Corporation, Publishing & Broadcasting Limited, and Fairfax all entered the top 100 by 1964; most spectacularly News Corporation entered at 82nd, rising to first by 1997, helped by its acquisition of early leader Herald & Weekly Times and its diversification strategies. In the related sector of paper manufacture, Australian Paper Manufacturers has largely maintained its early dominance. The leadership of air transport by Ansett (formed 1936) and Qantas (formed 1920) had begun to emerge by the time of the aviation boom of the 1950s although Qantas only officially entered the top 100 list in 1997, at position five, due to its being under state ownership from 1947 until completion of its privatisation in 1996.

In very recent years, there has been a strong influx of newly corporatised service industries, particularly communications and leisure. In 1997 five new firms associated with gambling entered the list, of which three were casinos (Burswood, Crown and Jupiters) and two corporatised betting shops (TAB and Tabcorp). Telstra has been the dominant non-government firm in telecommunications services since its recent and partial privatisation beginning in 1997. From Federation in 1901 to 1997, telecommunications took the form of a government monopoly. Its very recent movement to the private sector is too brief to include in our list.

Only two of the six firms that survived all six periods in the top 100 – Dunlop and British Tobacco/Amatil – could be considered predominantly a manufacturer, confirming the conclusions of Chapter 2 (Table 2.14) that the sector is only weakly represented among the most elite Australian corporate leaders, especially when compared with their dominance in many other nations. BHP (metals and minerals) and CSR (sugar, building materials) crossed the primary and manufacturing sectors. The others were service industry firms: Australian Gas Light Company (utilities) and Burns Philp (wholesale trading).

In spite of its absence from the top 100 companies list for methodological reasons, the finance sector generated many substantial firms. The sector incorporates a wide range of banks, life offices, insurers, finance companies, merchant bankers, building societies and credit unions. However, as Appendix B indicates, a few firms and their antecedents have dominated the sector throughout the twentieth century, notably four banks, National Australia Bank, Australian and New Zealand Bank, Commonwealth Bank of Australia and Westpac, and one life office, AMP. For example, National Australia Bank and its antecedent companies ranked in the top 10 financial firms throughout the century. Westpac and its main antecedent, Bank of New South Wales, have always ranked in the top four. AMP is the highest ranked life office in each year, well ahead of its nearest rival, National Mutual Life.

Market share

Market share is an important indicator of leadership, providing the size to yield scale and scope economies, the opportunity to build competences that might be used in international business, and the strength to exert direction over the industry. Historically, we lack precise figures of market share for most industries, but our evidence is strong enough to supplement quantitative data with qualitative judgements. We saw in Chapter 2 that big business has dominated the corporate economy to a greater degree in Australia than in many other nations.[22] In Table 3.4 we summarise the available historical information on concentration levels in order to generalise about the features of many of the main industries.

Concentration levels have been segmented into monopoly, dominant firm, duopoly, highly concentrated oligopoly, medium concentrated oligopoly and competitive, as defined in the table's note. There is a reasonable spread between the different concentration levels, except that only two industries, retail and shipping, have been competitive for part of the twentieth century. About half of the industries for which we have some information experienced a change in concentration category, reaffirming the frequent changes in corporate leaders, or at least their relative standings. Monopoly and dominant firms have mostly derived from manufacturing, consistent with the work of writers on industrial concentration, particularly Karmel and Brunt, quoted in Chapter 2, and Sheridan (1968).[23] Household consumables, materials, and engineering, were among the most concentrated, but in most cases their control weakened later in the century. By contrast, some of the initially less concentrated industries, such as newspapers, retail and brewing, became more concentrated over time with the emergence of strong national brands. It should also be noted that within a number of industries, particularly chemicals, appliances and fabricated metal products, the leading firms often concentrated upon different products, suggesting a higher degree of market share than might be apparent at first.

The food and drink industries contained many of the most dominant firms. CSR held a virtual monopoly of refined sugar output by 1907 and about 40 per cent of raw milling capacity.[24] Utilising science-based technologies in large-scale refineries, it was able to eliminate most of its rivals and achieve a near monopoly in the domestic sugar market for over 100 years. British Tobacco had a monopoly of the Australian tobacco market from 1904 until 1955, when new entrants appeared, most notably Rothmans and Philip Morris. Its market share

Table 3.4: Market share estimates

Industry	Concentration level*	Major firms (max & min % share)	Dates
Sugar	M	CSR	20th century
Cola	M	Amatil (80–99)	1980s, 1990s
Glass	M	AGM	Up to 1930s
	DU	ACI; Pilkington	1940s on
Paper	M	APM	Up to 1930s
	DU	APM, ANwsprt	1940s on
Tobacco	M	Br Tob	1904–55
	HO	Rothmans (40); Br Tob (30); Philip Morris (30)	1980s
Coffee/milk	D	Nestlé	1930s on
Concrete	D	Humes	To 1950s
Flour milling	D	Goodman Fielder	20th century
Fabric metal	D	Metal Manufacturers	1960s–90s
Vehicle parts	D	Repco	1960s
Rubber	D	Dunlop	Up to 1930
	M		1930 on
Soap	D	Unilever (55–70); Colgate-Palmolive	1928–65
	HO	Unilever; Cussons; Colgate-Palmolive; Procter & Gamble	1970s
Vehicles	D	Holden (45); Ford (15); BMC (10)	1960
	MO	Holden (22); Ford (13); Toyota (18)	2002
Life insurance	D	AMP (49–61); NML (12–13); MLC (13)	1905, 1920
	MO	AMP (33); NML (14); MLC (10)	1974
Beer	HO	CUB (31); Tooth (17); Tooheys (16); Castlemaine (16)	Pre–1979
	DU	CUB/Foster's (45); Lion Nathan (45)	1990s
Aviation	HO	Qantas, Ansett; TAA/Australian	1960s–92
	DU	Qantas, Ansett	1992 on
Newspapers	MO	HWT (33–43); Fairfax (14–19); Murdoch (3–7)	1936, 1956
	DU	News (25); Fairfax (14); HWT (61)	1976
	DU	News (66); Fairfax (22)	1991

Table 3.4: Continued

Industry	Concentration level*	Major firms (max & min % share)	Dates
Retail (grocery)	C	Woolworths (17); Coles (9)	1964
	DU	Woolworths (36); Coles (30)	1998
Mining/metal	HO	BHP; NBH; WMC; CRA; MIM	20th century
Building mats	HO	Hardie; CSR; Boral; Pioneer	1950s on
Petroleum	HO	Shell, BP, Mobil, Esso, Ampol	1960s on
Appliances	HO	AWA, Email, Clyde	20th century
Gas supply	HO	AGL; SAGASCO	20th century
Chemicals	HO	ICI; Monsanto; Union Carbide	1950s on
Construction/ property	HO	Lend Lease; Hooker	1960s on
Banking	HO	ANZ(22–30); Wpac(27–33); NAB (23–32); Cwealth (15–21)	1939, 1970
	MO	ANZ (13); Wpac (14); NAB (18); Cwealth (17)	1997
Shipping	MO	Adsteam; Huddart Parker; Howard Smith	To 1950s
	C	Also Australian National Line, BHP	From 1950s
Wholesale	MO	Burns Philp; Robert Reid; D. W. Murray; Harris Scarfe	20th century
Pastoral agents	MO	Dalgety (12–19); Elders (4–17); GMort (5–13); NZLMA (7–12)	1902–62

Note: * M = monopoly (one firm = 70%+); D = Dominant firm (40–70%, other firms <20%); DU = duopoly (two firms = 70%+); HO = high oligopoly (3–4 firms = 70%+); MO = medium oligopoly (3–4 firms = 40–70%+); C = competitive (concentration level below this).

Sources: Maxcy, 'Motor industry', p. 508; Langfield-Smith, 'Carlton and United Breweries, pp. 41, 99; Alemson, 'Advertising', pp. 282–306; Morkel, 'Amatil', p. 343; Fieldhouse, *Unilever*, pp. 72, 81; Brash, *American Investment* p. 319; Brown, Competitive Marketing', pp. 206–7 & 210–27; Nestlé, pp. 103–6; Sargent, *Foodmakers*, p. 268; Briggs & Smith, *Groceries*, pp. 16, 21; *Fair Market*, Table 4.1; Goot, 'Newspaper circulation', p. 214; Henningham, 'The press', p. 63; Butlin, Hall & White, *Australian Banking and Monetary Statistics*, p. 133; White, *Australian Banking and Monetary Statistics*, pp. 314–15; Reserve Bank of Australia, *Statistical Bulletin*, September 1997; Gray, *Life Insurance*, pp. 46, 127, 133, 264; Sinclair, *The Spreading Tree*; Ville, *Rural Entrepreneurs*, ch. 2; Fountain, 'Technology acquisition', p. 92; Hunter, 'Transport industry', p. 76.

dropped rapidly from 96 to 33 per cent during 1956–63 as its rivals flooded the market with new products.[25] British Tobacco's subsequent diversification as Amatil took it into a dominant position in the soft drinks market by gaining control of the local franchises for Coca-Cola.[26] Nestlé has held a dominant position in coffee and milk product markets for much of the twentieth century while facing more serious challenges from Cadbury, Fry and Pascall in confectionery.[27] The constituent firms of Goodman Fielder held dominant shares in flour milling. Henry Jones is believed to have dominated early jam production; by the early 1980s after some years of increased competition its share was 28 per cent.[28] Among other household consumables, Unilever dominated the soap market to 1965 with its share fluctuating between about 55 and 70 per cent. Cussons and Procter & Gamble have made strong challenges in toilet soap and dishwashing liquid since the 1970s.[29]

Australian Glass Manufacturers operated a virtual monopoly of bottle and other glass production in the early decades of the century until British multinational Pilkington entered the Australian market in 1936.[30] Dunlop controlled the market for rubber and related products; in 1959–60 it derived two-thirds of its income from tyre sales before its subsequent diversification.[31] Humes exerted a similar stranglehold over concrete pipes, at least in the first half of the century before the rise of the diversified building material companies. Australian Paper Manufacturers had achieved a near monopoly of paper manufacture by 1920. Associated Pulp & Paper Mills and Australian Newsprint, however, emerged as credible competitors in the 1930s, but thereafter Australian Paper Manufacturers became increasingly dominant with the former two specialising in fine paper and newsprint respectively. Vehicle production was led by General Motors-Holden's: in 1960 the firm was dominant with a 45 per cent share, ahead of Ford and the British Motor Corporation.[32] Today, General Motors-Holden's remains the market leader but the market has become less concentrated with its share halved due to competition from Toyota and Mitsubishi.[33] Repco controlled the market in vehicle parts by the 1960s, also exporting to many countries.

Each brewer was a dominant producer or monopolist in its own state by the 1920s and 1930s; exceptionally New South Wales had two powerful companies, Tooheys and Tooth. Tooth was the prime mover, originally established in the 1830s; its 1929 acquisition of Resch's consolidated its domination of New South Wales with 80 per cent of the market. Tooth consolidated its leadership with innovative marketing, particularly its 'pub art' of the 1930s, and through the tied house system, which raised entry costs. Tooheys, however, managed to increase its market share, especially in the move to packaged beer in the 1960s; Tooth's New South Wales market share reducing to 65 per cent by 1964.[34] By the 1990s Foster's and Lion Nathan dominated national market share, accounting for 40 to 50 per cent each.

The exploitation of scale and scope economies have driven successive rises in concentration levels in publishing, with metropolitan-based newspapers driving out smaller regional and rural competitors with higher costs. By 1936 the industry had become a medium oligopoly with the leading three newspaper publishers, Herald & Weekly Times, Fairfax and News Corporation accounting for 54 per cent of daily circulation. Forty years later this had risen to 100 per cent as they completed their stranglehold over the industry.[35] Similar increases in concentration occurred in the electronic media, led by News and the Packer family interests, although post-World War Two federal regulations on owner-ship constrained the same level of dominance achieved by News in newspaper sales.

Retailing moved from competitive to segmented duopolies: Myer and David Jones have come to dominate department store sales, while Woolworths and Coles have exerted strong control over chain store sales, particularly since the 1960s with their entry into the grocery trade and the construction of large suburban stores. The market share of both Woolworths and Coles more than doubled between 1964 and 1998, to produce a combined share of 66 per cent.[36]

Oligopoly has characterised many of the service and resource sectors, with a group of three to five firms leading the industry. Market share in the finance industries has been proxied using company assets, since these figures are dominated by borrowing and lending volumes. The big four and their antecedent firms accounted for at least 89 per cent of trading bank assets as early as the 1890s and rose further through the twentieth century to nearly 100 per cent by 1970.[37] Their collective share was diluted by the influx of foreign banks after 1985 and the end of the distinction between trading and savings banks in the early 1990s. There has been no dominant firm within the group and leadership has changed over time. Thus, the Bank of New South Wales (Westpac) and the Commonwealth Bank of Australia held the largest market shares before and after World War Two; by 1997 National Australia Bank was the leader, followed by the Commonwealth. AMP has been the market leader of the life office sector: its share of sums assured has consistently been two to four times the size of National Mutual Life. Together with Colonial Mutual Life, these three companies have accounted for perhaps two-thirds of the market over the long term.[38]

Our corporate leaders in commercial property development and manage-ment, Lend Lease and Hooker, have faced competition from a small number of other significant firms, particularly Frank Lowy's Westfield. In wholesaling, Burns Philp and Robert Reid have held significant market shares, but other notable firms included D. W. Murray in the early years, Harris Scarfe, McPhersons and Sleigh. Four or five pastoral agents dominated wool broking, although their relative standings fluctuated. Dalgety became the market leader in 1903 and maintained that position until it was surpassed by Elders in 1958. Goldsbrough Mort had been the leading wool broker in the 1890s, as the pioneer in moving the market to Australia, but slipped rapidly in the following two decades to fall out of the top five agencies at the end of World War One, before recovering to second or third.[39]

In the early days of commercial aviation between the wars, the market was shared among many regional airlines that came and went in quick succession. Concentration increased sharply in the postwar industry. Ansett acquired its major domestic market competitor, Australian National Airways, in 1957, and as a result shared the official two-airline policy with state-owned Trans-Australia Airlines. Between them they accounted for over 95 per cent of domestic passengers.[40] Further acquisitions made Ansett the largest domestic airline by the end of the 1960s. State-owned Qantas (1947) was the local provider of overseas services in competition with 37 foreign airlines flying into Australia. By the late 1980s it held a market share of 42–43 per cent but remained the only major international airline without a domestic network to feed its international services.[41] In the 1990s the privatisation of Qantas, its acquisition of Australian Airlines (1992) (the successor to Trans-Australia Airlines), and Ansett's overseas expansion created a duopoly in both domestic and international markets that remained largely unchallenged until the latter's collapse in 2001.[42]

Shipping has been able to accommodate somewhat more large-scale firms: five companies dominated market share by the 1890s, of whom three – Adelaide Steamship Company, Howard Smith and Huddart Parker – are among our list of corporate leaders by dint of sustaining their market share. Their declining influence in the coastal trade, however, was evident by the 1950s when state-owned Australian National Line and vertically integrated BHP together accounted for more than half of domestic tonnage coastwise.[43]

A similar number of firms have dominated mining and metallurgy.[44] BHP extended its leadership into steel production in Australia, especially after its acquisition of Australian Iron and Steel in 1935. Conzinc Riotinto Australia has dominated smelting and basic metal products following postwar consolidation in the industry, and WMC has held a large part of the gold market. A variety of firms periodically held a significant market share of different fabricated metal products including Containers Ltd and J. Gadsden (tin-plate can-makers), and Cyclone and Lysaght (steel fabrication). However, it was Metal Manufacturers that increasingly dominated postwar production, especially of copper and wire, tubes and cables, before going into relative decline in the 1990s to be acquired by American Marsh Electrical in 1999.

Regional gas companies monopolised state markets by dint of government franchises, including Australian Gas Light Company and South Australian Gas Company. Public criticism of the pricing behaviour and general service standards of Australian Gas Light Company led to legislation in 1912 and 1932 setting closer operating guidelines. The main effect, though, was to institutionalise its local monopoly.[45] The gas firms, however, did face periodic challenges to their market dominance. Electricity was threatening its lighting market by the early twentieth century, so the gas companies turned to the heating and cooking market. After World War Two, the increased availability of oil and the conversion to natural gas heightened competition and led to further strategy adjustments, as we shall see in the following chapter. In the 1990s, official deregulation of gas and electricity supply removed the previous regional monopolies.

The petroleum market was shared between Shell, Esso, BP, Mobil and Ampol. However, Shell, who established in Australia in 1903, dominated the early market and held the highest top 100 positions throughout the century.[46] Imperial Chemical Industries of Australia and New Zealand held the largest share of the market for a wide range of chemicals, followed by Monsanto Chemicals (Australia), a subsidiary of the United States firm that entered Australia in 1928. Union Carbide expanded in Australia in the 1950s.

Email initially specialised in the production of electric meters, a valuable niche market from which it expanded to achieve a dominant market share in many industrial and household appliances. Amalgamated Wireless Australasia was in a similar position in electronic products, particularly in the supply of television parts and traffic control equipment; it additionally benefited from its close working relationship with the Postmaster-General. Clyde Industries' position as one of the largest general engineering organisations in Australia derived particularly from its contracts to manufacture diesel and electric locomotives for the Commonwealth, New South Wales and Victorian State Railways.

National growth

The geographic growth of a firm is a strong indication of leadership, providing it with the opportunity to control rights over widely distributed resources and strategic assets, or to exploit larger factor and product markets. We now look to establish the extent to which the dominant firms also grew into national organisations. The question of subsequent international expansion is addressed in Chapter 4.

Most Australian firms remained localised or confined to a single state through most of the twentieth century, as a result of the problems of operating and communicating over long distances and the historical particularism of individual states. However, as the century evolved, most corporate leaders expanded across state borders to become regional firms, and by 1997 there were few that did not operate nationally.

The nature of their national expansion varied. In some cases it involved supplying a national market through a network of warehouses or distribution centres supporting a manufacturing base in a single state, particularly where low transport costs and significant plant economies of scale existed. Alternatively, production units located in individual states reflected the absence of these conditions or the importance of proximity to the market, most commonly in service industries. In some cases the strategic advantages of a national presence were achieved through franchises and other forms of inter-firm agreement or brand recognition.

Leaders in many service industries were particularly quick to seek national expansion, since this provided close contact with customers, an evolving reputation, and the opportunity to duplicate successful methods. Financial services firms had begun to build national, sometimes international, businesses before the turn of the twentieth century. Colonial Mutual Life had branches in all states in the year of its establishment, 1874. AMP, which had begun operating in 1849, completed a national network by 1884.[47] By 1892 six banks had branches across four or more colonies, including those who became the core of the Australian and New Zealand Bank, National Australia Bank and Westpac. A wave of bank mergers facilitated the further spread of national networks between the two World Wars.[48]

The leading pastoral agents had begun crossing state borders by the early twentieth century. Dalgety had offices in five states before World War One, Goldsbrough Mort following suit between the wars, and Elders achieving similar coverage after World War Two, could claim to be national firms. The other leading agents achieved regional status across several states. Representation through the leading pastoral districts and in the major port cities gave them enhanced leverage in the national wool auction system.[49] In construction and property, Lend Lease was concentrated in New South Wales and Victoria until the 1970s because it developed a profile of large commercial and residential projects for Sydney and Melbourne. L. J. Hooker completed a national network of real estate offices in 1960 and accelerated its national growth with the opening of the first franchised offices in 1968, at Bankstown, Miranda and Newport.

The leading transport firms quickly sought national growth in order to gain competitive advantage from providing a full service range, and to yield scale economies in the process. Adelaide Steamship Company operated along the south-east coast in 1875 but by the 1890s traversed most of the country's coastline with permanent offices in all major ports. By 1914 they had extended their national presence through the employment of agents in many secondary ports, a practice common among shipowners travelling to a diversity of destinations. Howard Smith and Huddart Parker operated around most of the Australian coast, with offices at major ports by the late nineteenth century. In land transport, Brambles was concentrated in central New South Wales for the first 70 years or so of its operations, before pursuing expansion from the mid-1950s that had achieved national operations within a decade.[50]

Air transport is naturally conducive to national, and international, operations. Qantas soon expanded beyond its Queensland and Northern Territory origins, while Ansett developed a national presence by the 1950s to provide the comprehensive domestic services needed to compete effectively. From the end of World War Two up to 1992, as we saw in the previous section, nationalised Qantas was confined to international services, although operating from airports across Australia. In retailing, the chain stores were quick to move interstate as might be expected from the nature of their business; Coles operated in all six states by the 1930s and Woolworths in three. The department stores served a single capital city or regional centre before World War Two. After 1945 they engaged in a series of takeover battles to establish a national presence, with Myer and David Jones leading the way. In publishing, newspapers were state-based until the 1920s when Keith Murdoch first began to build a national chain of newspapers. Each had its own local masthead until his son, Rupert, introduced a national paper, the *Australian*, in 1964. Frank Packer had launched the *Australian Women's Weekly* as a mass audience national magazine in 1933.

However, two major corporate leaders in the service sector, Australian Gas Light Company and Burns Philp, were slow to expand nationally. Australian Gas Light Company has led the utilities sector and been one of the six companies to survive through all six spot years, but was restricted in its geographic expansion by the state government franchise system for gas supply. Its activities were restricted to the Sydney area until the 1960s, when it spread through regional areas of New South Wales.[51] It was also typical of the utilities industries, in that there were few scale economies from geographic expansion, which required the building of additional production plants or lengthy additional pipelines. Recent deregulation has presented new opportunities for geographic expansion. Wholesaler and international trader Burns Philp originated in northern Queensland and supported its activities with an office in Sydney. This remained its focus for many years as it developed its international connections, but by the 1950s it had achieved a substantial trading presence throughout Australia.[52]

Firms in mining and metallurgy expanded to exploit resources widely available across Australia. National expansion strategies in metallurgy have been determined by the need for the co-location of plant with mineral deposits as a cost minimising strategy. Substantial plant scale economies and the availability of suitable infrastructure, especially deepwater shipping terminals, have produced a structure of production concentration to supply the national market. BHP has specifically focused on the Newcastle–Lithgow–Sydney–Wollongong corridor with notable steelworks in Newcastle from 1915 and Port Kembla from 1935. It also has blast furnaces in Whyalla (South Australia) and rolling mills in Kwinana (Western Australia). Consolidated Zinc Corporation's establishment in 1949 led to a national profile including plants in Queensland and Tasmania. Although it has operated mines in, for example, Victoria and Queensland, Western Mining Corporation has focused more on building upon its strong Western Australian base, initially in gold, then bauxite, nickel and iron ore.

In manufacturing, extensive opportunities for firm scale economies encouraged corporate leaders to seek out national markets. Whether these were sourced by a broad network of factories or localised production depended upon a range of factors, including transport costs, product mobility, plant economies and relative factor endowments between states. The small, scattered Australian population, divided by poor transport facilities, dispersed production by many national firms well into the twentieth century. Among food and drink companies, CSR had refineries in all state capitals except Hobart by the 1930s, while British Tobacco had interests across all capitals except Hobart and Perth by the early twentieth century as the holding company for the tobacco trust representing the major manufacturers. By the mid-1960s it had 61 factories across all states except Tasmania, as well as 121 warehouses nationally.[53] Rothmans also had a national presence by this time, although largely based upon distribution centres supported by a leaf processing plant in Queensland and factories regionalised in New South Wales and Victoria.[54]

As we saw in the previous section, brewers rarely strayed beyond state boundaries until the merger activities after 1979 that resulted in two national companies (Foster's Brewing Group and Lion Nathan). By the early 1990s Foster's had brewing capacity in every state except South Australia, and Lion Nathan everywhere but Victoria. Nestlé was early to establish a national network of factories and branches before 1939, beginning with Victoria in 1911 and New South Wales in 1918.[55] Lever Brothers expanded nationally in the early twentieth century; from its original Sydney branch of 1888 it expanded through the acquisition of soap manufacturers in Melbourne and Adelaide and thence to other states with its diversification into ice cream and canned foods after World War Two.[56] Petersville produced ice cream in most states by the

1920s using different locally registered 'Peters' companies. Henry Jones had established a regional presence in south-east Australia by 1919, manufacturing jam in Hobart, Sydney, Melbourne and Adelaide.[57] In flour milling, the three constituent firms of Goodman Fielder all had a national presence by the 1960s.[58] Australian Glass Manufacturers operated plants in all states by 1935. Australian Paper Manufacturers conducted a similar type of expansion to mining through the importance of vertical technical links between primary production and its downstream products. Thus, they located mills close to timber resources. By the 1950s it had mills in Victoria, New South Wales and Queensland, adding Tasmania and Western Australia by the following decade. Building materials firm James Hardie operated factories and subsidiaries in all mainland states by the 1960s.

The shape of concentrated urban development also influenced the location of oil refining sites, which were chosen close to major markets to exploit the relative cost advantage of transporting crude over refined products. The companies established a national presence from the 1950s through solo marketing techniques, which bonded petrol retailers to a particular company. In vehicle manufacture, General Motors-Holden's had plants in all mainland states by 1931 for local assembly of completely knocked down kits imported from the United States.[59] Repco operated a national distribution network in parts and accessories by 1960, and then expanded its manufacturing bases. Amalgamated Wireless Australasia did not expand manufacturing sites nationally, although it had a brand recognition that was national through its domination of radio and television parts. Email and Clyde Industries expanded in order to establish the minimum scales required in appliances production. Whether or not they developed as national firms, they certainly had a strong local presence.

Innovation

Innovativeness can distinguish a corporate leader by providing it with a strong source of competitive advantage. Chandler emphasised the role of technological innovation among many corporate leaders in America by facilitating economies of scale and scope. Innovation is broadly interpreted in the present study to include processes, products, managerial techniques, organisational advances and the development of intangible, as well as tangible, assets such as branding. These advances will gradually spill over or filter down to other firms in the industry, in the process shifting production functions and providing further evidence of industrial leadership. Thus, the innovating corporate leader has the ability to transform the performance of an existing industry or create a new, related sector. Australian firms drew heavily upon overseas partners and parents in larger industrial economies for scientific and managerial innovations.

It has been estimated that 83 per cent of the firms responsible for major innovations between 1939 and 1953 had overseas affiliations; in 1988–89, 80 per cent of payments by Australian firms for technical know-how went to related foreign enterprises.[60] Adaptation for the local market and production environment was, nonetheless, an important requirement; a sample of firms spent on average 42 per cent of their research and development budget on modifying foreign technology.[61] Domestic contributions to innovation were more important in product branding and designing local organisational systems.

This section does not seek to provide a comprehensive account of innovation among our corporate leaders; this would require a lengthy study in its own right. Rather, it is illustrative of the innovative nature of many of our corporate leaders. Further evidence of their innovation will emerge as part of the discussions of corporate strategy in subsequent chapters.

In manufacturing, the type of technological innovation identified by Chandler is most apparent. CSR fits the Chandlerian strategy effectively. Its early success rested on being the first to install technologically advanced refining plants on a scale that dramatically lowered unit cost. The vigorous application of science enabled the firm subsequently to improve refining technology. The firm's official history stresses technical efficiency as the company's watchword.[62] Organisationally, CSR developed a carefully conceived business structure, adopting aspects of U- and M-form as appropriate.

The rise of the breweries owed much to science-based advances in production techniques that were well adapted to large-scale production. The competition from Courage's entry into Australian production in 1968 also fostered strong branding skills, particularly by Carlton & United Breweries. Unilever and Nestlé benefited from importing the production technologies of the parent company without achieving much indigenous innovation. Humes, by contrast, sent employees overseas in search of leading edge technology. Andrew Reid toured Britain, Europe and the United States in search of overseas technology that enabled it to begin local production of asbestos cement sheeting during World War One. Goodman Fielder effectively exploited scale and scope economies in milling and baking, and combined this with marketing innovations, including product branding and the forging of new distribution channels, as bakeries evolved from home delivery to supplying supermarket chains. As we noted earlier, Amalgamated Wireless Australasia's growth was closely connected to its technological innovativeness in radio and television.

The strong role of service industries in the Australian economy has been helped by the innovativeness of their leaders. Retailing innovation can be classified under three broad headings. Suppliers to store changes have included integrating the purchasing function to deal directly with suppliers, backward integration into manufacturing as a credible threat, generic and home brand development, bulk purchasing for discount, centralised warehousing and outsourcing logistics, and the use of information technologies to connect sales registers with warehouses and suppliers. Innovations to in-store operations have included improved and systematic store layout, point-of-sale technology, suburban relocation, self-service and extended opening hours. Store to customer innovations have focused upon advertising, credit, loyalty techniques, home delivery, remote shopping, broader and more rapidly changing product choice.

The financial services industry has experienced extensive innovation in its product range, back office technology and organisational design. Corporate leaders pioneered many of these changes as a way of driving down their costs and maintaining their leadership. The deregulation of financial markets in the 1980s, accompanied by the application of information technology to back office and product technology, transformed the rate of innovation and the intensity of competition within the industry. New products have resulted, particularly card-based services (credit cards, ATMs, EFTPOS), phone and Internet banking, while computers have radically reduced the costs of capturing, processing, storing and retrieving information. Finally, the leading banks were among the earliest Australian firms to give careful thought to improved organisational design, as we shall see in Chapter 7.

The leading firms in the print, publishing and media industries have demonstrated considerable innovation. Australian Paper Manufacturers was seen as a key innovator by the 1930s when it enthusiastically espoused the use of Australian eucalyptus pulp in paper production and had the finance to support the shift. The newspaper proprietors followed innovations in Europe and the United States by investing in new printing technologies and changing the layout and content to reach a mass audience. As new means of disseminating information became available via radio and television, newspaper owners entered these fields, exploiting economies of scope, access to content and contacts with advertising agencies, to access a new stream of advertising revenue. Satellite and pay TV have also been rapidly embraced by the sector's corporate leaders, particularly News Corporation and Publishing and Broadcasting Limited. News Corporation, for example, moved into satellite television in the 1980s with the creation of its Fox Network, and distributes programs to independent television stations via satellite.

The advance of steam shipping from the later decades of the nineteenth century was embraced by leading Australian shipowners Adelaide Steamship Company, Howard Smith, and Huddart Parker. Steam, and later motor, ships greatly increased vessel productivity and the scale economies of ship-owning, and thus were a strong source of competitive advantage. The incremental nature of technological development in the industry required a leader to sustain its innovativeness over long periods of time. Adelaide Steamship Company was regarded as an innovative firm, regularly seeking out new opportunities. In 1964, for example, it was part of a joint venture, Associated Steamships, which arranged for the construction of the world's first cellular container ship, and had designed and built the world's first terminal container stacking system.[63] Australian Gas Light Company used technology to sustain its prime mover advantages and to legitimise its monopoly of gas supply to Sydney. When its heavily mechanised Mortlake gasworks commenced production in 1886 it possessed the greatest manufacturing capacity in the Southern Hemisphere, providing the opportunities to derive cost-reducing scale economies in supplying the expanding Sydney metropolis. It additionally kept down its costs and prices by the manufacture of by-products such as tar, oil, and sulphate of ammonia. In 1959 it achieved lower costs by installing 'one of the finest computers in Sydney'.[64]

Figurehead personalities

Personality can reveal additional evidence of leadership that is hidden from statistical and simple factual evidence. Charismatic or well-connected business figures may hold an influence disproportionate to the standing of their firm, facilitating leadership in, say, pricing, planning or industry representation with government and trades unions. Such figures can also provide the enthusiasm and drive to make the key strategic decisions upon which successful firms rely, such as product launches, technology augmentation, fund-raising, and suitable mergers and acquisitions.

Many leading Australian firms have been dominated or controlled by a particular entrepreneur or small group of decision-makers. This was particularly the case in the first half of the twentieth century before the 'managerial' firm belatedly began to supersede the 'entrepreneurial' model in Australia after 1950.[65] Reference to personality also helps to lift the 'corporate veil', that is, where the locus of economic leadership within the firm differs from its legal boundaries.[66] In the interwar period the Collins House Group of mining companies particularly illustrated the role of corporate personality. We shall look at this example in more detail in Chapter 5.

Although personality has generally played a lesser role in recent decades with the growth of managerial firms, some notable exceptions exist. The conglomeration movement of the 1970s and 1980s placed a number of our corporate leaders into the hands of organisations led by key strategic figures, particularly John Elliott and John Spalvins. Elliott exercised control over Henry Jones, Elders, Carlton & United Breweries and Foster's among other companies, while Spalvins' empire, based upon Adelaide Steamship Company, included David Jones, Woolworths, Tooth, Amalgamated Wireless Australasia and Petersville.

Probably the most widespread evidence of the role of personality has been in the publishing and media industries, which have been dominated by the Packer, Murdoch and Fairfax families. Their influence on the success of Publishing and Broadcasting Limited, News Corporation, and Fairfax Ltd is particularly important but also lifts the corporate veil on otherwise modestly represented public companies in our top 100 such as Daily Telegraph, Consolidated Press, and the South Australian Advertiser. The families' reputations often influenced the strategic paths taken by other firms. In addition, their connections with government and well-honed negotiating skills have been frequently used to effect in obtaining licences. On the other hand, the economic and perhaps cultural opposition to proliferation in sensitive industries had prevented even Murdoch and Packer from invariably achieving their political outcomes, as was indicated by the restrictions placed on numbers of television licences available to each interest (1956) and on cross-media ownership (1987).[67]

Strong personalities played an important role among many of our most enduring corporate leaders. CSR owed much of its prime mover success to its founding chairman Edward Knox, particularly his knowledge and connections in the industry and ability to obtain bank support. Essington Lewis, BHP's general manager from 1921, played a key role in the company's survival through the interwar turbulence – strong international competition in the 1920s and economic depression in the 1930s. In the process he reorientated the company towards steel production and particularly special steels that would be needed for wartime output.[68] James Burns and Robert Philp led Burns Philp from a general merchandise business in northern Queensland in the 1870s to a powerful trading and wholesaling business throughout the Pacific in the first half of the twentieth century. Henry James Holden was the driving force behind Holden. He effectively blended an understanding of vehicle technology with an ability to exercise close control over production. Holden saw the opportunities presented by World War One and proved an effective lobbyist for import controls.

In the pastoral agent industry there were many charismatic leaders of pastoral agencies, often ex-farmers well connected in politics, business and society that sometimes gave particular firms the upper hand on specific issues. Dalgety chief executive E. T. Doxat played a central role in the incorporation and modernisation of the company as preconditions for its leadership of the industry in the late nineteenth and early twentieth centuries.[69] The dominant retailers all benefited from the drive of their founders, David Jones, Joseph and Albert Grace, Sidney Myer, and George Cole. The entrepreneurial acumen of

Sidney Myer was evident through his ability to anticipate changing fashions and movements in the business cycle, the latter being particularly important to the firm's survival in the downturn of the early 1920s.[70]

The newness of commercial aviation required entrepreneurs with vision and adaptability. Reginald Ansett fits well that perspective. He was one of the pioneer aviators in Australia, having diversified into air services when his road services business was constrained by government legislation designed to protect the railways. Henry Jones provided highly innovative leadership for his company from the 1890s until his death in 1926. He achieved scale economies by expanding his production facilities and scope economies by widening his food product range. Very early on, he also developed a strong national brand name in IXL, which gave the company a strong competitive advantage over smaller domestic competitors, as well as multinational Heinz, who established a local factory in 1935. Herbert Gepp, managing director of Australian Paper Manufacturers from 1935, provided strong leadership in developing the company's reputation for technical expertise and innovation.[71] In a large and administratively complex public company like AMP, strong personal leadership nonetheless counted for much. Richard Teece, general manager from 1890–1917, has been described by Blainey as probably the most influential figure in Australian insurance and of carrying the company on his shoulders for several decades. He possessed both a keen understanding of business principles and strategic political connections, including a friendship with New South Wales premier and prime minister, George Reid.[72]

Prime movers and challengers in Australia

Having surveyed a range of evidence across sectors we can return to the broader question of prime movers and challengers. Three distinctive patterns emerge. In some industries, corporate leaders were firms who had established an early dominance and maintained that position throughout the twentieth century. CSR (sugar), Dunlop (rubber), AMP (life insurance), Email (appliances), Amalgamated Wireless Australasia (radio, television), Imperial Chemical Industries of Australia and New Zealand (chemicals), General Motors-Holden's (vehicles), Australian Gas Light Company (gas), Burns Philp (wholesale trade), Shell (petrol), and BHP (mining and metals) are the clearest examples. Serious challengers were encountered by the following prime movers: Dalgety (pastoral agency), British Tobacco/Amatil (tobacco), Herald & Weekly Times (media), James Hardie (building materials), Humes (cement), and Australian Glass Manufacturers (glass). The origins of challenger firms fits quite closely with Chandler's view that they were either the product of mergers in the industry (Elders, News) or diversifiers from other products or geographic areas (CSR,

Table 3.5: Prime mover and challenger firms, 1910–97

	1910	1930	1952	1964	1987	1997
1. Successful prime movers						
Sugar	CSR	CSR	CSR	CSR	CSR	CSR
Rubber	Dunlop	Dunlop	Dunlop	Dunlop	Dunlop	Dunlop
Life insurance	AMP	AMP	AMP	AMP	AMP	AMP
Appliances		Email	Email	Email	Email	Email
Radio, TV equipment		AWA	AWA	AWA	AWA	
Gas	AGL	AGL	AGL	AGL	AGL	AGL
Chemicals		ICIANZ	ICIANZ	ICIANZ	ICIANZ	ICIANZ
Vehicles		GM-Holden	GM-Holden	GM-Holden	GM-Holden	GM-Holden
Petrol				Shell	Shell	Shell
Wholesale		Burns Philp	Burns Philp	Burns Philp	Burns Philp	Burns Philp
Metal products		BHP	BHP	BHP	BHP	BHP
Mining		BHP	BHP	BHP	BHP	BHP
2. Successful challengers						
Pastoral agent	Dalgety	Dalgety	Dalgety	Elders	Elders	Wesfarmers
Tobacco	Br Tob	Br Tob	Br Tob	Br Tob	Rothmans	Philip Morris
Newspapers	HWT	HWT	HWT	Fairfax	News	News
Building materials	Wunderlich	Hardie	Hardie	Boral, CSR	Boral, CSR	Boral, CSR

continued over page

Table 3.5: Continued

	1910	1930	1952	1964	1987	1997
Cement		Kandos	Humes	Boral, CSR	Boral, CSR	Boral, CSR
Glass		AGM	ACI	ACI, Pilkington	ACI, Pilkington	ACI, Pilkington
3. Rotating leaders						
Brewing	CUB	Tooth	Tooth	CUB	CUB/LNathan	CUB/LNathan
Shipping	Huddart Parker	Howard Smith	Howard Smith	Adsteam	Adsteam	Howard Smith
Retail	Farmer	Myer	Myer	Woolworth	Coles	Coles
Aviation		Qantas	ANA	Ansett	Ansett, Qantas	Qantas
Paper		APM	APM, ANwsprnt	APM	Amcor	Amcor
Banking	Westpac	Westpac	Commonwealth	Commonwealth	Westpac	NAB

Note: Evidence is taken from a range of sources including top 100 asset data and market share information. Results for some industries and years are difficult to specify with any accuracy and so have been omitted.

Boral, Rothmans, Pilkington) rather than simply new firms. A third distinctive pattern relates to industries where leadership oscillated among several dominant firms such as in brewing (Carlton & United Breweries, Tooth), shipping (Huddart Parker, Howard Smith, Adelaide Steamship Company), aviation (Australian National Airways, Ansett, Qantas), retail (Myer, Woolworths, Coles), paper manufacture (Australian Paper Manufacturers, Australian Newsprint), and banking (Westpac, Commonwealth Bank of Australia, National Australia Bank).

Conclusion

In Chapter 3 we narrowed down our investigation into big business to focus upon key firms, the corporate leaders. These firms had both the size and the staying power to exert a significant influence on an industry and contribute to national economic change. Our selection methodology included refining our top 100 lists while also seeking some additional, more qualitative criteria. Corporate leaders generally held a significant market share, most expanded to serve a national market and were innovators, organisationally if not technologically. Dominant personalities helped to bring firms or groups of enterprises to the fore, particularly in the earlier part of the century.

Some important conclusions emerge. Most enterprises did not survive long in the top 100; only 63 of 354 endured for three or more benchmark years. This suggests, on the one hand, that relatively few companies were able to build up the organisational capabilities necessary to remain ahead of the pack. An alternative interpretation is that the corporate economy was sufficiently competitive to prevent too much entrenchment by prime movers, although concentration levels were high in many industries. When our corporate leaders disappeared from the list it was mostly due to takeovers, particularly by other leading companies, suggesting that there was a significant degree of continuity of corporate leadership.

Multinational enterprises again played an important role, accounting for around 25 per cent of corporate leaders. They were larger than the average firm, as we might expect to find, but tended to survive in the cohort for shorter than average periods. This may suggest that while they were effective at exploiting their initial competitive advantages, they were not as good as domestic firms at adapting to change in the Australian environment, particularly in the economy.

The spread of corporate leaders between different sectors reflects changes in the Australian macroeconomy with the early importance of mining, primary industries, utilities, transport, finance, wholesaling, and some basic consumer industries. As the economy broadened to include more manufacturing and new service industries, so did the spread of corporate leaders. Indeed, it appears that the spreading effect happened among corporate leaders before the economy as a whole, suggesting a pulling effect from the leaders. Some of the corporate leaders of the old sectors, however, were able to survive by diversification into new growth areas, Dunlop, CSR and Adelaide Steamship Company being good examples of this. Finally, the interplay between prime movers and challengers varied between industries. The growth strategies underlying the performances of our corporate leaders will be addressed in the following chapters.

CHAPTER 4

Paths of Corporate Development: Directions of Growth

In *Scale and Scope* Chandler explained the typical directions of growth followed by large-scale United States corporations which sustained their industry leadership.[1] This involved phases of horizontal and vertical integration to capture economies of scale and throughput, followed by product diversification in response to new scientific research and internationalisation to exploit their competitive advantages in foreign markets. This has not been a universal experience of all countries; successful British firms, for example, have been less vertically integrated and for many years Japanese firms were reluctant to expand overseas.

We now focus upon the growth directions of the Australian corporate leaders we identified in Chapter 3, to see if any common patterns emerge. We begin by reviewing the strengths and weaknesses of the different directions of growth.

Directions of firm growth

The choices of direction of growth are complex decisions that will change over time in response to alterations in the environment and the character of senior management. Firms choose between a range of growth directions. They can increase output of their existing products through horizontal integration, take on additional functions in the value chain – in other words, vertical integration – and they can diversify into new product lines, market segments, and geographic locations.

Each of these growth directions has both advantages and shortcomings. The benefits of horizontal integration are often associated with cost-reducing economies of scale at the plant level or greater specialisation between factories at the multi-plant level. An associated idea is that higher levels of output facilitate supporting activities that require a minimum scale to operate efficiently, such as product branding, and research and development. The product specialisation of horizontal integration brings greater expertise and accelerated learning opportunities, ideas commonly referred to as the experience curve, making it easier to replicate the firm's capabilities in different markets.[2] Finally, large size in a particular sector enhances a firm's market power, providing it with increased control over the market and greater negotiating strength.[3] The costs of horizontal integration include the concentration of risk upon a particular product, a limited knowledge of related products and functions, and the prospect of the firm attracting the attention of competition policy enforcement agencies due to its large market share.

Vertical integration can reduce transactions costs by bringing contractual negotiations, such as between procurement and manufacturing stages, under the single governance structure of the firm. Linked to this is the fact that vertical integration removes the risk of contractual 'hold-up' (also known as 'opportunistic recontracting'), where the firm has many specific use assets that cannot easily be redeployed if negotiations with another company break down. For the integrating firm, control of upstream and downstream functions increases market power over existing competitors and creates barriers to new entrants.[4] In terms of operations management, vertical integration can accelerate the throughput of products and mitigate the need to hold inventory stocks.

Where a firm is faced with irregular or non-existent upstream and downstream functions, vertical integration addresses this form of market failure and helps the firm to expand its production if horizontal integration is a growth strategy. Vertical expansion additionally provides a broad and integrated understanding of the extended value chain, how different parts of it work together, and it helps to prevent proprietary knowledge from leaking to competitors transacting with the same firms. On the negative side, vertical integration, as the 'make' rather than 'buy' decision, also concentrates the firm's risks into a particular industry and involves additional fixed costs.[5] Stages in the value chain often have different economic characteristics from each other, such as their optimal size, which may not easily be accommodated within a single organisation.

One of the major drivers of product diversification is risk-spreading to avoid a downturn in the industry, the emergence of a powerful competitor, the attention of the competition regulator, or simply to spread operating risks such as variable cash flow. Sometimes the company has grown too large for its existing product line. Diversification enables firms to pursue growth opportunities in sunrise industries, and generally access additional resources associated with other industries, including government incentives. Among these additional resources must be counted rich veins of information about different sectors, which allows the firm to act as a mini capital market, transferring funds internally according to the changing fortunes between industries. Where the new product lines are related to the firm's original output, cost-reducing scope economies are likely as tangible and intangible assets can be shared across the firm's different products.

Not surprisingly, there are costs associated with product diversification. Expertise is diluted as the firm shifts away from its core competencies; more so where it is unrelated diversification. Organisational costs and complexity may increase in managing an extended range of products with different techno-logical and marketing needs, as we shall see in Chapter 7. Where diversification has been driven by government policy, such as investment incentives or tariff protection, the firm may operate inefficiently and be vulnerable to changes in official policy.

Market diversification occurs where a firm seeks new markets for its existing product line; alternative market segments might include low or high income, urban against rural, household versus industrial customers. It provides some of the benefits of both horizontal integration and product diversification, notably economies of scale by selling more of the same product, and risk-spreading between markets that may be affected differently by changes in the environment. Thus, it is also a means of tapping into the rapid growth of par-ticular market segments according to demographic or income shifts. The dis-advantages relate to the potentially different marketing needs of alternative segments, thereby weakening opportunities for scope economies. Brand devel-opment may be different across markets and, further, product reputation may be diluted by going down-market, or difficult to build if moving up market.

Geographic diversification takes firms into new, spatially distinct markets. This is most significant when firms expand internationally, since it takes them across national boundaries and frequently into societies with different cultural, legal and institutional norms. Often firms move along a learning curve of inter-nationalisation from exporting, through contracting with a local firm, to foreign direct investment. An extensive literature exists on the internationalisation process of firms.[6] Essentially, firm-specific and country-specific advantages exist for firms going multinational. In the former case, international expansion exploits ownership advantages unique to the firm, such as superior technology or management systems, privileged access to finance or raw materials, greater market power and scale economies from larger size, and product branding and advertising. These advantages must generate an additional return for the firm that is greater than the extra cost of doing business in a foreign setting. These advantages are either location-bound or non-location-bound depending on the range of countries in which they can be exploited.

Country-specific advantages reflect conditions in the recipient nation that are conducive to local production, such as cheap or well-trained labour, high quality infrastructure, and preferential policies from governments keen to attract investment. They also derive from conditions in the sender nation – whether they have been conducive to the development of domestic firms capable of internationalisation. Large and competitive markets, for example, promote the emergence of efficient and sizeable firms likely to succeed internationally. As a geographical form of diversification, international expansion additionally promotes risk-spreading. The weaknesses of multinational activity particularly relate to the costs and challenges of cross-cultural and long-distance control and coordination of the enterprise.

Growth directions of Australian corporate leaders

We saw in Chapter 2 that Australian firms have faced an operating environment with a particular and probably unique combination of elements, most notably geographic remoteness, a small population, interventionist governments, high levels of inward foreign direct investment, a late developing capital market, and a strong comparative advantage in the primary industries. Together, these elements suggest an environment characterised by rapid change and high levels of uncertainty. Therefore, corporate leaders needed, above all else, to show adaptable qualities, reducing their exposure to industries in decline or subject to new multinational entrants, and seeking out new opportunities for growth.

As we can see from Table 4.1, corporate leaders changed their directions of growth several times over their lifespan. It was their responsiveness to the environment and speed of change that gave many their competitive edge over rivals. The most important of these environmental influences upon the directions of corporate growth were the small market, inward foreign direct investment, the dominance of the primary sector, and the active role of government, as we shall see below. In addition, since Australia is a small follower economy, its companies frequently responded to changes in the conventional wisdom of corporate growth imported from large, early developer nations such as the United States and Britain.

While there are unique firm and industry-specific elements to the pattern of growth among Australia's corporate leaders, we can broadly generalise about their directions of growth. Many firms established their early mover advantages through a decision to create scale (horizontal integration). Preservation of leadership often required subsequent investments in upstream or downstream activities (vertical integration). As firms outgrew markets and responded to new growth opportunities, product and geographic diversification provided a new lease of corporate life. In addition to firm life cycle patterns, there have been longitudinal trends arising from changes in the Australian macroeconomy, with

Table 4.1: Growth directions of the most enduring corporate leaders

Company	Horizontal integration		Vertical integration		Diversification		Internationalisation	
	Minor	Major	Upstream	Downstream	Related	Unrelated	Regional	Global
BHP		By 1900		1915	1960s			1970s
Br Tob/Amatil		1904			1960s	1950s		1990s
CSR		By 1900	By 1900		1930s	1970s	By 1900	1980s
Dunlop		By 1900			1920s	1960s	1970s	1980s
AGL		By 1900		1880s	1920s	1980s	1990s	
Burns Philp	By 1900	By 1900	By 1900	1930s		1970s	By 1914	1980s
AMP		By 1900			1950s		By 1900	1980s
BNSW/Wpac		By 1900			1950s		By 1900	1960s

Notes: Table consists of the six firms that endured for all six periods and the two leading financial institutions. This table seeks to generalise about growth directions rather than capture every event.

diversification particularly emerging from the 1960s, conglomeration in the 1970s, and internationalisation from the 1980s.

Achievement of early leadership: Appropriating scale advantages

It was the strategic decision to create scale that enabled many firms to capture early mover advantages that propelled them towards a position of dominance. These advantages included the appropriation of strategic assets such as natural resources, foreign patents, brands, and government subsidies, contracts and production licences.[7] Given the smallness of the market in Australia, where many industries could not support more than one or two large-scale enterprises, rapid horizontal expansion was vital to achieve the incumbency of a first mover.

Building scale lowers the costs of most production, especially in capital-intensive industries at the relatively low levels of output in Australia. While not driving down costs to the extent possible in larger overseas markets, horizontal growth yielded sufficient capacity to change a firm's cost schedules and in many cases transform the industry. Many Australian leaders were not in the technology-intensive manufacturing industries identified by Chandler in the United States; however, scale economies were yielded in other ways, such as in marketing, managerial deployment and information use. Perhaps most important was the ability of firms to lower learning costs by leveraging their cumulative expertise to establish new branches and plants across Australia.

Strategic assets: Mining, utilities and aviation

The leading mining companies moved quickly to appropriate readily available mineral resources. In the process, they cornered a limited market to establish prime mover advantages through lower costs in a capital intensive industry. BHP led the pack, as we will see below. Western Mining Corporation similarly built scale and low costs through extended horizontal integration from the 1930s to the 1970s. The expertise Western Mining Corporation developed in the process was reflected in its innovativeness in production and organisation: for example, it operated identical plants, centralised purchasing and amalgamated its Kalgoorlie mines for servicing by a single treatment plant.[8]

In the production and distribution of gas, Australian Gas Light Company and South Australian Gas Company built scale primarily by the ownership of the supply franchises from the governments of New South Wales and South Australia respectively. Their monopoly enabled them to yield scale economies in a capital-intensive industry and invest regularly in new equipment in a rapidly changing sector; for example, large vertical retorts and high pressure steel mains enabled them to extend their geographical coverage in the interwar period.[9]

The companies were alert to the political opportunities and challenges associated with their franchises. They were quick to defend their rights and fostered important connections. After World War Two, South Australian Gas Company saw major growth opportunities from providing supply to the public housing programs but faced a competitive threat from electrical suppliers. In response, it fostered close political connections with the State government and the South Australia Housing Trust.[10]

Government policy exerted a strong influence over corporate strategy in the aviation industry. Qantas relied heavily upon government subsidies and contract work to develop its earliest routes in the 1920s and 1930s, working closely with the Civil Aviation Department.[11] Subsidy to total revenue ratios varied between 50 and 80 per cent.[12] As domestic route subsidies were reduced in the 1930s, Qantas began expanding its interstate network and initiated the Empire mail service to Britain with government support.

Immediately after World War Two, Ansett began to build its position in the air freight market: by transporting passengers during the day and freight at night it significantly improved its airliner utilisation above a low 54 per cent.[13] The resulting scale economies, along with cost-cutting, enabled Ansett to be highly price competitive in establishing its market position in competition with other domestic pioneers, such as Australian National Airways and Trans-Australia Airlines. Ansett's 1957 acquisition of Australian National Airways was of major strategic importance. It brought the company within the government's two-airline policy, with further benefits flowing from the tightening of that policy in the following year, which was central to sustaining its fleet expansion and keeping out competitors.[14]

Scale economies: Manufacturing, the media and shipping

The dominant firms in the food, drink and tobacco sector drew heavily upon new technologies from Europe and North America and the development of branded product ranges to expand horizontally and claim first mover advantages. The rapidly expanding urban market for beer and the introduction of science-based advances into the industry by the turn of the twentieth century enabled brewers to grow horizontally by introducing capital-intensive, large-scale production at lower unit cost. Australian brewers honed their marketing skills, developing brand names to sustain their dominance. Tooth became known for its 'pub art' marketing in the 1930s, but the development of strong national brands came about more recently, in response to the arrival of British brewer Courage in 1968 and the absorption of the leading brewers into expansion-minded conglomerates in the following decades.[15]

Jam producer Henry Jones concentrated initially upon building scale by enlarging production facilities. This gave him double the capacity of all his rivals combined and drove down his production costs. He was an early user of branding techniques as a means to sustain a market for his large production capacity; all his products carried the IXL brand name from the mid-1890s.[16] Nestlé and Unilever were foreign multinationals that settled in Australia to exploit their reputation in branded food products. Unilever grew horizontally by dominating the branded soap market and Nestlé in powdered and condensed milk and milk drinks such as Milo.

The three dominant firms in building materials, Australian Glass Manufacturers (glass), Humes (pipes), and James Hardie (concrete and other building materials), built scale in their particular area before leveraging off these competences to add narrowly diverse products and to expand overseas. Each built scale through being a leader in technical innovation in the first half of the twentieth century. Humes pioneered the manufacture of concrete pipes, and James Hardie the manufacture of fibro-cement. Australian Glass Manufacturers pioneered many aspects of modern glass manufacture in Australia through the acquisition of foreign patents. The rapid growth of demand for rubber products, together with strong marketing of the brand name, provided Dunlop with ample opportunities for horizontal growth. Its factories were soon turning out a range of rubber-based products, predominantly tyres but also shoes, golf balls, valves, tennis balls, clothing and hot-water bottles.

Metropolitan-based newspapers, faced with expanding urban markets, had grown to sufficient size to introduce large-scale printing technologies from North America and Europe. In 1934 the Herald & Weekly Times was the first Australian firm to employ printing presses capable of producing 50 000 copies an hour at its new Flinders Street site.[17] The resulting scale economies and lower costs rapidly drove out smaller and regional competitors with shorter print runs. The capacity created by the new technology enabled the firms to expand horizontally to build national newspaper chains beginning in the inter-war period, as we saw in Chapter 3.

In addition to the adoption of scale-based technologies, size also generated information economies since journalism costs were spread over longer print runs. Central to these scale strategies, the strong-minded leaders of these media firms, particularly the Packers and Murdochs, modified the presentation and layout of their newspapers to popularise them and thus expand their market.

Horizontal integration dominated the early growth strategies of Australian shipping companies. This was to be expected in an industry of high capital intensity and scales of efficiency. In the age of steam and then motorised liners, the ability to offer regular, timetabled services across a wide range of routes was a strong source of competitive advantage. Adelaide Steamship Company, for example, built up a sizeable fleet in the late nineteenth and early twentieth centuries operating in the port, coastal and overseas sectors, serving the cargo, passenger and tourist trades. By 1914 it owned 29 ocean-going ships, eight steam tenders, and 23 hulkers and lighters.[18]

Leveraging knowledge in service industries

In many service industries, the leading firms rapidly multiplied their retail outlets across Australia by leveraging their early and cumulative expertise and reputation in setting up and operating such units. Horizontal expansion of retail products has been the predominant growth path of Australia's leading financial institutions. Banking and life insurance provide examples of technological economies typical of Chandler's large-scale United States manufacturing enterprises, particularly in product range and back office operations, as we saw in Chapter 3. Additionally, they achieved cost savings by leveraging their expertise in the provision of specialist services across a nationwide branch network, thereby telescoping the learning curve. The number of branches operated by the Bank of New South Wales, for example, rose impressively from 167 in 1891 to 789 in 1939 and continued to rise rapidly thereafter.[19] In a similar fashion, L. J. Hooker had built up the largest national chain of real estate offices by 1960, emphasising their brand name and experience. Thenceforth, they extended their network further by franchising from 1968, using the same competitive advantages but at lower cost. By the 1990s the company had over 600 offices located across Australia, Hong Kong, Papua New Guinea and New Zealand.[20]

The rapid expansion of wool output, with the extension of settlement, provided the opportunity for a group of about half a dozen pastoral agents to grow horizontally to yield economies of scale.[21] In addition to exploiting cumulative expertise, the fixed costs of their business – branch offices, auction sites, commercial information – were spread across a wider range of client farmers, facilitating relatively low-cost expansion into newly settled pastoral regions, such as parts of Queensland and Western Australia. As they expanded, the firms were able to offer farmers a full range of pastoral services – wool and livestock sales, finance, and technical and business advice – which yielded economies of scope by sharing physical assets and customer information. Broad transacting meant lower transactions costs for both agent and farmer, and the development of high degrees of trust between them. These large agencies additionally benefited from being able to offer their range of services as virtual joint products – for example, farmers needed short-term finance on their consigned wool, and business advice regarding the state of the market.

Sustained horizontal integration enabled a limited number of retail traders to grow rapidly from the early twentieth century at the expense of the established pattern of dominant wholesalers and small suburban retailers. The growth of capital city populations and improved transport systems provided the conditions for large-scale retailing. Department stores, Myer and David Jones, occupied centrally located sites in easy reach of customers and suppliers. Size gave them scope economies, convenience for customers, and bargaining power with suppliers. Chain store operators, Woolworths and Coles, used scale to offer low prices for an initially limited range of household items, and then leveraged their expertise, reputation and buying power into an expanding chain of outlets and broader range of merchandise. Each retailer drew heavily upon innovation to augment its standing and extend its horizontal growth; we saw in Chapter 3 that a regular flow of innovations characterised all stages of the sector including supplier-to-store, in-store, and store-to-customer operations.

Horizontal integration was extended rapidly in the 1950s as these largely state-based firms grew into national organisations. Coles moved into food retailing in 1958, and in 1960 established the first free-standing 'supermarket' with its own car park in Balwyn (Victoria). The supermarket was an international trend that began in the interwar period in the United States. It was driven by a range of social, spatial and technical changes, which included suburban expansion, the spread of the automobile, refrigeration, and double-income families. This enabled well-resourced retailers to build large out-of-town 'supermarkets' that offered a wide variety of foods conveniently located in a single store. Price competition was intensified by low land costs and buying power.[22] Closely linked to this was the postwar rise of the shopping centre ('mall'), led by property companies Lend Lease and Westfield. In a symbiotic manner, the success of these two companies owed much to the anchoring of a major retailer in each centre in order to attract business.

Consolidation of leadership: Developing vertical links

Vertical frequently followed quickly upon horizontal expansion to consolidate the firm's advantage. The small Australian market rarely sustained sufficient upstream and downstream firms to maintain the necessary throughput of a large firm, thereby necessitating vertical integration to overcome this market failure. Serious risks of 'hold-up' also existed because of the limited number of competing suppliers. Vertical integration enabled corporate leaders to build entry barriers against potential competitors for small markets. Some firms vertically integrated to pursue upstream or downstream growth opportunities, as in vehicle construction and oil refining. Transaction cost savings from integration motivated some firms, although few operated on a scale where significant economies could be yielded by internalising supply and distribution functions in the manner of United States corporations.

Contesting market power: Contractual hold-up and entry barriers in capital-intensive sectors

Contractual hold-up is particularly significant in industries with a concentration of ownership and a capital intensity of assets that are not easily redeployed ('asset specificity'). Mining and metallurgy fit these features particularly well. Zinc Corporation was established in 1905 to acquire tailings and process them into zinc through electrolytic and flotation techniques. It soon acquired a mine in Broken Hill to avoid any 'hold-up' of supplies. Further mines were acquired, as well as a timber mill in 1947 to supply pit props to their mines. The company formed a major part in the creation of Consolidated Zinc Corporation in 1949, an integrated lead and zinc manufacturer.[23] By the 1950s Mount Isa Mines had, by a similar process, become a vertically integrated copper producer as miner, smelter and refiner. The strategic benefits were reflected in its dominance of the copper industry by the 1970s, accounting for 88 per cent of refined production.[24]

It was their vertical integration strategies, throughout the company's history, that mostly sustained wholesale trader Burns Philp against contractual threats from upstream and downstream firms. Like many traders, the firm acquired its own vessels to overcome inadequate shipping services and to guard against predation by large shipping companies. In due course, it expanded its shipping operations, providing a network of regular inter-island services across the South Pacific. The company additionally acquired marine towage facilities and the coal supplies necessary to fuel its fleet. As they expanded their interests through the islands of the South Pacific, Burns Philp vertically integrated backwards into agency services and the operation of plantations, this partly reflecting inadequate supply and the risk of predation. Additionally, the company recognised the market growth in coconut, copra and rubber on which most of their plantations were based, and the increased cargoes they provided for the passage back to Australia.[25]

It was the downstream threat from the large retailers that proved more serious. The company was quick to recognise this, James Burns junior observing in 1931, 'the only way now for a wholesale distributor to expand is by means of a chain of tied stores in which the wholesaler has a controlling interest'. The following year, Penney's Ltd was formed to operate a chain of retail stores on behalf of the company, which by 1935 consisted of 25 outlets in

Queensland and northern New South Wales. Burns Philp went on to acquire many stores in rural New South Wales.[26] In the long run, however, the plantation policy proved more successful than the operation of retail stores. Although Penney's was said to be 'big and flourishing' in 1952, it was sold four years later to Coles. Many years later, Burns' assessment was that the company had lost out to the major retailers like Myer and David Jones by not investing more substantially in capital city retailing in place of country stores, thereby leaving them without a strong metropolitan base.[27]

CSR rapidly built vertical integration into milling, plantations and shipping, thereby ensuring the supply of its capital-intensive refineries was not held up by opportunistic suppliers or the lack of a market in the specialised shipping services it required. One of CSR's customers was the astute jam producer Henry Jones, who was alert to the threats from his two main upstream suppliers, shipping and sugar: both were highly concentrated industries, thereby increasing the risk of hold-up for his large-scale, capital-intensive operations. His solution was to integrate backwards into shipping by establishing his own fleet and, additionally, acting as agent for other lines in order to improve working relations and reciprocity of dealing. Jones additionally sought to integrate backwards into sugar with an abortive attempt to acquire a Queensland refiner. Although unsuccessful, his action sent a credible threat to CSR that it should not press this customer too hard. Jones also integrated backwards into saw-milling to provide timber for packaging, and into fruit and hop growing to supply his factories, as well as for export.[28]

While the firms discussed above took a strategic decision to integrate in response to upstream and downstream risks, several corporate leaders did so in order to erect entry barriers against potential competitors. The most celebrated example of this came in the form of 'tied house' agreements, which gave the leading brewers control over the principal retail outlets for beer. This created a powerful entry barrier for Carlton & United Breweries, particularly when the number of liquor licences on issue in Victoria was capped from 1907 until the mid-1950s. These agreements were finally outlawed by trade practices legislation in the 1970s.[29] Likewise, upstream integration secured supplies and increased the probable entry price for new firms. Thus, Carlton & United Breweries had an equity position in Joe White Maltings from 1910 until the 1930s and invested in its own malting production facilities in 1952. There is rarely a single explanation of strategic decisions and it should be noted that efficiency explanations also ranked in the vertical integration of Australian brewers. They integrated forwards into distribution, transporting their own products and acting as agents for other beverages and supplies to hotels. Given the bulkiness of beer and the importance of careful and prompt handling, integration of these functions was also an efficient mode of operation.

Principal growth strategy: Oil, automobiles and property development

In several industries, vertical integration was the dominant strategy after World War Two. The key to the commercial success of Lend Lease from its establishment in 1958 was its introduction of the concept of 'design and construct' into the building industry. Design and construct was based upon the notion that a vertically integrated building and property management company could control all stages of the building process – from initial design through construction to ownership of the building, leasing and selling the property. In this way, costs and quality could be more closely controlled than had commonly been the case in the industry.[30]

Working with its parent company Civil and Civic, Lend Lease adopted the strategy of gaining market dominance by tendering successfully for major contracts that would raise the profile of the firm – this included the Sydney Opera House, Australia Square (Sydney), the MLC Centre (Sydney), sporting stadiums (Sydney Football Stadium, Olympic Aquatic Centre), Darling Harbour, Russell Defence Offices (Canberra), and the Academy of Sciences building (Canberra). The enormity of the construction task that began in 1962 with the Australia Square project motivated Lend Lease to extend its vertical control to ownership of the manufacturing companies that supplied lifts, windows and building materials.[31] The benefits came from transaction cost savings, especially coordination costs which could be reduced with fewer suppliers, enabling the company to operate on a tight construction schedule.[32]

General Motors-Holden's leadership of the automobile industry was built upon taking the correct 'make or buy' and locational decisions at different stages of the industry and firm's development. The industry featured high minimum scales of efficiency that early twentieth-century Australia's small market could not meet. Therefore, General Motors-Holden's initially imported completely knocked down units for assembly in Australia, drawing upon the scale economies of General Motors and then minimising transport costs from the United States. With high interstate transport costs, the earliest vehicles were assembled at regional plants around Australia. As local content increased, centralised assembly plants became more cost effective, most tasks being completed in Melbourne and Sydney.

Government policy had influenced the structure of the automobile industry in many respects, perhaps most notably tariff protection's encouragement of local production by foreign firms. In 1944 the federal government announced that it would grant preferential tariffs and scarce US dollar exchange to firms prepared to manufacture a car completely in Australia. Accompanying such incentives was the threat that the Commonwealth might commence vehicle production.[33] General Motors-Holden's, along with Ford, Chrysler and International Harvester accepted the challenge. In circumstances where there were no reliable local suppliers of particular components, the firms were obliged to 'make' not 'buy'. Thus, General Motors-Holden's established its own foundry facilities to produce engine castings, since the domestic foundry industry was incapable of satisfying their technical requirements. As Maxcy has noted, 'the company ended up more integrated than it perhaps would have wished – at least at that time'.[34] Nonetheless, General Motors-Holden's showed an awareness of the benefits of using local firms where they could work with competing suppliers to mitigate the risk of 'hold-up', policies which contributed to the rise of a local components industry led by Repco.[35]

Holden's model 48-215 became the first Australian-built car in 1948. It drew upon the design experience and test facilities of General Motors, along with the local subsidiary's knowledge of Australian road conditions. General Motors-Holden's also vertically integrated forwards from 1948 with its own dealer network, believing that control over the quality and presentation of the vehicle could thus be more effectively managed than through general retailers who had no loyalty to a specific manufacturer and were not easily monitored. By the mid-1950s Holden had achieved a 50 per cent share of the local vehicle market for its range of models, reversing the initial postwar dominance of British firms which had benefited from the dollar shortage and the 1949 devaluations.[36]

The petroleum multinationals, Shell, BP, Esso, Mobil and local firm Ampol concentrated upon integrated exploration, production, refining, marketing, and the operation of service stations. Since petroleum has a high bulk to value ratio and its markets and supply sources are widely dispersed, vertical integration helps to minimise disruptions to the extensive product flows required to make the industry operate efficiently.[37] As we shall see in Chapter 5, a range of vertical relationships were adopted by the petroleum companies. Subsidiaries and associated companies were used to connect exploration, production and transport. Forward vertical integration has variously involved acquiring or developing service stations, or solo marketing relationships that prevent the service station owner selling rival products.[38] While the need for efficient throughput has weighed heavily upon the integration decision, so has the desire for corporate leaders to protect their interests in a highly concentrated industry with very high levels of minimum scale and capital intensity serving a small but fast-growing local market.

Securing sequential activities in emergent industries

In relatively new industries the problem of insufficient suppliers in a small economy was accentuated. Amalgamated Wireless Australasia sought vertical integration as their strategy in the 1910s and 1920s. The firm grew initially on the back of the expansion of the demand for radios. Besides the production of radios and their components, it vertically integrated forwards to service and repair radio sets and, additionally, entered the operation of radio stations. It integrated backwards into the manufacture of major components such as radio valves and, later, television tubes. Its domination of these new technologies meant Amalgamated Wireless Australasia was best placed to provide highly integrated production and services. It leveraged its core competences in these technologies to foster a close working relationship with the federal government, acting as the major supplier of traffic control equipment and, from 1922, as provider of the Beam Wireless service until its sale to the federal government in 1946. This included the design and manufacture of equipment, as well as operating the service. In this role it was responsible for several important innovations including the introduction of overseas telephone services in 1930.[39] Australian Glass Manufacturers' experience was similar. Its vertical integration strategy promoted a holistic view of technological change in the industry and the consequent ability to apply learning-by-doing advantages.[40]

Australian Gas Light Company and South Australian Gas Company vertically integrated the production and distribution of gas. This made sense on a number of levels – a lack of alternative suppliers, the risk of hold-up if any firm gained leadership in gas production, and technical non-separabilities in the production and distribution of gas.[41] They further integrated into retail and marketing, including the sale and lease of gas cookers and the provision of cookery lessons, demonstrations and competitions, operating their own show-rooms by the 1920s.[42] With the introduction of natural gas in the 1970s, both companies withdrew from the manufacture of gas, now being provided by the oil companies, and concentrated upon distribution and marketing. This enabled them to avoid the major investments required to extract natural gas, and helped to dispel their old image as manufacturers of 'grimy' town gas. On the other hand, they lost some of their strategic influence over the industry and vigilance was required to prevent producers bypassing them to supply major industrial users. While South Australian Gas Company fell out of the top 100 list after 1964, Australian Gas Light Company has been able to maintain its position, helped by its return to upstream vertical integration, particularly after Ron Brierley's Industrial Equity Limited acquired a large share of the company in 1986. Today, it remains a major energy player with investments in oil and gas exploration and production.

Renewed expansion through diversification

Diversification came at a later stage of development for most corporate leaders as they outgrew their small local markets. Related product diversification built upon their existing competences within the Australian market to yield scope economies. In the more scientific industries, related diversification was a response to similar policies overseas from the interwar period, as Chandler has particularly noted of the United States.[43] Local subsidiaries of foreign multinationals were well placed to diversify along the lines of their parent, as occurred with Imperial Chemical Industries, British Tobacco and Unilever. Others, however, were less diversified in the face of constraints imposed by their parent companies and by the limitations on their legal rights to acquire other Australian companies.[44] The earliest diversifiers, such as CSR, began in the interwar years, but it became a more common strategy after 1945 with the broadening manufacturing base of the economy.

Unrelated diversification has enabled some firms to enter new growth industries and risk spread away from declining industries, or from the real or credible threat of a multinational competitor, where divestment was seen as the best strategy.[45] 'Conglomeration', as unrelated diversification is sometimes known, was additionally an imported 'fad' of the 1970s and 1980s, based on the optimistic belief that good managers would excel in any industry. The poor performance of many Australian conglomerates has led to frequent divestment of these additional activities in the 1990s and a return to 'core competences' in order to survive.

Development of new products in science-based industries

The emergence of new or modernised products, often based upon imported technological knowledge, motivated related diversification by the corporate leaders of science-based industries able to yield scope economies. ICI applied the same strategy in Australia as it had elsewhere, diversified growth building on its research reputation and the wide range of technological innovations in the chemicals industry in the middle decades of the century. This took the company into such areas as paint, explosives, alkalis, fertilisers, dyes, fabrics, plastics, non-ferrous metals and petrochemicals.[46]

The innovativeness of radio producer Amalgamated Wireless Australasia enabled it to diversify into stereo equipment and radar products in order to yield scope economies. It has been estimated that the company held as many as 3000 patents for radios and radar products. The advent of television gave the firm another set of related products and markets to which it could apply its expertise in electronic equipment design and manufacture. By 1960 it was described as being in the 'envious position' of the leading television producer, and the only provider of key components such as tubes.[47] In the following decades it diversified into a series of new products including electric fans, film projectors, communications equipment, air-conditioners, refrigerators and washing machines.

Postwar diversification was common in mining and metallurgy, and provided firms with a broader revenue base and new growth opportunities, particularly during the mineral boom of the 1960s and the rapidly expanding market for bauxite and uranium. This was mostly narrow related diversification within the resources sector. With limited opportunities for vertical integration in gold production, Western Mining Corporation embarked upon extensive diversification into other minerals, particularly nickel, bauxite, copper and iron, from the 1950s. Bauxite was discovered in the Darling Downs in the late 1950s, copper in the Warburton Ranges in 1965, and nickel in Kambalda (WA) in 1966. The company played an important role in the establishment and operation of aluminium company Alcoa from 1961, and also began mining iron ore and talc in the same decade.[48]

From the late 1930s Mount Isa Mines had used diversification into copper, which could also be mined at Mount Isa, to overcome its lack of scale and efficiency in lead and zinc. With its Townsville copper refinery dominating postwar national output, Mount Isa Mines was able to expand its range of copper products including billets, wires, bars and rods.[49] Diversification was vigorously pursued by Conzinc Riotinto Australia's predecessor firms for similar reasons. The creation of Consolidated Zinc Corporation in 1949 integrated Zinc Corporation's lead and zinc manufacture. By the early 1960s it was exploiting improved processing technologies to produce sulphuric acid for chemical companies and phosphoric acid for use in agricultural fertilisers. The firm also diversified into mineral sands, uranium, oil, coal and natural gas from the 1940s onwards. Finally, Consolidated Zinc Corporation entered aluminium production with the discovery of bauxite at Weipa and created Comalco in 1956 to develop the deposit.[50]

The leading media organisations achieved scope economies by using a sizeable production capacity to diversify their stable of publications, offering both morning and afternoon papers, together with magazines and colour printing services. Thus, from the early 1920s the Herald & Weekly Times began publishing a morning paper, the *Sun News-Pictorial* and several editions of the evening *Herald*. There followed a bi-weekly *Sporting Globe*, a weekly country oriented the *Weekly Times*, along with magazines such as the *Australian Home Builder*. Scope economies of news content were generated when related stories were used in several publications and across media forms.

The Herald & Weekly Times was the first newspaper group to diversify into radio, setting up 3DB in Melbourne in 1929.[51] In 1955 it moved into television with the establishment of HSV7. Packers' Consolidated Press diversified into television through Channel Nine in 1956.[52] The more recent growth of satellite and pay TV has been dominated by News Corporation, particularly with the formation of Foxtel in 1994. These new types of media provided the companies with a large increase in advertising revenue since radio, then television, became ideal channels for modern 'persuasive' advertising.[53]

Diversification was, however, limited by federal regulations regarding ownership. The *Broadcasting and Television Act 1956* limited the number of licences a firm could own. Substantial amendments to that legislation in 1987 capped the overall audience any television network could reach and prohibited cross-ownership of print and electronic media in the same city.[54] As a result of these measures, the companies sought specialisation within print, television or radio.[55] In particular, News Corporation was obliged to divest its network television channels, Ten and Seven.[56] Government policy appears to have been a factor behind broadening its diversification strategy to include book publishing, film-making, farming and transport.

Reinforcing core service activities

Diversification by corporate leaders in several service industries was strategically designed to reinforce their core activities. Narrow diversification by Australian Gas Light Company and South Australian Gas Company exploited scope economies and boosted their strategic standing. They manufactured by-products of gas by the 1920s, including sulphate of ammonia, coke, tar and its derivatives, which drove down the production cost of gas. They sought market diversification for gas, from heating to lighting, cooking, and in vehicles, and from household to industrial consumption. It was only after 1986 that Brierley drove Australian Gas Light Company to much broader diversification into gold exploration and property development, a strategy that was wound back in the 1990s in favour of narrower diversification into electricity, to take advantage of privatisation policies.

Reg Ansett had diversified into airline operations within a few years of establishing his taxi service in 1931. Diversification would become a postwar watchword of the company as it responded to the limited opportunities for further horizontal expansion resulting from the virtual monopoly of overseas flights by Qantas. In the two decades after World War Two, diversification yielded scope economies in support of its national air services network. This particularly involved the establishment of a chain of holiday resorts and hotels, beginning in the Whitsundays in 1947. In addition, it operated helicopter services and facilitated intermodal conveyance by becoming the largest road freight operator. From the 1970s, Ansett diversified very broadly into finance, credit cards, television stations, furniture removals, restaurants and stationery. Although mostly unrelated to its core aviation, some lines such as finance, credit cards and removals, provided synergies.[57] Again, many of these additional layers of activity had been peeled away by the 1990s.

From the mid-1950s the banks diversified their product range to support their core trading business. After more than half a century of horizontal expansion establishing national networks across Australia, they turned to new products to sustain their growth. Thus, the Bank of New South Wales began savings banking in 1956, followed a few months later by the Australian and New Zealand Bank. They then moved into hire purchase, nominee companies, and later into merchant banking, insurance, funds management, as market maker in the United States bond market, and bullion dealing. This closely related diversification enabled the banks to leverage their skills in financial intermediation into new products. The timing of these moves and the extent of the banks' involvement also resulted from closer regulation of their core activities. AMP crossed the traditional divide among insurance companies by adding fire and accident to their life insurance business in 1958 and then followed the banks into the short-term money market in 1959.[58]

Retailers saw narrow diversification as a means of yielding sizeable scope economies and shoring up their dominance. The boundaries within the industry were breaking down in the 1960s and 1970s. Helped by trade practices legislation, particularly the ending of resale price maintenance, the leaders moved aggressively into the discount market, building huge stores and relying upon volume sales to win supplier discounts and drive down their prices. Myer achieved this through its Target stores, Woolworths through 'Big W', and Coles by using the K Mart brand. They continued to diversify their portfolio of retail services in the final decades of the century. This has included the 'killer category', stores specialising in a narrower range of products than department stores, while competing with discount stores on price. In the case of Coles Myer this included World 4 Kids, OfficeWorks, and Mega Mart. However, as the most diverse retailer, it has struggled in recent years to manage its different market segments.

Countering decline in traditional industries and markets

Diversification was used in industries suffering long-term decline or where the opportunities for growth had been stunted by increased competition, particularly from well-resourced multinationals. National transport systems of aviation and motorised road haulage emerging in the interwar years represented serious competition for the coastal shipping routes around Australia. Shipowners responded through closer cooperation, as we shall see in Chapter 5, and by diversifying into other industries. Adelaide Steamship Company moved into air services, believing this to be 'the way of the future', with their establishment of Adelaide Airways in 1935, leveraging many of their managerial skills in transport.[59]

By the 1960s, the company was diversifying more broadly into investment and property ownership, wineries, optical goods and engineering. By targeting faster growing industries, it was able to stem its fall from corporate leadership. Like other leaders discussed in this chapter, however, they were forced to retreat from diversification in the 1990s. In 1991, with debts of more than $7 billion, recession and high interest rates triggered the collapse of the group. The company survived, however, by avoiding an immediate fire sale, with the strategic sale of over 30 businesses during the next few years. By 1997 it had returned to a focus on marine services as Adsteam Marine.

Huddart Parker failed to diversify sufficiently and, overcommitted in particular to the coasting trades, fell from the top 100 group after 1952. Howard Smith had diversified from early in its history as a part founder of Australian Iron and Steel in 1928. While recognising the pressures for change in the second half of the century, it has focused upon vertical integration and narrower, related forms of diversification than Adelaide Steamship Company. This has particularly involved marine towage, line boat services, salvage operations, shipping agency, and stevedoring as a means of shoring up its position in the maritime sector. In the 1980s and 1990s Howard Smith diversified into engineering and the distribution of hardware and industrial products while seeking to minimise its ownership of non-core assets.

From the interwar years, pastoral agents considered new products and markets in light of a severe cyclical downturn and the relative decline of the rural sector in the face of expanded manufacturing and substitute fibres for wool. They saw opportunities to gain scope economies by marketing a wider range of products, particularly merchandise, through their branch networks to a ready-made clientele of farmers.[60] The continued expansion of manufacturing after World War Two and the intensification of competition among the agents for a stable or contracting market produced diversification into unrelated complex manufacturing and service industries including engineering, property, construction, home appliances, alcohol, metallurgy and international trading. Market diversification built upon product diversification since they could sell consumer products to a wider national market beyond farming communities. Further, they diversified by function, trading rather than serving as commission agents, a strategy justified by the larger volumes of products and wider range of customers.

Internal discussion documents indicate that the agents had some reservations about broad, unrelated diversification and they were sometimes ineffective at handling a wide range of products. However, in the 1970s and 1980s the pastoral agents were all swallowed up by the large conglomerate enterprises of the time. Divestment occurred in the 1990s, most notably the separation of Elders from the Foster's Brewing Group in 1993. Today, the two leading pastoral agents, Elders and Dalgety (now Landmark), are divisions of other company groups (Futuris and Australian Wheat Board respectively). The industry, a much diminished sector of the Australian economy, no longer boasts a corporate leader.[61]

British Tobacco's dominance of the local tobacco market resulted from its position as the holding company for the major local importers and manufacturers. As we saw in Chapter 3, its market share fell sharply when faced with foreign competition after 1955, suggesting it had made little headway in developing efficient growth directions. Medical reports in the 1960s linking smoking with cancer exacerbated the firm's problems. Its response was broad diversification, beginning in 1964 with printing, vending machines, tenpin bowling, pastoral properties, and food and drink interests. Among these various new directions, however, the company dominated the snack foods market and cornered the highly valuable local Coca-Cola franchise, activities that it focused upon after 1989. The latter, in particular, provided the firm, now Coca-Cola Amatil, with the leverage to expand into the Pacific, Asia and central Europe, 17 countries in total by 1996. Unilever, also faced with increasing competition from other multinationals such as Colgate-Palmolive, Cussons, and Procter & Gamble, began to diversify into the foods market from the 1960s.[62]

Dunlop pursued closely related diversification in the interwar period into other rubber products, including foam and latex, in response to strong competition from three other companies including recently arrived Goodyear. After World War Two, Dunlop identified further competitive threats, especially from Japanese tyre manufacturers, and opted for broader and increasingly unrelated diversification, which included bedding, automotive batteries, medical products and foods.[63] Some of these ventures have fared better than others. The adverse impact of trying to manage a diverse range of products was reflected in their gradual loss of the car tyre market, a core area of the firm, to foreign competitors. Arguably rather late and resulting from investor pressure, Pacific Dunlop began a major program of divestment in the late 1990s and now concentrates on healthcare products under the Ansell brand and company name. Even in this area, faulty pacemakers exposed the technical problems of unrelated diversification.

Repeated phases of diversification have been central to Boral's success over half a century. Formed in 1946 to refine bitumen from imported crude oil, it recognised the scope economies from producing fuel and diesel oil. As Hutchinson has pointed out, this was probably a poor decision since the company faced tough competition from multinationals, which were able to establish very large-scale refineries yielding low-cost oil.[64] However, Boral redeemed itself by actively seeking out alternative markets for oil by-products, which involved product and market diversification combined with vertical integration.

Vertical integration in the 1960s was deployed to strengthen its position and utilise its core competences in bitumen, upstream into quarries to secure supply and downstream into road surfacing operations, ready mix concrete, and hot-mix asphalt to develop new markets.[65] By the end of the 1960s, however, the company recognised the need to diversify out of bitumen if it was to sustain a pattern of growth. Exploiting scope economies again, it turned to other building materials such as reinforced steel, concrete products and brick plants. As the commercial property market turned downwards in the early 1970s, Boral once more showed nimbleness of strategy by diversifying into the residential construction and renovation sectors, and bolstering this with the development of a national brand.[66]

Global leaders: Belated internationalisation

We saw in Chapter 3 that interstate expansion was a common experience among our corporate leaders, particularly in the middle decades of the century. Expansion overseas as multinationals, however, came later in the life cycle of most Australian companies, if it came at all. The small and fragmented local market made it difficult for firms, particularly in manufacturing, to grow to a scale of efficiency necessary to compete in many larger overseas markets. Geographic distance often presented insurmountable managerial challenges. The lateness of Australian industrialisation additionally meant local firms frequently faced entrenched international oligopolies.

While Australia has long been a leading exporter of primary products such as wool, butter, meat and grain, there were few countries where the specialist skills of Australian firms of the primary and related sectors could be leveraged to advantage. Official policy in the form of import tariffs and a weak domestic competition policy constrained the development of efficient Australian firms who were likely to be successful in foreign markets. Local subsidiaries of foreign multinationals might have been expected to embrace internationalisation more enthusiastically. In practice, many of them were limited to exporting by parental strategies designed to mitigate competition with other subsidiaries.[67]

Before the 1970s, overseas growth was heavily location bound, being largely limited to New Zealand and the Pacific Islands. These locations can most obviously be explained by their geographic proximity. Psychic proximity was also important as Australia and New Zealand shared colonial, cultural and institutional similarities. The Pacific Islands, on the other hand, provided opportunities for resource-oriented multinationals such as Burns Philp, with its branches and plantations across the South Pacific.

Several of the larger pastoral agents, particularly Dalgety, operated in Australia and New Zealand, reflecting the importance of farming in both nations. The belated industrial development of New Zealand and the Islands additionally provided a market for expansive Australian manufacturing firms such as Henry Jones, and one that was of a smaller and more manageable size in comparison with many other foreign markets. While expansion into New Zealand and the Pacific Islands provided a relatively easy first jump overseas, it was a poor springboard to other international locations, especially larger and more distant industrial nations.[68]

Several exceptions to this constrained internationalisation should be noted. As the designated national air carrier, Qantas expanded rapidly overseas from the 1930s. The company's first overseas passenger flight was to Singapore in 1935 and to the United Kingdom by 1938. However, it was the postwar period that witnessed the main growth of its overseas network, including Japan and Hong Kong from 1949, South Africa from 1952, and North America from 1953. While many airlines ordinarily operate as international businesses, a more significant early example is Humes. It exploited its patent over the manufacture of concrete pipes to establish production facilities in Singapore as early as 1922, in New Zealand by the following year, and additionally reached the United States, United Kingdom, Japan, Germany, Brazil, South Africa and several Asian nations by the end of the decade.[69]

In the last few decades of the twentieth century, however, Australian corporate leaders were much less location bound, venturing into a far wider range of countries across Asia, Europe and North America. Table 4.1 (p. 83) indicates that all of our principal corporate leaders have now internationalised, and only Australian Gas Light Company would not be considered a global company. This has arisen for a number of reasons. The diversification of the Australian economy away from its primary resources base has fostered firms with competences in products and industries that could be leveraged to many overseas locations. Globalisation has extended the reach of firms worldwide. Australian firms have been able to exploit improved international communications technology in order to mitigate the informational and control drawbacks of remoteness. The deregulation of financial markets, tariff reductions, and the strengthening of competition policy have all contributed to the accelerated internationalisation of Australia's corporate leaders by providing improved home country-specific advantages.[70]

International leverage in new industries and products

News Corporation is the outstanding example of an Australian company leveraging its skills in new products globally over the last three decades. This example is examined in detail in the subsequent section. Lend Lease has also leveraged its innovative skills overseas, applying its firm-specific advantages in project design, construction and management in many overseas nations, particularly targeting growth economies. A frequent pattern of internationalisation pursued by Lend Lease has been to win a major overseas contract in order to establish a beachhead, then pursue additional contracts with the aid of a local joint venture partner. Further expansion leads to the establishment of a local office in that country. Thus, for example, the move to New Zealand was initiated by a major contract in Wellington, followed by a joint venture with Wright Stephenson in the name of Challenge Properties. By 2003 Lend Lease could boast operations in 43 countries on six continents, with a significant presence in the United States, Europe and Asia.[71]

Boral expanded overseas in more conducive conditions from the 1970s, including into the United States, United Kingdom, Indonesia, Continental Europe and North Asia.[72] They sought to exploit their innovative product diversification of the previous couple of decades. For example, they acquired Californian Tilemaker Incorporated in 1978–79 at a time when the United States market for roof tiles was in its infancy. As concrete roof tiles expanded to 75 per cent of the market by 2000, Boral emerged as the second largest producer in the United States. The company had also become the leading brick producer in the United States by 1994 and pioneered plasterboard production in a number of Asian nations including Malaysia, Indonesia and China.[73]

Cuts in tariff protection and export incentives in 1974 provided the impetus for Dunlop to seek lower-cost production locations including the Philippines, China and Malaysia.[74] In the 1980s it extended its overseas production to the United States, Thailand and New Zealand. Like Boral, it leveraged its diverse product range in global markets. At the same time, the company used international strategic alliances and ventures to enhance its expertise, and foreign acquisitions to extend further its product range. The 1987 acquisition of Bioser Medical SA, a French surgical glove-making company, was to add an important new dimension to the company's product range.

Enhanced opportunities in established industries

Shifts in the operating environment discussed above provided new opportunities for internationalisation in some long-established Australian industries and products. Australian mining companies have acted as resource-seeking multinationals in recent decades, applying their competences to exploration and extraction opportunities across an increasingly diverse range of natural resources. Western Mining Corporation has built up its overseas investments in nickel, copper, lead and zinc, particularly in countries on the American continent such as Canada, United States, Brazil and Chile in the 1980s and 1990s.

Conzinc Riotinto Australia has followed a similar pattern of overseas invest-ments, being described by Tsokhas in the 1980s as, 'a transnational corporation with increasingly global interests'.[75] The company has particularly focused on Europe, acquiring zinc smelting plants in the United Kingdom that have allowed it to produce and sell within the European Union, thereby avoiding the latter's common external tariff. In a similar fashion, Australian Gaslight Company has expanded overseas in recent years in pursuit of energy resources with investments, for example, in Chile and New Zealand.

While sharing many similar strategies to the pastoral agents, the banks have differed significantly from them by pursuing extensive overseas expansion. By offering services that are not specific to the primary industries but are in demand worldwide, they have competed successfully in an international market for banking services. The Bank of New South Wales, for example, opened a London office as early as 1853, and then proceeded to develop an extensive network of overseas correspondents. (All the major banks had London offices by 1914, along with extensive correspondent banks.[76]) It then opened branches in Fiji in 1901 and Papua New Guinea in 1910.

The next wave of international expansion began in the 1960s and was far more global in scope, with representative offices or branches opened in such nations as United States, Singapore, Hong Kong and Japan. These new locations reflected the need to be represented in the world's financial centres, particularly after the rise of eurocurrency markets, and the shifting pattern of trade away from the United Kingdom and towards the United States and Asia.[77]

The brewers exported bottled beer to Pacific neighbours from the earliest days and Carlton & United Breweries consolidated their position with the establishment of a brewery in Fiji in 1958. However, it is in more recent times that the leading brewers have looked overseas to leverage their skills, scale and powerful brand names in an era of globalising tastes for alcoholic beverages.[78] Foster's lager established a strong market position in Britain beginning in the 1960s. Carlton & United Breweries' focus on overseas markets has strengthened considerably in the last two decades, after ownership passed to Elders, with acquisitions in the United Kingdom and Canada. In the 1990s expansion by Foster's went further afield into the developing markets of China and India, with the aim of becoming a global player and combining this with product diversification into other drinks (wine, whisky, non-alcoholic drinks), property management and entertainment.

Firm focus

Below we highlight the growth strategies of three corporate leaders with a focus on vertical, conglomerate and global growth respectively.

BHP: Vertically integrated resources and metallurgical products

BHP had positioned itself as the leading silver, lead and zinc miner by the early twentieth century through capturing important mining leases. This proved to be an important prerequisite to forward vertical integration into steel production, which began with the opening of its Newcastle steelworks in 1915 and was extended with the Port Kembla works from 1935. Chairman Essington Lewis made this the core value-adding growth strategy of the firm from the 1920s, supported both by tariff protection and the lower costs achieved by the initial horizontal integration.[79] BHP's forward vertical integration into steel production positioned it well to diversify into a range of related downstream products including steel alloys, tools, fence posts, drums and hot-water systems. In addition, the company used downstream investments and joint ventures to combat foreign competition; for example, agreements with Rheem Manufacturing Company (1937) in producing steel containers, and Cleveland File Company (1939) for machine tools.[80]

Somewhat more broadly, BHP leveraged its competitive leadership in steel products to establish a shipbuilding yard at Whyalla in 1941, and by 1960 operated the largest shipyard and non-government shipping line in Australia. Since the 1960s, BHP has leveraged its general expertise in mineral extraction into the booming offshore gas and oil exploration industries. The extent and success of these activities can be seen by the profits of the company's oil division, which were ten times that of steel-making by 1974.[81] By the 1990s there was evidence of divestment taking place to slim down and focus some of the diverse resources interests. BHP had begun discharging non-strategic assets as early as 1987 with the sale of Blue Circle Southern Cement.

BHP has achieved important overseas expansion since the 1970s as a resource-seeking multinational. This has included coal mines in New Mexico, the commissioning of Escondida, a major copper mine in Chile, and the Ekati diamond mine in Canada. However, it also operated globally as a fully integrated steel-maker, with steel-making and downstream operations in Asia, North America and the Pacific region. Its recent international growth has been focused on flat products for the construction industry in the Pacific Rim.

CSR: Sugar and building materials conglomerate

CSR initially expanded horizontally, eliminating rivals with its low-cost, large-scale and technically advanced refineries, and then vertically integrated to protect itself from unstable sugar prices and the opportunism of suppliers. By the 1930s, with its virtual monopoly of sugar production well established

and the sugar market mature and slow growing, CSR turned to related diversification to maintain expansion. Its research laboratories, helped by visits to
overseas plants, foreign licences and international joint ventures, led the firm
to new products.[82] Substantial economies of scope were available through the
use of by-products of sugar refining to enter the alcohol and chemical industries, and the production of building materials from waste sugar cane. The
related diversification into building materials continued strongly through the
postwar period, including the production of vinyl flooring (1949), insulation
and hardboard (1959), particle board (1960), pre-mixed concrete (1965),
terracotta tiles, asbestos, cement products and architectural metal products
(1969). CSR followed the trend towards unrelated diversification in the 1970s,
investing widely in the energy and minerals sectors, particularly in oil, gas,
coal, iron ore and bauxite.

Many of these unrelated ventures incurred very large losses in the 1970s
and early 1980s, requiring the firm to reconsider its growth direction. It faced
falling commodity prices in the recession of the early 1980s and these problems
were compounded by diversified investments in businesses whose cash flows
and earnings were highly volatile. Fortunately, the company recognised these
directional mistakes and took steps to correct them. A strategic review in 1983
led to the divestment of most of CSR's energy and mineral interests, except
aluminium, to focus on sugar and building products as its core competences.
Most of its growth in the following decade was in building materials, whose
share of company assets rose from 18 to 63 per cent, 1983–93.[83] By contrast,
sugar, the company's original product, had shrunk to 16 per cent of profits by
1995 and fell further to 6 per cent by 2002 as the company began to focus
heavily upon building materials.[84]

Another solution to CSR's rapid saturation of the Australian refined sugar
market was to tap into overseas markets. As early as the 1930s it exported more
than half of its output, a figure that had risen to 80 per cent by the late 1980s.[85]
In addition to exporting, the company had acquired sugar mills in Fiji and an
interest in an Auckland refinery in the nineteenth century. However, like many
other resource-based Australian multinationals at this stage, there were limited
opportunities to expand further. Instead, it is only in recent decades that it has
become a significant global company. Bulky building materials are mostly
unsuitable for large-scale exporting and provide broader leveraging opportunities than sugar milling and refining. This motivated significant offshore
acquisitions by the company, particularly in the United States from 1988, and
the United Kingdom, Canada, Taiwan and China in the 1990s. The extent of its
overseas operations can be seen from the fact that over 60 per cent of its assets
are now located in the United States.

News Corporation: Global media empire

News Corporation stands apart from the Fairfax and Packer media empires in that it has become a global player. It ranks as one of the world's largest media firms, acquiring a string of overseas newspapers, magazines and book publishing businesses, Twentieth Century Fox film studio, a string of TV stations in the United States and satellite operations for pay TV. By September 2002 its total assets were worth approximately US$40bn, with annual revenues of US$16bn.[86] News grew rapidly within Australia from the 1950s and 1960s through strategies of horizontal integration and diversification. By the 1980s it published the only national newspaper, the *Australian*, two national magazines, over 20 provincial newspapers, with related interests in publishing, television, film-making and record production. Central to the business strategy of the Murdochs who controlled News was to concentrate upon down-market mass media to build circulation and therefore advertising revenues.

It initially expanded beyond its Australian base with the purchase of popular mass circulation British newspapers, the *News of the World* in 1968 and the *Sun* in the following year, using the same strategies that had proved successful in Australia. In the following decade, News moved into the United States market and proceeded to acquire a series of foreign newspapers, magazines and publishers. By the mid-1980s it had begun to realign its activities around television and film. By the end of the decade, News was acting like a global company using a standardised and integrated approach to its satellite services beamed to many parts of the world. In 1990–91 News' revenues were severely affected by an economic downturn in its three major markets, the United States, United Kingdom and Australia, while its costs were still projecting upwards through expansion and acquisition. Murdoch undertook substantial asset sales, particularly in its printing and magazine interests, which were seen as the least strategic part of its portfolio of businesses. The company recovered and continued to build its global presence through the 1990s.

Norton and Wilcocks argue News' global strategy was based upon a, 'belief that tastes, income levels, technologies, and even political philosophies around the world were converging on the American model, producing strong demand for American-style films and television programmes'.[87] While this statement probably overstates the degree of convergence, News had clearly transcended the problem faced by many Australian multinationals of country and firm-specific advantages that had little relevance for much of the world.

Conclusion

In Australia, as in many other economies, the strategic course was set for many corporate leaders by expanding their scale of production on a rising market in order to drive down unit costs. Early incumbency has been particularly important in the Australian context. Firms sought early control over the small local market where scale economies were limited and few efficient firms could be accommodated. In addition, strategic assets existed for exploitation by industry pioneers. For service industries closely linked to the pattern of population settlement, early leaders were furthest along learning curves, and so well placed to replicate their expertise. Vertical links can consolidate a firm's position and short circuit predatory behaviour. Insufficient upstream and downstream firms was a constraint on growth in the small, developing Australian economy and a source of opportunistic threats. In a few industries, vertical rather than horizontal expansion drove growth. Our investigation suggests that vertical integration or, at least, vertical links were relatively common in the Australian corporate economy, if not the predominant growth strategy, particularly in the second half of the century.

Diversification was motivated in some cases by the science-based generation of new products, which provided scope economies similar to the experience in new manufacturing industries overseas. In many of the service industries that were a notable feature of the Australian economy, diversification was designed to shore up their core activities rather than change direction. Given the rapid rate of structural change in the Australian economy and the proliferation of foreign multinationals, diversification provided some businesses with a different growth trajectory to mitigate these threats. Taking a lead from overseas, many firms built conglomeration onto their narrow diversification with, in most cases, the same disappointing results and subsequent divestments. Most corporate leaders did not operate overseas until quite recently. Local environmental influences in Australia militated against outward foreign direct investment, including the small and isolated home market, an official policy unconducive to competitive conditions, and a national specialisation in the rural and related industries that was not easily transferable overseas. When changes in these conditions, together with globalisation forces, took hold from the 1970s, there was a stream, and then a veritable flood, of leaders migrating to many destinations, confirming their ability and willingness to exploit favourable opportunities when they arose.

CHAPTER 5

Paths of Corporate Development: Methods of Growth

Firms must choose a method of effecting the types of directional growth strategies described in Chapter 4. The three principal methods of firm growth are by internal expansion, merger and inter-firm agreements.[1] Thus, for example, a firm may acquire another that is a competitor to support horizontal expansion, or a supplier (vertical integration). Acquisition of firms in another industry or country would likewise facilitate diversification and internationalisation. Chandler acknowledged that mergers have been important in both the United States and Britain, but in the former they typically led to a large, centralised and integrated organisation, while in the latter the result was more often ownership of a collection of small personally run firms. German and Japanese big business have long been known for their inter-firm cooperation; more recent research has identified similar habits in other nations, including Britain and Australia, and globally across national boundaries.[2]

In this chapter we focus upon the growth methods of our corporate leaders. We begin by reviewing the strengths and weaknesses of alternative methods of growth.

Methods of firm growth

Each of the three growth methods brings both benefits and shortcomings. Internal expansion, sometimes referred to as greenfield investments, involves growth through continued expansion of the firm's own internal resources. It provides full control over the development process, affords protection of proprietary knowledge, and avoids the cultural clash and integration costs associated with mergers and inter-firm associations. On the negative side, internal growth tends to be slower than by acquisition, particularly for the purposes of unrelated diversification, since the firm has to learn about the new product or industry and seek out suitable human and physical resources. Internal growth additionally lacks the synergies, shared experiences and general institutional cross-fertilisation associated with the other growth methods.

Mergers provide something akin to instant corporate gratification. Ready-made companies are acquired thereby telescoping the growth process. Tangible and intangible physical and human assets, including expertise, equipment and market position, are purchased together with exposure to alternative corporate practices. In the process, the performance of the individual firms can be transformed, filling production and market gaps in larger firms and adding value to the performance of junior partners. Where mergers are spread across an industry they can transform its competitive position, as rationalisation eliminates duplication and excessive competition, and drives down costs.

The public visibility of mergers can also have a demonstration (or pro-liferation) effect across an industry, inducing similarly efficiency-enhancing moves by rivals. Acquisition of suppliers and customers may also reduce trans-actions costs and the threat of contractual opportunism. Where a competitor is acquired, the firm's market power and general influence over the industry is strengthened.

However, acquisitions are generally expensive because of the premium share price paid to convince sceptical shareholders. Acquiring a controlling share rather than full ownership provides a lower-cost strategy but may require ongoing transactions with other owners. The acquired or merged organisation generally comes as a package, containing weak or unsuitable elements that have to be reformed or disposed of, as well as appealing ones. Integration of the organisations to achieve enhanced efficiency can be an expensive and time-consuming business, and has to be weighed against the benefits of maintaining some of the corporate identity of the acquired firm.[3] Where significant synergies fail to emerge, shareholder value is normally reduced. The act of acquisition may expose a firm to the glare of competition regu-lators more readily than creeping internal growth. The potential efficiency gains at the industry level discussed above must also be set against the con-sequences of increased market power that may raise prices to consumers and other firms.

A wide variety of inter-firm relationships provide an intermediate strategy between internal growth and merger. They range along a continuum from relatively loose licensing arrangements between firms, through agencies, strategic alliances and franchises, to the tightly organised joint venture as a separate company owned by the partner firms.[4] What these arrangements all have in common is the opportunity to acquire expertise and yield synergies through only a partial surrender of corporate sovereignty and at a generally lower cost than merger or internal growth. They are particularly suited to firms with similar or complementary resources and they provide an ongoing and flexible way of gaining synergies in contrast to the once-only merger 'event'.

Partners to inter-firm agreements particularly seek to share market and technical information and infrastructure costs, thereby allowing reasonable autonomy of production for individual firms. They are particularly suited to industries where these types of costs are very high. They also favour periods of sectoral downturn when firms seek to trim costs, or where prevailing high levels of uncertainty can be shared. Where optimal scales of efficiency vary between operational stages, cooperation permits production sharing between firms and mitigates the risk of contractual hold-up. Besides boosting operational efficiency, some agreements, normally collusive in nature, are designed as rent-seeking strategies, either by enhancing market power or by acting as political lobbyists.

The costs of inter-firm relations are largely those associated with building and sustaining the trust that underwrites the relationship, most particularly ingratiation and sensitive monitoring. The failure to sustain high levels of trust leads in many cases to the breakdown of the agreement. With such a break-down, each firm has surrendered know-how to the other that may now become its rival. Tighter forms of inter-firm relationship, most notably the joint venture, help to provide a permanency to the relationship, but can run into organi-sational problems if the culture of the partner firms is quite different and therefore their view of how the joint venture should operate. Exit costs will also be higher if the joint venture breaks down. Where cooperative behaviour among firms becomes, or is perceived to be, collusive action, this may incite adverse responses from affected parties and the possible attention of com-petition regulators.

Growth methods of Australian corporate leaders

In a similar fashion to directions of growth, corporate leaders recognised the need to select growth methods attuned to their operating climate. Indeed, trends in growth methods over time are the predominant pattern here. In this case the key environmental influences were a small local market, the belated develop-ment of the capital market, government competition policy, and inward foreign direct investment. As a result, we can see longitudinal secular and cyclical changes in growth methods over time, with internal growth being common in the early years of the century, mergers becoming of greater significance from mid-century, though fluctuating in waves, while inter-firm groupings appear to have grown in importance in recent decades.

Industry and firm life cycle features are also somewhat discernible, with the early stages of each often being associated with internal growth and sometimes inter-firm agreement. Later on, acquisitions became more important. Finally, the directions of growth selected by a corporate leader influenced its method of expansion. Thus, acquisitions provided a rapid method of capturing share in a limited market or telescoping the learning process when diversifying into new and unfamiliar industries. Similar to our findings in Chapter 4, corporate leaders demonstrated flexibility, switching their growth methods in response to these various influences, rather than adhering slavishly to a preferred approach.

Keeping it in the family: Internal growth

Most firms rely upon the internal growth method for at least part of their corporate history. Internal growth was important for many corporate leaders in the first half of the twentieth century. The limited sources of external finance available to Australian firms in the absence of a sizeable public stock market or robust investment banks constrained the large-scale fundraising necessary to purchase firms, particularly large rivals. As we will see in Chapter 6, firms at this time relied more heavily upon retained earnings and private equity finance, which were suitable means to fund incremental increases in their internal operations.

In the small Australian domestic market, suitable acquisition targets were scarce due to the limited number of competitors and suppliers. This was particularly the case for established prime movers in the early stages of an industry's development, who rarely needed to look beyond their boundaries for best practice; later entrants, or challengers, had more to gain from acquisition and better financial and informational means to do so. Where a single firm continued to dominate the industry as it evolved, internal expansion would remain the main growth method. Firms that perpetuated their early technical leadership were similarly inclined to grow internally to develop their competencies. Finally, multinationals often favoured internal growth, drawing upon the resources of their parent company.

Thus, internal growth was particularly associated with prime movers who maintained a monopoly or dominant market position for a lengthy period. These firms can be identified from tables 3.4 (pp. 60–1) and 3.5 (pp. 75–6). CSR relied upon internal growth for much of its early history to sustain its leadership. As a virtual monopolist in sugar refining there were few opportunities for merger or inter-firm agreements. Neither did its related diversification strategies in the 1930s draw heavily upon acquisition: much of it was designed to yield production scope economies from its existing output and used technology in which the company was already a leader in Australia.

Dunlop similarly drew upon its internal resources as a powerful multinational, constructing a rubber factory in 1902. However, it also purchased Pioneer India Rubber Works from Barnett Glass Rubber three years later and, in 1929, when faced with intense price competition, merged with one of its main rivals, Perdriau Rubber. After World War Two, Dunlop again grew by internalisation in order to restructure: it closed down obsolete factories and established new, smaller factories, retreaders and a wide range of dealerships.

The predominant growth path for Australian Gas Light Company through most of its history has been internalisation. It had established a virtual monopoly around Sydney in the nineteenth century and much of its subsequent expansion in the twentieth century was about technological modernisation, and expanding and diversifying its markets. Aided by its expanding revenue base and additions to its subscribed capital, the company undertook major new building works and mains extensions on a regular basis, such as at Mortlake and Haymarket, beginning in 1912.[5] In these circumstances, there were very limited opportunities for merger or inter-firm agreements. Periodically, it acquired local gas companies in its path, including Liverpool Gas Company (1928), Katoomba and Leura Gas Company (1957), and a range of gas businesses around New South Wales in the 1960s, particularly in Wollongong, Grafton, Casino and Singleton.[6]

Corporate leaders who sustained their technical dominance by internal expansion included Humes, James Hardie and Amalgamated Wireless Australasia. The latter's domination of the new technologies of electronic equipment, especially radio and television, was achieved by leveraging its core competences in their design and manufacture. It had little to gain from acquiring other companies when it held most of the appropriate patents. Clyde Industries, on the other hand, concentrated upon the light manufacturing and household appliance markets. It did not control technological change in these older industries in the same manner, and focused upon mergers and acquisitions to aid its competitive position and build market share. In addition, the company developed a 'buy-rebuild-sell' approach, where it would acquire a controlling interest in a light engineering company and then sell it again several years later after a restructure designed to build additional value. Examples included Trugarde Cotton Waste and Australian Stockinette, both bought in 1949 and sold in 1951.

Humes' pioneering international expansion from the 1920s was largely achieved through greenfield sites, although joint ventures were sometimes used as an initial beachhead. After World War Two, James Hardie pioneered breakthroughs in a range of building materials, which drove its internal expansion.[7] To this list we might add Lend Lease, whose competitive advantage, as we saw in Chapter 4, lay in its pioneering 'design and construct' strategy. Thus, its growth was based upon replicating a strategy not prominent elsewhere in the industry.

Subsidiaries of foreign multinationals drew upon internal resources, particularly technical know-how. Imperial Chemical Industries of Australia and

New Zealand relied heavily upon internal growth since its main source of competitive advantage was the technical knowledge and innovativeness of its parent. The automobile industry leader, General Motors-Holden's, has grown largely by internal expansion, drawing heavily upon the technical knowledge, corporate expertise and resources of General Motors, one of the largest global companies throughout the twentieth century. General Motors-Holden's made regular investments to support the growth directions discussed in the previous chapter. In the 1950s, for example, it embarked upon four major expansion programs costing A£57 million to support its plans to build a complete car in Australia. These projects included building a new assembly and construction plant at Dandenong, Australia's first testing ground at Lang Lang (Victoria), and developing the first entirely new model in a decade.[8] Mergers have been of little importance to the company since its main competitors are also large multi-national enterprises. Limited numbers of local supply companies have existed, requiring General Motors-Holden's to draw upon its parent for components and then increasingly develop integrated activities in Australia, as we saw earlier.

Internal growth periodically found adherents in less concentrated industries with fewer technical innovations. The major retailers largely followed a pattern of internal growth in the early years of the century and of their corporate development by leveraging their competitive advantages discussed under 'directions'. For Myer and Coles, this enabled them to expand within Melbourne and Victoria respectively in the first half of the century. While mergers became of greater importance later in the century, corporate leaders still needed the internal growth path when implementing industry innovations, such as the construction of shopping centres and free-standing supermarkets. The major banks concentrated upon internal expansion interspersed with merger cycles, with the latter contributing less than half to the increase in branch numbers. Since their corporate strategy largely avoided diversification, this eliminated one significant reason for mergers. However, there was an upturn in the number and size of acquisitions between 1917 and 1931, the Bank of New South Wales, for example, acquired three major banks at this time, the City of Sydney Bank in 1917, the West Australian Bank in 1927, and the Australian Bank of Commerce in 1931.[9]

Buying leadership: Mergers and acquisitions

Various estimates of merger activity have been made for Australia, including the number of de-listed companies, and the number and value of takeover bids and of actual mergers, which together point towards a major secular expansion in merger activity from the 1950s onwards, interspersed with cyclical fluctuations.[10] Merger activity rose in the 1950s, before falling away sharply in the first half of the 1960s, rising again to a further peak in 1969–72, falling away to the middle of the 1970s, with further peaks in the early and then mid to late 1980s, and mid-1990s.[11] De-listings provide the longest single run of data from the 1940s, as indicated in Figure 5.1.

Initial acquisitions

The limited number of listed companies meant acquisitions in the first half of the twentieth century were largely of private companies, which was a time-consuming business, based on incomplete information, and normally requiring the cooperation of the acquired firm. As a result, Australia does not appear to have experienced the cyclical merger booms of the United States and Britain in the first half of the century, where the public stock market was much larger.[12]

While internal expansion was therefore the default method for corporate leaders, some firms became adept at managing the takeover of unlisted companies, in spite of the risks. Pastoral agents Elders and Goldsbrough Mort acquired many small local firms from the interwar period as they sought to build up a national network to compete with Dalgety. As the early prime mover, Dalgety relied upon internal growth for much of its history, establishing offices in new areas to follow the movement of settlement. As a result of a series of acquisitions in the 1920s, Goldsbrough Mort increased its share of the national wool market from 5 to 11 per cent and its location of wool auctions from two to five states.

Until about the 1960s, most of the acquired firms were small private agencies rather than listed companies. In some cases this made for expensive and drawn out negotiations, especially in the evaluation of the firm's 'good-will', a significant part of the value of local agencies being their list of loyal customers. However, on many occasions the two firms had previously worked in cooperation, the national leader selling the wool of the local firm's customers and often providing finance and market information. This made the process of due diligence easier to complete.

In addition, it was frequently the case that the local firm initiated a proposed takeover when adversely affected by one of the severe cyclical downturns that characterised the industry or when faced with a succession crisis. Elders, as one of the most acquisitive firms, became expert at assessing the appropriate-ness of an acquisition, and handling the integration of merged firms into their business, a process they referred to as 'Elderising'.[13] Burns Philp was an effective operator in the takeover market prior to the rise of the listed company. Buckley and Klugman's detailed history of the firm indeed indicates that they completed many successful acquisitions in the South Seas trade, beginning as early as the 1890s.[14]

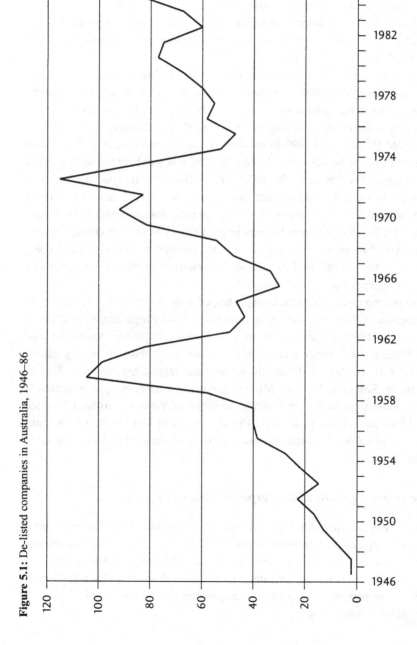

Figure 5.1: De-listed companies in Australia, 1946–86

Source: Bureau of Industry Economics, *Mergers and Acquisitions*, pp. 25–6.

The media barons relied heavily upon acquisition as their method of national growth from the start. Applying their ideas, such as focusing upon popular mass circulation newspapers, and their general expertise in newspaper management, together with the substantial scale and scope economies available, they could add significant value to acquired small, local newspapers, and as a result transformed the cost structure of the industry as a whole. The Herald & Weekly Times, the initial industry leader, built its national presence with the aid of a number of major regional purchases, including the *Advertiser* in 1929 and the *Courier Mail* in 1933.

Mergers have been a key leadership strategy in brewing from the outset. Waves of merger activity have played an important role in resolving periodic overcapacity in the small domestic market. The corporate leaders have taken the initiative in these waves. Among the most notable was the formation of Carlton & United Breweries in 1907 to resolve a crisis of overcapacity in Melbourne as a result of the introduction of new and more efficient brewing techniques in the previous two decades. Thereafter, they periodically mopped up local and regional brewers. Helped by improved transport facilities and the growing portability of beer, the company acquired and then closed a series of breweries. This included three regional brewers in the 1920s. The process continued after World War Two, with further acquisitions and closures in 1947, 1958 and 1962, a strategy that was repeated throughout the country with regular acquisitions by the leading brewers.

In mining and metallurgy, mergers helped firms to achieve scale rapidly by the capture of strategic assets in an industry with very high minimum levels of efficiency. BHP's acquisition of its major steel competitor, Australian Iron and Steel, in 1935 firmly established its control of the industry and, by adding a firm half its size, BHP rapidly became the largest non-financial firm in Australia. Similarly, Western Mining Corporation used mergers to establish rapid dominance in the gold mining industry of Western Australia between the 1930s and 1950s, particularly the acquisition in 1949 of its parent company, Gold Exploration and Finance Company of Australia, along with Gold Mines Australia.[15]

The postwar growth of the corporate takeover market

The process of acquisition was made easier, quicker and more widespread from the 1950s by the availability of increasing numbers of listed public companies to purchase and expanded sources of corporate finance. More information is available about public than private corporations and, as we will see in Chapter 6, equity or part equity funded most acquisitions in the 1950s and 1960s, and external debt after 1970.

The postwar expansion of corporate takeovers provided a new and accelerated growth path for firms. Challenger companies emerging by this time in many industries and, eager to catch up with the prime movers, were likely to view merger as the preferred growth method. Acquisition enabled firms to pursue their plans to diversify rapidly into other fields. An active mergers market also accelerated the process of rationalisation in the declining primary and related industries, thereby facilitating industrial restructuring.

The importance of merger activity to the continued expansion of corporate leaders in the 1940s and 1950s can be seen from the work of Bushnell in Table 5.1. He focuses upon a top 103 companies list using different measurement criteria from the current authors but which, nonetheless, includes many of our

Table 5.1: The importance of mergers to increased company value, 1947–56

Company	Mergers' share of company growth (%)
David Jones	82–95
Peters	9–87
Coles	52–84
Elders	55–65
NAB	31–61
Clyde	42–44
Repco	33–43
Email	29–42
HWT	33–38
GM-Holden's	15–34
Myer	29–30
Dunlop	9–17
Howard Smith	5–13
Woolworths	7–11
Burns Philp	3–9
Humes	7–8
AGL	1

Notes: Two alternative measures are used: (i) Market value of ordinary shares plus par value of preference shares and long-term debt; (ii) shareholders' funds plus long-term debt. These figures somewhat understate the contribution of mergers since they compare the value of mergers at the time of acquisition with total growth of the company over nine years but do not allow for the growth of acquired sections over the remaining part of that nine years.

Source: Bushnell, *Australian Company Mergers*, pp. 108–11.

corporate leaders. Among this group as a whole, 23–29 per cent of company growth was attributed to merger activity, but the figure rises to 38–50 per cent if one only looks at those firms who were involved in any mergers.[16] Among the latter group, the importance of mergers varied considerably from David Jones and Coles, where it was critical, to Burns Philp and Australian Gas Light Company, where it was negligible.

In the 1960s corporate leaders were again among the most acquisitive of Australian companies, most notably Dunlop, CSR, Brambles, Peters and Repco.[17] CSR and Dunlop used mergers to pursue diversification strategies. Dunlop's 1960s acquisitions included Frankwil Engineering, Ansell, Universal Textiles, Hollandia Shoes, and Taft Australia. Later, in 1980, Dunlop consolidated its position in the tyre industry with the acquisition of Olympic Tyres. Repco achieved its postwar dominance of the automotive parts industry with the aid of regular acquisitions in the industry.[18]

Buildings products firms that had relied heavily on internal growth earlier in the century now used the merger tool to diversify. In 1978–79 James Hardie bought Reed Publishing and FowlerWare (bathroomware and basins), followed by further acquisitions in the 1980s. Australian Consolidated Industries' diversification was achieved through the acquisition of box companies, plastics and cardboard manufacturers; by the end of 1960 it possessed 32 subsidiaries and eight associate companies in Australia, New Zealand, Singapore and Thailand.[19]

However, the highest aggregate value of takeovers of the 1960s occurred in the department store category.[20] The national growth of the leading retailers was largely based upon a series of takeover battles of smaller, mostly private retailers. Coles strengthened its position in a number of states. It acquired Selfridges (1950) for its stores in New South Wales and Western Australia, Foy & Gibson Stores (1952) in country Victoria and southern New South Wales, Penney's (1956) in northern New South Wales and Queensland, and the Beilby chain (1958) in South Australia. These acquisitions accounted for around 30 per cent of its stores by 1958. Myer extended its department stores across capital cities and states through acquisition: these included Brisbane (McWhirter in 1955, Allan & Stark in 1959), Hobart (Johnston & Miller, and Brownells in 1959), New South Wales (Farmer & Co, 1961, Clutterbucks 1962, Mortimers 1967, The Western Stores 1967), and Western Australia (Bairds 1969).

When the dominant variety chains, Coles and Woolworths, moved into food retailing from the late 1950s, acquisition was an important part of their strategy: Dickens' 54 self-service grocery stores in Victoria were acquired by Coles in 1958 and 250 grocery stores in New South Wales were purchased from Matthews Thompson in 1960. The subsequent rush by all the leaders into discount retailing was again helped by acquisitions; the purchase of Lindsay & McKenzie by Myer in 1968 was used as the foundation for its Target discount stores, although Coles entered into a joint venture with United States retailer K Mart Corporation to set up K Mart stores in Australia in the same year. When Coles decided to diversify further into department stores, its merger with Myer in 1985 was its key strategic event.

Merger activity was particularly important to the fastest growing corporate leaders, confirming this method's value to those firms seeking speed of change. Boral's rapid ascent to corporate leadership drew heavily upon a strategy of mergers and acquisitions to vertically integrate in the 1960s and diversify in the 1970s and 1980s. It bought companies in downstream markets in road surfacing, concrete and asphalt together with its diversified production of LPG and building products.[21] The choice of acquisition gave Boral the speed to change direction rapidly when it realised the mistake of competing with the petroleum companies and then the limited growth prospects of bitumen production. In particular, it enabled the firm to expand effectively into a full line of building products.

Ansett's rapid postwar advance up the top 100 list was also achieved through a policy of growth by acquisition. The importance of gaining market share and raising load factors quickly in a capital intensive industry drove Ansett to acquire many competing domestic carriers, including Butler Air Transport (1958), Guinea Airways (1959), and MacRobertson Miller Airlines (1963). Most important for Ansett, however, was the acquisition of Australian National Airways in 1957, which had been one of the parties to the emerging two-airlines agreement, along with Trans-Australia Airlines. Subsequent acquisitions enabled Ansett to pursue its diversification strategy; for example, furniture removals (Wridgways Holdings, 1972) and restaurants (Denny's, 1982).

Mergers were also used to transform whole industries where rapid restructuring was needed. Intense merger activity effected a major reorganisation of the brewing industry in the 1980s, resulting in a virtual duopoly of Lion Nathan and Foster's, as we saw in Chapter 3. In particular, Lion Nathan acquired the Bond brewing assets during 1988–92, and the Hahn Brewery and South Australian Breweries in the following year. Foster's and Carlton & United Breweries had been merged into Elders IXL by 1983, which was renamed Foster's Brewing Group in 1990, with Carlton & United Breweries as its Australian brewing arm. Similar to overseas experience, improved logistics and distribution, together with an extension of branding practices, drove consolidation.[22]

The pastoral agent industry was long overdue a major restructure by the 1960s: intense competition meant that the farmer was being over-serviced and the firms' costs were far too high relative to their earnings. In 1963 the four leading firms merged into two, Dalgety joining with New Zealand Loan & Mercantile Agency, and Elders with Goldsbrough Mort. This enabled significant cost-cutting, particularly in the duplication of local branches and head offices, which released spare funds for diversification into growth industries.

Further sorting and consolidation in banking recognised opportunities for cost-cutting, especially as a means of competing effectively with foreign banks licensed in Australia, to produce the big four banks of today. Australian and New Zealand Banking Group was formed in two stages – the merger of the Bank of Australasia and the Union Bank of Australia in 1951, adding the English Scottish and Australian Bank in 1969. Westpac was the product of the merger of the Commercial Bank of Australia and the Bank of New South Wales in 1982, while the National Australia Bank originated from the merger of the National Bank of Australasia and the Commercial Banking Company of Sydney in 1982.

While the majority of acquisitions were horizontal, vertically related mergers helped address the problems of contractual hold-up discussed in Chapter 4, and sometimes this was undertaken through buying a strategic block of shares rather than attaining full control. This provided strategic influence at lower cost, although the ability to control and direct partially acquired firms has been limited in some cases. BHP effectively used downstream investments to combat competitive threats from foreign companies in the 1930s. After World War Two it took equity shares in downstream companies in order to get in early to areas of product growth such as hot-water systems and steel tools.[23]

Raiders and conglomerates

In the 1970s the balance between public and private company acquisitions shifted further and decisively towards the former and the number of takeover bids as a percentage of listed companies increased.[24] The market in corporate control strengthened as banks showed a greater willingness to finance acquisitions, including hostile bids, through the acquisition of blocks of shares in public companies. The credible threat of acquisition exposed poorly managed firms to the discipline of the capital market. Emergent conglomerates showed particular interest in acquiring weak firms, believing they could add value through better management, irrespective of the industry in which they were located.

Several of the conglomerates were spearheaded by 'corporate raiders', acquisitive opportunists who were thought to prey upon companies with undervalued assets that were suitable for asset stripping.[25] Of particular note among our corporate leaders was the fate of Adelaide Steamship under John Spalvins' command in the 1980s. As well as being one of our corporate leaders, Adelaide

Steamship acquired partial ownership of several other companies in our study, including David Jones, Tooth, Woolworths, Howard Smith, and Petersville. BHP, Amalgamated Wireless Australasia, Myer and several of the leading banks were also targeted. By controlling these companies with less than a 50 per cent share, Spalvins was able to conceal many of his strategies, including profit inflation, rising debts, and defence tactics, to guard against acquisition by other raiders, particularly Howard Smith.[26]

Other corporate leaders became caught up in the acquisitions frenzy. Many of the pastoral agents were absorbed into John Elliott's Elders-IXL. Industrial Equity Limited's acquisition of a share in Australian Gaslight Company changed the latter into a much more acquisitive firm under the influence of Ron Brierley, acquiring for example TMOC Resources (1987–78) and CSR Petroleum (1988). Corporatisation of the electricity market in many states in the 1990s provided Australian Gas Light Company with the opportunity to acquire electricity companies, including Solaris Power in Victoria (1995–98) and the Electricity Trust of South Australia (2000).

The stock market collapse in 1987, an ensuing economic recession in the early 1990s, and poorly conceived organisational design put paid to conglomerate Adelaide Steamship Company and its ilk in the 1990s. Allegations of asset stripping by the corporate raiders appear to have been largely ungrounded, with no detrimental effect on shareholder values in either the bidding or target company.[27] It is clear, though, that most conglomerates did not bring the managerial benefits expected of them.[28] However, the credible threat to weak and under-performing companies had been established. An ambitious but abortive bid to control BHP by another raider, Robert Holmes à Court, failed in 1987. Nonetheless, it sounded a warning that even the 'Big Australian' could be a takeover target. This may have sounded a wakeup call to the company whose performance dramatically improved in the following years.

De-merger activity continues to be important as firms seek to increase value by separating businesses with different strategic plans. BHP's OneSteel was floated off in 2002. De-merger plans received a further fillip in 2002 with legislation providing for capital gains tax relief at the shareholder and firm levels. CSR has announced plans to separate its sugar and building materials businesses into two firms; Western Mining Corporation has divided aluminium from other production, and AMP intends to separate its loss-making United Kingdom operations from its Australian operations.

International merger activity

It was noted above that multinationals in Australia were better placed to expand rapidly through the internal growth method. Indeed, Bushnell, commenting on their relative inactivity in the merger market, observed that the ability of multinationals to grow rapidly by internal means motivated many domestic firms to enter the merger market to try and keep pace with these foreign competitors.[29]

Stewart's study of mergers in the 1960s provides us with closer details of multinationals. In spite of the growth of multinational activity in the local merger market in the 1960s, domestic takeovers outnumbered foreign by a multiple of 5.5.[30] However, takeovers by foreign multinationals were relatively more important in other respects. The average value of takeovers was always greater by multinationals; they often purchased the largest domestic firm in their industry, and their acquisitions were concentrated upon manufacturing.[31] At its decadal peak in 1965–66, the average takeover by a foreign company was valued at nearly six times that of a domestic one. British multinationals also appear to have been more acquisitive than American, with the main focus of their attention being foods, industrial machinery and fabricated metal products.[32] There were also mergers between Australian subsidiaries of United Kingdom multinationals, such as Dalgety with New Zealand Loan & Mercantile Agency (1963), and Australian and New Zealand Bank with English, Scottish and Australian Bank (1969).

British Tobacco, urgently seeking to diversify away from competitors and the negative publicity of smoking in the 1960s, chose the merger method to achieve a rapid shift in strategy. Its 27 acquisitions in that decade created a figure greater than any other foreign or domestic firm in Australia.[33] Its acquisition of the Coca-Cola franchises in Australia, beginning in Perth in 1965, provided much greater opportunities for merger and joint ventures, particularly when it expanded into the Pacific, Asia and central Europe in the 1980s and 1990s to exploit the franchise. Since its overseas expansion was designed to exploit intangible assets, notably the Coca-Cola franchise and an evolving expertise in operating bottling plants, the company concentrated upon acquisitions rather than seeking to set up new greenfield plants. In some cases, where an international joint venture was successful, Coca-Cola Amatil subsequently bought out its local partner, for example, Budapesti Likoripari Vallalat in 1991–93.

While British Tobacco had operated in Australia for half a century before embarking upon this merger wave, other multinationals viewed merger with a local company as an effective way of establishing an initial beachhead. In 1962 Consolidated Zinc Corporation merged with the Australian subsidiary of Rio Tinto Company of the United Kingdom. The local company provided access and exploration rights to the Pilbara, while the foreign company was strongly armed with financial skills and resources. The new company, Conzinc Riotinto

Australia, proved to have the strength to evolve as a powerful multinational corporation itself, thereby overcoming the size and distance problems that constrained many Australian companies seeking to expand overseas.

News Corporation provides the converse experience to most of the companies mentioned in this section, as a highly acquisitive Australian firm expanding in overseas markets. We detailed in Chapter 4 the growth directions of the company, diversifying within the media and entertainment sectors in order to build circulation, advertising revenues and synergies between media forms. Under Rupert Murdoch's leadership, News pursued a broad policy of aggressive acquisition in print and related media, entertainment and cable television in Australia and global markets, which enabled the firm to ascend up the list of corporate leaders from 82nd in 1964 to 3rd in 1986.

Applying the synergies foreshadowed above, Murdoch sought to buy under-performing companies cheaply and then rebuilt them. In the 1950s and 1960s News acquired an impressive array of local and regional newspapers in Australia, ultimately acquiring former leader, Herald & Weekly Times, in 1987. News added many of the national newspapers in Britain, including the *Times* and *Sunday Times* in 1981 and major United States regionals, including the *New York Post* (1976) and *Chicago Sun-Times* (1983). Acquired book publishers included Angus & Robertson in Australia in 1981 and William Collins in the United Kingdom in 1989. Television stations purchased included Australian regionals such as WIN4 TV in Wollongong (1963) and Sydney Channel 10 (1979), along with overseas stations, most notably a large stake in London Weekend Television (1973).

Recent internationalisation by other Australian firms has involved many acquisitions. Under Elliott's control, Foster's aspired to become a global player and 'Fosterise' the world. In these circumstances, acquisition became a key policy by giving the firm close control over its international expansion. Thus, by 1986 it was acquiring major foreign brewers, including Courage in the United Kingdom and Carling O'Keefe in Canada.[34]

Mount Isa Mines presents an interesting picture of a company that had suffered from capital deficiencies and low operational efficiency when the American Smelting and Refining Company acquired a major share in it in 1928–30. By the 1950s Mount Isa Mines was growing from strength to strength, with higher mineral prices, successful diversification, and heavy reinvestment of retained earnings, such that it began to acquire a growing share of its erstwhile parent company in the 1980s. As Tsokhas has noted, 'so we are presented with a picture of a vulnerable, struggling subsidiary growing to such financial strength and commercial stature as to become one of the single most important shareholders in its erstwhile parent.'[35]

Beyond the firm: Interorganisational expansion paths

A major publication at both the beginning and at the end of the twentieth century indicates the enduring importance of inter-firm linkages in the Australian business environment. In 1914 Wilkinson drew attention to the large number of trusts covering various sectors of the Australian economy, many of which were colluding to control output or raise prices.[36] In 1995 the Bureau of Industry Economics surveyed the extensive cooperation that existed between many firms, citing the benefits that it yielded in terms of firm performance and competitiveness.[37]

While the publications deal with the same subject, the pejorative tone of 1914 contrasts with the official encouragement 80 years later. This reflects a broader disagreement among writers about the value of inter-organisational expansion paths, but it may also indicate a change in their nature over this period. Wilkinson was concerned with what he saw as Australian corporations acting as collusive rent-seekers to the detriment of consumers and other firms. The Bureau argued that cooperating firms generate sustainable improvements in their efficiency with consequential benefits for the cost structure of the industry in which they operate. While smaller firms frequently work together to overcome their size disabilities, cooperation among larger and fewer firms is easier to administer and therefore more likely to succeed. Since Australian corporate leaders are, at the same time, minnows on the world stage, the incentive for them to cooperate is two-fold.

Negotiating the external architecture

Inter-firm agreements designed to enhance operational efficiency have been commonly used by corporate leaders throughout the twentieth century. Indeed, a number of firms, including BHP, have become adept at developing and sustaining agreements with suppliers, customers and competitors; that is, in negotiating their external architecture.[38] Such agreements have helped firms enjoy some of the benefits of scale in the small Australian market, particularly where synergies can be derived without challenging the competitive instincts of firms, such as in infrastructure and research and development, where there is a strong public good element. The mitigation of uncertainty and addressing different optimal scales in the value chain have also motivated cooperation.

The clearest evidence we have of why and how major Australian firms cooperated lies in the report of the Bureau of Industry Economics in 1995, foreshadowed above. Based upon over 1000 returns from five industrial sectors, it established that at least one-third of the firms were involved in cooperative arrangements and that they were particularly large-scale, high growth, exporting companies in advanced technology capital goods industries.[39] The

predominant inter-firm arrangement was bilateral (84 per cent), and this was conducted most commonly with a customer (40 per cent) or supplier (33 per cent).

Similar numbers of agreements were formal in nature, normally involving
a written contract, or informal, based largely upon trust and reputation. Only
11 per cent of agreements were with overseas partners, although these were
believed to bring the strongest benefits to the participants, particularly in terms
of enlarged markets. Overall, 75 per cent of firms believed their agreements
yielded critical benefits especially in terms of market-related gains and production efficiency improvements. Many firms also received unintended benefits
as a result of interaction with their partner.[40]

Inter-firm cooperation in relation to infrastructure costs and research and
development are clearly illustrated in the pastoral agent industry. The major
firms shared the costs of developing and operating a national wool market.
Their pooling of resources was critical in establishing an Australian wool
auction system that largely replaced the London market, bringing with it a
range of benefits to farmers and to the broader Australian economy. The companies cooperated in the diffusion of new techniques where spillover benefits
between agents and their farmer clients were clear, particularly countering the
spread of rabbits and other forms of crop and animal feed infestation.[41]

In shipping, the aims of the Australasian Steamship Owners Federation
(1899) were to share information and establish a code of practice. From this
developed other mutual benefits, such as ticket interchangeability, shared
advertising, and a system of deferred rebates and pooling arrangements similar
to the operations of the collusive shipping rings which dominated international

Table 5.2: Key features of inter-firm agreements in the 1990s

Type of arrangement	Per cent
Formal	50
Informal	50
Customer	40
Supplier	33
Other	27
With one other firm	84
Two or more other firms	16
Overseas firm	11
Domestic firm	89

Source: Bureau of Industry Economics, *Beyond the Firm*, p. 15.

shipping in this period. These arrangements remained with minor changes until World War Two.[42] The major banks were brought together in industry bodies such as the Australian Bankers Association, formed in 1954, and its predecessor, Associated Banks of Victoria, which provided a representational role and facilitated cooperation in relation to such matters as clearing house arrangements.

Mineral exploration and metal production have attracted many agreements. These have largely been motivated by the need to mitigate the uncertainty associated with huge exploration costs in risky projects, and to address differences in optimal scale between processes, particularly the achievement of scale in refining. The Collins House Group of mining companies was the most extensive and sustained cooperative working relationship among Australian firms.[43] Lasting from 1915 to 1951, it centred upon three of the leading mining companies, whose headquarters were located in the Collins House building at 360–66 Collins Street, Melbourne, notably North Broken Hill, Broken Hill South, and Zinc Corporation. Other companies were periodically part of the group, either as participants or as partial or wholly-owned subsidiaries.

The original motive for the Group was to fill a vacuum created when pre-war German dominance of the base metal mining and metallurgical industries was terminated under the terms of the *Enemy Contracts Annulment Act 1915*. However, the scale of operations now required, particularly in smelting and refining, was beyond the resources of any single Australian company. As often during wartime, inter-firm collaboration provided a possible solution. In spite of changed conditions after World War One, the companies found it in their interests to continue and extend the work of the Group and in the process created, 'a non-ferrous metal group of international importance'.[44]

The Group established a monopoly of lead, silver and zinc production at Broken Hill and went on to invest in English companies to secure involvement in zinc smelting in that country. Their interest extended outwards from here into metal fabrication, chemicals and beyond: in 1936, for example, the Collins House Group joined with BHP, General Motors-Holden's, Imperial Chemical Industries of Australia and New Zealand, and P&O Steamship to found the Commonwealth Aircraft Corporation.

Part of the reason for the continuation of the group for over 30 years was that none of them had the resources to take over one of the other dominant players, particularly in the context of an underdeveloped capital market. However, between them they were able to take control of, or eliminate, many of the smaller players. There were also many positive reasons for the Group's continuation. Key figures in the Collins House Group were close friends, or even relatives in the case of the Baillieu family. This was reinforced more formally by interlocking directorates and cross-shareholdings among the firms.

The Collins House Group provided a flexible and lightweight structure in a rapidly changing industry. Decisions could be made to acquire and dispose of subsidiaries on a regular basis, while complex organisational structures could be developed by the companies, not the Group. The broad-ranging nature of the inter-firm relations reinforced their appeal to each firm. This included joint ventures, marketing arrangements, technological collaboration, along with a range of supporting financial, legal and secretarial services.

Broken Hill Associated Smelters was formed in 1915 among the three companies and, for a while, BHP, before it turned to steel production. Since German markets for their lead concentrates were lost as a result of World War One, local cooperative smelting and refining by the three companies through the purchase of BHP's Port Pirie lead smelter provided the solution.[45] Broken Hill Associated Smelters rapidly became one of the principal world lead producers and endured for many years.

Burn's study of the 'July 1930' contract between the same three mining companies and zinc smelters Electrolytic Zinc and Imperial Smelting Corporation provides further evidence of the multi-layered inter-firm agreements and the benefits they brought. In this case, the high trust environment generated by multiple dealings enabled the firms to design a flexible contract that left room for future negotiations over prices and production.[46] The alternative would have been a more rigidly specified contract, designed to mitigate opportunism among parties employing highly specific assets. As a result, the agreement, with periodic modifications, worked effectively in a highly uncertain environment in the 1930s of falling zinc prices, volatile exchange rates, and fluctuating government policies.[47]

The success of the 1930 contract can be contrasted with the failure of a later inter-firm mining venture in Western Australia between Western Mining Corporation and United States miners Hanna Mining and Homestake Mining. The agreement between the firms was signed in 1962 to meet the rising demand of Japanese mills for iron ore. Western Mining Corporation's local knowledge and contacts complemented the United States firms' resources and technical expertise. However, in the absence of the close personal connections or broad-ranging sets of agreements discussed above, a very general memorandum between the companies was insufficient to avoid recurrent opportunism, the breakdown of trust, and the collapse of the agreement.[48]

The Collins House Group had effectively broken up by 1951: the close friends who had sustained the company links had now died and the interests of the companies had diverged. While nothing as encompassing and enduring replaced the Collins House Group, inter-firm agreements remained central to the resource industries. The major postwar expansion in demand for oil and natural gas stimulated exploration for new sources. Joint ventures and consortia enabled firms to share the high costs and risks of exploration. A major discovery by a competitor could impact seriously on a firm's relative standing in the industry, and therefore involvement in joint ventures was also a hedge against discoveries by other firms. Such joint ventures were frequently international in nature, combining the resources and technical expertise of foreign multinationals with the local knowledge and connections of Australian firms.

Immediately after World War Two, Zinc Corporation established joint ventures with a number of overseas companies, including with Standard Vacuum Oil of the United States and BP to search for oil and natural gas, and with Newmount Mining Corporation, also American, in silver and lead exploration.[49] BHP's joint venture with Esso to drill for oil in Bass Strait in 1960 ensured a full transfer of leading edge drilling technology from the United States company. CSR and Australian Gas Light Company are other notable corporate leaders who have been drawn in recent years into joint ventures in mineral exploration.

Like mining, petroleum firms faced high costs and risks in exploration and large-scale economies at the refining stage. At every major point of the value chain the firms cooperated in a more or less formal manner. Ampol, Shell and Caltex participated in a joint venture exploration company, West Australian Petroleum, which led the increased interest in exploration in the 1950s. Driving this expansion in exploration was the opening of new oil refineries in Australia, requiring huge scale economies beyond the small fragmented regional markets of Australia. In order to drive down production costs as far as possible and minimise transport costs, therefore, the companies cooperated in several ways: sharing refineries and conducting output exchanges where particular firms operated refineries in different states.

A similar set of operational credits and debits operated in distribution in order to maximise load capacities. Finally, at the retail stage, solo marketing agreements were introduced in 1951 between the oil companies and petrol retailers, wherein the latter covenanted only to stock and sell the producer's petrol. By concentrating sales upon a limited number of exclusive outlets, the companies reduced their distribution costs. Drawing upon similar practices used by the companies in North America and Europe, solo marketing, like exploration, provided a guaranteed throughput for the new Australian refineries.[50]

Chemical producers, facing similar problems of capital intensive production under conditions of high minimum scales of efficiency, cooperated with the oil producers in the manufacture of petrochemicals. The construction of local oil refineries in the 1950s was partly justified by the opportunity to make use of by-products, particularly ethylene, which is used in the manufacture of polythene, polystyrene, PVC and synthetic rubber. Much of the petrochemical industry was localised in Altona, Victoria, facilitating local cooperation between petrol and chemical companies. In Sydney an agreement between Shell and Imperial Chemical Industries of Australia and New Zealand provided for the production of heavier chemicals from petrol – ammonia and nitrogen fertiliser. While several other inter-industry agreements developed, cooperation within the chemical industry was less noticeable than in minerals, reflecting the dominance of particular chemicals by individual firms drawing upon their parent company expertise.[51]

After World War Two, the leading shipping companies faced a highly uncertain environment, particularly through the impact of air and motorised road transport on the demand for coastal shipping, the emergence of a government-owned carrier, and waves of new technology that raised further the capital intensity and minimum efficient scale in the shipping industry. Great risks accompanied increasing investment in an industry under these circumstances, so the companies developed a series of joint ventures designed to share costs and enable them to withdraw gradually from the industry or at least retain the funds to diversify. Bulkships was established in 1959 among the leading shipping companies to build and operate bulk carriers. Five years later Associated Steamships was formed to operate the coastal services of the companies. In both cases, Adelaide Steamship Company was the largest partner with a 40 per cent share rising to 50 per cent; by 1970 virtually all of its tonnage was jointly owned. In 1967 Associated Steamships in turn formed Seatainer Terminals, with a group of British companies, to operate container cargo terminals in Australian ports.[52]

Corporate leaders who were unable to draw upon the expertise and resources of a foreign parent sought opportunities to yield similar benefits through international agreement. Australian Glass Manufacturers, for example, operating in a technologically innovative industry, sought close relationships with foreign manufacturers of glass-making equipment to facilitate technology transfer. It fostered a high trust relationship with Hartford Corporation in the United States that gave it early access to new developments and provided support for Australian Glass Manufacturers in a dispute over patent rights.

This example additionally indicates the manner in which the threat from a powerful multinational entrant into Australia can be handled. In the 1930s, following Pilkington's entry into Australia, the two companies became involved in market sharing, cross-shareholdings and joint venture activities. Australian Glass Manufacturers managed to maintain its strong position in the Australian market and its agreements with Pilkington were still evident 30 years later.[53]

Australian firms venturing overseas have faced particular challenges of high costs and uncertainty associated with different and much larger markets. Inter-firm agreements have often provided a solution, at least in the early phases of a firm's internationalisation, as we saw in Chapter 4 with Lend Lease. Qantas, as the pioneering airline in Australia, grew by internalisation in the early years before World War Two. As it began to develop an overseas network from the 1930s onwards, however, it sought inter-firm agreements with other international airlines, particularly Britain's Imperial Airways, in order to operate a joint route between the two countries. The two companies jointly established Qantas Empire Airways Ltd in 1934, each owning 49 per cent. An 'umpire', Sir George Julius, owned the remaining 2 per cent.[54]

After 1945 cooperation continued between the national airlines of the two countries. More recently, this has been formalised through British Airways' 25 per cent stock ownership of Qantas. By the late 1980s, Qantas extended its cooperation to a group of other international lines, including Lufthansa and American Airlines, as part of the 'One World' strategic alliance. By sharing routes, known as code sharing, Qantas could offer its customers direct travel to more overseas destinations and with greater frequency, and at the same time could withdraw some of its own overseas flights. Cooperation has been extended to cover shared reservation systems, frequent flyer schemes, and preferred hotel, credit card and car hire companies.[55]

News Corporation, conversely, acquired many firms during its initial foreign expansion in the 1970s and 1980s. Its subsequent moves into film and satellite required very large funds, a situation made more difficult by a downturn in News' main markets in the early 1990s. Part of the solution was asset sales, especially of publishing and newspaper interests, but additionally through the formation of joint ventures to share the costs and also the risks. Examples included an alliance with Telstra to form Foxtel in 1994, a joint venture with MCI Communication in 1995 to create and distribute electronic information, education and entertainment services worldwide, and a series of international joint ventures in 1996 to expand the company's sports coverage. The joint venture mode provided the additional benefits for internationalising Australian corporate leaders of drawing upon foreign know-how while limiting financial exposure in developing nations with higher levels of political and economic uncertainty. This has proved particularly important for Coca-Cola Amatil in Indonesia, Czechoslovakia and Hungary. Foster's also used joint ventures as part of its move into China in the early 1990s, notably in Shanghai and Guangdong in 1993, although with limited success to date.

Laying claim to strategic assets

Cooperating firms were strongly placed to lay claim over particular strategic assets, notably market power and the nature of regulation over the industry.[56] Market power was influenced by agreements that sought to control output, prices or entry to the industry. The lobbying of governments through industry bodies was intended to achieve preferential regulation of the industry, such as the protection afforded by import tariffs. At the beginning of the twentieth century, inter-firm agreements existed in many industries, including the building supplies, confectionery, sugar, tobacco, jam, flour, dried fruit, fresh produce, mineral oil, coal, and shipping industries.[57]

Although identifying individual companies was often difficult in light of the secrecy surrounding collusion, a range of corporate leaders can be identified or are suspected of participating in such arrangements, including CSR, Henry Jones, Carlton & United Breweries, Mount Lyell, British Tobacco, Adelaide Steamship Company, Huddart Parker and Howard Smith. In many cases, price-fixing occurred at the expense of the consumer and other firms. Suspicion particularly centred upon large and powerful foreign enterprises that might threaten the evolving Australian manufacturing base.

It was the collusive agreement between a United States firm, the International Harvester Company, and a local firm in 1905 that led to the introduction of legislation on competition policy. The *Australian Industries Preservation Act (1906)* outlawed many collusive practices. While it may have contributed to the collapse of an agreement among the Newcastle coal companies, the Act soon became a dead letter despite not being repealed until 1965.[58] The absence of effective competition policy until the last third of the century, with the *Trade Practices Act (1967)* and the *Australian Competition and Consumer Commission Act (1995)*, enabled inter-firm agreements to continue to flourish after World War Two. Butlin, Barnard and Pincus observed that, 'all the restrictive practices known to man were exploited in the Australian economy'.[59]

Britain faced a similar situation, which triggered legislation in 1948 requiring the registration of agreements. British and Australian experience contrasted with active competition policy in the United States throughout the century, which had forced the break-up of many trusts, such as Standard Oil, and drove others into full merger. As we saw in the previous section, merger activity was less common in Australia until the 1950s.

We have a clearer picture of the nature and extent of inter-firm agreements in Australia when registration on a secret register was required by the *Trade Practices Act (1965)*. By 1969, 11 882 agreements had been registered covering all divisions of the standard trade and industry classification, suggesting a broadening of coverage since 1914; 3083 were horizontal agreements between competing firms, 6460 were distributional, particularly dealing with cases of resale price maintenance. Miscellaneous agreements included supply arrangements, licensed agreements, and lease agreements tying the use of business premises.[60] Only 49 cases had been acted upon by the trade practices commissioner and, of these, only one referred to the tribunal.[61] While this may partly reflect limitations in the new investigative mechanisms, which were strengthened in 1974, it is also suggestive of most agreements being along the lines discussed in the previous subsection to improve performance, rather than serving an uncompetitive purpose.

The extent to which agreements served an anticompetitive motive has been a matter for dispute and interpretation. The oil industry included many such arrangements that might be viewed from either an efficiency enhancing perspective, as we saw earlier, or perceived as anti-competitive. The practice of solo marketing or tied outlets, for example, reduced the companies' distribution costs but provided for the sale of only a single petrol brand at individual service stations.[62]

The role of trade associations has been the main focus of alternative viewpoints on inter-firm agreements. By 1969, 1001 trade associations were registered and they were involved in 1422 agreements of the total of 11 882, or just 12 per cent. In practice, many of the more notorious sectors for restrictive practices lacked a trade association, which tends to confirm Freeman's view that 'many associations have little or nothing to do with restrictive practices'.[63] Arbitrating disagreements among firms in the industry, setting professional standards, and establishing codes of practice have also been counted among their functions.

The representational function of trade associations was likely to have been most significant. We saw in the previous section how industry bodies in shipping, banking and wool-broking were able to improve coordination among firms. In addition to this, they viewed their role as representing the industry in most forms of external relations. Using industry bodies to influence government policy in particular was a smart strategy in a country where governments had played a proactive role in industry policy since the later decades of the nineteenth century.

Close relations between Australian governments and industry associations have been used to explain several sustained policy orientations including the maintenance of high tariffs and the absence of effective competition policy for at least half a century. The Greene Tariff of 1921 established high rates of protection in Australia and in the following years the Tariff Board was receptive to most industry claims for further increases. It gave little thought to the risk of protecting inefficient firms or limiting foreign competition, where high entry costs restricted local entrants. The extension of regulation and direct controls by the 1950s, such as on prices, capital issues, foreign exchange, and a range of taxes, increased the potential returns to industry lobby groups. The case-by-case approach adopted by governments, particularly in the interwar period and the 1950s, enabled industry groups to target their lobbying more effectively. Mancur Olson's institutional sclerosis hypothesis, wherein 'distributional coalitions' (well-organised lobby groups) hijack government policy, had a certain resonance for Australia up until the 1970s, when high tariffs and centralised regulation began to be wound back.[64]

The dominance of government by the Liberal and National parties, sympathetic to industry pleading, in the initial postwar decades contributed to the emergence of a form of *clientism*, particularly between John McEwen at the Department of Trade and Industry and the Australian Chamber of Manufactures.[65] McEwen was on particularly close terms with many of the chairmen and senior executives of our corporate leaders. Armed with their resources and political connections, corporate leaders made unilateral representations to government, additional to those of industry bodies.

The introduction of highly protectionist local content plans for the vehicle components industry during 1962–65 has been attributed to representations by Repco, particularly the influence of its Chairman Charles McGrath in Liberal party quarters.[66] General Motors-Holden's was first to be consulted about plans for an Australian-built vehicle at the end of World War Two. Imperial Chemical Industries of Australia and New Zealand is thought to have used its influence to delay a tariff review of the chemicals industry in the 1970s.[67] Corporate leaders were also heavily represented on government industry bodies: the Board of Australian Industry Development Corporation, established in 1971, was dominated by representatives from BHP, CSR, Repco, Mount Isa Mines, BP and Ampol.[68]

On the other hand, corporate leaders would have had to share benefits from price maintenance and tariff protection with many other Australian firms, thereby conferring no particular competitive advantage within the domestic market. In addition, other firms in an industry were not slow to react to unilateral bargaining by corporate leaders. BHP successfully negotiated tariff reductions in 1981 that applied only to itself, although the government backtracked in the following year under pressure from other sectors of the industry.[69]

Some of the negative consequences of long-term protectionism and other forms of industry support for corporate leaders should also be noted, particularly the sustenance it provided to small and inefficient firms. Building corporate leaders that could maximise their scale economies and international competitiveness was not helped by such policies. While ineffectual competition policy may have permitted corporate leaders to maximise their market power, this diverted their attention and resources away from a concentration upon generating sustainable competitive advantages.

The success and competitive efficiency of most corporate leaders indeed made them wary about the apparent levelling effects of cooperative action.

Goldsbrough Mort was a reluctant member of the Sydney Woolbrokers Association, which 'submerged our traditional individuality and elected to fight from the same level as do the least of our opponents'. Thus, when the reformation of the Association was being contemplated in 1894, Goldsbrough Mort favoured only broad policy agreements, leaving firms free in the conduct of their internal business.[70] In 1896 they recommended a two-year rate war so that some of the excessive numbers of Sydney firms 'who are rapidly establishing themselves under the wings of the Assn can be "blotted out" and the trade "purified"'.[71]

The work of Tsokhas has drawn attention to a further range of divisions within the corporate distributional coalition, which weakened its effectiveness.[72] He distinguishes the differing interests of the manufacturing, mining, pastoralism, importing and retailing, and finance sectors. For example, pastoral and mining interests were sceptical of the value of tariffs in light of the impact on imports of capital equipment used in these sectors. In addition, miners and pastoralists sought to export to countries such as Japan, whose governments threatened retaliatory tariffs. The manufacturing sector was the strongest supporter of tariffs, although disagreements existed among some firms. Mining and manufacturing interests also clashed over foreign investment. Tsokhas additionally points to the mixed interests within corporations like BHP, whose operations spread across manufacturing and mining.

Conclusion

Internal growth, acquisition and inter-firm agreement were all widely used as growth avenues by our corporate leaders. The internal path was particularly used by firms in the early years of the century and in the initial phases of their expansion when both the resources and the public market in takeovers were thin on the ground. Foreign multinationals and firms that dominated their industry, especially in terms of technological innovation, also relied heavily upon the internal method. Acquisition, particularly of listed companies, expanded rapidly after World War Two, serving the needs of diversification strategies, fast-growing challengers, and corporate 'raiders' in search of undervalued businesses.

Inter-firm agreements were a consistent part of the Australian corporate economy throughout the century. There were good efficiency reasons for this, especially the yielding of scale economies through cooperation, as a beachhead for overseas expansion, and as a means of bringing order and a set of standard practices to each industry. Writers have also identified market power motives through the reduction of competition and the extraction of rents for the industry through the organised lobbying of government.

Not surprisingly, individual examples of anti-competitive and pressure group tactics are more difficult to identify but they are seen as broadly behind particular policies, especially the persistence of high tariffs and weak competition policy for much of the century. Such market power tactics tend to be ephemeral and not yield the sustainable competitive advantages; nonetheless by weakening the competitive environment, they may have delayed the emergence of efficient corporate leaders in Australia and overseas until the later decades of the twentieth century.

CHAPTER 6

Financing Corporate Strategies

The financing decisions for our corporate leaders were influenced over time by a range of macroeconomic and firm-specific factors (for example, the institutional structure of finance markets, the size of the firm, current sources of finance, ownership structure). The availability of finance from private and public markets affects the cost of capital for the firm, and dictates the extent to which it must fund growth from internally generated sources. Financial regulations, tax regimes, the openness of the economy to international capital flows, and investor sentiment (to name a few), all influence the nature and structure of the domestic finance market. At the firm-specific level, the financing decision involves judging whether to retain earnings for growth, or to raise new capital from debt or equity. Alternatively, firms might draw on networks of relationships to fund expansion and growth. If external sources are chosen, management is required to address more complex questions associated with the maturity and seniority of finance, and the nature of future payments (for example, fixed or floating interest rates, the currency of denomination, and dividend payouts).

In this chapter we examine the sources of finance utilised by Australia's corporate leaders. We begin by describing the sources of finance available to firms: retained earnings, networks, equity and debt. We then examine how each of these sources were used to finance corporate strategies and sustain competitive advantages. We conclude with an examination of the rise of financing operations in the corporate head office of two corporate leaders: Dunlop and BHP.

Sources of finance

Firms can finance strategic growth from a range of sources, which fall into four general categories – retained earnings, networks, equity and debt. Retained earnings are the earnings available to management for growth after paying all financial claimants – variable costs of production (wages, raw materials, other expenses), interest payments on debt, and dividend payouts to equity holders.

The level of retained earnings depends upon the developmental stage of the firm, the competitive rivalry of the firm's markets, and the capital structure of the firm. Early stage firms may not have the ability to generate earnings sufficient to provide for growth, and will rely more upon equity financing. By contrast, established firms with relatively high market share have the ability to pay all claimants (including regular dividend payments) and retain earnings for growth.

From a manager's perspective, retained earnings are the easiest form of finance to source because the manager does not need to provide as strong a justification for funding as that required to convince debt or equity holders to provide additional money. The decision to hold back dividends from share-holders can be made by administrative fiat; and by definition, as the firm's dividend payout ratio declines, the level of retained earnings rises.

Another source of finance that does not require the formal, external capital market is the network of relationships that the firm builds up over time in its normal course of business. The most common form of network finance comes from the 'loose network' of trade participants. Trade credit is usually short-term in nature, and allows the firm to manage financing requirements so that retained earnings, for example, can be allocated to long-term strategic initiatives rather than paying short-term liabilities. The nature of trade credit is determined by the conventions and business practices of the industry. Convention dictates the period of credit and discounting rules. The reputation of the firm and its prior history in commercial relations provide cost-effective monitoring and reduces the likelihood that trade credit provisions are abused.

The amount of trade credit available in any one period is determined largely by the level of activity in the industry. Trade credit between firms, therefore, will be associated with macroeconomic conditions in the economy by the extent to which an industry is pro-cyclical or counter-cyclical. Trade credit provides a 'loose' finance network for firms by reducing asymmetric information between a lender (such as a raw material supplier) and a buyer (the firm). The long-term business relationships create a premium on trust, reputation, and 'fair and reasonable' business dealings.

Network finance also comes from the 'tight network' that may exist between the firm and related parties. The network may be formed initially through trade and commercial relationships. Over time, the long-term nature of the com-mercial relationship leads to a network form of organisation in which inter-dependence, reputation and reciprocity rise in importance. The network may be informal (reinforced through ongoing trade) or formal (through joint ventures or cross-equity holdings). In terms of finance, a network allows the firm to source finance from knowledgeable groups who have access to 'thick', quality information flows on the strategic development of the firm.[1] Thus, the finance

provided by network partners may be long term and the requirement for repay-
ment is sensitive to start-up costs and longer lead periods before profitability.[2]

Retained earnings and networks play an important role in financing organic
growth and relatively small capital expenditures. Corporate strategies that
require substantial capital injections will be more likely funded by equity or
debt. Equity finance can be obtained by the firm from private or public sources.
The early stage of firm development can often be funded by private shareholders, as the amount of funds required is not great. However, as the firm
grows and requires more finance, the limited pool of private shareholders can
face liquidity constraints.

One exception to this is the case where a private shareholder is an overseas
company that itself has recourse to various sources of finance. The limited pool
of risk capital therefore drives the firm to raise public equity through an initial
public offering on the stock market. The choice of which stock market to list on
is one that is made by management and existing shareholders, with reference
to the relative costs and benefits of different exchanges (in Australia and/or
international markets such as London or New York). Once the firm is listed, it
can issue 'seasoned' equity to finance growth. This equity may be ordinary
shares, permitting the purchaser to exercise all rights and responsibilities of a
shareholder, or a range of preference shares that may have different rights than
ordinary shares (for example, preferential claims of recovery of monies during
financial distress, differential voting rights, guaranteed dividend payments).
The ability of firms to raise finance through seasoned equity offerings has
varied over the course of the twentieth century in the world's major stock
markets as institutional developments have influenced the attractiveness of
equity investment.[3]

Like equity, debt can be obtained through private or public sources and
may be of different maturities, depending upon the financing requirement. The
major providers of long-term debt in the economy are trading banks and
insurance companies, and more recently wholesale providers such as merchant
banks, superannuation funds and mutual funds. Firms can also raise debt
directly on the stock market through publicly listed debentures or debt notes,
usually for fixed terms such as three, five or ten years. Given that the majority
of debt raised by a firm is secured over its assets, the level of tangible assets and
firm size have been found to be related to debt (or leverage) levels. In addition,
the level of profit (and its certainty) often influences debt levels, as firms that
have volatile cash flows will be perceived as higher risk investments.

Our examination of the sources of finance for corporate strategies is complicated by the interplay between the demand and supply of capital. There were
major changes in Australian financial institutions during the twentieth century,
and these changes influenced the supply of equity and debt. To this we must add

important regulatory and tax changes, allowing firms to expense interest payments (increasing the attractiveness of debt) and make depreciation allowances. The relative importance of the source of finance, therefore, changed as the corporate leaders exploited changes in relative prices.

Another question that arises in an Australian study of the development of big business is whether the domestically-owned corporate leaders had different financing options from subsidiaries of a multinational corporation. Multinationals have a greater opportunity set from which to raise equity, debt and trade credit, and may be able to operate internal capital markets efficiently across their subsidiaries. However, there may also be particular biases in the sources of finance adopted by multinationals. For example, it can be argued that they will have a preference for retained earnings and local debt as these sources of finance allow the multinational parent to match local currency denominated income to capital requirements (thus reducing exchange rate risks of financing the subsidiary). Furthermore, the parent would be unlikely to raise equity locally as it wishes to maintain ownership rights over strategic assets of the multinationals.

The next four sections of this chapter investigate the methods adopted by our corporate leaders to finance their strategies. We begin by describing the enduring link between a strong market position and retained earnings, and the importance that network relationships have played in a relatively under-developed capital market. We then turn to describe how equity financing was available to firms with a reputation for earnings reliability. Market developments were slow, and equity financing was always ancillary to other sources of long-term finance ('hot' issue public markets aside). Finally, we trace the growth in the use of debt to finance strategies. It is in this section that we see most clearly the linkages between institutional (including tax regulation) development and changes in the demand for funds.

Virtuous circle: Market dominance, retained earnings and organic growth

Underdeveloped capital markets place a brake on corporate development by limiting the ability of firms to fund all net present value projects. Not only is the price of capital high (reducing the number of viable projects), but quantity constraints mean that not all profitable strategies are funded. A conservative capital market stifles emerging industries, making technological development less likely. The first 50 years of Australian corporate development was characterised by relatively underdeveloped domestic capital markets and limited sources of finance.[4] Retained earnings and network sources of finance were therefore important in allowing the corporate leaders to implement their growth strategies. Public issues of equity were more important than debt capital during these years, and, as Forster states, banks played only a 'small role ... in the provision of funds for industry'.[5]

The attainment of corporate leadership had important implications for the firm's ability to fund expansion. Market strength provided the ability to influence prices for goods and services, and deliver strong financial performance. Market dominance meant that the firm could create a virtuous circle, whereby it could satisfy shareholder demands for a constant dividend and retain earnings for organic growth. It also meant that the underdeveloped nature of the local capital market worked in the corporate leaders' favour by limiting entry into markets from competitors.

The ability to generate retained earnings depends crucially on the firm's profitability and sustainable competitive advantage. Obtaining empirical data on firm profitability in Australia is a difficult task, especially for the years of our study. Indeed, the long-term profitability of Australian firms has attracted little attention from researchers. In order to estimate how profitable firms were, and how retained earnings could be generated, we have constructed a profitability series covering 1921 to 1986. The time series measures net profit as a percentage of shareholders' funds for all industrials (being manufacturing, wholesale and retail trade, and services).[6] Net profitability fluctuated between 6 and 8 per cent up to the 1960s, when a rise in profitability occurred. While there are noticeable peaks and troughs (the large fall in the early 1930s being most evident), the ability of firms to generate consistent profits over 65 years leads us to conjecture that shareholders could be satisfactorily rewarded with dividends, and earnings could be retained for growth opportunities.

Reliable data on the sources of finance for the corporate leaders is provided by Hall's seminal research on Australian company finance between 1946 and 1954, and later data from reviews of the financial system by Matthews and Harcourt, and Ma and Matthews.[7] Hall's list of 100 companies includes no fewer than 51 per cent of our corporate leaders, and 71 per cent of the top 28 firms (that is, those that were in our benchmark years four to six times). All industries are well represented, except mining and pastoral services. The data for 1955 to 1971 comes from official sources covering Australia's largest firms.

Table 6.1 shows that retained earnings provided 10–30 per cent of finance up to the 1970s. The proportion of retained earnings averaged 19.6 per cent during the 1950s, and 16.8 per cent during the 1960s. Internal sources (retained earnings and depreciation allowances) were even more important (see Figure 6.1), providing 40–60 per cent of capital injection in any one year. Given the importance of these sources, it is no wonder that a strategy designed to attain market leadership was seen as crucial.[8]

Table 6.1: Net sources of financing, 1946–71 (%)

Year	Shares	Long-term debt	Short-term debt: creditors	Short-term debt: bank overdraft	Retained earnings	Depreci-ation allowances
1946/47	10.5	2.1	16.0	16.4	18.5	20.3
1947/48	17.2	2.5	14.5	20.5	16.2	16.2
1948/49	27.5	2.9	17.1	7.3	15.7	18.6
1949/50	18.9	12.3	19.8	0.0	17.9	17.9
1950/51	22.5	7.7	19.3	14.0	13.3	10.8
1951/52	26.9	8.6	0.5	25.8	10.2	12.3
1952/53	11.6	11.9	0.0	0.0	16.2	16.9
1953/54	12.5	13.6	18.2	0.0	20.7	21.5
1954/55	–	–	–	–	–	–
1955/56	20.2	13.6	10.8	2.6	23.9	20.5
1956/57	19.2	12.6	3.1	–0.6	28.4	28.0
1957/58	11.8	19.5	6.4	–2.3	29.2	28.0
1958/59	10.3	19.3	8.9	0.6	27.0	26.0
1959/60	10.7	21.6	14.3	4.8	21.3	18.8
1960/61	19.8	25.9	–0.6	5.8	15.1	26.8
1961/62	22.5	20.5	–5.2	–8.3	18.8	35.5
1962/63	–	–	–	–	–	–
1963/64	–	–	–	–	–	–
1964/65	–	–	–	–	–	–
1965/66	21.0	16.7	6.5	1.0	15.7	36.7
1966/67	11.3	13.0	7.5	1.3	18.6	43.9
1967/68	6.8	15.0	7.9	0.3	19.1	36.7
1968/69	14.4	17.5	12.1	1.8	16.5	28.9
1969/70	14.1	14.7	13.7	4.0	14.1	29.1
1970/71	6.8	15.2	12.8	5.8	16.8	32.5

Sources: 1946/47 to 1950/51 – Hall, *Company Finance*, pp. 43–4 ('1946 Companies');
1951/52 to 1953/54 – Hall, *Company Finance*, pp. 43–4 ('100 Companies'); 1956/57
to 1961/62 – Mathews & Harcourt, 'Company finance', Table 4; 1955/56, 1965/66 to
1970/71 – Ma and Mathews, 'Company finance', Table 2.7.

Which corporate leaders relied on retained earnings to finance strategies
and what type of strategies were funded in this way? The first group of corporate leaders (those in leading market positions between 1910 to 1950) used
retained earnings primarily to finance organic growth and small capital expenditures (we shall note several exceptions). Burns Philp adopted a retained
earnings policy after over-reliance on short-term bank finance during the 1890s

Figure 6.1: Net sources of financing 1946–71: Internal sources, equity and long-term debt (%)

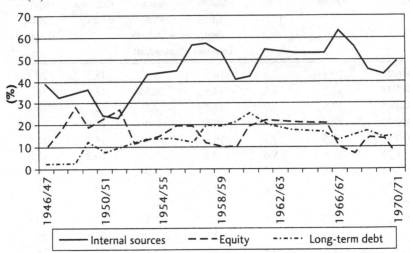

Note: The data series has been made continuous by interpolating for the following years: 1954/55, 1962/63, 1963/64, and 1964/65.

Source: 1946/47 to 1950/51 – Hall, *Company Finance*, pp. 43–4 ('1946 Companies'); 1951/52 to 1953/54 – Hall, *Company Finance*, pp. 43–4 ('100 Companies'); 1956/57 to 1961/62 – Mathews & Harcourt, 'Company finance', Table 4; 1955/56, 1965/66 to 1970/71 – Ma and Mathews, 'Company finance', Table 2.7.

depression. In 1899 Burns Philp resumed placing half of their earnings in a reserve fund 'to strengthen and expand the business of the Company'.[9] This strategy was continued until the 1930s and allowed Burns Philp to survive the depression on the strength of reserves.[10]

Stock and station agents were also able to use retained earnings to expand organically. Profits from successful branches were used to cross-subsidise branch expansion and the inevitable losses in early years. In a similar vein, the Bank of New South Wales financed branch networking from retained earnings until the 1980s – equity issues were predominantly used to maintain a rough ratio of paid capital to deposits of ten per cent.[11] As a mutual fund, AMP also funded expansion from profits.

Market dominance in the food, drink and tobacco industries provided strong cash flows and corporate liquidity for expansion. Between 1890 and 1950, CSR funded most growth from profits, 'savings' and asset sales while continuing to pay 85 per cent of profits each year to shareholders. Carlton & United Breweries' acquisition of Victorian-based rivals, brewing plant upgrades and improvements in tied hotels were financed from the combine's annual cash flow. Minimal competition from other beverages (until the 1960s), the use of the tied house system to deter entry and collusive pricing agreements ensured that retained earnings were available. In mining, retained earnings took on a slightly different role in the capital structure. New discoveries and successful extraction provided mining companies such as Western Mining Corporation and Mount Isa Mines with annuity streams that could be applied to new exploration activities. Retained earnings were never sufficient to fund the substantial capital expenditures required for mineral extraction. An exception is BHP, which financed expansion throughout the 1920s and 1930s with internal funds and a bank overdraft.[12]

The emerging corporate leaders of the 1950s and 1960s also grew from internal sources. In the embryonic airline industry, Ansett built up reserves and utilised depreciation allowances to contribute to the purchase of Australian National Airways (1957).[13] Brambles drew upon profits and depreciation allowances to finance organic growth in the transport industry. James Hardie's new product developments in Hardiflex, new applications for fibro-cement and related diversification into brake linings and friction materials were possible through 'extensive reinvestment of earnings' (an exception was the 1959 acquisition of Better Brakes).[14] Boral's acquisition of companies between 1973 and 1981 were also largely funded from profits; despite this funding requirement, Boral managed to pay out 64 per cent of profits in 1956, 85 per cent in 1966 and 63 per cent in 1976.[15] In real estate, L.J. Hooker's expansion into pastoral properties was financed through ploughing back their income for two or three years, and Lend Lease mastered the use of project financing and design-and-build strategies to become the pre-eminent commercial property developer.

The final group of corporate leaders that adopted retained earnings as a major finance source was the multinationals. As we have noted, multinationals have recourse to additional sources and methods of finance. General Motors-Holden's, Shell, BP and Imperial Chemical Industries of Australia and New Zealand Ltd reinvested heavily into capital works to maintain their market position (these firms were also adept at attracting government finance to subsidise new plant). The use of retained earnings to fund growth in multinationals served several purposes. They could arbitrage between developed and underdeveloped capital markets to provide the cheapest source of capital. They had access to deeper equity and debt markets given their international reputation. Ploughing back profits also served a useful control mechanism to limit agency costs. Major capital expenditures required domestic managers to mount a case to head office (either for additional capital or cessation of dividend payments to the parent), and provided opportunities for review and monitoring. General Motors-Holden's is a case in point. Apart from an equity issue in 1924 (to fund technological improvements in its production process), General

Motors-Holden's reinvested the majority of its profits and paid its parent a modest dividend rate (the equity issued in 1924 was bought back in 1959–60, ending 'direct participation by Australian shareholders' in the operations of the company).[16] Retained earnings funded assembly plants in Melbourne, Sydney, Brisbane, Adelaide and Perth, the acquisition of Holden Motor Body Builders Ltd (1931) and a new head office.[17]

Imperial Chemical Industries of Australia and New Zealand Ltd also survived on domestically generated earnings. The first opportunity for domestic shareholders to fund growth and participate in ownership of the company was not until 1938 (ten years after the firm was established in Australia), with a £1 million float of preference shares.

Network financing: The benefits of long-term relationships

Network financing through trade credit (loose network) and related parties (tight network) played an important role in financing the strategies of our corporate leaders. Networks did not suffer from the same level of incomplete information associated with external equity and debt markets. Long-term trade and business relationships were based on trust and reciprocity of 'fair' business dealings. Finance provided within the firm's network did not require a premium to compensate for the risks associated with managerial agency behaviour. By contrast, the principal–agent relationships between external debt and equity providers and managers could lead to finance being used for projects that maximised managerial welfare at the expense of other parties (for example, projects that increase the 'empire', consumption of perquisites). Agency costs were minimised in the network relationship through a combination of close monitoring, reputation and the benefits of repeated interaction.

Trade credit provided short-term financing for most corporate leaders. The level of credit was determined by the norms, conventions and discount rules in the prevailing industry. As Schneider has shown, changes in the use of trade credit in Australia were determined by the volume of industrial sales and activity, rather than by external factors, such as the price of credit, broad macro-economic trends or business confidence.[18] Thus, we find industry variations with our corporate leaders' experience.

In the stock and station agent industry, trade credit was drawn onto smooth cash flows. Dalgety, Elders and Goldsborough Mort (to name three) were both providers of trade credit to farmers (locking in customers and obtaining useful information on the client) and users of trade credit from banks. The network relationships were crucial to this type of financing; without bank support the role of the stock and station agent as a financial intermediary would have been severely curtailed.[19] Wholesale trader Burns Philp also had recourse to trade credit to smooth irregular cash flows associated with consignments and cyclical industry demand. Burns Philp's banking relationship was less secure than the stock and station agents, and the company switched banks several times. A conscious strategy to reduce reliance on trade credit from the mid-1890s was driven by the arbitrary provision of finance. The supplier–provider network here was loose, and banks were not prepared to invest in a long-term relationship.

Cyclical industries in retail and construction were strong providers of trade credit. CSR was able to exploit timing differences between the receipt of revenue and payments to growers. Carlton & United Breweries used trade credit in the tied house system and building products companies such as James Hardie, Boral and Lend Lease smoothed cash flow variability with inter-industry credit conventions. Multinationals such as General Motors-Holden's could also exploit their international, intra-company network to provide short-term finance.

In sum, short-term financing through these loose networks formed an important function in providing working capital. As Table 6.1 shows, short-term finance varied in importance between 1946 and 1971, and bank overdrafts in particular declined in use relative to other financing sources. New sources of short-term debt would arise due to changes in financial market regulation (we describe these later). In 1962, for example, the Reserve Bank of Australia made special arrangements with trading banks to allow them to make fixed term loans for three to eight years to finance expenditures by rural, manufacturing and commercial enterprises.[20] Other network forms of finance were more enduring, however.

A tight financing network provided longer-term finance for capital expenditures. Two types of tight networks are examined here: related company networks and government–company networks. Related company networks have a long history in Australian corporate development. In the shipping industry, inter-company loans and guarantees were common between Adelaide Steamship Company and Elders. The relationship had roots in cross-shareholdings from the 1870s and led to Elders advancing or guaranteeing funds for several capital expenditure items, including coastal steamers.[21] In airlines, both Ansett and Qantas received network support from groups dependent on aviation services – pastoral stations and graziers were early finance providers in the 1920s and 1930s. Post-1945, Ansett's acquisition of Australian National Airways (for £3.3 million) was partly financed by £500 000 from each of Vacuum (now Mobil) Oil and Shell. In addition, both companies provided special fuel guarantees for similar amounts.[22]

Finance networks in the mining industry are perhaps the best example of the way in which close business relationships allowed expansion and growth. Major mining development projects often involved a consortia of corporate leaders. In the 1960s the Mount Newman iron ore project was financed by BHP (through its subsidiary Dampier Mining Company Ltd), CSR (through Pilbara Iron Ltd), United States multinationals and Japanese steel mills. This network successfully lobbied Australian, Japanese and United States governments to secure debt, tax concessions and bank relief from statutory reserve requirements. Intra-company cooperation and heavy rent-seeking (especially by BHP and CSR) resulted in further entrenchment and market dominance for these firms.[23]

BHP replicated these intra-company networks in other major projects in the 1970s and 1980s – its alliance in the oil industry with Esso (US); bauxite with Reynolds Metal Company (US), Kobe (Japan) and Billiton (South Africa); and aluminium at Worsley (again with international partners). Western Mining Corporation was also embedded in the exploration, development, financial network with joint projects with BHP (Yilgarn iron deposit), and North (bauxite and copper). Wider intra-company relationships were often harder to develop, as seen in the failed attempt to exploit similar synergies in its joint venture arrangements with Hanna Mining Company and Homestake Mining Company Ltd (both American).[24]

Regulatory changes affected the ability of some corporate leaders to engage in inter-company financing. In 1974 the *Financial Corporations Act* permitted firms to register as 'Intra-Group Financiers'. By 1991, 13 companies had developed formal relationships allowing the transfer of funds within the corporate groups. These internal capital markets again solved important asymmetric information and agency issues associated with debt financing. Notable corporate leaders using the intra-group financiers system were Conzinc Riotinto Australia (via CRA Finance) and Santos Finance; and Consolidated Press, Elders IXL, Foster's Brewing Group and Pacific Dunlop. The deregulation of financial markets during the 1990s reduced the transaction cost benefits from these intra-group structures. By 2002 not one corporate leader was a registered financier.

A distinguishing feature of the development of Australian corporate leaders was the tight network in finance that firms formed with governments. This relationship was part of a wider political economy encompassing industry policy through tariff protection, subsidies and incentives.[25] The government–company relationship has been the topic of much debate in Australia. One manifestation of the relationship is the close dealings corporate leaders had with public officials in tax, regulations and accounting procedures. Depreciation allowances (and rates of depreciation) and, more recently, research and development tax benefits were the topics of debate and negotiation between corporate finance departments and public officials. As we reported in Table 6.1, depreciation allowances provided 10–40 per cent of net finance to replace the existing capital stock of the company. While these are important, we focus here on how the corporate leaders exploited the government–company network to finance strategies to sustain competitive advantages.

Firms in the key infrastructure industries had close relationships with federal and state governments that extended to financial arrangements. In the gas industry, Australian Gas Light Company's ability to finance capital expenditures was restricted by the requirement to pay out dividends. Monopoly rights, sliding scale arrangements for fees and tax benefits to debt were negotiated in the company's favour, providing a major barrier to entry. In 1966 amendments to the *Gas and Electricity Act* gave Australian Gas Light unlimited borrowing power, which it exploited into the 1980s.

In airlines, Ansett and Qantas enjoyed government subsidies for a range of expenditures. The establishment of the Department of Civil Aviation in 1939 organised government involvement in the financial support of terminals, upgraded airstrips and mail delivery services. Qantas would not have attained its corporate leadership were it not for its strategy of securing government assistance on key airline services. Between 1923 and 1934, government subsidies provided, on average, 64 per cent of total revenue.[26] Further lobbying in 1936 guaranteed revenue through the duplication of airline services to Singapore (which provided 25 per cent of total revenue in 1950).[27] Corporate leadership was ensured when Qantas management and shareholders encouraged state ownership in 1947; the nationalised corporation established a position of market dominance and funded major capital expenditures from the federal government's consolidated revenue. From 1993, Qantas emerged as a privatised corporation with sustained corporate advantages in the local market and the power to withstand challenges from new entrants (most evident in the late 1990s).

Government initiatives to help finance the growth in the mining industry included the establishment of the Australian Resource Development Bank (1967) and the Australian Industry Development Corporation. Both institutions were designed to provide funds in order to keep mining, exploration and downstream industries in Australian ownership. The major iron ore projects at Mount Newman (BHP and CSR), and Western Mining Corporation's nickel project at Kambalda are examples of the tight financing network.[28]

Equity finance: Risk capital in a small developing economy

The size and depth of an equity market is crucial to provide finance for the growth strategies of firms in an economy. There is now convincing evidence that developed capital markets are associated with robust economic growth, a well-developed corporate sector, and more efficient allocation of resources.

Australian corporate leaders faced difficulties in raising equity finance for much of the twentieth century. Indeed, there was a clear advantage in being large and dominant in an industrial sector – size and leadership provided a reputation and access to equity not available to rivals. We examine this phenomenon and the experience of the emerging corporate leaders in raising equity.

Privileged access: Reputation and the equity market

Organic growth and small capital expenditures for the corporate leaders could be financed by retained earnings. Larger projects, however, required a more substantial change in capital structure. The major corporations of the 1920s and 1930s were able to tap into the local equity and debt markets due to their size and reputation. Corporate leaders were known to investors and were analysed by the leading stock brokers. Low information asymmetries meant that the corporate leaders would more likely be successful in raising external capital and not be required to issue shares at a discount to par. Mergers and acquisitions were the most common strategy funded by equity raisings.

In the finance industry, the Bank of New South Wales funded its acquisition of Western Australia Bank (1927) and the Australian Bank of Commerce (1931) with previously unissued stock.[29] In the mining industry, BHP's acquisition of Australian Iron and Steel Ltd in 1935 was financed through the issue of 750 000 shares. CSR and the newly-formed Carlton & United Breweries also undertook seasoned equity raisings. CSR's vertical integration into plantations, sugar-crushing plant and shipping in Australia, New Zealand and Fiji required large amounts of capital. Between 1887 and 1907 it made seven equity issues to raise £1.12 million. The acquisitions of the Victorian Sugar Company and the Australasian Refining Company were funded by equity and debt, with debentures being offered in 1887 and 1894. Carlton & United Breweries listed in 1913 with the issuing of 1 000 000 £2 ordinary shares, which were held by the six constituent breweries. Corporate leaders who raised capital via equity issues in the early postwar period included the Herald & Weekly Times (to fund the acquisition of News Ltd of Adelaide in 1947), and Australian Paper Manufacturers (£19 million in shares and debt between 1945 and 1953).

Shipping industry corporate leaders were listed on the domestic stock exchange. Adelaide Steamship Company was incorporated as a public company in 1875 when it offered £100 000 to shareholders at 10 000 £10 shares. As was common at the time, shares were partly paid up to £1, with 10 shillings due per month. Although Huddart Parker was established in the 1850s it did not list on the domestic stock market until 1912 when it offered preference and ordinary shares totaling £1 000 000. Equity raising was important for the shipping companies. Horizontal integration via acquisition involved purchasing high tangible asset companies; growth via internalisation similarly involved high physical capital expenditures. Retained earnings were insufficient to fund growth in the industry; Adelaide Steamship, for example, increased equity in 1882 to fund acquisitions of Spencer Gulf Steamship Company (1882), and Anderson and Marshall (1883). In 1915 it acquired Coastal Steamships Ltd with cash and £30 000 of seasoned equity.[30] In 1920 (and 1935) it restructured its balance sheet with more equity to finance internal growth and the establishment of Adelaide Airways Ltd (1935).[31]

Equity financing post-1945 remained available to the established firms. Notwithstanding this, equity declined as a source of net finance for the corporate leaders between the late 1940s and the late 1950s. This decline is largely attributable to the rise in the use of debt. When firms did use equity it was opportunistically to fund mergers and acquisitions or to exploit new issue markets. Equity and equity–cash combinations were popular mediums of exchange in mergers and acquisitions to the 1970s.[32]

Equity was used extensively by several firms to achieve horizontal integration, related diversification and, in the 1960s, unrelated diversification. Dunlop Australia made a number of related acquisitions in the 1950s with equity: Kenworth Rubber Ltd, Trilby Footwear Pty and Busset and Bills Bros Pty.[33] Australian Consolidated Industries, Clyde Industries, and Repco made similar financing decisions in their attempts to achieve scale and scope economies. Hot issue markets allowed the issuing of equity at high prices to maximise fund raisings. One clear example of this is the use of equity financing by BHP, Conzinc Riotinto Australia and Colmalco in 1969 and 1970. These established corporate leaders commanded equity premiums during the hot issue market of that time. Shareholders were willing to pay BHP 2.47 times nominal value ($47.0 million for $19.0 million shares), Comalco 5.5 times nominal value ($35.75 million for $6.5 million shares) and Conzinc Riotinto 29 times nominal value ($29.0 million for $1.0 million shares). Such premiums reduced the per share transactions costs of fund-raising, effectively providing 'cheap' finance for capital expenditures.

Equity raisings by the new growth firms: Solving information asymmetries

So far we have concentrated on the equity raising ability of the 'early' corporate leaders. The emerging corporate leaders faced a more difficult task of raising equity finance to pursue their strategies. The lack of a deep public debt market forced firms to try to issue equity in order to fund large capital expenditures. These new growth firms had to convince investors to hold risk finance.

Investors needed to assess the impact on firm growth of technological developments in new industries, and a range of firm-specific competitive risks. In order
to give investors some comfort on the risk profile of the new investment,
emerging corporate leaders attempted to solve information asymmetries by
signalling quality earnings ability and low risk through a constant dividend
policy and high payout ratio.

The expansion of manufacturing in the 1920s called forth greater equity
financing than had been used previously. Prior to 1914 investors had the option
of taking up government bonds, or subscribing for seasoned equity offerings
on the stock market by public utilities or mining firms. The financing requirements of manufacturing firms led to a greater number of initial public offerings
in the 1920s from 'non-traditional' capital raisers. Forster has estimated that, in
aggregate, the majority of finance was provided by new and seasoned equity
(48.7 per cent), retained earnings (20.4 per cent), debt (both through banks and
creditors) (19.5 per cent) and bonus share issues (11.5 per cent).[34] If we combine equity raising and bonus share issues, then the shareholders provided
60 per cent of the new capital raised by manufacturing firms during the decade.

Several corporate leaders achieved critical mass during the 1920s and 1930s
through horizontal expansion. These strategies were often financed by equity
rather than retained earnings as the firm moved beyond its state boundaries to
increase market presence. Unlike the more established corporate leaders in the
financial services, mining and shipping industries, these corporations had to
convince shareholders that equity provided an adequate return for the level of
assumed risk. The technique of adopting a constant dividend payout signalled
confidence in the new corporate strategy.

Several examples are worthy of mention. Qantas issued new equity to
purchase aircraft, and once it had reached profit by the late 1920s declared a
constant 4 per cent dividend, which it maintained for most of the 1930s. The
Herald & Weekly Times raised equity finance to fund expansion through new
publications (such as the *Sporting Globe*) and new buildings in the 1920s, and
to establish new subsidiaries in the 1930s. Throughout these decades the Herald
& Weekly Times honoured a dividend rate of 6.5 per cent on its cumulative
preference shares, and maintained a high payout ratio on ordinary shares.
Australian Paper Manufacturers Ltd issued shares in 1920, 1922, 1925, 1926
and 1937 to private shareholders to fund its strategy of horizontal expansion
through mergers with the Sydney Paper Mill (1920) and Cumberland Paper
Board Mills Ltd (1926). The most common form of equity were cumulative
shares earning 8 per cent per annum; the success of this signal of quality is
illustrated by the company's first public issue in 1937 (1 000 000 ordinary
shares), which was oversubscribed within two hours.[35]

Not all corporate leaders were successful in raising equity to fund growth. Several firms' growth strategies were stunted by a lack of domestic risk capital, especially in cases where the firm could not offer dividends in the short term. Western Mining Corporation's early years is a case in point. Gold Mines of Australia (from 1933 Western Mining Corporation) was established in 1930 by a syndicate of domestic and multinational mining companies (New Consolidated Gold Fields Ltd of South Africa, the Zinc Corporation and the Imperial Smelting Corporation) and private shareholders. Due to a lack of risk capital in Australia, the company formed investment vehicles domiciled in London to obtain the requisite finance for exploration activities. In 1935 and in 1938–39 the company raised over £2 million from overseas investors – only a few years earlier (in 1934) it had been forced to withdraw its Australian prospectus when it received interest for £150 000 out of a £1.12 million raising.[36]

Equity market consolidation and international integration

The Australian Stock Exchange was formed on 1 April 1987 by the merger of the six former state exchanges based in Sydney, Melbourne, Brisbane, Perth, Adelaide and Hobart. The national market provided a more efficient way of accessing the liquidity base from which firms could raise equity. Furthermore, the national exchange now stood in a position to introduce listing requirements that would standardise the level of information available on registered public companies. The new level of transparency and timeliness (especially after the introduction of continuous disclosure rules in the 1990s) and the greater provision of information (accounting information, industry and geographic segments information) improved the pricing of equity on the exchange (potentially lowering the cost of capital).[37] Domestic equity raisings increased fourfold between 1984 and 1987 as firms exploited the hot issue market to fund growth (see Table 6.2). Listed debt also increased in absolute value, although debt listings were less popular as a percentage of total listings between 1986 and 1989.

Three features of the 1980s and 1990s equity market are worth noting. First, equity raisings in 1986, 1987 and 1988 were driven by an increase in the number of initial public offerings. While the corporate leaders certainly raised seasoned equity, new firms came to the market in unprecedented numbers. Second, the listing of new debt on the market was constrained by regulation until the mid-1980s. Previously, only brokers could underwrite debt issues and their size meant that many of the corporate leaders could not raise enough funds domestically.[38] This was to change as merchant banks and other institutions

Table 6.2: Equity and debt raised on the Australian Stock Exchange, 1984–91 ($b)

Year	Shares	Fixed income	Shares (%)
1984	3.5	0.4	89.7
1985	3.6	0.6	85.4
1986	7.0	0.2	97.2
1987	16.1	1.3	92.5
1988	13.4	1.2	91.8
1989	11.0	1.0	91.7
1990	9.1	2.2	80.5
1991	6.6	1.8	78.6

Source: Calculated from Drake and Stammer 'Stock exchange', Table 8.1 p. 286.

were permitted to underwrite debt. We shall examine the impact of the avail-ability of debt on corporate leaders in the next section. Third, corporate leaders could exploit developments and linkages between the domestic and overseas stock markets to cross-list their firms and improve the cost of equity. We briefly examine this feature below.

The dual listing of corporate leaders and other prominent companies has fuelled debate in recent years that the cost of equity on the domestic capital market is higher than that obtained on large overseas markets. This is despite consolidation of the stock markets, increased transparency through listing and disclosure rules, and an increase in institutional (largely superannuation) shareholdings. Dual listings have been shown to lower a firm's risk (and cost of capital), improve investor recognition, provide access to more liquid markets, and offer opportunities to arbitrage tax laws between countries. There have been over 150 dual listings from Australia since 1985, with several firms listing on more than one exchange (the exchanges include Berlin, Frankfurt, London, New York (the New York Stock Exchange and NASDAQ), New Zealand, Tokyo, Toronto and Vancouver).[39] Corporate leaders altering their capital structure by dual listing through American Depositary Receipts on the New York Stock Exchange include Australian and New Zealand Bank, BHP-Billiton, Coles Myer, James Hardie, National Australia Bank, News Corporation, Telstra and Western Mining Corporation. Dual listings on the London Stock Exchange have been undertaken by Ansell (previously Pacific Dunlop), BHP-Billiton, Coles Myer, CSR, Foster's Brewing Group, National Australia Bank, and News Corporation. The equity markets available to the corporate leaders of the 1990s are increasingly integrated across national boundaries, leading to improvements in corporate governance and financing options.

Debt and the certainty of cash flows

Debt raisings have been used to finance expansion throughout the twentieth century, although the ability to raise external debt in the form of debentures was limited in the early decades to the largest firms. Debt holders sought evidence of reliable cash flow to lower the risk of debt provision in a small local market. Debt was attractive to managers because it allowed the funding of strategic development without diluting equity and facing the scrutiny of new shareholders.

A preference for debt over equity is explained by the pecking order theory of Myers and Majluf.[40] When a firm has assets in place and a new project needs finance, management will only issue equity if the transfer of wealth from old to new shareholders is more than offset by the value of the new project.[41] An information asymmetry between managers (who know the value of the new project before financing) and potential equity holders (who must form expectations about the new project) means that equity finance will be issued at a discount, and will decrease the wealth of existing shareholders. Thus, managers who wish to maximise the value of existing shareholders' wealth will finance projects and new strategies in ways that do not make current shareholders worse off.[42]

Gas and electricity suppliers were one of a limited group of corporate leaders in the 1920s and 1930s that could obtain debt financing, because these companies had large capital requirements and could exploit local monopoly conditions to maintain strong cash flows. Retained earnings would not provide the levels of funding needed to establish a fixed asset base of land, buildings, plant and machinery and a distribution network.[43] Australian Gas Light Company and South Australian Gas Company preferred debt to equity and were regular issuers on the nascent domestic debt market. As early as 1904 South Australian Gas had established a borrowing program to finance capacity expansion and physical capital upgrades.[44] Australian Gas Light issued seven-year debentures in 1926 and by 1927 had over £2.0 million in debt.

More generally, Forster shows that electricity and gas companies were able to source between 65 and 85 per cent of their requirements from external markets in the 1920s; total long- and short-term debt comprised 46.2 per cent (electricity) and 36.6 per cent (gas) for these companies in stark contrast to the 19.5 per cent raised in aggregate by manufacturing firms (see Table 6.3). On the whole though, corporate leaders were more likely to raise debt through networks than on the external market until after the Second World War.

A significant change in capital structure decisions by managers of Australian corporate leaders took place in the 1950s with a move to issue debt finance, largely in place of equity. Long-term debt was approximately 2.5 per

Table 6.3: Sources of finance: Electricity and gas companies, 1920–29

Source	Electricity (%)	Gas (%)
Equity (new, seasoned and bonus)	40.2	53.6
Debentures	23.1	31.4
Mortgages/Government loans	17.1	–
Retained earnings	13.7	9.8
Other liabilities	6.0	5.2

Source: Forster, *Industrial Development*, pp. 204–5; *Jobson's Investment Digest*, various years.

cent of funds raised between 1946 and 1948, but this increased to 12.3 per cent in 1949–50. By 1955–56, long-term debt made up 20 per cent of capital raisings. The increased use of debt is illustrated in Figure 6.2 below, where external debt raising is expressed as a percentage of total external financing. Debt comprised 20–30 per cent of external sources during 1950–52, and 55–70 per cent by the late 1950s.

Commentators have attributed the rise in debt financing to the emergence of long-term mortgage finance from insurance companies, the tightness of the new issue market in the 1950s, and changes in regulation favouring the tax benefits to debt.[45] Traditional and new debt issuers exploited the new sources of debt. Australian Gas Light issued debentures in 1950, 1951 and 1953 to fund capital works (a new gas works at Chullora), and to benefit from the tax shield on

Figure 6.2: Debt as a proportion of capital raised per year, 1949–85

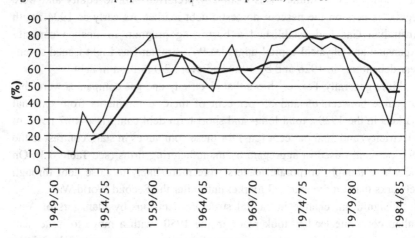

Note: The fitted line represents a five-year moving average.

debt.[46] Boral raised debt finance in 1950 from the City Mutual Life Society (a local life insurance firm) to finance their new strategies refining crude oil.[47] Lend Lease funded its establishment with equity in 1959, but also saw the benefits of the merging debt market by offering successfully its first public debenture.[48] Other important corporate leaders to enter the market included Dunlop and BHP. We examine their experience separately in our description of the emergence of the corporate centre and financial policy.

Corporate leaders have had access to new sources of domestic and overseas debt in more recent years. Most of these sources have been made available by the financial deregulation of the 1980s (such as removal of interest rate controls, banking deregulation, and the floating of the Australian dollar), increased specialisation in the provision of financial services, and the integration of the domestic capital market with major world markets (particularly aided by improvements in information technology). New financial instruments (bank bills, swaps, options, eurobonds, corporate bonds, convertible notes, depositary receipts and dual listings), and greater access to overseas debt and equity markets widened the set of debt–equity combinations.

Figure 6.3 illustrates the change in debt levels of Australia's public companies between 1955 and 1997. The figures are derived from the Reserve Bank of Australia Company Supplement data drawn from the balance sheets of Australian corporations. Using the debt–equity ratios, we have constructed a measure of leverage (the debt-to-total firm value – equity plus debt). Figure 6.3

Figure 6.3: Aggregate leverage ratio, 1955–97

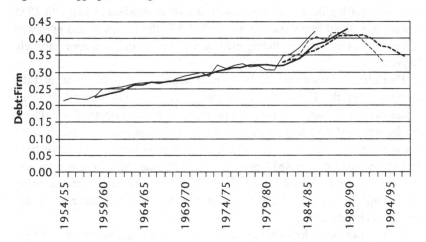

Note: The bold fitted lines represent a five-year moving average.

Source: Calculated from Reserve Bank of Australia data series, various years.

traces a rise in leverage, with the five-year average peaking in the early 1990s. Corporate leaders operated with leverage ratios of around 30 per cent in the early 1970s and these had risen to 40 per cent by 1990.[49] The implication of higher leverage was a decrease in interest coverage throughout the 1980s. Lowe and Shuetrim report interest coverage falling in 1980–83 from 7.1 times to 3.8 times, while Davis shows that median interest coverage between 1982 and 1990 dropped from 3.7 times to 1.9 times (the orders of magnitude are similar). Thus, increased debt and lower interest coverage implied an increase in the financial risk of corporate leaders due to changes in the probability of default. The 'decade of debt' was an apt description for the experience of several of the corporate leaders.

Indeed, the 1980s were to mark the demise of several major firms that had created and maintained competitive advantages throughout most of the century. The availability of new sources of debt and increasing acceptance of higher leverage ratios placed in sharp relief the trade-off corporate leaders could make between debt (and its attractiveness through tax deductibility of interest expenses) and the costs of financial distress. In theory, firms must decide how much debt is appropriate and estimate the costs associated with the probability of default (and potentially bankruptcy).[50] In practice, estimating the certainty of cash flows servicing the debt is an imprecise science.

Acquisitions and market expansions were the most common strategies funded by debt in the 1980s and early 1990s. News Corporation faced debt servicing crises in 1990 and 1991 as downturns in key markets left a gap in working capital and high short-term debt. As share prices fell, the company's bonds were downgraded to near default by Moody's Investor Service. CSR increased gearing during its acquisition and diversification strategy. In 1955 gearing was about one-third. By the early 1980s the company had borrowed heavily so that gearing (including off-balance sheet items) was approximately 50 per cent.

Divestitures during the late 1990s have helped reverse this trend, and the de-merging of the United States building products division from the Australian operations has decreased the pressure of debt servicing. Burns Philp, too, has reversed international expansion after debt was used to acquire bakery and spice businesses internationally. Debt-to-shareholders equity grew from 75 per cent in 1994 to 4674 per cent in 1998, and the company's interest coverage ratio went from 3.4 to 1.3 times. Recent divestitures and restructuring has brought Burns Philp back to reasonable debt levels at the cost of dis-illusioned shareholders.[51]

Two corporate leaders were not able to survive the consequences of a high debt capital structure. Elders IXL funded an aggressive expansion strategy in the 1980s through highly levered transactions. Elders' purchases of Henry

Jones IXL and Carlton & United Breweries in the early 1980s were the start of a strong wave of increasingly audacious manoeuvres. Elders IXL's strategy to 'Fosterise the world' was one example; the role Elders IXL played in the defence of BHP was another. In 1990 the company imploded under heavy debt servicing liabilities and its divisions were divested.

Adelaide Steamship Company also exploited the availability of debt to fund a diversification. Its group structure (see Chapter 7) involved cross-shareholdings between many of the corporate leaders, as we saw in Chapter 5. Adelaide Steamship's CEO, John Spalvins, adopted a strategy of substantial minority controlling positions in these companies, and used inter-company loans, investments and related-party transactions to present the company in a better financial position than it was.[52] Leverage rose substantially at the consolidated company level – debt was 23 per cent of total assets in 1982 and 95 per cent of total assets in 1991, the year of the company's collapse. As Trevor Sykes stated, 'Adsteam for years had been pyramiding debt and disguising the extent through its minority-controlled empire … [It was] increasingly at the mercy of its bankers'.[53]

The increase in demand for debt also had important spillover effects on the domestic finance sector. While it is difficult to determine causation, there is no doubt that the rise in debt was associated with increased financial engineering and specialisation in the finance sector. One example is the rise of merchant banks, which provided financial and corporate advisory services to the corporate leaders.[54] In 1953 merchant banks held less than 0.1 per cent of financial assets in the economy, and by 1989 this share had risen to 8.5 per cent. The major activities of merchant banks were treasury risk management products, helping companies with swaps and options, foreign exchange services (currency trading, currency risk products, futures contracts), futures market trading and trade finance (for example, trading through short-term trade bills).[55]

The entrance of merchant banks into the provision of corporate financial services resulted in a competitive response from the major trading banks to offer such services. Westpac, National Australia Bank and Australian and New Zealand Bank developed new competencies in merchant banking and corporate financial services. AMP also extended its financial services to this market, especially after the merger with Henderson Global (UK). The removal of banking controls and increasing international competition prompted the facilitation of bank bills, swaps, eurobonds and corporate bonds.

The development of the bank bill market allowed borrowers to construct a sequence of short-term bills at preferential interest rates to gain a long-term loan with a floating rate. Bank bills were available for the corporate leaders who had strong relationships with their banks, and raising debt in the bank bill market provided the firm with a 'bank certification' of high quality.[56] Secondary private debt markets have also developed to satisfy a demand by institutional investors for quality non-government debt. Shell Australia raised $150 million in the first corporate bond in January 1988 at a coupon rate of 12.5 per cent for three years. In the next two years there were 58 corporate bond issues by 21 separate issuers – the majority were financial institutions and finance companies and all but a few had high credit ratings (AA– or better).[57]

The capital structure decision: The role of the head office and the emergence of a corporate financial policy

Since the 1950s, finance market developments have provided corporate leaders with opportunities to financially engineer funding and increase the value of the firm. Corporate leaders could leverage the firm to a greater extent than before to exploit tax shields and fund expansion at more acceptable terms. It was no longer necessary to construct synthetic debt instruments using equity and a constant dividend ratio – debt was available (at least for public firms) in the capital structure decision. The evidence in this chapter is that Australian corporate leaders took the opportunity to increase leverage presented by changes in market regulations and the public's willingness to invest. However, retained earnings, depreciation allowances and trade credit were still the most important sources of finance for many firms, and firms with less tangible assets called on the equity market for finance. We should not give the impression that the 1950s and 1960s were decades of debt. But when Comalco and Hamersley Holdings issued eurobonds for the first time in late 1970 and 1971 no one could argue that Australian corporate leaders were not slowly obtaining the financing options only previously available to their United States' and United Kingdom counterparts.

Two corporate leaders exemplify the way in which corporate financing was becoming a value-added exercise in itself, and the choice between equity, debt and retained earnings was made with reference to the firms' ability to arbitrage between the relative costs of capital. However, in one case – Dunlop – management's experience in the new era of highly geared organisations proved inadequate. In the other we see how a judicious use of debt by a monopoly – BHP – could add value.

Dunlop's diversification strategy was designed to widen the company's earnings base away from rubber products. From the early 1960s the company increased exposure to footwear and garments, bedding, automotive products and flooring. These acquisition activities were financed with debt. Unsecured notes were issued in four tranches in 1966 at between 7.25 per cent and 7.75 per cent, payable in various years from 1973 to 1986. Dunlop returned to the debt market in 1969 and 1971, issuing secured debentures at rates varying between 7 per cent and 8 per cent.[58] As debt mounted and cash flows were directed towards financing the debt burden, the management of Dunlop was forced into a cost-cutting strategy to maintain profitability. Between 1966 and 1972 the company reduced its dividend payout ratio from 95 per cent to 65 per cent. Interest coverage (calculated here as profit after tax divided by interest on fixed-term loans) fell from 20 times in 1966 to 5.35 times in 1969 and 2.35 times in 1972. In 1974–75 Dunlop closed factories, put companies into liquidation and withdrew from textiles and fashion-related industries.[59]

BHP had a strong history of financing expansion through retained earnings and periodic equity issues. From the mid-1960s it was involved in a number of mineral ventures, which formed part of a diversification strategy into iron ore and pellets, crude oil and natural gas exploration and production. The company's development of the oil and gas discoveries in the offshore Gippsland Basin was undertaken in partnership with Esso Exploration and Production, a subsidiary of Standard Oil (USA). The Esso partnership gave BHP access to finance 'on reasonable terms … without in any way affecting the company's equity in the venture'.[60] Additional requirements would be funded from retained earnings and a new capital raising source – debentures.

Debentures were not commonly used by BHP before the 1960s. The first public debenture was issued in March 1962 (£21.6 million at 7 per cent maturing in 1977 and 1987) on the Australian market, and June 1962 (£A9.2 million in sterling at 6.75 per cent) on the London market. Debt was used more frequently from that year, with further issues in 1966 and 1968 to fund the diversification strategy.

Unlike Dunlop, BHP's use of debt did not increase the company's debt burden to a point where interest payments were a major concern. BHP's leverage ratio (long-term debt to long-term shareholders' funds – shareholders' funds plus long-term debt) increased from 14.1 per cent in 1959 to 20 per cent in 1968. However, net tangible assets per share increased from $3.32 (1959) to $6.22 (1968) and interest coverage was approximately four times (reduced from 20 times in 1959; 4.5 times in 1963 and 3.9 times in 1968). These data show that asset growth and profitability supported the higher debt burden. In addition, throughout the 1960s BHP continued to pay a dividend between 6 per cent and 9 per cent and a return on shareholders' funds of 6 per cent to 7 per cent.

Conclusion

The financing decisions of Australian corporate leaders were influenced by the institutional structure of domestic finance markets, the Australian regulatory regime, and the ability of firms to exploit market positions to generate retained earnings. The four major sources of finance varied in relative importance during the twentieth century, although retained earnings and other internal sources of finance were the major source of finance throughout the period. Also important were network sources of finance. We have described how the corporate leaders used loose and tight networks to fill gaps in the external capital markets.

Equity finance was used to finance large capital expenditures for the first half of the twentieth century. In order to reduce the riskiness of equity for shareholders, firms adopted high dividend payout ratios. This behaviour provided equity holders with constant dividend streams and gave equity debt characteristics. From the 1950s, however, firms increasingly choose debt over equity and the proportion of equity financing declined from approximately 25 per cent of capital raising in 1950–61 to 10–15 per cent during 1967–71. Again, the use of equity finance varied by industry, with some industries able to exploit windows of opportunity on equity markets to raise finance. Debt financing rose in importance between the 1950s and 1970s. In terms of external sources (equity or debt), debt was preferred – debt as a proportion of total external capital raising rose from 13 per cent in 1949–50 to between 60 and 70 per cent in the late 1960s. A second wave of debt financing took place in the 1980s as the Australian economy was deregulated. The average leverage (debt-to-firm value) ratios rose from 30 to 40 per cent, placing great strain on the cash flows of large conglomerate firms.

The patterns of financing adopted by corporate leaders to achieve their corporate goals can be explained by the desire to exploit a hierarchy of funding options (a pecking order), and limit the level of agency costs in the firm. Retained earnings, debt and equity were used in decreasing importance to fund corporate growth. Prior to these developments, managers were limited in the choice of financing options (due to underdeveloped debt and equity markets) and had to signal to equity holders high quality through their dividend payout reputation. More recently, the international integration of domestic equity and debt markets has relieved the financing constraints on the corporate leaders.

CHAPTER 7

Organisational Configuration and Corporate Governance

Organisational configuration consists of the structures, processes, relationships and boundaries through which a company operates. They are influenced by the strategic options adopted by managers, the technological features of the company and its industry, the stage of life of the company, and its external environment. Thus, we have left the analysis of organisational configurations to the end of our study in order to examine the features of design and structure that are associated with longevity and big business.

Australian corporate leaders demonstrated many of the trends identified in studies of overseas developments in the corporate economy. Corporate leaders in several sectors invested in science-based technologies to exploit economies of scale, and expanded into products and markets through the use of multi-divisional structures. We describe these developments in organisational con-figuration as companies developed core and related markets through horizontal and vertical integration.

Australian corporate leaders also faced unique geographical conditions that meant they had to deal with coordination problems and information flows over large distances if they wished to achieve national coverage. Pastoral agents, banks, retailers and property companies leveraged core competencies and repli-cated expertise across multiple sites, leading to an 'organic' multidivisional organisation. The size of the local market prevented companies from estab-lishing scale in any other way.

Another point of differentiation from international experience was the position of multinational subsidiaries in providing demonstration effects to domestic firms. While these corporate leaders were constrained in growth strategies by overseas parents, they provided a window to international best practice in production organisation and management techniques. Finally, we examine the trend of unrelated diversification in Australia in the 1960s and 1970s, and discuss how the poor estimation of benefits and costs for these structures led to their demise.

The second section of the chapter examines the interrelationships between strategic decisions, organisational configuration and the governance of the company. We examine the basic features of the governance of the corporate leaders to assess the extent to which external review of management behaviour has changed over the period. Data on share ownership concentration, the structure of remuneration contracts for management and directors, and the size and composition of the board of directors, all suggest that Australian corporate leaders faced greater scrutiny by a market-based corporate governance system by the 1990s.

Organisational configurations: Some concepts

Organisational configurations involve the physical location of production and office space, work activities (the performance of tasks of the company), the processes of delivering product to market, structural design factors (the roles and boundaries of responsibility of managers and staff, and lines of reporting), and information systems (the coordination of horizontal and vertical information in the company and between the company and its market environment).

Organisations have received attention from researchers in such diverse fields as economics, finance, law, organisational theory and organisational psychology. As a result, we know much about the benefits and costs of various configurations and their impact on human behaviour.[1] One aspect of organisational configurations worth dwelling on is the organisational structure adopted by companies in the allocation of resources.

Functional groupings and divisional groupings are the two most common forms of organisational structure. Unitary functional structures (often termed U-forms) are based upon the primary activities that have to be performed by the company in order for it to maintain profitability. The structure involves a single department responsible for each of the basic business functions – production, research and development, sales and marketing, finance and accounting, and personnel. The focus is on individual business processes suitable to a stable environment where there is a low level of uncertainty. The functional structure allows the company to exploit economies of scale with functional departments, promote in-depth skill development (and concomitant professional training, staff manuals and so forth), and add new tasks as the company grows. Functional responsibilities can be clearly defined and mapped into key performance criteria (often leading to the establishment of performance indicators, functional budgets and statistical reports). Internal control for the head office is made easier by the fact that individuals are grouped within a common department and come to share similar backgrounds, norms of behaviour, goals and performance standards. However, the functional structure can be inefficient in dealing with the diversity and requirements of coordination between departments. Over time, functional structures may face decreasing benefit–cost ratios as the company alters strategy.

Multidivisional structures (M-forms) comprise a set of autonomous divisions led by a corporate head office. Divisions may be organised by product, customers, geography or related business units (or a combination of these). Divisions, in turn, may be a grouping of inter-related sub-units organised along functional lines (or again, on a divisional basis). A multidivisional corporation, for example, may divisionalise by geography (American, European and Asia-Pacific) and then by product and function. The benefit–cost ratio of M-form structures rises as the company increases in size and faces a changing market environment and moderate to high levels of uncertainty.

The M-form allows the company to focus on strategic business units, satisfy market-specific demand and adapt to new competitive challenges. Resource allocation in the company is facilitated by improved measurement of overall performance at the divisional level. The reduction of exogenous factors (to the division) influencing performance allows a more efficient use of pay-for-performance compensation and a reduction in agency costs. Divisional accountability and resource allocation across divisions are undertaken by a corporate head office that provides strategic advice and parenting.

The extent of head office involvement in divisional operations will vary depending upon a range of factors, including information dissemination, location, strategic importance to the company and interpersonal relationships. In sum, the M-form provides transactions cost minimising advantages to a company as it increases in size, but may introduce bureaucracy and agency costs associated with scale (for example, added management process complexity, competition and rent-seeking within the company).

Several other organisational structural types fall under the functional and divisional groupings. Matrix structures can take the form of product and geographical divisions operating in tandem, because knowledge of both areas is important for the company to achieve strategic growth. A multinational may structure itself as individual working groups that have product and geography lines of reporting in order to complete a particular project or provide a service (for example, mining projects requiring country-specific skills and technology skills). The matrix structure arises when the economies to scale and scope provide a rationale to organise along more than one division. It permits the allocation of scarce human specific capital to various products and improves the company's ability to deal with diverse market demand.

A holding company structure (H-form) is further decentralised than the M-form. It consists of a single investment company with shareholdings in a variety of businesses, often unrelated to each other. The H-form offers benefits to the constituent divisions through autonomy in decision-making and opportunities for greater brand recognition. The holding company head office has little strategic or operational involvement in the underlying businesses, and most often relinquishes control after a threshold financial return is achieved. Holding company structures can be driven by legal and taxation benefits or through their ability to diversify income streams to lower risk for ultimate owners. However, such structures can sometimes lack internal strategic cohesion and involve the replication of functional tasks across businesses.

Determinants of organisational configurations

The decision by management to configure the company in a particular way is determined by the company's life cycle, external environment, technology and strategic direction. The life cycle of the company is linked closely to organisational configuration because company growth and development have implications for the level of formalisation and elaboration of activities. As the company increases in size, the number of management levels increase, leading to vertical complexity and greater formalisation of communication. The installation and use of rules, procedures and control systems alter human interaction and create internal labour markets. Management control functions are introduced to better coordinate departments and the allocation of rewards and promotions. Our study here, by design, focuses on companies that are deemed to be corporate leaders because they are large and manifest longevity. Many of the managerial decisions associated with configuration as the company grew from its establishment to possess a leadership position are therefore out of our gaze. Where life cycle impinges upon strategy and configuration we shall pause to comment.

The external environment has a major impact on the benefit–cost ratio associated with various organisational configurations. The environment impacts on the needs of managers for information about internal processes (and external markets) and the need for resources in order to sustain competitive advantage. Environmental uncertainty may be driven by the features of the economy, social patterns, technological developments (both at an industry and economy-wide level), law and regulation.

Corporate leaders faced change over the twentieth century in all these areas. Thus, post-World War Two population growth created different environmental factors in comparison with the 1920s. Similarly, deregulation increased openness of the economy and the information technology advances in the late twentieth century meant that managers in the 1990s faced different constraints on configuration decisions than previously.

Apart from these broad structural changes, companies may face different levels of change and uncertainty as determined by demand factors, industry specific technology and so forth. The speed of change in markets alters the relationships between suppliers and customers, and may break down barriers to entry. A new competitive rivalry and the strategic responses by firms imply re-examination of the most appropriate organisational configuration. Chandler, in *Scale and Scope*, examines organisational capabilities and configurations according to how companies experienced technological change or were able to create market stability through oligopolistic structures. Similarly, we shall analyse how the corporate leaders adopted configurations that allowed them to deal effectively with unstable environments (where relevant) and uncertainty. In a small, mixed industrial economy the organisational configuration utilised to sustain competitive advantage may well be different from those commonly adopted for the United States, the United Kingdom and Germany.

The technological features of the company and its industry imply different organisational configurations. The characteristics of technology influence the nature of task interdependence in the company, and the requirements for efficient processing of information. Manufacturing firms may apply high levels of specialisation to the production process, and organise in a sequential form where interaction between individuals and/or divisions is determined by the completion of tasks from one stage to another. Originally a functional structure (U-form) may be the best configuration. However, over time the need for an M-form arises. As technology and external market factors change we may observe the necessity for a new organisational configuration. Rapid changes in market demand may dictate a new strategy of differentiating products or working more closely with customers. The M-form structure allows for changes to an unstable environment, where decentralised decision-making has a higher benefit–cost ratio than the functional form. Thus, technology (capital intensive production, assembly lines) and information processing are suitable for multi-functional, multidivisional, multi-product structures operating in different geographical regions (as Chandler shows). The addition of new units (geography, markets, products) allows maintenance of 'a long term rate of return on investment by reducing overall costs of production and distribution'.[2]

Strategy influences organisational configuration because it determines the application of costs and benefits to various features of the configuration. Chandler's description of the changes in industrial capitalism in the United States after 1920 shows that the U-form possesses a lower benefit–cost ratio than the M-form as companies grew in size, specialised in function, and sought expansion into multi-products and new markets. The strategy of product diversification required a flexible organisational configuration in order to improve response times to market changes, permit decentralised decision-making and streamline control systems via the establishment of profit centres and head office specialisation. A strategy of mass product delivery and standardisation in retail, however, is better configured through franchising (as we have seen in fast food, service delivery and so forth) than by a multidivisional structure that may have high information coordination costs across divisions.

Organisational configurations of Australian corporate leaders

We have examined how corporate leaders captured scale economies through investment in science-based technologies, sought control of strategic assets and leveraged knowledge in service industries. These strategies provided corporate leaders with a market dominance that proved difficult to compete away. Scale economies were generated in technologically intensive manufacturing (although not to the extent seen in the United States) and in marketing, management deployment and information use. Corporate leaders consolidated early mover advantages by developing vertical linkages in the economy. These linkages enabled corporate leaders to secure sequential activities in emergent industries (to secure supply or maintain marketing and service standards), avoid contract hold-up (given asset specificity in production) and create barriers to entry.

Both horizontal and vertical integration had important implications for the management of corporate leaders. New strategic directions required careful implementations to ensure the firm would be successful, and that the strategy provided the required financial objectives once bedded down. Corporate leaders' organisational structure, internal processes and management activities needed to be revised and improved in order to ensure a smooth transition to scale, or to coordinate the production process (and information flows) between stages in the supply chain.

The organisational configuration of corporate leaders was linked to the path of strategic growth. Most corporate leaders adopted functional organisational configurations in the early phase of their growth in order to obtain operational efficiencies at each stage of the production process and management of the firm. Achieving scale brought with it new challenges, most commonly the geographical diversification of the organisation to seek strategic assets, reap economies of scale through multi-plant operations, or leverage knowledge.

For many corporate leaders, a multi-site U-form was sufficient to maintain market leadership. This was the case for corporate leaders in industries where scale allowed the erection of barriers to entry. The small scale of the local market, however, meant that many corporate leaders achieved scale through geographical diversification early in their life cycle. A multidivisional organisational configuration was part of organic growth and a logical development for the firm. This 'organic multidivisionality' was the appropriate structural design for corporate leaders investing in strategic assets or leveraging knowledge.

A third organisational configuration can be seen in the unrelated diversification strategies adopted by corporate leaders as they attempted to counter the decline in traditional markets. Multidivisional structures were adopted by default by corporate leaders in order to diversify income streams or capture economies of scope. At the extreme, holding company structures were adopted for financial and taxation purposes, and disparate divisions held on the basis of the specific investment case.

Scale, geographical expansion and multidivisionality

The strategic decision to create scale and capture early mover advantages involved analysing the benefits and costs of geographical expansion. The size of local and state markets were often insufficient to warrant the company investing in production capacity. A larger, national market permitted corporate leaders to adopt techniques and facilities that would lower average production costs and increase the minimum efficient scale of the firm. Some corporate leaders were able to achieve scale and specialisation by concentrating production to a few key locations. We will examine mining and gas to illustrate these corporate leaders. For others (financial services, retail and wholesale trade, and real estate), the organisational configuration for scale involved a functional structure that allowed the replication of technology and knowledge across branches. Finally, we examine how multinational subsidiaries in the transport and chemical industries achieved scale and the benefits and synergies from being located within a larger organisational configuration.

'Let's get physical': Scale and capital intensity

A small number of corporate leaders in Australia were able to obtain scale by investing in physical capital. Their organisational configuration was initially functional, with a hybrid multidivisional structure evolving as new projects and specific sites were developed. The leading mining companies invested heavily in industrial and management science to improve their competitive position. BHP expanded horizontal and vertical boundaries simultaneously. Its CEO, Essington Lewis, implemented a cost-oriented strategy to focus attention on scale and transactions economies. This involved appropriating overseas technology and modifying it to local conditions. Over time, the core competencies associated with 'experience, technical know-how and financial skills' (along with its ability to access political circles and negotiate with governments), allowed BHP to 'dominate the management of new mining projects'.[3] In gold mining, Western Mining Corporation also extracted economies across separated operations (usually mines) by centralising treatment plants and duplicating standard processes.[4] New techniques applied to gold mining included aerial and geological surveying and below-surface exploration methods.

Business growth involved expanding the boundaries of the firm as new mineral deposits and market opportunities arose. This growth involved geographical expansion on a project basis due to the fact that mineral deposits and other strategic assets (for example, harbours) were scarce resources. BHP, Western Mining Corporation, Mount Isa Mining and Conzinc Riotinto Australia developed organisational configurations that permitted efficient knowledge transfer between project sites and stages of the production process, and yet provided devolution of decision-making to enable the solution of immediate problems. Functional configurations allowed specialisation and experience benefits to be captured and exploited in these firms. BHP duplicated functional departments across steel mills in Newcastle and Port Kembla.[5] Western Mining Corporation operated identical plants, centralising the purchase and distribution of plant and spares.[6] Conzinc Riotinto Australia's specialities in smelting processes were extended across new plants as they were acquired or constructed.[7] So long as core markets were the focus of the business, mining companies maintained functional organisations. Related diversification in the 1960s was to lead to reconfiguration.

In the gas industry, early mover advantages from government franchises and capital intensity provided Australian Gas Light Company and South Australian Gas Company with incentives to extract economies from specialist functions. In the early twentieth century, Australian Gas Light established departments such as gas sales, testing and research, and general services to reap economies. Further functional specialisation took place in the 1920s and the 1930s with the formation of general management positions. Staff training and management information systems were introduced to provide better coordination of office methods and procedures (and in the 1930s to improve monitoring in a difficult economic climate).[8]

South Australian Gas Company faced a different market environment in South Australia, leading the company to be slower to devolve management tasks across departments. Senior management was dominated by a close oligarchy well connected in South Australian industry and politics. Even after nationalisation in the late 1940s the company's board experienced little turnover. A strong local market position and lack of need for shareholder accountability (apart from to the government) allowed South Australian Gas Company to perpetuate a simple functional structure longer than would have been the case in a more contestable market.

Scale and organising across multiple locations

Scale and geographical expansion are intricately linked for Australian corporate leaders. A small economy and dispersed groups of local markets created coordination and organisational complexities early on for firms wishing to capture scale advantages. While geography created the need for replicating core competencies across locations, it also provided a barrier to entry of an early mover that had obtained national coverage.

Shipping companies were among the earliest corporate leaders to establish economies of scale and adopt national coverage as a barrier to entry. Adelaide Steamship Company, Huddart Parker and Howard Smith enjoyed legacy positions in shipping from the late nineteenth century. They maintained single function configurations during much of the twentieth century to exploit economies from their shipping fleets. Adelaide Steamship Company, for example, appointed local branch managers in ports where traffic levels justified a corporate presence – Fremantle, Sydney and Melbourne. At other locations they used non-company agents, a cost effective method of competing with emerging transport technologies such as road and air transport, at least until the period after World War Two.

Financial service providers, such as pastoral agencies and banks, operated branch networks to capture early mover advantages from scale. Knowledge and service skills were replicated across the company. This expansion and sub-sequent diversification into related products required these corporate leaders to configure as multidivisional structures early in their strategic growth. Pastoral agencies diversified services in the early twentieth century and maintained functional departments such as livestock, wool and produce, in addition to finance. These departments were interdependent, in that the provision of pastoral services involved coordination to satisfy market demand. Manage-ment information systems were developed to enable vertical information flows from head office to branch managers and between agents in the branch. This facilitated accurate measurement of client risk.[9] Horizontal information flows were less efficiently organised, with agencies often repeating mistakes in different parts of the organisation.[10] Nevertheless, hybrid functional and geo-graphical M-form structures permitted agencies to develop specialist know-ledge and techniques that could be institutionalised and codified. Branch networking added management complexity as pastoral agents introduced additional tiers to the organisation.

During the interwar period, state branches were used to decentralise the responsibility of service provision, and (much like Australian Gas Light Company in the gas industry) allow clear monitoring of regional performance. Task specialisation was increased, with corporate head office taking on a greater strategic management role. Elders, for example, built up a corporate head office staff in the 1940s and increasingly differentiated this from the South Australian state branch. Dalgety was a pioneer of manager conferences in the 1920s – a forum that brought state managers together to discuss corporate issues. Management conferences were a regular feature of most pastoral agencies by the 1950s. Standard practice manuals were also developed in the 1950s to delineate responsibilities within the company, routinise tasks and maintain continuity of practice.[11]

Banks obtained national coverage of retail products by establishing new branches and acquiring smaller competitors. Each branch operated independently of the others, with head office ensuring the company exploited economies and learning advantages. The Bank of New South Wales board were able to coordinate the activities of an extensive branch network that spanned Australia, New Zealand and the Pacific Islands by the 1950s.

Banks were forerunners in constructing centralised bureaucratic structures in Australia. Knowledge was codified and manuals written to ensure that branches followed the rules of business and reported regularly to centralised headquarters. Head office was supported by a series of state offices that had oversight of activities within their territory and which maintained an internal audit function through state 'inspectors'. While the organisational configuration was relatively flat in a structural sense (head office, state offices and branches), reporting and staff roles were very hierarchical. Banks operated complex internal labour markets and invested in staff training, performance review procedures and career development.[12]

Functional specialisation in banking (and insurance) also led to the pioneering of back office mechanisation. AMP was using punched cards to process data as early as 1924; computers were applied to insurance functions in the 1950s.[13] Ledger machines were used in some banks before World War Two, and were commonplace in the 1950s. The ability of these machines to 'read' magnetic tape presaged the widespread use of computers in trading banks from the 1960s. Indeed, both banks and insurance companies now rely on computers to capture, process, store and retrieve information in ways that allow them to offer a wider range of products and reduce processing costs.

Early movers in the retail and wholesale trades were also faced with replicating technology and knowledge across multiple locations. Wholesale traders like Burns Philp operated geographically dispersed businesses, given their competencies in logistics and trade. A branch network not dissimilar to that in the financial services sector was adopted to coordinate trading stations across the South Pacific. By 1935 Burns Philp reported having 'nearly sixty branches ... about a dozen small businesses and eighteen to twenty chain stores'.[14] Similarly, Robert Reid operated trading houses in each state capital, although the company refocused to the Sydney and Melbourne markets by 1940.

Wholesale traders may have been structurally similar to financial services, but they were less successful in implementing and operating multi-location functional divisions. At Burns Philp, each branch manager was required to submit an annual report to head office, receiving periodic inspections and appraisal. But the range of tasks and functions for a wholesale trading company was far greater than the process and function-driven banking environment. It was difficult to codify reporting or to obtain timely information on the activities of the branches. Burns Philp experienced 'grave management problems ... Remote control from Sydney was frequently unsatisfactory' and inspections of remote locations went amiss.[15] Burns Philp's response to these management challenges was to eschew centralised management and devolve responsibility with a multidivisional structure.

Retailers moved organically to multidivisional structures as they sought scale to secure competitive advantage. As we have described earlier, centrally located department stores were able to establish brand advantages and greater variety over suburban rivals as mass transit systems delivered increased store numbers. Specialist functions in department stores included buyer functions, warehousing and delivery, store layout and design, as well as the application of science to customer relations and human resource management. These skills were then leveraged across the new chain store structure. Myer and David Jones established national coverage after World War Two in order to exploit economies of scale and scope. Related diversification in the 1960s into the grocery trade required a move to a multidivisional form – a move we shall examine soon.

The experience of L. J. Hooker and Lend Lease (in real estate), and Humes (building products), in establishing economies of scale and national presence differed from the patterns we have described thus far. L. J. Hooker pioneered franchising in 1968 as an organisational configuration to leverage brand in the real estate market. Franchises allowed L. J. Hooker to exploit the local knowledge of real estate agents, and solve agency problems by encouraging links between ownership and control. It gave the company economies of scale in marketing and promotion, and permitted head office (or the master franchiser) control over a geographically dispersed network.

Lend Lease adopted a product-based approach to organisational growth, which had a major impact on the configuration of the company. Critical paths in design and construction of buildings were not dissimilar to those faced by the mining industry. Lend Lease configured itself in the late 1950s to support the 'Design and Construct' strategy: functional divisions associated with various stages of the construction process to ensure minimisation of hold-up in key phases. Priority was placed on the application of leading edge management and financial techniques to Lend Lease's operations.[16] Chief executive officer Dusseldorp's experiences of management education courses (with Harvard) in 1957 inculcated a belief in the importance of expanding the company's human capital (from 1962 professional management courses were a permanent feature of Lend Lease training).

International expansion involved the replication of the design and construct model, usually through the award of a major construction contract. In building products, Humes Ltd pioneered centrifugal technology for the production of reinforced concrete pipes. After replicating its technology in production sites around the country (using a functional configuration), Humes internationalised.[17] Overseas subsidiaries in Singapore (1922) and New Zealand (1923) were managed in similar fashion to Australian state plants, given similarities in political systems and cultural outlook derived from a common colonial link to Britain.

Scale and multinational subsidiaries

Multinational subsidiaries were restricted in changing their organisational configurations by the broad set of strategic goals of the parent. While these companies became some of Australia's largest corporate leaders, they did not adopt the multi-product divisional configurations of successful big business in the United States, the United Kingdom or Continental Europe. To this extent, the multinational subsidiaries had no demonstration effect on domestic firms in terms of structure. What the multinational subsidiaries did provide was an open window to international management practices that influenced the non-structural aspects of a company's configuration – the rules, procedures, information systems, and the application of management science. Furthermore, as several authors have demonstrated, the subsidiaries facilitated the transmission of new technology and knowledge to the Australian economy.[18]

The corporate leaders of the automobile industry maintained functional configurations as part of American-owned corporations. General Motors-Holden's was closely monitored by the General Motors Corporation to avoid agency problems; senior managers were sent to Australia from head office, and approval was required for major capital expenditures and new models.[19] Only after a period of time did head office acknowledge local skills and ability, and harnessed that human capital for the rest of the organisation.

General Motors-Holden's has been 'functionally divided' throughout its history. Directorships of manufacturing, marketing and finance existed in 1931, and the first chief engineer position and the Supply and Materials department were created in 1934. Later, design, quality control and 'reliability' were separate departments.[20] The production techniques and plant design transferred to Australia from United States experience dictated close functional relationships between departments. Sequential dependence in the production process was high, in order to economise on transaction costs associated with coordination and information flows. Thus, a functional organisation provided a configuration 'equilibrium' for the company.

Coordination failure did occur however. Local management, striving to operate the company in the Australian conditions, had to tread carefully. In the late 1940s, for example, CEO Hartnett's insubordination led to his departure from the firm.[21] Other managers felt constrained but worked within the multinational structure. Perhaps the most notable coordination failure was a decline in quality in the late 1970s and early 1980s that almost bankrupted the company. Head office–subsidiary relationships were more than once strained over design issues and market strategy in Australia. The parent replaced managing directors, rationalised product ranges (causing the subsidiary to rationalise plants across the country), and forced adoption of international technology. Demonstrations of local market knowledge and the strategic benefits of an Australian base for Asian exports changed the balance of power between head office and subsidiary in the 1990s, making General Motors-Holden's an integral part of the multinational's future international presence.

Chemical and petroleum companies operated continuous production facilities based upon exploiting strategic assets. Most of Australia's corporate leaders in this industry were multinational subsidiaries whose strategic development was determined by the broader regional aspirations of the parent organisation. In petroleum the functional divisions within the production process were managed and coordinated by cross-shareholding relationships of separate companies. Thus, the Esso–Mobil grouping saw different marketing companies operating at the retail end of the market (Mobil Oil Australia and Esso Australia) while refining and exploration were jointly owned. Chemical companies made up the affiliates to exploit petrochemicals, synthetics and related markets. Similar relationships can be seen between multinationals such as British Petroleum, Caltex and Imperial Chemical Industries, and Australian subsidiaries of affiliated companies. Product developments and technological innovations were transferred from overseas markets to Australia through the subsidiary-affiliate network. Benefits in terms of project financing, capital transfer, and management of supplies were captured by the Australian industry. Imperial Chemical Industries of Australia and New Zealand, for example, undertook major related expansion into paint, explosives, dyes, plastics and other chemicals.

The ability of Australian chemical and petroleum companies to adopt a strategic growth path outside the wider corporate plan was severely limited. Most often, economies of scale in production were limited by the local market and parent companies limited growth outside Australia. One exception was Boral, the bitumen manufacturer that pulled itself out of its strategic relationship with Caltex to expand into related markets in refining, LPG distribution, and road surfacing.[22] Boral's 'transformation' to a major building products manufacturer operating a multidivisional, international company was based upon capturing industry-specific knowledge and having the flexibility to adapt products to new markets. Freedom to take management decisions in the face of changes in market conditions was not given to other companies in the chemicals and petroleum industry. These corporate leaders have been constrained to their core markets.

Vertical integration and related diversification: Creating synergies between divisions

Vertical integration and hybrid configurations

Corporate leaders vertically integrated to consolidate early mover advantages. As we described in chapter 4, the small Australian market rarely provided sufficient supply or demand to sustain a single large firm at one stage of the production process. Vertical integration also built entry barriers against potential competitors. In order to achieve vertical integration, the organisational configuration of the corporate leaders needed to efficiently coordinate stages in the supply chain. Thus, we find hybrid functional structures in many industries as companies tried to reconcile the specialisation advantages of scale and investments in technology with new divisions. There was often no conscious managerial decision to reorganise the company along a pure multidivisional structure. Rather, hybrid multidivisional configurations (with mixtures of geography, product and function) evolved in an organic way to reduce agency problems across related divisions. The belated internationalisation of the corporate leaders from the 1980s (we have already noted the exceptions to this) added nuances to these configurations.

Food, drink and tobacco companies maintained functional and hybrid M-form structures up to the 1950s. These companies obtained scale and competitive advantage by adopting a 'pure' Chandlerian strategy of being first to install science-based high technology and improved efficiencies by the application of science. CSR placed technical efficiency high in the set of corporate goals. Chemical engineers made several scientific discoveries in the 1880s and 1890s that resulted in major cost reductions and improvements in product quality. From 1884 the company commenced 'a system of chemical book-keeping in regard to the work of the mills' and chemical staff were given more responsibility in the control and organisation of manufacturing.[23] Colonial Sugar Refinery expanded into related products in the 1930s in order to exploit markets for by-products from the refinery process. By the 1950s the company was configured as a hybrid functional organisation with many 'classic' U-form attributes (see Figure 7.1).

Figure 7.1: Organisation of CSR headquarters

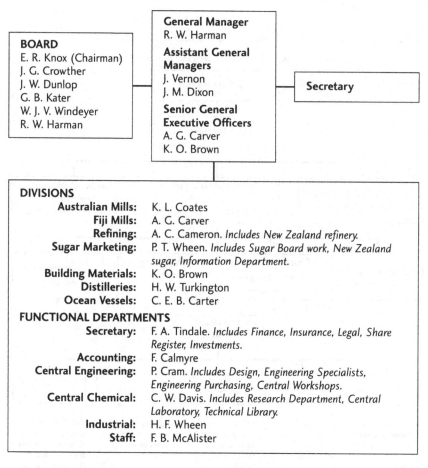

INDUSTRIAL CHEMICALS
The company's interests are represented by 60% ownership of CSR Chemicals Pty Ltd.
Board: E. R. Knox, Chairman; R. W. Harman; J. Vernon; Sir Graham Hayman (Alternate – L. J. Thompson); E. Stein (Alternate – L. W. Sweetman); **General Manager** – A. J. Jarratt.

Source: Harman in Lowndes (ed.), *South Pacific Enterprise*, p. 242.

It had seven divisions and six functional departments at head office. Each division was organised by function. Functional specialisation also existed at the divisional level where the company operated multiple sites. The Australian milling division's (see Figure 7.2) responsibilities were organised in two tiers – divisional tasks (that appeared across all mills) and mill tasks (at the specific site). This functional specialisation implied a developed internal labour market in the company, with 65 per cent of salaried staff engaged directly from school 'to become chemists, clerks or engineering apprentices'. There were 19 staff categories in 1956 for the 1056 salaried staff; a further 9000-odd workers were contract waged.[24]

Figure 7.2: Organisation of CSR Australian milling division

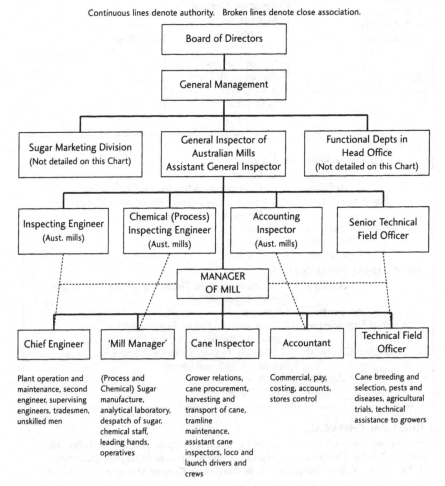

Continuous lines denote authority.   Broken lines denote close association.

Source: Harman in Lowndes (ed.), *South Pacific Enterprise*, opp. p. 242.

Carlton & United Breweries operated in a relatively stable competitive environment. The formation of the brewery combine allowed the introduction of superior capital-intensive, science-based technologies in brewing and packaging. The organisational configuration was designed to enhance managerial control over the integrated production process. In the 1950s the company operated with specialist managers in brewing, engineering and property, reflecting the process of getting beer to market. Little had changed by the 1980s, except that the levels of hierarchy had increased due to the company's size. New functions such as marketing, industrial relations, personnel and public affairs reflected increased managerial specialisation and the use of management techniques in all aspects of the business.

Stable monopoly market conditions also allowed British Tobacco to organise along functional lines. The original holding company was formed by the principal importers and manufacturers in 1904 to control the market and avoid 'destructive competition'.[25] It operated with a single distribution company and forced single line selling and sale of goods conditions on retailers until the 1950s, when the tobacco multinationals entered the market. By the mid-1960s the company had factories across all mainland states and a national network of warehouses. Nevertheless, its configuration did little to protect it from the more efficient international competitors, and it rapidly lost market share, forcing a new, unrelated diversification strategy.

In paper, Australian Paper Manufacturers integrated backwards in the 1920s with mergers and acquisitions into paper mills. The strategy was motivated by a desire to reduce reliance on imported pulp and establish Australia's first integrated pulp and paper mill. During the early stages of strategic growth little decision-making power was delegated to senior managers. As Sinclair reports, the 'board habit of acting a management role lasted a long time' in order to transfer scarce paper-making and management skills.[26] By the 1940s, however, functional departments had been established and management responsibility delegated to departmental managers of research and development, financial, sales, engineering and personnel. In research and development matters, departmental managers reported to two chemists in head office who were assisting the managing director.

Scientists were also closely involved in the organisational development of Australian Consolidated Industries. Functional divisions were established early (in the 1910s and 1920s) to facilitate specialisation in glass manufacturing. The company's ability to secure domestic patents of key overseas technology, and transfer skills to a domestic workforce from overseas specialists cemented its industry position. Specialist technology and know-how was transferred to the firm from the early appointment of United States experts to manage local plants.[27]

In media, the Herald & Weekly Times and News Corporation maintained functional specialisation between departments in the company. The time schedules involved in print media implied that transaction cost benefits could be obtained from specialisation. Thus, production (purchases, journalism, advertising, printing) and distribution (newsagents, delivery) were well delineated. Both companies expanded horizontally via acquisition, creating geographically diverse operations. Functional structures could be overlaid on new divisions to maintain economies of scale in printing and content production.

News Corporation's related diversification into magazines, book publishing, television, film and satellite by the 1980s posed greater structural issues. Unlike other Australian corporate leaders, the management and organisation of News has not taken on the bureaucratic and highly formalised configuration we would expect from multidivisional companies. Rather, Rupert Murdoch's personal management style (supplemented by an efficient reporting system) ensures goal alignment and efficient management of the company. Murdoch has been described as disliking committees, bureaucracy and red tape.[28] Weekly reporting meetings against budget, regular communication between Murdoch and divisional heads on specific problems, and 'unannounced parachute trips' by Murdoch to check in person, characterise management processes.

Organic multidivisionality and related diversification

An organic multidivisionality can be noted for many corporate leaders as they undertook related diversification. In terms of timing, these configurations clustered around the 1950s and 1960s as post-World War Two population changes, new products (from technological advances) and changes to the external market environment provided new growth opportunities. Sometimes hubris of management led to a more unrelated diversification, which we shall examine separately.

Pastoral agents and banks diversified product lines once they had established scale from national coverage. Elders and Dalgety had long provided a range of services to the pastoral sector and we have described the hybrid functional configuration they adopted to leverage skills and knowledge in the firm. Trading banks like the Bank of New South Wales diversified into savings bank functions, hire purchase, and nominee company services in the 1950s.

Financial deregulation in the 1970s and 1980s provided further scope with the establishment of international transaction markets, merchant bank and funds management. Westpac's ability to reduce agency problems within a larger diversified organisation was duly tested. A highly centralised structure based upon geographical territory with a standard product line was increasingly inappropriate to manage such new lines of business. New product and service divisions were created (for example, segmentation on the basis of retail and commercial) and divisions were given greater responsibility to meet market needs. It was the lack of experience in managing a complex multidivisional structure that almost brought Westpac to its knees in the early 1990s.[29] The mantle of corporate leadership in banking passed from Westpac to the National Australia Bank as the former failed to manage the risks in the non-bank businesses (especially in its finance subsidiary AGC).

BHP's vertical integration process meant that it was a forerunner in operating multidivisional structures in Australia. As Wills has described, BHP maintained a line command approach that permitted clear reporting between divisions.[30] Its diversification into gas and oil was managed as separate divisions in the same way as earlier projects.

Other resource companies were required to make greater changes to their structure as related diversification was adopted. Western Mining Corporation's group structure in 1936 (see Figure 7.3) represented the classic resource company's project configuration. Each company in the structure was associated with one product or a set of projects in a region. Accountability could be determined in a relatively straightforward manner. The companies aligned exploration, output, sales and financing in a way reminiscent of later 'profit centres' of the 1980s and 1990s. By 1974, Western Mining Corporation's diversification strategy was organised by product and function (see Figure 7.4). Economies of scope were exploited in exploration, new projects and investments. Similar trends are observed in Mount Isa Mining, North Ltd and Conzinc Riotinto Australia.

Utilities and airlines reconfigured operations as emerging products and changes in regulation presented new market opportunities. Australian Gas Light Company had devolved power from the board to senior managers in the 1950s and created regional managers and divisions to better meet local demand conditions.[31] New divisions for LPG and gas exploration were created as vertical integration was pursued. South Australian Gas Company also moved into bottled gas and autogas as markets for these products emerged, although government ownership of the company restricted new initiatives.

Australian Gas Light Company restructured again in 1985 to demarcate clearly between market structures. A new holding company was established with two broad categories of company – those regulated under state gas and electricity legislation ('regional' companies supplying energy and services) and non-regulated companies across a range of areas including LPG operations, exploration, consultancy, finance and investments, and real estate.[32] Non-core divisions were divested and longer term projects upstream (in gas pipelines) were undertaken, leading to an improved financial position.[33]

In airlines, Qantas maintained a functional structure and focused on a single product with geographically dispersed activities. It followed international trends

Figure 7.3: Group structure of Western Mining Corporation, 1936

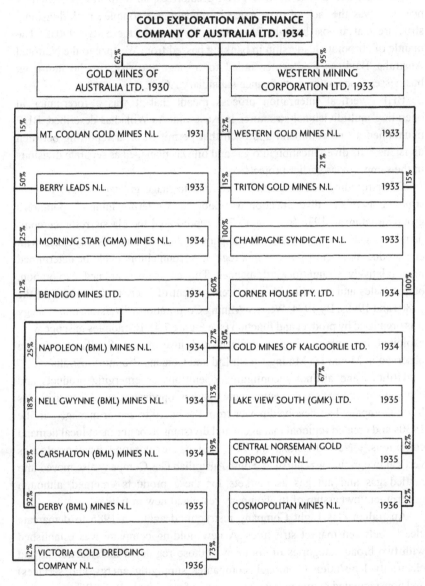

Note: Dates shown indicate year of incorporation. Percentages shown are approximate.

Source: Clark, *Built on Gold*, Appendix.

Figure 7.4: Group structure of Western Mining Corporation, 1974

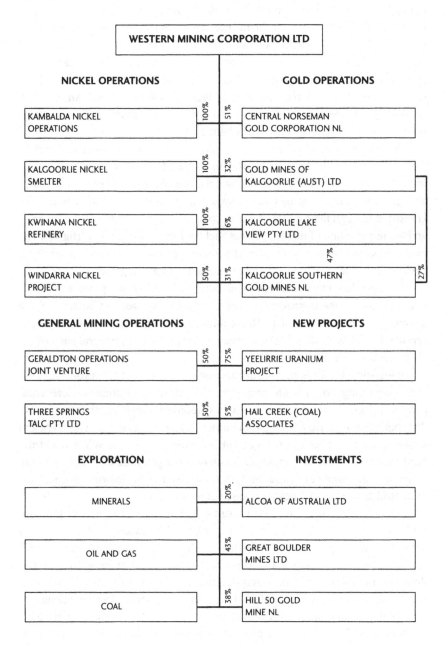

Source: Clark, *Built on Gold*, Appendix.

by adopting the hub and spoke transportation system, making the Brisbane–Sydney–Melbourne link one of the world's busiest passenger routes. Ansett, by contrast, diversified early in its life cycle in the shadow of the Qantas dominance. New divisions from the late 1940s included the Ansett Travel Service (retail and later international), Aviation (manufacturing aircraft accessories), Insurance, Cargo (to handle air and road freight), and holiday resorts. The successful management of these divisions ensured Ansett's survival until the 1990s, when airline deregulation, new entrants and poor capital refinancing decisions caused the company's demise.

The corporate leaders in retailing extended organisational boundaries in the 1960s and 1970s through the establishment of chain stores in the grocery trade. Coles and Woolworths broke down the boundaries between variety chains and grocery. Large suburban supermarkets and malls altered the competitive landscape through the capture of scale economies in purchasing and marketing, and the introduction of discount stores such as Target, K Mart and 'Big W'. The most important developments in the organisational configuration of these companies related to human resource management and logistics.

Retailing has been involved in a continual and broad process of technological innovation to provide cost efficiencies, as we saw in Chapter 3. Store layout, recording of products (bar-coding and scanning), check-outs, self-service, EFTPOS, trading hours, and car-parking now seem integral parts of the shopping experience.

In logistics, the large purchasing accounts of Coles and Woolworths altered their bargaining power with suppliers and delivered customers more competitive prices. The change in logistics (preferred suppliers, 'home brands', distribution warehouse and electronic ordering) has led to the development and application of proprietary management information systems. While the structural aspects of these corporate leaders have changed little over the years (an increase in the number of stores and related divisions), the internal mechanisms of control have provided new core competencies.

Diversification often arose as a result of the emergence of new or modernised products based upon imported technological knowledge. Multidivisional structures based upon products were logical changes for corporate leaders. CSR applied new science to the waste products from sugar refining to establish divisions in building materials and distilleries (alcohol and other chemicals). Once these divisions had exploited learning economies, they expanded to capture dominant market positions in their own right. CSR's building products division embarked on a major process of acquisition in the 1960s and internationalisation in the 1980s.

Conzinc Riotinto Australia diversified markets as new minerals were discovered and used in post-World War Two production processes. Uranium, zircon and other 'glamour' mineral sands were the basis of joint ventures that allowed Conzinc Riotinto to lower the costs of technology acquisition and establish new expertise. Again, a project-based structure was best suited to the company's strategy.

In paper, Australian Paper Manufacturers' strategy in the 1960s and 1970s (and its internationalisation from the 1970s) led to a greater number of subsidiaries as paper declined in importance and packaging became the company's focus. In 1963 the company had 12 subsidiaries and associated companies; by 1989 it had 60 separated businesses functioning as autonomous profit centres, and operated through Europe, Asia and the Americas.[34] In 2000 Amcor, as it had become, de-merged its paper manufacturing and distribution businesses to concentrate on packaging. The configuration remained a product/geography hybrid with geographical divisions (Australia, Asia) overseeing product subdivisions (for example, aerosols, cartons, glass recycling), and product divisions (flexibles, closures, PET (polyethylene-based) packaging) configured by region (Europe/Asia, North America, Latin America).

In glass manufacturing, technological innovations in Australian Consolidated Industries led to diversification in a range of packaging markets. By 1960 the company had 32 subsidiaries and eight associated companies across related markets and products in boxes, plastics and cardboard. However, like many corporate leaders of that era, the distinction between related and unrelated divisions was blurred in executing growth strategies. Australian Consolidated Industries' expansion into finance, quarrying, insurance, engineering, white goods, and building products was heralded as affording 'valuable protection against the vagaries of competition'.[35] But the holding company configuration increasingly failed to transfer core competencies from glass and packaging to new divisions.

A similar fate can be seen in the building products company James Hardie. It was configured as two holding companies in the 1920s to allow focus on building materials (asbestos, slate and builder supplies) and merchandising (tanning, laundry, dyes, chemicals, engineering and rubber).[36] Functional divisions such as Pipes, Building Products, and Research and Development were the next layer of organisation. New product developments and the establishment of new markets led to organic multidivisionality, with James Hardie operating a hybrid structure based on products and geography.

A conscious diversification program in the 1970s added a Publishing and Leisure Division (with the acquisition of Reed Consolidated Industries), and by the mid-1980s the company had three key divisions: Building Products, Paper Merchanting and Converting, and Technology and Services.[37] Wider diversification failed to reap economies or income smoothing benefits, leading to a divestiture program in the late 1980s and 1990s.

Unrelated diversification and 'forced' multidivisionality

The rise of unrelated conglomerates in Australia was almost without exception a defensive move by corporate leaders to counter decline in traditional industries and markets. Few corporate leaders were successful in this strategy, if we are to judge success by the longevity of the conglomerate firm. By the late 1990s almost every corporate leader that adopted an unrelated diversification strategy had been acquired (and broken up) or had implemented a divestiture program to return to a core area of business. At the time, however, unrelated diversification was motivated by a set of expectations that operating a group of unrelated divisions would provide shareholders with benefits from leveraging managerial skills in new markets, smoothing revenue streams across the business cycle, and allocating capital to efficient uses within the firm. The empirical evidence on the benefits of diversification has since shown us that only under certain circumstances does the benefit–cost ratio exceed zero.[38] Firms may gain advantages if external markets are underdeveloped and have poor information on the firm.[39] More commonly (and this has been the case in Australia), management over-estimated their ability to manage a multi-divisional configuration that was forced on a group of divisions.

Dunlop and Adelaide Steamship Company present two examples of the failure of conglomerates in Australian business history. Both corporate leaders faced downturns in their core activities. As we saw in Chapter 4, Dunlop had expanded as a diversified rubber products company between 1903 and the 1950s (although it was still heavily reliant on revenue from tyres).[40] Japanese competition in the key tyre market prompted a conscious diversification strategy in the 1960s and 1970s in order to maintain profitability. Adelaide Steamship Company took a similar path. Originally a corporate leader in the shipping industry, the company was in decline by the early 1970s. Under the leadership of John Spalvins it was to become 'the very-model-of-a-model-conglomerate' through a complicated cross-shareholding structure.[41]

By 2002 both companies had disappeared from Australian corporate leadership. Pacific Dunlop refocused on its Ansell rubber products (and changed to that name) after one of the largest local divestiture programs. Adelaide Steamship Company endured a break-up at the behest of a syndicate of banks in 1991, and faced corporate and class actions over accounting irregularities throughout the 1990s. Pacific Dunlop and the Adelaide Steamship Company pushed up against the logical boundaries of unrelated diversification and multidivisional configurations.

Dunlop's initial diversification process was cemented by an organisational restructuring in 1963 to reflect the new strategy. Five divisions were created housing assets and companies under automotive (including tyres), industrial, footwear and weatherproofing, flooring and sporting goods.[42] The acquisition program was highly profitable for much of the 1960s, with capital works centred on acquisitions in fields with growth opportunities. In 1968 the chief executive officer, Eric Dunshea, described the strategy as 'selective diversification', the benefits of which were outlined in a board paper in October.[43]

But Dunlop's acquisitions were to become anything but selective. After a major financial crisis in the early 1970s (and an attempt at restoring operational performance by factory closures and divestitures), Dunlop extended the conglomerate structure to include domestic and international divisions in electrical, consumer products, latex and medical products. Major acquisitions in the late 1980s and early 1990s included Bonds (clothing), Nucleus (pacemakers and ear implants), Repco (automotive products), and Petersville Sleigh (food brands). By 1993 the company had nine operating groups across unrelated products and geographical markets.

Adelaide Steamship Company's strategy and conglomerate structure were formed by a complex web of cross-shareholdings.[44] It was regarded as 'one of the most active of the 1980s entrepreneurial companies' and was heralded for its corporate success story.[45] The company's unrelated diversification strategy was rationalised as focusing on 'basic businesses' such as food, ship towage, building and retailing. In practice, the strategy was driven by the financial gains obtained by acquiring 'controlling' (but less than 50 per cent) interests in major companies. Its group structure by 1990 (see Figure 7.5) contained controlling positions in many of the corporate leaders already examined.[46]

The cross-shareholding structure covered retailing, food, meat, wine and small goods, real estate and property investments, towage and port services, and manufacturing. Adelaide Steamship Company was able to work within prevailing accounting and other regulations to create financial gains from inter-company loans (for income tax benefits) and create a 'corporate financial health' that was greater than the constituent parts.[47] That the multidivisional configuration did not satisfy the basic tenets of strategic logic or provide transactions cost advantages in organising production was not the point. Here strategy and configuration were one and same. Eventually, poor investment decisions (especially in Bell Resources and Industrial Equity Ltd) and a more active monitoring by debt holders called in the Adelaide Steamship Company venture. A major reported loss in 1990–91 (of an unprecedented $1.35 billion) led to the unravelling of the conglomerate.

Unrelated diversification was followed by other corporate leaders but with less dramatic outcomes. Pastoral agents countered decline in rural markets by expanding into new products and markets. Elders and Dalgety moved beyond their core activities in the 1960s to be hybrid conglomerate configurations diversified by function (trading, processing), market (outside the traditional

Figure 7.5: Group structure of Adelaide Steamship Company, 1990

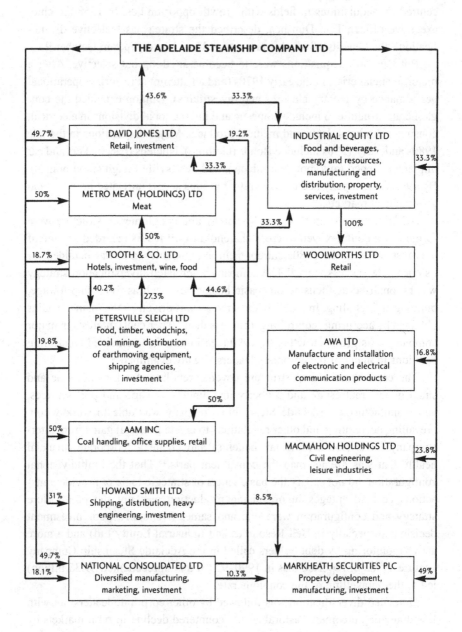

Source: *Australian Financial Review*, 8 November 1990, p. 18.

farmer clientele) and product (consumables, hardware and complex sealed technology).[48] Both were casualties in the conglomeration movement of the 1970s and 1980s. Elders formed part of the Elder IXL conglomerate in 1981 and Dalgety Australia was acquired by Wesfarmers in 1993.[49]

British Tobacco fared little better in unrelated diversification. It faced intense competition in tobacco in the late 1950s as major multinationals entered the Australian market, and diversified broadly, as described in Chapter 4. Such a defensive strategy meant a virtual holding company structure, which was successful to the extent that it reduced the company's reliance on tobacco to approximately one-quarter of profits by the late 1980s. The holding company configuration also provided a set of 'strategic options', one of which paid dividends. Its non-alcoholic beverage division acquired numerous fragmented Coca-Cola franchises around Australia – a market position that grew to a 99 per cent market share in 1990. A major new shareholding by the Coca-Cola Company of Atlanta and divestiture of unrelated divisions provided an organisational re-engineering for the company. It expanded franchises into Asia and central Europe to become one of the largest 'anchor bottlers' in the Coca-Cola system. However, the difficulties of operating across several continents led the company to de-merge its European division in 1998 and concentrate on the Asia-Pacific region, which included operations in Australia, New Zealand, Fiji, Papua New Guinea, Indonesia and South Korea.

Corporate governance

The changes in organisational structure and internal operations for the corporate leaders were motivated by the requirement to align the workings of the firm with its strategy. We have seen in this chapter that corporate leaders achieved this alignment in different ways. The choice of structure was embedded in a set of principal–agent relationships between owners of the corporation and their managers, debt holders, and between managers within the divisional hierarchy. The concern for senior management was to ensure that internal resources were allocated efficiently, notwithstand-ing that the costs and benefits of various resource allocation combinations altered according to market contestability, public (especially industry) policy, and prevailing business norms. At a higher level, ownership structure and corporate governance posed a different set of questions about how the corporation was owned and managed on behalf of its owners as a profitable, surviving enterprise.

In this section we turn to the governance of our corporate leaders in order to understand how ownership and control changed during the twentieth century.

General trends

Corporate governance entails a set of mechanisms by which the owners of the firm ensure that managers undertake activities consistent with the firm's goals. The agency relationship between owners and managers gives rise to the possibility that managers may act opportunistically to improve their welfare at the expense of owners. Given incomplete information between the owner (outside the corporation) and managers (insiders), it is costly to write contracts to bind managers to shareholder value maximising behaviour, and to monitor their behaviour subsequently. Large shareholders may be expected to incur monitoring costs because the benefits to doing so (in terms of shareholder wealth gains) outweigh the transactions costs. Increases in ownership concentration, therefore, and a rise in the number of block shareholders (those holding greater than 5 per cent) can serve small shareholders well by increasing the level of review of company management.

Other control mechanisms include the ability of directors to oversee the behaviour of management (the structure and role of the board of directors), the design of executive remuneration (aligning interests through incentive-based pay), and the threat of takeover from the market for corporate control. Of these, the most important for the governance of the corporate leaders were ownership concentration, block-holders, remuneration and board structure. The operation of the market for corporate control in Australia has long been regarded as relatively less important as a constraint on management, at least until the 1980s and 1990s.[50]

Australia's corporate leaders in the first half of the twentieth century are best characterised as 'family capitalism' as opposed to 'managerial capitalism'. Separation of ownership from control was minimal. Firms bore family names and continued to draw their directors and managers from within the family circle. There is little evidence of hierarchies of salaried managers outside the banks, pastoral companies or mining houses. Indeed, it is the separation of ownership from control that distinguishes some of the largest corporate leaders from their rivals between 1900 and 1950.

Companies such as BHP, CSR, and Burns Philp had scales of operation and organisational complexity that were a feature of Chandler's managerial capitalism. But relative to the United States, the proportion of such firms in the group of corporate leaders was small. Indeed, in the 1950s a study of the largest 102 companies in Australia (including financial institutions and subsidiaries of multinationals) indicated the founding families were in a position to control the majority of those companies through their board positions and shareholdings. Only one-third of domestic companies could be identified as management controlled.

The nature of the separation of ownership from control changed dramatically in the second half of the century. Broad indicators of ownership are available for 1952 and 1995 from Wheelwright's study of ownership of Australian companies, and Davies and Peacock's review of the Australian stock market (see Table 7.1 below). The data is not strictly comparable, given that Wheelwright's focus was on voting shares issued by companies whereas Davies and Peacock report the market value of shares by ownership type. However, trends are discernible.

Individual share ownership has fallen substantially since the 1950s. They comprised the largest shareholder type in 1952 (75.6 per cent) but had declined to third in 1995 (22.8 per cent). By contrast, financial institutions have risen in importance over the 40 years covered by the data. All financial shareholders were 8.9 per cent of the total in 1952, and 34.8 per cent in 1995 (combining life and pension funds, and banks). Ownership of Australian corporations by overseas shareholders is difficult to ascertain. Wheelwright's study did not identify foreign owners as a separate group (owners are included in individuals and nominee, or financial categories). In 1995 foreign owners comprised 32.0 per cent of shareholders, and it is reasonable to expect that the figure was lower for 1952.

The trends in Table 7.1 impacted on the governance structure of corporations. Individual shareholders did not have the resources to actively monitor the managers of Australia's largest companies. Indeed, Wheelwright concluded that one-third of the companies in his sample were 'in the hands of management, over whom shareholders can have little control'. The diffuse ownership structures of the 1950s (and of later decades, as reported by Wheelwright and

Table 7.1: Ownership of shares by individuals, companies and institutions, 1952 and 1995 (%)

Owner	1952	1995
Households/persons	75.6	22.8
Rest of world	–	32.0
Companies	15.5	8.8
Life and pension funds	–	23.8
Banks and other	–	11.0
All financial	8.9	–
Government	–	1.5

Source: Wheelwright, *Ownership and Control*, Table III C, p. 46; Davies & Peacock, 'The role of the stock exchange', Table 4.11, p. 110.

Miskelly (for 1962–64) and Lawriwsky (for 1974–75)) meant that managers faced less scrutiny than would be the norm today.

Companies were the only other shareholder type of any importance (15.5 per cent of shares), and typically inter-company share ownership tended to be supportive of incumbent management. Close personal relationships and reputations at the board level often meant that the company representatives (as shareholders) would not act in the best interests of the smaller individual shareholder when questions of priority arose.

Financial institutions held 8.9 per cent of shares in 1952. In their 1962–64 sample of manufacturing firms, Wheelwright and Miskelly estimated that institutions could, if they combined as a single bloc of like-minded investors, control 30.6 per cent of surveyed companies (effectively replacing the one-third managerial control). However, 'non-action by institutions' meant that managers were not subject to external review from this group. By the 1990s, financial institutions had risen in importance to provide a countervailing balance to managers. At this broad level of analysis we can conclude that the corporate governance of Australian corporations has improved.

The experience of the corporate leaders also shows a change in ownership structure and governance relationships. Detailed information is available on ownership for approximately half of the firms under examination (excluding the financials). In Table 7.2 we report the summary statistics for corporate leaders in 1964 and 1997 for the percentage of shares owned by the top 20 share-holders, top five shareholders and largest shareholder.

The sample sizes for both years were 23 corporate leaders, representing 42 per cent of the list in 1964 (23 out of 55) and 62 per cent in 1997 (23 out of 37). All measurements of ownership concentration show that the corporate leaders experienced increased concentration. The top 20 and top five

Table 7.2: Ownership concentration of Australian corporate leaders, 1964 and 1997 (%)

| | Top 20 | | Top 5 | | Largest | |
	1964	1997	1964	1997	1964	1997
Mean	39.2	65.2	29.9	46.4	15.9	20.5
Median	30.6	64.5	15.4	44.8	7.3	16.6
Standard deviation	26.9	15.8	28.4	15.7	17.9	15.6
Count	23	23	–	–	–	–

Source: Calculated from Wheelwright, *Ownership and Control*; Connect4 Annual Report database.

shareholders in 1964 held, on average, 39.2 per cent and 29.9 per cent respectively. By 1997 the corresponding groups held 65.2 per cent and 46.4 per cent.

Also noticeable is that the variation in corporate leader experience declined between 1964 and 1997. The standard deviation of top 20 and top five shareholdings reduced from 27–28 per cent to 15 per cent. Thus, in 1964 there was a greater dispersion of ownership, and corporate leaders adopted a range of ownership and corporate governance mechanisms to reduce agency issues between shareholders, debt-holders and managers. By 1997 the lower dispersion meant that the governance functions were more likely to be undertaken by the same groups. Indeed, one important group – the largest shareholder – increased in size, from an average 15.9 per cent of shares in 1964 to 20.5 per cent in 1997.

While the average experience of the corporate leaders is informative, the nature of averages can be influenced by the experience of one or two firms with high ownership concentration. For example, Comalco and Metal Manufacturers were both 100 per cent owned by their top 20 shareholders – Comalco by Conzinc Riotinto Australia and the Kaiser Aluminum and Chemical Corporation (United States), and Metal Manufacturers by British Insulated Callender Cables, Broken Hill South and North Broken Hill. These firms are included in the samples, and influence the average if the experience of the remaining firms is different. The median shareholding for each ownership concentration is also reported in Table 7.2 as a more robust measure. All median data show at least a doubling in ownership for our corporate leaders. Top 20 shareholders held 30.6 per cent in 1964 and 64.5 per cent in 1997; the top five shareholders became even more important, with a rise from 15.4 per cent of shares in 1964 to 44.8 per cent in 1997. The largest shareholder also increased its holding from 7.3 per cent to 16.6 per cent.

A sub-sample of corporate leaders (13 firms) that appear in both years is reported in Table 7.3. A comparison of the smaller sub-sample summary statistics with the larger sample shows that these firms are reasonably representative. Ten out of the 13 corporate leaders experienced increases in top 20 shareholdings. Two corporate leaders that had decreases in this measure – Comalco and Metal Manufacturers – remained in concentrated ownership, while Boral saw a diffusion of ownership of its shares. We have already noted the increase in top five shareholdings and largest shareholder. The ratio of top five to top 20 shareholdings provides another measure of change in concentration, and highlights the increased importance of large shareholders (or block-holders) in the governance system. Relative to the top 20, the top five are now much more powerful in controlling the voting in corporate leaders. The top five to top 20 ratio rose (as a median) from 0.63 to 0.71 between 1964 and 1997. Similarly, the size of the largest shareholder (on median) rose from 9.5 per cent to 14.5 per cent.

Table 7.3: Changes in ownership concentration, 1964–97: Select corporate leaders (%)

Company	Top 20		Top 5		Ratio Top 5 to Top 20		Largest	
	1964	1997	1964	1997	1964	1997	1964	1997
BHP	12.4	56.7	6.3	39.1	0.51	0.69	1.9	16.6
Amatil	45.4	88.0	39.3	73.1	0.87	0.83	31.4	33.4
CSR	30.6	47.6	18.5	34.3	0.60	0.72	8.3	11.1
Amcor	21.5	46.3	12.3	26.3	0.57	0.57	3.3	9.7
Mt Isa Mines	59.9	73.7	56.1	53.8	0.94	0.73	53.7	19.0
Dunlop	31.3	57.3	20.7	34.7	0.66	0.61	10.8	8.7
North Ltd	14.5	53.8	6.4	37.8	0.44	0.70	2.5	12.5
Comalco	100.0	94.1	100.0	79.1	1.00	0.84	50.0	67.0
James Hardie	72.2	64.0	60.9	45.8	0.84	0.72	46.6	28.2
Email	22.4	52.3	9.6	34.1	0.43	0.65	2.2	9.6
AWA	22.3	54.7	12.3	36.1	0.55	0.66	3.5	14.2
Boral	43.9	38.2	34.7	24.5	0.79	0.64	19.0	7.6
Metal Manufacturers	100.0	92.5	99.2	81.8	0.99	0.88	49.6	61.2
Average	41.0	63.4	33.0	45.8	0.69	0.71	21.1	21.6
Median	31.0	57.0	19.6	38.4	0.63	0.71	9.5	14.5
Standard deviation	28.4	16.6	30.9	17.6	0.21	0.09	21.9	18.0

Source: Calculated from Wheelwright, *Ownership and Control*; Connect4 Annual Report database.

Thus, a strong minority shareholder is now more common. Combined with an active group of top five shareholders, the implication is that the review and monitoring of management has increased substantially.

Ownership and control: Were foreign-owned corporate leaders different?

The corporate governance experiences of multinational subsidiaries could be expected to be different from Australian firms in a number of ways. First, the fact that more foreign-owned corporate leaders were managed as subsidiaries in a wider, international corporate structure (rather than as stand-alone firms) meant that domestic managers were closely monitored by corporate head office.

Second, until the 1990s financial disciplines were greater under a system of internal capital markets (where head office had more information on day-to-day operations) than in a firm with diffuse ownership and a more market-based relationship with debt-holders. Finally, there was a more rapid transfer of the best international practices of governance mechanisms such as the operation of the board, functions of corporate officers and remuneration (and increasingly the cross-fertilisation of ideas through the experiences of Australian managers overseas in the larger organisation).

Domestic and foreign ownership of the top 100 companies at each benchmark year were presented in Chapter 3 and discussed in some detail. Table 7.4 reproduces some of that data in summary form to examine the importance of foreign ownership. As stated earlier, our measurement of foreign ownership understates the actual figure by using the country of registration or majority ownership as an indicator. Foreign ownership accounted for nearly 25 per cent, on average, of the top 100 companies throughout the twentieth century. Prior to 1964 this ownership was concentrated in retail/wholesale industries (for example, pastoral agents such as Dalgety or New Zealand Loan & Mercantile Agency, or traders such as Robert Reid or Farmer). By 1964 foreign ownership was largely in the chemicals and petroleum sectors due to the entry of

Table 7.4: Foreign ownership of corporate leaders, 1910–97

Panel A: Domestic versus foreign ownership (% of corporate leaders)						
	1910 %	1930 %	1952 %	1964 %	1986 %	1997 %
Australia	72	87	86	67	77	73
Overseas	28	13	14	33	23	27

Panel B: Foreign ownership by industry (% of corporate leaders)						
Sector	1910 %	1930 %	1952 %	1964 %	1986 %	1997 %
A	12.5	20.0	–	–	–	–
B	–	–	14.3	11.0	–	9.0
C	12.5	–	–	78.0	100.0	91.0
F	75.0	80.0	85.7	11.0	–	–

Note: For a full description of ASIC classifications see pp. 237–8.

Source: Various issues of: *Australasian Insurance and Banking Record*; *Jobson's Investment Digest*; *Official Melbourne Stock Exchange Record*; *Delfin Digest*; *Business Review Weekly* 6.11.1986, pp. 89–116, and 16.11.1998, pp. 108–60.

companies from the United States and United Kingdom such as ICI, Shell, BP, Mobil and Esso (not to overlook Ford and General Motors-Holden's which had been Australian multinational subsidiaries through much of the century).

These industry concentrations are important to recognise when examining corporate governance relationships. The operation of the pastoral companies in Australia involved close correspondence between Australian managers and the London boards; after all, these companies relied upon the London finance markets for the provision of capital. Control over Ford and General Motors-Holden's, by contrast, was through strong internal hierarchy (General Motors-Holden's, for example, was held on a tight financial leash by its United States parent during prosperity and times of crisis).

The chemical and petroleum companies operated in Australia as two intercompany groupings. The Caltex group (comprising California Texas Oil Company and Monsanto Chemicals) held cross-holdings in Boral and Ampol, and in smaller firms such as H.C. Sleigh, Australian Petrochemicals and Australian Oil Refinery. The Esso-Mobil group (Standard Oil New Jersey and Mobil Petroleum Company) owned their subsidiaries and companies such as Petroleum Refineries, Altona Petrochemicals and Australian Synthetic Rubber. Only the cross-holdings observable in the BHP group compared at the domestic ownership level. Cross-holdings and control by multinationals were driven by strategic purposes and involved close governance of Australian firms (indeed, most were privately owned). However, the close-knit nature of these holdings did not provide a positive spillover (or demonstration effect) to domestic corporate governance practices between 1910 and the 1970s.

Aligning interests and monitoring the company: Share ownership, board characteristics and block-holders

We have argued in this chapter that the increase in ownership concentration of the corporate leaders has had a major impact on the nature of the corporate governance process. Further evidence for this position is presented by examining three related governance mechanisms – the level of managerial (and director) share ownership, board size and composition, and the number and type of block-holders (groups with more than 5 per cent of shares).

Recent research has shown that these mechanisms can be complementary and/or substitutable in resolving agency issues in the firm, and that their use is influenced by ownership concentration. For example, the composition and operations of the board of directors depend upon the claim on positions by major ownership groups. In cases of majority owners, other corporate governance mechanisms may have to be used to protect the interests of minority shareholder groups.

Share ownership by key decision-makers in the company can be used as a corporate governance mechanism to ensure that the interests of all shareholders are protected. Managerial and director shareholding aligns interests on share value maximisation and decreases the probability that managers act opportunistically or that directors monitor ineffectively. Empirical evidence from studies of companies in the United States, Europe and Australia suggest that managerial shareholding is associated with higher firm value over time (although not performance in any one year), and that managers are unlikely to empire build, claim excess pay, or consume excess perquisites.

While it is difficult to obtain data on management shareholdings for Australian firms before the 1990s, information on directors is more readily available. Table 7.5 shows the share of equity held by directors in the years 1952, 1962–64 and 1974–75 for samples of Australian firms. The data show that there were few majority control positions held by directors, and that diffuse share ownership was the norm.

Indeed, director share ownership was usually in the form of small parcels of shares, the aggregate of which was less than 10 per cent of company equity. The proportion of minority holdings had increased by 1974–75, but remained less important than diffuse holdings.

Director share ownership for the corporate leaders was also at low levels, and did not exhibit large changes between 1964 and 1997. The average director share ownership remained relatively constant at 0.2 per cent, although median ownership rose and the variance (or differences between firms) decreased (see Table 7.7, p. 198). In addition, we must bear in mind that almost all companies used director share ownership as a remuneration alignment tool by 1997 (by contrast, only four out of 13 companies did in 1964). Share ownership of

Table 7.5: Share of equity held by directors, 1952–75

Directors/Group	Per cent	1952	1962–64	1974–75
Majority	>50	–	8.4%	7.6%
Minority	>10<50	#33.3%	25.8%	42. 0%
Diffuse	0<10	66.6%	65.9%	50.3%
Sample size		72*	299	157

Note: # This figure refers to both minority and majority categories.

    * 'Industrials' only.

Sources: Wheelwright, *Ownership and Control*, p. 120; Wheelwright & Miskelly, *Anatomy of Australian Manufacturing*, Table 29, p. 40; Lawriwsky, *Ownership and Control of Australian Corporations*, Table 5, p. 19.

0.2 per cent (on average) of a large corporation in the 1990s could also be expected to have a real economic effect on directors' welfare. By contrast, holdings in 1964 (and earlier) were in companies substantially less capitalised. In sum, we can conclude here that the alignment of interests between decision-makers and other shareholders in the sub-sample of Australian corporate leaders improved, and there is no reason to expect this not to hold for other firms.

Board size and board composition have long been regarded as important components of the governance process. Board size is positively associated with company size due to the fact that as a firm increases in size and complexity, directors with a variety of human capital skills are needed.[51] Smaller firms have less complex control and decision-making systems, implying that directors require general managerial skills. As the firm increases in size, non-executive and executive directors play important roles in monitoring and strategic formulation. There are costs, however, to larger boards. Jensen, and Lipton and Lorsch argue that as board size increases it becomes difficult for an additional director to increase value. A larger board negatively affects the amount of time available at typical board meetings and has a negative impact on group dynamics by leading to greater formality and less frankness and openness in strategic discussion.[52]

Board composition refers to the number of non-executive and executive directors on the board. Executive directors hold both a board position and a senior management or executive position within the company. Owing to this dual role, executive directors have the potential to make a valuable contribution to the board, as they are able to bring firm-specific knowledge to board deliberations. Notwithstanding the benefits of executive directors, their independence from management may be impaired. Executive directors display greater loyalty to management than do their non-executive colleagues and, given their position, they are subject to greater influence by the company's CEO than are outside directors.

The selection and reporting process of executive directors reduces independence, as directors are charged with the responsibility for monitoring the performance of the CEO and also report to the CEO.[53] In cases where the chair of the board is also the CEO, the governance and oversight of senior appointments can be compromised. This results in a potential conflict of interest for such directors and the presence of too many executive directors on a board may invite scepticism about the independence of such a board, especially with regard to reviewing the performance of management.

Unlike executive directors, non-executive directors are only employed by a company in the capacity of a director on the board. Non-executive directors are typically appointed in view of their industry expertise and their decision-making abilities. The role of these directors differs somewhat from that of their executive counterparts in that non-executive directors may be under-taking strategic, independent monitoring and representative roles.[54] Despite the fact that non-executive directors are not employed in other positions by the company, there may be circumstances where their independence is threatened. For example, many authors have questioned the independence of outside direc-tors, given the dominance of a company's CEO in making such appointments, or directors' previous connections with the firm.[55] In some cases, important positions, such as the chair of the board of directors, are held by previous executives of the firm so that independence in name does not necessarily translate to independent actions.

Tables 7.6 and 7.7 show the board size for the sample of Australian cor-porate leaders in 1964 and 1997. Median board size increased from seven to 11 directors between our benchmark years, consistent with what we would expect from theory and previous empirical evidence. However, this fact tells us little about what may have happened to the operation of the board and its governance role over time. After all, corporate leaders increased in size during that period so that it is difficult to ascertain from board size alone whether boards behaved better. What we can say from examination of individual companies in Table 7.7 is that several firms (Mount Isa Mines, Comalco, Boral, Metal Manufacturers, Amcor and Dunlop) experienced stable or declining board size. This suggests that firms found different ways to allocate managerial and governance resources over time.

Information on the composition of boards is more difficult to locate. Table 7.7 shows the prevalence of an independent chair on the board of directors for the 13 corporate leaders. Eight of the 13 boards between 1945 and 1980 had chairmen who were either the CEO or had held executive positions previously. We would conjecture that independence was compromised, especially in cases where previous management decisions were under scrutiny. By 2000 we report quite a different picture. Boards of the corporate leaders at the turn of the

Table 7.6: Monitoring the company: Board size and block-holders

	Board size		Block-holder	
	1964	1997	1964	1997
Mean	7.5	10.4	1.0	4.0
Median	7.0	11.0	1.0	4.0
Standard deviation	2.1	3.0	1.2	1.4
Sample size	–	–	23.0	23.0

Source: Calculated from Wheelwright, *Ownership and Control*; Connect4 Annual Report database.

Table 7.7: Monitoring the company: board size, block-holders and director share ownership: select corporate leaders

Company	Board size		Independent chair			Block-holder		Largest financial block-holder		Director share ownership (%)	
	1964	1997	1945–80	2000		1964	1997	1964	1997	1964	1997
BHP	7	12	✗	✓		0	3	1.9	4.3	0.0	0.1
Amatil	9	12	✗	✗		1	4	3.0	6.8	0.0	0.1
CSR	7	13	✗	✓		1	4	4.8	11.1	1.3	0.2
Amcor	11	11	✗	✓		0	2	3.3	9.7	0.4	0.4
Mount Isa Mines	10	7	✗	✓		1	5	0.5	19.0	0.1	0.0
Dunlop	11	11	✗	✓		1	6	3.6	8.7	0.0	0.5
North Ltd	7	13	✓	✓		0	4	2.5	12.5	0.9	0.5
Comalco	8	5	✓	✓		2	1	0.0	3.3	0.0	0.0
James Hardie	7	8	✗	✓		1	3	2.7	6.6	–	–
Email	5	11	✓	✓		0	4	2.2	9.6	0.0	0.2
AWA	5	7	✗	✓		0	2	2.7	9.4	–	–
Boral	7	7	✓	✓		2	3	2.7	7.6	0.0	0.1
Metal Manufacturers	11	7	✓	✓		3	4	0.2	5.9	0.0	0.0
Mean	8.1	9.5				0.9	3.5	2.3	8.8	0.2	0.2
Median	7.0	11.0				1.0	4.0	2.7	8.7	0.0	0.1
Standard deviation	2.1	2.8				1.0	1.3	1.4	4.0	0.4	0.2

Notes: Independent chair measures whether an executive director and/or the CEO was or became chair of the board of directors.

Source: Calculated from Wheelwright, *Ownership and Control*; Connect4 Annual Report database.

twenty-first century appear much more independent, at least in terms of the chair of the board.

Composition of the board in terms of executive and non-executive directors also illustrates changes in the governance process. We have collected data for the six companies that appeared in our lists throughout the twentieth century to give a longer term perspective on governance patterns. Tables 7.8 and 7.9 show board size and board composition for BHP, CSR, Dunlop, British Tobacco/ Amatil, Australian Gas Light and Burns Philp from 1913 to 1997.

Examination of these top six corporate leaders shows that board size remained relatively stable until the 1960s. Only Dunlop increased board size substantially by 1964, most likely as a result of previous mergers and acquisitions. Smaller boards may have worked efficiently between the 1910s and the 1950s, as the demands of external investors for rigorous oversight and review was low. Alternatively, the data suggest that these companies were not subjected to high levels of outside scrutiny and could persist with CEO (or chairman) appointed boards of limited size. The rise in board size is by no means uniform for this group, as with our larger sample. Board size increased at BHP, CSR and Dunlop, but not for Amatil, Australian Gas Light or Burns Philp.

Table 7.9 adds further insight by presenting the composition of the board (the percentage of non-executive directors) for the six companies. All companies initiated a change in composition over the period to include a greater number of executive officers on the board. This change suggests that board operation and strategic formulation improved as executives played an increasingly important role in board deliberations. Noticeable too is the fact that every corporate leader maintained a majority of non-executive directors, due in large part to the professionalisation of governance practices in large organisations. (It is another question whether these directors were independent non-executives.

Table 7.8: Corporate governance of Australian corporate leaders: Board size

Company	1913	1928	1964	1997
BHP	7	6	7	12
CSR	5	5	7	13
Dunlop	6	5	11	11
Br Tob/Amatil	10	10	9	14
AGL	12	6	*	8
Burns Philp	7	6	*	7

Note: * indicates no data available.

Source: Calculated from Wheelwright, *Ownership and Control*; Connect4 Annual Report database.

Table 7.9: Corporate governance of Australian corporate leaders: Board composition (% non-executive directors)

Company	1913	1928	1964	1997
BHP	100	83	86	67
CSR	100	100	86	77
Dunlop	100	100	73	73
Br Tob/Amatil	90	100	100	86
AGL	100	100	*	88
Burns Philp	100	67	*	86

Note: * indicates no data available.

Source: Calculated from Wheelwright, *Ownership and Control*; Connect4 Annual Report database.

Anecdotal evidence would suggest that they were not.) While only conjecture, we suggest that the rise of a market for professional non-executive directors and the increased importance of director reputation has served these firms well in improving monitoring, decision-making and governance practices generally.

Improvements in governance practices are also suggested by the rise of block-holders; the third mechanism which may lead to greater monitoring and lower agency costs. Block-holders are willing to incur the transactions costs associated with monitoring companies because the economic benefits to doing so are large. Block-holders often have more specialised resources to devote to monitoring shareholdings, and have access to greater levels of information than smaller, individual shareholders. In many cases, block-holders are able to engage in dialogue with incumbent management over the operations of the firm and adopt a 'voice' strategy in communicating dissatisfaction with performance (as opposed to an 'exit' strategy of selling equity positions). Therefore, smaller shareholders are able to free-ride on the actions of block-holders and enjoy improvements in performance, better strategic decision-making, and the greater likelihood of disbursements of excess cash.[56]

Tables 7.6 and 7.7 indicate that the number of block-holders increased for the corporate leaders between 1964 and 1997 (when we define block-holders as holders of an equity position greater than 5 per cent of ordinary shares). Typically one block-holder existed in 1964, but this had increased to four block-holders by 1997. The sub-sample of companies in Table 7.7 shows that only Comalco had a decline in block-holder positions. For these companies we also show the size of the largest financial block-holder in both benchmark years. The data is consistent with our findings of increased ownership concentration and the rise of financial institutions as equity holders. The largest financial block-holder held an average 2.3 per cent of equity in 1964 and 8.8 per cent in 1997 (there were similar increases in median equity holdings). Overall, we contend that the level of external monitoring by block-holders has improved to the benefit of all shareholders, notwithstanding that recent commentators have indicated that institutional shareholders are often passive in exercising true shareholder decision-making.[57]

Conclusion

The organisational structure of the corporate leaders was determined by the strategies adopted to sustain competitive advantages. We find that firms achieving scale through physical capital investment were most likely to adopt hierarchies based on functional structures. But the geography of Australia also impacted upon structure. Corporate leaders that gained market presence by achieving scale across multiple locations were required to operate branches and leverage information and technology. We also described how related and unrelated diversification led to multi-divisional structures that were difficult to manage and pushed local managerial capabilities to their limits. Managers of the multinationals were more attuned to managerial developments overseas and new techniques were fed to local subsidiaries.

Corporate governance has improved markedly in the corporate leaders, especially since the 1970s. An examination of the basic features of the governance mechanisms of these firms shows that share ownership concentration, the structure of remuneration contracts for management and directors, and the size and composition of the board of directors all led to managers facing greater scrutiny by a market-based corporate governance system.

CHAPTER 8

Corporate Leaders, Big Business and the Economy

This chapter draws together much of the material presented in the previous chapters to consider two central questions regarding the 'big end of town' in twentieth-century Australia: was Australian experience unique in comparison with the United States, Britain and Germany with respect to the location of large-scale firms in the economy, the timing of their emergence, their growth strategies and organisational design? What contribution did this new type of business organisation make to the creation of national wealth?

Sources of national differences 1900–50

Alfred Chandler's magisterial *Scale and Scope* identified three distinctive forms of large-scale enterprise that emerged in the world's leading industrial economies in the first half of the twentieth century. These were: 'competitive managerial capitalism' in the United States, 'personal capitalism' in Britain and 'cooperative managerial capitalism' in Germany.[1] They have been extended, refined and contested in their application to those three countries and many others.[2] Much of the debate has revolved around whether 'competitive managerial capitalism' was an inherently superior form compared with 'personal capitalism' and 'cooperative managerial capitalism'. While the evidence to support such a contention is ambiguous in many respects, identifying the key characteristics of each type provides a stylised template against which Australian experience can be compared.

A summary of the characteristics of the largest industrial enterprises in the United States, Britain, Germany and Australia at around 1950 is shown in Table 8.1. Chandler's purpose was to highlight the differences between the structures and behaviour of large-scale enterprises in the three countries of his study. Six of the key issues discussed by Chandler have been selected to permit comparisons across the four countries. Each will be discussed in more detail below.

Table 8.1: Characteristics of Australian enterprises compared with the United States, Britain and Germany: From distinctiveness to convergence, 1950–2000

Feature	USA 1950	USA 2000	Britain 1950	Britain 2000	Germany 1950	Germany 2000	Australia 1950	Australia 2000
Origins of entrepreneurs	Domestic Multinational	Domestic Multinational	Domestic & Multinational	Domestic & Multinational	Domestic & Multinational	Domestic & Multinational	Multinational & Domestic	Domestic & Multinational
Sources of competitive advantage	Organisational capabilities	Organisational capabilities	Weaker form & proprietary assets	Organisational capabilities	Organisational capabilities	Organisational capabilities	Weaker form & proprietary strategic assets	Organisational capabilities
Managerial hierarchy	Strong	Strong	Modest	Strong	Strong	Strong	Modest	Strong
Organisational structures	M-form & U-form	M-form & U-form	U-form	M-form & U-form	Weaker M-form	M-form	U-form & organic M-form	M-form & U-form
Growth strategies	HI; VI; R&D; Diversification: Product; Export/FDI	HI; VI; R&D; Diversification: Product; Export/FDI	HI; Weak R&D; Diversification: Weak Product; Export/FDI	HI; VI; Modest R&D; Diversification: Product; Export/FDI	HI; VI; R&D; Diversification: Product; Export/FDI	HI; VI; R&D; Diversification: Product; Export/FDI	HI; Weak VI; Weak R&D; Diversification: Weak Product; Export/Regional FDI	HI; VI; Modest R&D; Diversification: Product; Export/FDI
Challenger route	Market growth Niche		Market growth Niche		Market growth Niche		Government assistance	Market growth Niche

Source: Adapted from Chandler, *Scale and Scope*, 1990; Chandler, Amatori and Hikino (eds), *Big Business*.

In brief, Australian companies were similar in many respects to the leading enterprises in these other nations, while being different in several ways as well. Australian experience was furthest from that of the United States and Germany and closer to that of Britain. That it should bear a greater resemblance to Britain is not surprising, given the close economic, institutional and cultural ties between the two countries. Yet even between these two closely connected countries there were many important differences.

In summary, Australian corporations relied more heavily on foreign entrepreneurship through the involvement of multinationals than did any of the other countries; its companies relied more on the possession of proprietary and strategic assets and less on the development of organisational capabilities to achieve competitive advantage; they had less strongly developed managerial hierarchies; they had less clearly articulated administrative structures, whether U- or M-form, and their organic M-form structure was designed to manage distance rather than separate product markets; their growth strategies relied less on research and development, product diversification and vertical links; going abroad was a less important part of their growth strategies; and challengers to the entrenched first movers, particularly in manufacturing, relied more heavily on government assistance to gain a footing than was the case elsewhere. The first order conditions that stood Australia apart, it will be argued below, were the lateness of its industrialisation, the smallness of its domestic markets and the great distances between them, and its geographic isolation.

The differences in business systems shown in Table 8.1 reflect in large part differences in the underlying economic structures and stages of development of these countries. Timing was crucial to the emergence of large-scale enterprise in Australia. While the United States, Britain and Germany were the world's most powerful industrial economies at the outbreak of World War One, Australia was still predominantly a producer and trader of commodities and minerals. Australia's first wave of large-scale companies that emerged in the late nineteenth and early twentieth centuries were located more in services and publicly-owned utilities than in manufacturing firms spawned by the second industrial revolution. As a late industrialiser, Australian manufacturing firms faced major difficulties generating sufficient scale or scope, given the entrenched presence in world markets of dominant first movers from the early industrialising nations of the United States, Britain and Germany.

Australia's small population and physical isolation left a powerful impress on the evolution of its corporate leaders and big business in general. The new technologies in communication and production processes of the second industrial revolution allowed unprecedented economies of scale to be realised in a wide range of industries. In spite of widening markets, regional, national and international, the new industries consolidated as fewer firms could satisfy demand. Latecomers in small home markets faced significant competitive disadvantages. An inability to achieve scale, particularly in production, meant higher costs. In Australia's case, this disadvantage was compounded by the lack of proximate foreign markets that were of any consequence for its manufacturers. Another legacy of lateness was that other more advanced nations had already accumulated superior managerial capabilities forged by experience and, increasingly, by formal management education. The many multinationals that entered the Australian market gained a competitive advantage from their access to better management skills, as well as more advanced technologies.

Sources of entrepreneurship

Entrepreneurial endeavour was the driving force behind the creation of the new giant companies in all the countries in which they appeared. Australia had no lack of individuals who were prepared to take risks and start new ventures. The opportunities it offered in terms of material self-advancement drew a flood of highly motivated immigrants to its shores who started their own businesses. More importantly, many of these risk-takers were also inventors and innovators who found new ways of doing things or new products to sell. Australia has a long history of indigenous invention and technical progress.[3]

However, whatever technical advances were made by entrepreneurs in various industries within Australia, few could match the scientific knowledge of those who made significant contributions to the emerging technologies of the new chemical, electrical and mechanical industries that arose in the United States and Germany through the late nineteenth and early twentieth centuries. Increasingly, invention and innovation in these industries resulted from the application of applied science by those with formal training. Neither Australia nor Great Britain, the primary source of immigrants, possessed the institutions necessary to provide such training. Only a handful of Australian firms, most notably CSR[4] and BHP,[5] engaged scientists and operated research laboratories before World War Two. However, a number of Australian manufacturers showed great initiative in acquiring and adapting technology from abroad.[6]

They appear to have been in the minority. A government report published in 1937 argued that the gap between industrial technologies in Australia and overseas was so great that it could only be bridged by a nationally funded body.[7] It was the development and commercialising of new technologies, a rare activity by Australian firms, that was the wellspring of growth to giant industrial enterprises in the United States, Germany and, to a lesser extent, Britain.[8]

Foreign firms had a head start in the technology stakes. The number entering Australia accelerated sharply after World War One. They were responsible for the establishment of many key industries including oil refining and distribution, automobile assembly, metal fabrication, electrical equipment, chemicals and parts of textile and apparel.[9] Foreign and domestic entrepreneurs vied to establish and gain a dominant position in emerging industries, the rubber tyre industry being a case in point.[10] As a late starter in the industrialisation process, local firms were not well placed to withstand the foreign invasion. As we noted in Chapter 6, local firms were handicapped in their ability to raise funds compared with subsidiaries of multinationals by the immaturity of the Australian capital market. The entrepreneurial function within Australia passed decisively in those capital-intensive, science-based industries to foreign firms that had already established first mover advantages in their large home markets.[11]

Australian entrepreneurs fared better in those industries that depended less on scale and were less technologically complex. The list of the top 100 firms in 1910 shows that local entrepreneurs dominated the establishment of a number of industries: brewing, sugar refining, baking, meat packing, soap, jam-making and rubber. The 1930 and 1952 lists reveal local firms thrusting forward in a wider range of industries: iron and steel, automobile assembly, automobile parts, rubber products, glass, paper, fertilisers, building materials, textiles, food products, electrical equipment, petroleum products and general engineering.

Foreign firms held sway in many industries by the 1950s and 1960s, in spite of the actions of local entrepreneurs. A key exception was base metal mining, smelting and downstream fabrication of both ferrous and non-ferrous products. This industry continued to be dominated by BHP and its subsidiaries, and by the 'Collins House Group' of companies. However, the emergent aluminium industry relied heavily on the involvement of foreign firms such as Alcoa, Alcan and Comalco. Public debate about the extent and consequences of foreign direct investment in Australian manufacturing was fuelled by revelations that foreign firms accounted for the greater part of value added in many industries.[12] Foreign entrants acquired Australian top 100 pioneers such as CresCo Fertilisers, J. Kitchen & Sons, Queensland Meat Export Agency and MacRobertsons.[13]

In comparison, local firms were better able to prevail or at least hold their own in several non-manufacturing sectors. Pastoral stock and station agents, important providers of a bundle of inputs and services to woolgrowers, were an amalgam of local and British firms, with the balance in favour of the former. Australian banks and insurance firms coexisted with British and American-owned rivals with domestic institutions, the Bank of New South Wales and AMP, winning out decisively in the longer term.

Retailing was transformed from the 1910s onwards by local entrepreneurs, particular the Myer and later the Coles family. Sidney Myer took the department store into new territory in terms of scale and merchandising, while the

Coles brothers were leaders in the development of variety chain stores before World War Two. Local entrepreneurs, the Fairfaxes, Packers and Murdochs, drove a transformation of their newspaper and publishing businesses, becoming leaders of an increasingly consolidated and national industry.

That so many industries were dominated by foreign firms points to an important difference between the Australian experience and that of the United States, Britain and Germany. Firms from these three leading industrial powers had inter-penetrated one another's markets through foreign direct investment from before World War One, resulting in a mingling of foreign and domestic entrepreneurship.[14] However, it is generally true, especially for the United States, that domestic firms provided entrepreneurship in the sense of creating new industries and remaining at the forefront of those industries. In this sense Australia is an outlier, in that it was foreign rather than domestic firms that played a disproportionately important entrepreneurial role, especially in higher technology and capital-intensive industries.

Sources of competitive advantage

Entrepreneurship was required to get a business up and running. Sustained competitive advantage relied on much else besides. If the enterprise was to continue to grow, Chandler informs us, its founder and managers needed to undertake a number of critical and inter-related tasks.[15] These included an understanding of the commercial potential of new technologies and an ability to raise the capital to build a plant or multiple plants of sufficient capacity to allow the exploitation of economies of both scale and scope. Additional invest-ments had to be made in distribution and purchasing that allowed access to customers and suppliers on a national scale. Moreover, a managerial hierarchy needed to be recruited and trained so that it could integrate and coordinate the complex sequential activities of the firm.

In sum, this combination of physical plant and managerial skills gave rise to 'organisational capabilities' that Chandler identified as the principal source of competitive advantage to a firm. He argues that the skills of the managers 'were the most valuable of all those that made up the *organisational capabilities* of the new modern industrial enterprise'.[16] Strategic and operational decisions, initially undertaken by the entrepreneur, passed to hierarchies of salaried managers, whose jobs became increasingly specialised to embrace middle and top management roles, with the latter planning and allocating resources across the organisation.

The longer-term survival of the firm depended on the constant renewal of its organisational capabilities. Moreover, gaps in capabilities could appear as a result of changing technologies and shifting markets. The 'three-pronged investments' in production, distribution and managerial hierarchy required constant upgrading and adaptation. In many respects, Chandler's ideas resonate with the literature of the resource-based theories of the firm and the idea that sustainable and dynamic competitive advantage derives from capabilities in using a unique bundle of resources.[17] Many of these capabilities derive from organisational routines that generate a stock of know-how, a mixture of codifiable and tacit knowledge, that is difficult for rivals to imitate.[18]

In *Scale and Scope*, Chandler argues that United States and German entrepreneurs and salaried managers in firms in key sectors of industry made the necessary investments to build organisational capabilities to the point that they became the source of competitive advantage. As shown in Table 8.1, he argues that British entrepreneurs and salaried managers in similar types of industries failed to do so.

What of Australian firms that made up the top 100 or 25 lists? Were organisational capabilities critical to their becoming corporate leaders? The available data allows only an impressionistic judgement. On one hand, there were no companies in Australia that could match the resource base of the leading industrial firms in the United States, Germany or even ICI in Britain, in terms of their size, breadth, complexity and the sophistication of their administrative structures. On the other hand, the organisational capabilities developed by the leading local companies, albeit partial in comparison with those abroad, gave an advantage compared to those rivals whose organisational capabilities were less well developed.

As was argued in Chapter 7, local firms did make investments that increased capacity and linked production with distribution before the middle of the twentieth century. Moreover, tasks were increasingly specialised within the organisation, with responsibilities being allocated to departments with a manager. The potential was there to generate organisational capabilities to confer a competitive advantage through the realisation of economies of scale and scope. These took on a distinctive Australian quality, in that firms which learnt to coordinate activity across multiple locations and vast distances, through learning to develop 'organic' multidivisional organisational structures, could reap the rewards associated with operating in a national market.

Despite these developments, hierarchies of salaried mangers, with little equity stake in their firms, were probably less common among Australian corporate leaders in non-finance sectors at mid-century than was the case in either the United States or Germany, and possibly even less so than in Britain. While more detailed research on a large number of firms is required, the evidence about the organisational form of the corporate leaders discussed in previous chapters suggests that hierarchies were still embryonic in many cases.

As late as the 1920s, Herbert Gepp, the newly appointed general manager of Electrolytic Zinc Company of Australasia, turned in desperation to the field service handbook of the British Army to find a model of organisational design.[19] The steel producer, BHP, and the sugar refiner, CSR, had clearly defined highly centralised structures in which senior executives monitored the work of numerous functional departments in the mid-1930s and 1950s, respectively,[20] but they would seem to be the exception rather than the norm. While salaried managers were increasingly employed by Australian firms, it is unlikely that the degree of specialisation in managerial function, particularly in the design of middle management and general management roles, was comparable to the largest United States or German industrial firms.

The slower emergence of large and specialised managerial hierarchies, a defining characteristic of 'managerial capitalism' in Australian corporate leaders, was in large part a reflection of the types of markets in which these firms operated. The decisions of Australian entrepreneurs in respect of their investments in hierarchies were commercially sound. It was not entrepreneurial failure in the broadest sense but the constricted set of choices open to them that determined their choices of industries in which to invest, at what scale to operate, and how to structure their organisations.

That Australia began its process of industrialisation roughly 30 years after the beginnings of the second industrial revolution, placed its entrepreneurs at a disadvantage in attempting to enter a wide range of key industries that were already approaching maturity, and whose global markets were dominated by stable oligopolies. Moreover, the size of the local market, even with the bonus of state enforced import substitution, was far too small to allow firms to reach a size that would enable them to realise the economies of scale and scope available to established firms in the United States, Britain and Germany.

Adapting to this local environment gave Australian corporate leaders a distinctive set of organisational characteristics that approximated more to 'personal capitalism' than to 'competitive managerial capitalism' of the United States mould. Because Australian firms emerged as leaders in the less technologically advanced or complex manufacturing industries, they were not required to build the types of organisational structures or the managerial information systems, as described by Chandler in *The Visible Hand* and *Strategy and Structure*,[21] to sustain a competitive advantage. Smaller firms could be managed by entrepreneurs or their families and associates, who mingled functional and strategic roles, and who relied more on direct personal supervision than delegating to managers.

Data shown in Table 8.2 provides an indication of the extent to which founders, directors and their family associates still controlled corporate leaders in the non-financial sectors. Directors and associates held five or more per cent

Table 8.2: Characteristics of a sample of top 100 companies at mid-century

	Mining	Manufacturing	Wholesale and retail	Transport	Leisure
Firms	[8]	[38]	[14]	[4]	[1]
Horizontal integration	–	23	9	2	–
Vertical integration	1	18	5	1	–
Both HI and VI	–	13	2	–	–
Cooperation	3	8	3	–	–
Research and Development	1	6	–	–	–
Diversification	6	18	11	3	–
Export	6	12	3	–	–
FDI	1	21	7	3	–
Block-holder	–	17	9	1	1

Notes: The sample is derived from those firms in the 1952 list of top 100 companies for whom data could be found about these characteristics. Data on all characteristics were not found for all firms. Foreign companies have been excluded from this estimation. These include those firms registered overseas and an additional nine locally registered firms whose foreign parents owned a majority of voting stock, as shown in Wheelwright, 1957. These included ICIANZ, British Tobacco, General Motors-Holden's, Nestlé, Standard Cars, Taubmans, Kraft Holdings, Chrysler Australia and Rootes (Australia). Block-holder refers to the position where the directors and associates hold 5 per cent or more of voting stock.

Sources: Data from a variety of sources including company histories. Data about foreign direct investment drawn from Block, 1964; exports and diversification from Potter, 1972; Research and development from *Technology in Australia*, 1988; block-holder data from Wheelwright, 1957, Appendix, pp. 123–206.

of voting stock, enough for control where the largest shareholders were often nominee companies which held stock in trust and where personal holdings tended to be very small, in 17 of the 38 manufacturing leaders from the 1952 list of the top 100 and in nine of the 14 leaders in the wholesale and retail category. It was not uncommon for members of founding families still to be holding top executive positions in these firms.

'Organisational capabilities' were the principal but not the only weapon in the arsenal of those firms seeking competitive advantage. There were other second order instruments that could reinforce advantages already gained or provide an opportunity for firms that had not yet generated 'organisational capabilities'. With respect to the latter, Chandler argues that manufacturing firms in Great Britain sought competitive advantage from their patents, advertising and inter-firm cooperation through holding company structures and trade associations.[22] Each of these firm strategies was designed to confer some element of monopoly power rather than to reduce cost. If Australian companies had less fully developed 'organisational capabilities' than the leading industrial giants in the United States and Germany, did they follow British firms in relying more heavily on actions that conferred a degree of market protection rather than greater efficiency?

Once again, it is difficult to come to a clear-cut answer. Our judgement is that patents would have been a comparatively less important source of competitive advantage in Australia than in the other more advanced industrial nations, simply because Australian firms were so heavily dependent on imported technology. This was applied directly through subsidiaries of multinationals or paid for through licensing agreements. In spite of the many notable technical innovations undertaken by Australian firms,[23] manufacturing had become heavily dependent on foreign technology by mid-century. Importantly, the inflow of foreign direct investment into manufacturing represented a transfer of technology, part of which would have been protected by foreign patents registered locally. At an aggregate level, Australia's patenting activity was comparatively low in the 1950s, a high proportion of those registered were foreign-owned, and a comparatively low ratio of patents registered locally were also patented abroad.[24]

How important were brands and trademarks as a source of competitive advantage to Australian firms? Local companies advertised extensively.[25] However, it is unlikely that Australian firms spent as much on advertisements as a proportion of sales, or ran as effective campaigns, as their United States and British counterparts, who had begun earlier and could draw on the services of the world's leading advertising agencies.[26] For example, one of the first widespread advertising campaigns in Australia, comprising radio, print media and point of sale material, for Aeroplane Jelly began in 1930.[27] Moreover, the value of brands was weakly developed compared with countries such as the United States[28] and Great Britain, as many were still known only within regions of Australia rather than nationally before World War Two.

Australian firms relied heavily on inter-firm cooperation in domestic markets to gain a competitive advantage, perhaps more so than they did on having patents or branding. This cooperation took several distinct forms. The first resulted from lobbying governments through trade associations that conferred a degree of monopoly power on all companies in the industry. High trade barriers provided protection to manufacturers. Local consumers lost out

further as firms in many industries routinely agreed on market sharing, production quotas, prices, full line forcing to retailers, exclusive dealings and collusive
tendering.[29] In an important sense, Australian manufacturers relied more on
what Kay has termed 'strategic assets', benefits conferred by market position
or regulation that are industry rather than firm-specific, than leading firms
from other advanced industrial nations.[30] That strategic assets are less able to
generate sustainable competitive advantages for firms than the heady brew of
organisational capabilities, was shown by the contraction of Australian manufacturing in the 1970s when trade barriers fell and anti-competitive behaviour
was outlawed.

Other types of inter-firm cooperation gave rise to more sustainable
competitive advantages, in that they resulted in efficiency gains. In the primary metals and petrochemical industries, as we saw in Chapter 5, it was not
economical for each firm to integrate upstream and downstream because none
could reach minimum efficient scale. Companies could be exposed to 'hold-up'
if another firm at another stage in the production chain could renegotiate the
contracts under which it purchased or sold materials. Firms responded to this
situation by negotiating joint ownership of key production points, such as the
Broken Hill Associated Smelters.[31]

The basic metals industries were characterised by cooperative relationships between smelters, refiners and fabricators, through a system of cross-
directorships, cross-shareholdings and technical exchanges.[32] There have also
been cooperative arrangements between the four petrol refiners and chemical
companies in the production of ethylene, a feedstock for the petrochemical
industry in 1960.[33] Firms, particularly in the mining and primary metals
industries, became adept at negotiating long-term relational contracts with upstream and downstream parties. Joint ventures, particularly between domestic
and foreign firms, became vehicles for important new developments in the
chemical industry from well before World War Two[34] and played a key role in
the exploitation of Australia's mineral industry in the 1960s.[35]

It would seem that negotiating cooperative agreements with suppliers and
competitors, the so-called 'external architecture',[36] was a skill acquired by
many leading Australian companies. Data in Table 8.2 shows that a significant
number of the 1952 corporate leaders in the mining, manufacturing and distribution trades – nearly a quarter – were engaged in some sort of cooperative
relationship with their competitors, suppliers or customers. Much of this
cooperative behaviour was a response to industry-specific problems, particularly the threat of opportunism in the metals industry, but it was also a
distinctively Australian solution to problems resulting from trading in a small
and fragmented market.

Comparative growth strategies

Were Australian corporate leaders 'outliers' in the type of growth strategies they pursued, compared with those of first movers in the United States? Chandler's research on industrial giants of the United States revealed a series of steps as firms altered their strategies. Those firms that first applied the new technologies in communication and production swiftly captured market share. Early growth of those firms who became corporate leaders was often facilitated by horizontal integration. However, the creation of the giant and integrated industrial enterprise also involved vertical integration where upstream and downstream activities were brought under common ownership. Firms continued to seek out growth opportunities to exploit the economies of scope through diversification. New technologies generated by in-house research and development had the capacity to create new markets. Firms continued to expand by adding new product lines and seeking fresh markets abroad.[37]

In the broadest terms, the leading Australian manufacturing firms, and those from other sectors to a lesser degree, had grown by moving through a similar set of steps to mid-century. Table 8.2 shows that many firms had expanded their operations as a result of horizontal and vertical integration, or both. A number of firms in mining and manufacturing had undertaken research and development through their own research laboratories that spawned new process and product technologies.

Diversification was widespread in terms of new product ranges and new markets through exporting and foreign direct investment. The data need to be treated with caution in two respects. First, data show whether firms have or have not integrated in various ways, undertaken research and development or diversified. The important qualitative issue that cannot be divined from Table 8.2 is the scale and importance of these moves in enabling growth. Second, data about foreign direct investment, diversification and exports come from 15 to 20 years later than the other information. It may well have been influenced by the dramatic changes in the postwar environment, rather than representing the character of corporate leaders in 1950.

Our judgement is that Australian corporate leaders pursued a somewhat different set of growth strategies than those observed in the United States. The flipside of the data in Table 8.2 is that some firms had become leaders without following the Chandlerian steps. There is reason to be cautious about the extent of both the nature and contribution of both horizontal and vertical integration as a source of leadership. Horizontal integration resulting in the achievement of scale economies for dominant firms was important in industries such as iron and steel, brewing, glass, chemicals and newspapers. However, the efficiency gains from the concentration of production into larger units was attenuated by the widespread use of labour-intensive technologies, at least until the 1920s.[38] It may well have been the case that integration led to increased market power, more than it did greater efficiency. Beyond the automobile, basic metals, glass, brewing, electrical equipment and sugar industries, few firms built a commanding position within an industry by integrating either upstream or downstream. Both BHP and the Collins House Group retained control over downstream activities through cross-directorships and minority cross-shareholdings rather than through internalisation.[39] Wholesalers survived later in Australia than in the United States, continuing to play a critical role as intermediaries in the distribution of groceries and electrical appliances until after World War Two.[40] Subsequently, there were more direct dealings between manufacturers and department and variety chain stores but little formal integration.

It is difficult to get a sense of the importance of the reported diversification. Our judgement is that most corporate leaders, particularly in manufacturing, generated 80 per cent or more of their sales from a core product. For example, before World War Two, the sugar refiner, CSR, diversified into building materials, alcohol and chemicals, all by-products of its milling and refining processes, before entering unrelated industries in the 1950s. However, its 1955 balance sheet revealed that 83 per cent of its fixed assets were directed towards its sugar business.[41] In similar fashion, Dunlop Australia still generated about 70 per cent of its profits from its rubber tyre operations in the mid-1960s.[42]

The data reported in Table 8.2 show that in the 1960s and 1970s, many companies found markets beyond Australia by exporting and through foreign direct investment. However, the fragmentary evidence at the firm level suggests that these activities were still generally peripheral for most, apart from the mining companies, in terms of share of sales and deployment of resources.[43]

Routes for challengers

New firms became corporate leaders over the period from 1910 until 1997. Of the 78 identified in Table 3.1 (on pp. 47–50), 29 made their first appearance in 1910, 10 in 1930, 15 in 1952 and another 16 in 1964. The issue is whether these firms were challengers to first movers in the same industry or were striking out into new territories and becoming first movers themselves? The data shown in Table 8.3 shows few true challengers meeting first movers head on before 1964. For example, in the mining industry the entrants in 1930, North Broken Hill and Broken Hill South, were part of the Collins House Group of companies, as was CRA, which first appears in 1952. The two other new miners in 1952, Mount Isa Mines and Western Mining Company, were involved in copper and gold, respectively.

Table 8.3: New corporate leaders by industry, 1910–64

ASIC	1910	1930	1952	1964	Total
A	2	–	–	–	2
B	2	2	3	–	7
C21–22	7	2	–	2	11
C26	1	1	1	1	4
C27	–	–	3	5	8
C28	–	1	2	–	3
C29	–	–	–	2	2
C31	–	–	–	1	1
C32	–	1	1	1	3
C33	1	1	2	–	4
C34	1	–	–	–	1
D36	2	–	–	–	2
E41	–	–	–	2	2
F46–47	9	–	–	–	9
F48	1	2	2	–	5
G53	3	–	–	–	3
G54	–	–	1	–	1
H56	–	–	–	1	1
Total	29	10	15	15	69

Notes: Corporate leaders are those firms that appeared in three or more lists of the top 100 non-financial firms. For a full explanation of ASIC categories, refer to pp. 237–8.

Sources: *Australasian Insurance & Banking Record*; Butlin, *Australian Monetary System*; Gray, *Life Insurance*; Butlin, Hall & White, *Australian Banking and Monetary Statistics*, pp. 98–101 & Tables 54(ii), 56(ii), 57(ii), 58(ii) & 59(ii); *Australian Banking and Monetary Statistics*, Table 70, p. 503; Block (ed.), *Delfin Digest 1964*, pp. 102–5 & 108–11; *Business Review Weekly*, 20 November 1987; *Business Review Weekly*, 16 November 1998; Various issues of: *Australasian Insurance and Banking Record*; *Jobson's Investment Digest*; *Official Melbourne Stock Exchange Record*; *Delfin Digest*; *Business Review Weekly* 6.11.1986, pp. 89–116, and 16.11.1998, pp. 108–60.

Of the seven original firms in the ASIC group C21–22, most were breweries, along with CSR and British Tobacco. There are no new challengers to the brewers, only consolidation. British Tobacco alone faced a challenger, Rothmans, but only after World War Two. New leaders in the C21–22 group that appeared in 1930, Nestlé and Peters, were in 'new' industries of dairy and confectionery products. Once again, the influx of new corporate leaders into the chemical and petroleum industries, C27, in 1952 and 1964 reflects the growth of new industry segments, petrol refining, for example, rather than challengers to Imperial Chemical Industries of Australia and New Zealand in its core business. While in retailing, F48, the two leading department stores, David Jones and Myer, and the variety stores, Woolworths and Coles, began their operations in different cities.

Was Australian experience atypical? In *Scale and Scope*, Chandler sug-gests a number of routes by which successful challengers may emerge.[44] First, a first mover may dissipate its advantages through managerial negligence and incompetence. Second, government policy can assist the growth of late starters through the provision of funding, guaranteed purchases, licensing, subsidies and trade barriers. Antitrust policy can provide new opportunities to challengers by forcing divestment or moderating the predatory use of market power. Third, the continued growth of the market allows new firms to establish themselves in niche positions that eventually became large enough to warrant those firms making the three-pronged investments to generate organisational capabilities. Fourth, the rate of growth of national markets mattered. Periods of prosperity and high growth rates were more conducive to the creation and development of challengers than periods of poor macroeconomic performance. Finally, challengers could seize the opportunities that arose from discoveries of new sources of supply of sufficient magnitude and importance that they redrew industry boundaries.

Taking a comparative view, as shown in Table 8.1, government policy seems to have been disproportionately important in assisting new challengers among Australian manufacturing firms. There was little to distinguish between the four nations in terms of the broad contours of national growth that would lead to differing outcomes in terms of the ability of a new generation of challengers to come forth. The sources of the differences lay elsewhere. Bigger markets in the United States and Europe encouraged greater specialisation by firms and more intra-industry trade. By way of contrast, the relative immaturity of Australian manufacturing and the many 'gaps' in its product base up to World War Two[45] severely limited the opportunity for domestic challengers to emerge at the margins of industries dominated by first movers.

The role of governments in assisting challengers differed significantly across the four nations. A vast and complex literature suggests the ideas for the following bold pronouncements. The United States government's antitrust policies acted as midwife for the birth of new challengers. Further, its post-World War Two defence and space programs had huge spin-offs for the next generation of high-tech industries. High levels of state-sponsored higher education and research and development in the United States, Germany and, to a lesser extent, Britain, provided a critical resource for the generation and management of new technologies.

By way of contrast, the Australian government tolerated anti-competitive behaviour among firms until the mid-1970s, and comparatively spent significantly less per capita on technical and higher education. It did not continue support for local defence industries beyond the mid-1950s,[46] and it was parsimonious in its support of private sector research and development. On the other hand, Australian governments had offered protection to manufacturers since before World War One through a combination of tariffs and import quotas. The indiscriminate awarding of 'protection' assisted in the creation of new industries in which additional corporate leaders emerged, for example, the automobile, chemical and petroleum industries. Subsidiaries of foreign firms often captured the premier positions in these new industries as they could deploy their parent's superior technology and, in the consumer goods industries, leverage existing brand equity.

Mid-century assessment

At mid-century, big business in Australia with the corporate leaders at its apex had a distinctive national flavour. The differences revolved around its location within the economy and its structural and behavioural characteristics. Australia's corporate leaders bore the stamp of the country's past.

At the time of the second industrial revolution, Australia was one of the wealthiest countries in the world. Its wealth derived from an extensive natural resource base whose exploitation necessitated massive investments in both rural and urban infrastructure and the provision of a wide range of specialist services. Its trade pattern was to export commodities and import manufactures. High per capita incomes and a rapidly growing local market provided opportunities for local providers of services and manufactured goods.

The first wave of large modern businesses occurred in the distributive trades, pastoral and financial services, particularly banks, mining and consumer goods manufacturing. The largest enterprises in the country at the beginning of the century were government-owned utilities such as posts and telegraphs, railways, tramways and later gas and electrical generation and distribution. Services remained important bastions of big business and corporate leadership despite losing some ground in the top 100 lists to the growing number of manufacturers.

These industrial enterprises became the centre of gravity of corporate leadership a full half-century later than in the United States, Britain or Germany. Having done so, they displayed many attributes that set them apart from the giant industrial enterprises of those more mature economies. Those businesses that had been created by local entrepreneurs were largely confined to industries that were not of the first rank technologically. They were located in the consumer rather than the producer goods industries and they lacked the extensive managerial hierarchies of the world's largest firms. However, they were also successful in transferring technologies from overseas and in making their own advances in process and product technology. Corporate leaders found organisational solutions to the pressing problems of multi-unit operations ranged over great distances through the evolution of an organic multidivisional structure. Further, they negotiated cooperative relationships with suppliers, customers and rivals such as networks, alliances, joint ventures and long-term contracts that were effective substitutes to horizontal and vertical integration.

Converging towards the Anglo-Saxon model, 1950–2000

The next 50 years saw remarkable changes in the scale and nature of Australia's largest corporations, reducing their differences from similar firms in the United States, Britain and Germany. Their growth strategies and organisational design were less uniquely Australian in any sense. Table 8.1, using the same set of comparative characteristics for 2000, shows more or less complete convergence.

A number of Australian corporate leaders adopted growth strategies of unrelated diversification through the 1970s and 1980s. For the most part, these conglomerates performed disastrously in the longer term, as discussed in chapters 5 and 7. While the national market remained the largest source of sales for manufacturers, local firms became engaged in global markets to an unprecedented degree. By the turn of the twenty-first century, Australia's largest domestically owned firms in both manufacturing and services were converging towards an Anglo-Saxon or Anglo-American model of 'shareholder capitalism', with its focus on maximum returns in the short term.

Sources of entrepreneurship

It was argued above that Australia had been an outlier, in that foreign firms had made a disproportionate contribution as entrepreneurs in the sense of starting new industries and making innovations that shaped industry boundaries. Domestic entrepreneurship became more important in the second half of the century, particularly in mining and non-financial services. A crude measure of this shift is that the number of foreign firms in the top 100 firms (see Table 2.2, p. 17), fell from a maximum of 36 in 1964 to 24 in 1986 and 30 in 1997.

The aggregate figures mask significant shifts within and across industries. For example, manufacturing's share of the top 100 fell from 71 in 1964 to 46 in 1997. Yet new firms such as Pioneer, Woodside, Southcorp, Goodman Fielder, Pratt Holdings, Smorgon Consolidated Industries, Murray Goulburn

Cooperative, Bonlac, and the Crane Group, entered the top 100 list between 1986 and 1997. This pattern was repeated in the resurgent mining sector with new local firms in oil, gold, diamonds, coal and bauxite entering the top 100 list in both 1986 and 1997, while the number of foreign firms fell.[47]

Domestic firms also led the charge in growth, creating very large service enterprises, particularly in construction and property management, transport, media, entertainment, fast foods, and gambling. On the other hand, as shown in Table 2.9 (p. 25), deregulation of the financial industry in the 1980s led to a sharp rise in the number of foreign-owned entities in the top 25 firms by 1997.

Sources of competitive advantage

Large firms and corporate leaders generated competitive advantages from a variety of sources. Insofar as generalisations are possible, there was a shift towards more reliance upon Chandlerian organisational capabilities and a dramatic decline in the importance of collusive agreements and government assistance. Market position rested more on delivering what the customers wanted than had been the case previously.

The increased scale and scope of leading firms shifted the balance decisively in favour of salaried executives taking over the role of management from the founding entrepreneur, their heirs or pioneering managers. There was a generational aspect to this transition as many of the older captains of industry retired or died in the 1950s. In the introduction to his perceptive biographical essays about inter-war business leaders, Kemp notes that 'development [of their companies] depended less on organisational methods and more on the dynamic drive, vision and all-round ability of gifted individuals ... big decisions were based more on the personal predilections and intuitions'. None, he suggests, 'would have fitted comfortably into the more rigid procedures and tighter rules of the modern, large-scale organisation'.[48]

In some cases, family dominance declined. For example, the direct influence of members of the Coles and Myer families in running these massive retailing empires lessened over time. On the other hand, some families, most notably the Fairfaxes and Packers, have maintained their control over generations, while new founders and family-dominated firms emerged, including the Murdochs, Smorgons, Lowys and Pratts.

These examples notwithstanding, the skills of professional salaried managers became an important source of organisational capabilities. This was largely a consequence of the enhancement of managerial quality. The breadth and depth of skills of salaried managers was significantly greater after World War Two. War service had provided an unprecedented training in administration for many thousands of young men who became career managers. The numbers graduating from universities and technical colleges rose sharply, particularly after the Commonwealth government assumed responsibility for university funding after 1957. Professionals such as engineers, geologists, accountants, chemists, economists, and lawyers rose up through the ranks of an increasingly specialised middle management to assume general management positions. A later generation of marketing, finance and IT professionals followed.

The organisational capabilities of Australian firms improved in the second half of the twentieth century. The pool of skills available to employers from shop floor to management was swollen by increased government funding of education and the arrival of skilled migrants. Firms increasingly undertook formal on-the-job training themselves or through outsourcing to specialist providers, partly in response to government policy initiatives. Much of this training was linked in the 1980s and 1990s to the introduction of Japanese shop floor practices such as kanban systems and just-in-time, and quality assurance.[49] Manufacturing firms benchmarked themselves against best practice elsewhere to diagnose weaknesses.[50]

Although still low by international standards, research and development expenditures rose as more Australian firms became participants in this activity. Tax concessions by government provided the spur. Australian firms narrowed the still considerable gap between themselves and the rest of the world in their ability to generate new knowledge, innovate and become internationally competitive.[51]

The accumulation of deeper sets of administrative skills underpinned the emergence of larger, more complex and geographically diverse businesses. Employee numbers, a proxy for the scale of tasks facing management, tell the story. In the mid-1960s, BHP was the largest employer with nearly 45 000 employees. By 1997, Coles Myer had 148 000 employees, and was one of 16 private sector non-financial firms with more than 20 000 employees.[52]

Building managerial hierarchies facilitated diversification as a wider set of skills within the firm enabled it to pursue new growth strategies, most notably diversification to exploit economies of scope. One measure of the strengthening of organisational capabilities of corporate leaders was the extent to which these and other large firms aligned this strategy with an appropriate multidivisional structure. A pioneering study of the strategy and structure of large Australian-owned manufacturing and service firms in the mid-1970s revealed that of the 146 manufacturing firms in the study, 131 were using an M-form or divisional structure.[53] However, this result probably overstates the extent and importance of diversification strategies and the use of M-form structures. The divisionalised firms had on average only 1.6 divisions. Moreover, most of these firms had adopted a divisionalised structure only after 1960, and it was the result of an evolutionary process of adjustment rather than a major reorganisation.[54]

Comparative growth strategies

Growth strategies pursued by corporate leaders increasingly approximated those of the largest firms in other countries. Integration, both horizontal and vertical, became even more important, although cooperative inter-firm relations were still used widely as well. Firms diversified into new product and geographic markets. A number of underlying environmental factors impacted on the changing portfolio of growth strategies. An expansion of the domestic market was very important. Population rose from around eight million in 1950 to 19 million by the turn of the twenty-first century.

While the local market grew significantly at the aggregate level, its effect was magnified significantly by the progressive integration of state or capital city-based markets into a national market by improvements in transportation. Manufacturers generally concentrated production in the major cities in the eastern states to realise the maximum plant economies of scale and built a national network of distribution centres.[55] Population expansion, market integration, and rising income levels allowed firms to increase their scale closer to the point where they needed to make the Chandlerian three-pronged investments. A national market allowed the development of national brands, an increasingly important element in the battle for competitive advantage.

To expand scale in production and to link production and distribution, many corporate leaders actively sought to merge with or acquire other firms. The early postwar decade and a half saw Australia's first merger wave in which firms absorbed rivals in the same product markets and many went interstate to build up national representation.[56] Further flurries of merger activity in the 1970s and 1980s resulted in a redrawing of the corporate landscape as many corporate leaders acquired one another. As discussed in Chapter 7, most of the conglomerates created by these mergers failed to create value for their shareholders. Many went into liquidation.[57]

The rapid rise and fall of leading companies through the 1980s and early 1990s had two lasting consequences, both of which were associated with a sea change in the nature of corporate governance. For most of the previous quarter of a century, hierarchies of salaried managers effectively controlled the allocation of corporate resources. Able to control the flow of retained earnings and having long-term relationships with their bankers, they adopted 'retain and retrain' strategies with respect to their funds and, more importantly, workers.[58] The shift to free-market ideologies and the associated micro-economic reforms, to be discussed below, shifted the balance of power towards shareholders in the 1980s and 1990s.[59]

Managers were under pressure to maximise shareholder value. One way of maintaining earnings was to 'downsize and distribute' surplus capital and labour back onto their respective markets.[60] The swollen corporate carcasses of the 1980s were rapidly dismembered, often through leveraged management buyouts. Downsizing and outsourcing became the order of the day as corporates, including the newly privatised publicly-owned businesses, focused on core activities. Australia's largest corporations shed tens of thousands of jobs, with 52 of the top 100 firms downsizing their workforces between 1992 and 1997.[61]

From the 1970s, the minds of directors and executives were concentrated towards maximising shareholder value by the emergence of a market for corporate control. Prior to this time, nearly all mergers and acquisitions involved only willing sellers. Hostile bids were limited by two important considerations. First, directors were not required to disclose offers to their shareholders until the amendment to the *Uniform Companies Act 1970*.[62] Second, financial institutions, notably trading banks, were reluctant to finance hostile bids. Changes to legislation mandating greater transparency in acquisition activity, together with financial deregulation, combined to create an environment in which hostile bids became commonplace. The rise of institutional shareholders,[63] reflecting the introduction of compulsory superannuation contributions in the early 1990s, added pressure on corporations' earnings. Firms that lost their way faced effective shareholder revolts that resulted in, for example, the departure of the chairman and several directors from Coles Myer and the replacement of directors and senior executives at Westpac, Orica (formerly part of Imperial Chemical Industries of Australia and New Zealand), BHP, Australian and New Zealand Bank, and Pacific Dunlop.

The strategies followed by corporate leaders were shaped by major changes in government policies on a wide number of fronts. For most of the twentieth century, Australian governments had followed highly interventionist policies to achieve a mix of social outcomes including national development, defence, population growth, and social security linked to a minimum wage and the pursuit of full employment.[64] In the 1980s Australian governments accepted the free-market ideology of the Reagan and Thatcher governments.[65]

Some of the policy reversals, which became known colloquially as microeconomic reform, had begun under the Whitlam government (1972–75), particularly with respect to reductions in trade barriers and the extension of trade practices legislation. The rhetoric of the Fraser government (1975–83) about reform exceeded its actions.

It was the Hawke–Keating Labor governments (1983–96) whose reforms swept aside most of the protective and regulatory apparatus that had shielded Australian product and factor markets from competitive pressures since before World War One. Trade barriers were largely removed. The financial system was released from its wartime restrictions in the early 1980s. It was also opened to international pressures with the floating of the dollar and the removal of exchange controls. Important reforms also occurred in labour markets with the introduction of enterprise bargaining. Furthermore, nearly all of the government-owned enterprises – financial services, air, road and rail transport, gas and electricity, ports and harbours, and water – were sold to private investors in the 1990s.[66]

In short, managers of Australia's largest firms found themselves in a very different environment than had been the case in 1950. Prices for goods, services and factors increasingly reflected supply and demand. Markets became more competitive in spite of the continued existence of pockets of market power. The removal of trade barriers, the lifting of regulatory suppression of competition and the end of monopoly rights conferred on state-owned enterprises, eroded the value of strategic assets enjoyed by protected firms.

Managers needed alternative sources of competitive advantage, such as organisational capabilities or proprietary assets that underpinned leading corporations in the United States, Great Britain and Germany, if they were to survive. Other consequences followed. Vigorous enforcement of competition policy from the mid-1970s put paid to collusive inter-firm cooperation. Moreover, the withdrawal of widespread protection by government increasingly forced challengers to compete with incumbents by entering niche markets or waiting for markets to become large enough to support new entrants. As noted above, the expansion of the local market in the 50 years after World War Two provided opportunities for new challengers to emerge.

Australian businesses entered foreign markets on an increasing scale after the mid-1970s as managers responded to the new environmental pressures. Australian firms sold a greater proportion of their produce overseas than they had done a generation earlier. The ratio of exports of goods and services to GDP rose from 15.2 per cent in 1975–79 to 19.0 per cent in 1992–96. More significantly, manufacturing and services, traditionally net importers, became important contributors towards the rising export totals.

Manufacturing's share of exports rose from 9.0 per cent in 1975–79 to 17.6 per cent in 1992–96, while services rose from 14.3 per cent to 22.4 per cent over the same period.[67] Thirty-two of the 46 manufacturing firms from the top 100 list for 1997 can be identified in a list of Australia's leading exporters.[68] Moreover, Australian firms undertook outward foreign direct investment on an

unprecedented scale, driving the ratio of outward stock of foreign direct
investment to GDP from 1.4 per cent in 1975–79 to 11.5 per cent in 1992–96.[69]
Twenty-nine of the 1997 top 100 non-financial companies were operating
as multinationals in the 1990s,[70] while there were eight multinationals from
among the 16 domestically-owned financial services firms from the top 25
list of 1997.[71]

In spite of this shift towards internationalisation, Australian manufacturers
and service providers still relied more on their domestic market than did comparable firms from the leading industrial economies, smaller European countries
and Canada. Australian firms had been slower to embark as multinationals
and some were not particularly successful when they had done so. National
Australia Bank lost heavily through its purchase of Homeside Mortgage, a
United States mortgage firm. AMP has fared poorly from its acquisition of
Pearl Insurance in Britain. BHP had a series of disappointments offshore
ranging from its involvement in the ill-fated Ok Tedi mine to the divestment
of copper mines in Arizona in 1999.

Poorly performing or loss-making subsidiaries reflected deep-seated systemic issues facing Australian managers. A small, distant and heavily protected
economy was not an encouraging environment in which to build the economies
of scale and scope necessary to underpin international expansion. Just as
importantly, by focusing on domestic markets Australian managers had little
opportunity to acquire the skills needed to run multinational enterprises. In particular, they lacked experience in operating across different national markets.[72]

Century's end

By the end of the twentieth century, therefore, Australia's largest corporations
had lost much of their unique national identity as they converged towards a
western 'business model'. The historical dependence on imported technology
was extended to the import of business 'software'. Many of the leading firms
in resources, manufacturing and services were foreign owned or at least controlled. However, the influence of United States, European and, to a lesser
extent, Japanese business models was far more pervasive. More frequent travel
and almost instantaneous access to news and information from around the
world made Australian managers less insular in their outlook. Moreover, nearly
all of the providers of business services were subsidiaries of foreign firms.

Australian managers bought services from foreign-owned management con-
sultants,[73] executive recruiters, accountancy and audit firms, merchant banks,
market researchers and advertising agencies.[74] The curriculum and textbooks
of the ubiquitous MBA programs taken by aspiring middle managers were
replicas of the United States. The mindsets and skills of Australian managers

were heavily reflective of the dominant management paradigms of the leading industrial economies.

In terms of Chandler's taxonomy of national business systems, Australia had shifted from approximating British 'personal capitalism' at mid-century to becoming closer to the 'competitive managerial capitalism' of the United States at century's end. The characteristics of big business in Australia early in the century reflected the distinctive nature of its economy and the commercial relationships between it and the rest of the world. Australia was a late starter in the process of industrialisation. The half a century of high trade barriers did little to develop organisational capabilities. The last quarter of the twentieth century saw a rapid and extensive change in the allocation of resources between sectors, a strengthening of organisational capabilities and a far greater international orientation by managers. Shareholders became the dominant stakeholder. Where corporate leaders were located within the economy, how those businesses were managed and what strategies they pursued were more and more like those of the other advanced industrial economies. The differences revolved primarily around degrees of internationalisation and, as discussed in the last section of Chapter 2, organisational scale.

Big business, corporate leaders and the creation of national wealth

Our interpretation of variations in long-term growth trends owes much to Chandler's arguments about systemic differences between national business systems. He made the case that the supremacy of the United States economy in the mid-twentieth century rested above all on the superior performance of its system of 'competitive managerial capitalism'.[75] This section of the chapter analyses the relationship between the emergence of big business and corporate leaders, in particular, and the absolute and comparative performance of the Australian economy in the twentieth century.

Current explanations of Australia's long-term macroeconomic performance appeal to aggregate models and national accounts data.[76] Growth, in absolute and comparative terms, is explained in terms of stocks of resources, rates of capital accumulation, and broad demographic factors. For the most part, government policies and exogenous factors beyond Australia were seen to have had a negative impact on the rate at which the economy could expand and its productivity increase. Chandlerian issues about the potential efficiency gains associated with new institutional forms have yet to be considered in this literature. To those scholars operating in a neo-classical economics paradigm, the firm has remained a hermetically sealed black box.

It is very difficult to model the relationship between the behaviour of the largest companies and long-term macroeconomic outcomes. The problem arises because the largest companies behave in ways that result in both 'goods' and 'bads'. Their beneficial effects include the superior efficiency with which they transform inputs into outputs, reduced transactions costs by substituting internalisation for problematic market exchange, and greater innovation. On the other hand, largeness is often associated with market power, and concomitant higher prices, poor quality, and slower rates of innovation.

There was no simple correspondence between the rise of large-scale enterprise and the trend performance of the economy in the last century. Australia enjoyed one of the highest per capita incomes in the world in the late nineteenth century, predating its industrialisation from the 1920s. Previously, Australia's wealth derived from its abundant natural resource base. The accumulation of additional labour and capital to exploit these resources mattered more than increases in productivity resulting from new forms of economic institutions. Early in the century, small-scale firms could still provide the merchanting and intermediating functions necessary to link miners, primary producers and manufacturers with their suppliers and customers. It was an economic system in which neither scale nor scope at firm level had yet become critical sources of competitive advantage.

Over the twentieth century, the economy expanded as the population more than doubled and real per capita incomes rose strongly. By any measure, living standards and the quality of life enjoyed by the majority of Australians was far higher in 2000 than 1900. However, the growth of Australian per capita incomes had been eclipsed by that of many other countries.[77] In the first half of the century, per capita incomes in this country showed little advance from 1890 to 1940.[78] Australia slipped down the OECD league ladder from fourth place in 1950 to tenth in the mid-1980s, its decline being explained more in terms of catching up by the rest rather than any absolute failing by the Australian economy to generate faster growth in productivity.[79] It is only in the last two decades of the century that Australian growth has risen comparatively and that there has been a sustained increase in total factor productivity.[80]

One can pose the counterfactual: would Australian living standards have risen more slowly than they did if no large-scale enterprises, run by hierarchies of salaried managers, had emerged in the resources, services and, most importantly, in the science-based, capital-intensive parts of manufacturing? The preceding chapters, discussing the emergence and longevity of our corporate leaders, support an answer in the affirmative: more large firms made a positive contribution.

It is improbable that Australia could have advanced as it did with what Chandler describes as the traditional enterprise.[81] The argument rests on the premise that the firms which became corporate leaders did so because their scale and organisational form underpinned their sustainable competitive advantage. This line of reasoning derives from two sets of literature. First, from the resource-based theories of the firm that link the creation of core competencies from organisational routines and learning to the achievement of sustainable competitive advantage. The second comes from the transaction costs literature and emphasises the economising aspect of the internalisation of activities.[82] Together they provide a *prima facie* argument that firms which become part of big business will, *ceteris paribus*, have an efficiency advantage over those which do not. Those advantages come from the exploitation of both scale and scope, together with a minimisation of transactions costs and, further, a greater capacity to innovate and diversify in the longer term.

Innovation and scale went hand in hand. At one level, this is nothing more than a restatement of Chandler's argument that new technologies in transport and communication, and process technologies, brought forth large-scale industrial enterprises in the late nineteenth century.[83] However, there is another dimension. The new technologies often dictated that large-scale organisations came to dominate markets. New organisational forms were necessary to exploit the possibilities of mass production and mass distribution, strategy and structure were thus inter-linked. These same large organisations, particularly in the science-based sections of mining and manufacturing, possessed the financial and technical resources to create or adapt to new technologies. It was the largest firms in Australia, many of them corporate leaders, that were in the vanguard of innovation, and whose cumulative effect was to make a significant and positive contribution to building national wealth. The gains flowed from economising on resource use and by extending the range of goods and services available in the market place.

Figure 8.1 presents a highly stylised illustration of the role of corporate leaders in introducing technological change. Two conclusions emerge. First, it shows that innovation and technological changes have taken place in different parts of the economy at different points in time. Second, it shows that the most important developments have occurred in the resources and intermediate goods industries, raw materials and components, rather than final consumer goods parts of manufacturing. Moreover, very significant technological advances and innovation have also taken place in business services, broadly defined, and the infrastructure supporting business operations.

Reading the diagram from left to right rearranges the industry ASIC into a crude value chain, starting with raw materials from farms and mines through to first-stage transformations in food, paper, chemicals and petroleum, glass, rubber and plastics, and basic metals, and then on to more end products and finished consumer products, fabricated metals, textiles and clothing, wood products, transport equipment, especially motor cars, and other industrial machinery, equipment and household appliances.

Figure 8.1: Interconnection of technological change

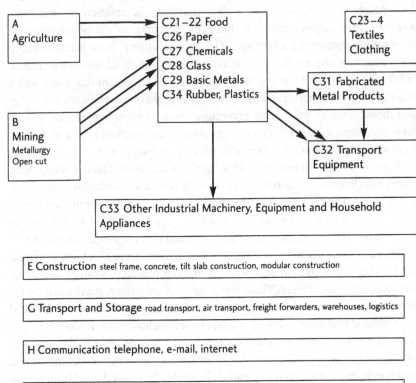

Significant technological innovation transformed the mining and food industries in the late nineteenth and early twentieth centuries.[84] This included the separation of complex mineral ores and innovations such as roller milling, refining, canning, pasteurisation and refrigeration in the food and beverage industries. Unlocking the mineral wealth of the New South Wales mines had important flow-on effects in the emergent non-ferrous basic metals and fertiliser industries after World War One.

The interwar period saw important advances on a number of fronts. The basic metals sector was fleshed out by the establishment of an iron and steel industry, which, in combination with non-ferrous metals, underpinned the expansion of fabricated metals. There were also major technical developments and innovations in chemicals, rubber, glass, and paper industries that impacted beneficially on downstream users.

Another wave of major innovations occurred after World War Two, most notably in automobile, aluminium and the chemical and petroleum industries. The latter were fundamental to the development of synthetic compounds that generated a new wave of products, including plastics. It was in the final consumer goods industries, notably textiles and clothing, wooden products, household appliances, electronic goods and so on, that technical advances were more modest in their frequency and impact.

Innovations were also taking place outside large-scale manufacturing enterprises in business services and infrastructure. Most of these major innovations in technologies came after World War Two, the substitution of electrical power for gas and steam, telephones for letters or the telegraph, new modes of transport, road and air travel rather than rail and ship, and new materials and construction technologies for buildings and infrastructure. The wholesale and retail trades were transformed, initially by the emergence of innovations in retailing including department stores and then variety chain stores. The application of information and computing technologies from the 1980s enabled the linking of retailers to wholesalers and manufacturers in a new fashion through integrated supply chains.[85] Mechanisation and the application of computers transformed clerical and administrative procedures, revolutionising back office work in financial service firms such as banks and insurance firms from the 1960s.

This account of the introduction of new technologies, often creating a 'new' industry, is broad brush in the extreme. It is not to deny that many of these technologies were applied earlier in other countries, that the state played a key role in science and technology in Australia, that local firms acquired technology under licence from abroad or that much was transferred to Australia through subsidiaries of multinationals, or that some of the imported technologies were inappropriate in the small local market.[86] The substantive point is that innovations were implemented by large firms in many industries, whose effects cascaded further afield, encouraging and supporting innovations elsewhere. This process of innovation, in pursuit of profit and competitive advantage, generated higher productivity growth than would have been the case in its absence.

Distributing wealth

If larger firms and corporate leaders possessed superior ways of creating value, how was it distributed among their various stakeholders? How did these large corporations interact with their workers, creditors and owners, and suppliers and customers? An institutional framework that defined and enforced property rights set the parameters for the outcomes of competing claims for shares of the wealth.[87] Government legislation and tribunals impacted on the nature of wage bargains, defined acceptable standards of corporate behaviour towards suppliers and customers, and defined the rights of creditors and owners, including the responsibilities of directors. These laws, enforced by the courts, were shaped by a dynamic political process, in which organised labour played a key role, and by shifting ideologies about the role of the state.

Workers

Large companies transformed work practices and labour relations in Australia. This is not to deny the long history of adversarial and confrontational relations between employers and trade unions in this country. Rather, the point is that larger organisations were the trail blazers towards what Jacoby has termed 'good jobs'.[88] They offered career paths, especially in white collar jobs, greater job security and non-wage benefits[89] than smaller firms. The defining character of labour management in many of these larger organisations was the creation of an internal labour market.[90] The retention of a stable labour force was a neces- sary condition for developing organisational routines, particularly those relying on tacit knowledge that generated firm-specific competencies.

Job security was a highly desirable attribute of any employment bargain in the first half of the century, particularly in the 1930s depression. The threat of job loss lessened during the 'golden age' of full employment from the end of the war until the mid-1970s. Yet, non-wage benefits, seniority payments, on-the-job training, and internal promotion continued to attract bright young, usually better educated, women and men into the big companies and govern- ment public service. However, the very substantial job losses associated with the privatisation and downsizing of the past two decades have signalled a very different attitude towards the wage bargain on the part of employers.[91]

What proportion of workers were employed by the largest firms offering better employment conditions? The available data allows only a speculative answer before World War Two. If the definition of big business is relaxed to include the government-owned businesses, there were a number of very large employers. For example, the Post Office had nearly 44 000 employees in 1930, and the state rail and tramways employed more than 100 000 people.[92] Vic- toria's electricity generator and distributor, the State Electricity Commission of Victoria, employed nearly 7000 persons in 1937–38.[93] Firms in the private sector were smaller, only 12 businesses in the 1930s had more than 2000 employees. Of those, only BHP, the Collins House Group, General Motors- Holden's, Australian Glass Manufacturers and Myer had more than 5000.[94]

Taken together, the public and private sector employment in the largest organisations accounted for about 16 per cent of the civilian workforce, excluding farming and domestic service, at the 1933 census.[95]

The full flowering of big business after World War Two meant that the numbers employed by the largest private and government-owned businesses increased substantially. However, the figures need to be treated with caution. The *Delfin Digest* 1967 list of just under 900 of the largest companies and government trading agencies shows that they employed more than a quarter of the workforce.[96] Employees of the top 500 manufacturing firms in *Delfin Digest* accounted for more than a half of total employment in the industry.

Similarly, the *Business Review Weekly*'s 1986 list of the top 1000 businesses in Australia and Zealand, ranked by value of sales, shows the same broad result. After deducting the New Zealand numbers, the remaining Australian firms employed about a quarter of the workforce.[97] These data suggest that one in four Australians were employed in the population of firms from which the corporate leaders were drawn in the 1960s and 1980s.

Owners

How successful were these largest companies in creating wealth directly for their owners, the shareholders? Over the long term, equities offered higher returns to investors than other financial assets. However, how widely were such benefits shared across the Australian community? Once again, long-term data is lacking. What information exists relates to the post-World War Two period.

In the 1950s individuals held three-quarters of the shares on issue in more than 100 of Australia's largest companies. Unfortunately, the number of persons or households owning shares at that time is unknown. Our judgement would be that share ownership was confined only to the better off, a small proportion of the population. By 1995, individuals held less than a quarter of the market value of shares, losing their once dominant place to institutional and foreign investors.[98] Despite this long-term downward trend, the proportion of householders directly owning shares more than doubled between 1980 and 1994, rising from 7 to 16 per cent.[99] Many households first entered the market buying shares in the initial public offerings of the newly privatised government businesses. In the 1990s, nearly all employees came to have an indirect beneficial interest through their compulsory participation in superannuation funds.[100] The ability of large firms listed on the stock exchange to create and distribute wealth through dividends, share price growth, bonus issues and share buy-backs has become a matter of material importance to Australia's ageing population.

Creditors

Creditors were also important stakeholders. The providers were lending institutions such as banks, direct financiers who held the firms' securities, and trade
creditors. In the absence of solid data, our view is that default rates were low.
Of course, firms failed and creditors' debts were not fully recovered. Some of
the failures, and associated losses, were spectacular.[101] Of these, many were
spiced with fraudulent behaviour as well as directorial and managerial incompetence. However, there is no compelling evidence to suggest that Australian
large firms and corporate leaders were less well managed, in the sense of
preventing failure, than firms in the United States, Britain or Germany.

Suppliers

How did large corporations deal with their suppliers? Many of the firms from
the top 100 lists were service firms that relied less on their suppliers than
manufacturers. In the case of manufacturers, were suppliers exploited by buyers
that operated, as will be discussed below, in highly concentrated markets?[102]
Once again, this question must be answered in a somewhat speculative fashion.
It might well be that investigation on an industry-by-industry basis would
reveal that buyers exerted monopsonistic power, and likewise that a supplier
was in a position to extract monopoly rents.

Two observations lend support to the view that large corporations may have
shown forbearance to their suppliers. First, manufacturers shared rents in many
industries through vertical price maintenance schemes with suppliers, at least
until the 1970s.[103] Secondly, where large manufacturers faced large distributors,
such as supermarkets from the 1960s onwards, a countervailing power, almost
bilateral monopoly, prevented one party from extracting rents from the other.[104]

The ability of large firms to pressure suppliers to reduce prices and increase
quality has been strengthened in the past 25 years. The Commonwealth government's legislation to outlaw anti-competitive behaviour broke the vertical and
horizontal agreements that once protected margins for suppliers, producers
and distributors in many industries. Moreover, the shift towards downsizing
and outsourcing in the 1980s and 1990s has placed a premium on competitive
tendering.

This broad generalisation must be qualified by exceptions. One was the
emergence of supply chains between component makers and automobile
assemblers that involved very close and almost quasi-permanent relationships.
Even in these circumstances, there was pressure from the buyers, who enjoyed
lower levels of government assistance than they received in the past, for continuous cost reductions and quality improvements.

Customers

To what extent did customers receive a share of the productivity gains resulting from innovation and rivalry through some combination of lower prices, higher quality and new products? The ability of large corporations to generate productivity increases was limited, particularly by the small scale of the market, as discussed above, when compared with the gains generated by firms in similar industries in the larger industrial economies. That observation notwithstanding, some economies of scale were evident in many parts of manufacturing and in financial services, and wholesale and retail distribution. Mass production, in brewing for instance,[105] and mass distribution, through department and variety stores, had a significant displacement effect on smaller businesses before World War Two.

Many commentators have argued that large corporations in Australia operated in highly uncompetitive markets from before World War One until the microeconomic reforms of the 1980s. For example, Karmel and Brunt's pioneering study of concentration drew attention to the high levels of concentration in both national and regional markets. They went on to argue that the 'kind' of industries that were highly concentrated was a matter of great consequence. In short, their findings were that the producer goods industries were more heavily concentrated than those in consumer goods. These producer goods industries were identified as having the most significant impact on efficient resource allocation because 'the further back an industry is located in the vertical sequence of processes leading to the consumer the more its behaviour, and in particular its cost-price relationships, will affect the structure of the economy as a whole'.[106] This same group of industries were the ones identified in Figure 8.1 as the most important source of innovation and dynamic efficiency improvements.

Can these seemingly contradictory positions be reconciled? If the existence of only a few firms in many industries weakens competitive pressures, how much of the cost reductions resulting from innovation would be passed on to customers, particularly final consumers, rather than be absorbed into higher profits? The weakest proposition is that some part of it was. While competition might have been muted, it was not entirely absent in most markets. Apart from industries that were government monopolies or where private operators enjoyed statutory monopoly rights, there were few cases where firms enjoyed prohibitive and permanent barriers to entry or faced no substitutes. Reductions in the numbers of competitors through mergers and acquisitions were often offset by new entrants, many of whom were subsidiaries of foreign multinationals.[107] Rivalry existed even where there were few sellers. A recent estimate of the welfare loss due to monopoly in Australia indicates that the burden was the equivalent to 'only one-half of one per cent of turnover'.[108]

Falling real prices and quality improvements measured consumers' benefits from the struggle among big business for their custom. For example, the local car industry never achieved the efficiencies of those of larger economies because of the small size of the market. Moreover, the high levels of protection offered to it by governments from World War One onwards further encouraged too many assemblers to enter. Yet, this highly protected and inefficient industry by world standards offered consumers a stream of cars whose functionality and durability increased significantly over time. New models of Holden cars embodied significant advances in technology and comfort.[109] The number of vehicles produced per person employed in the industry, while comparatively low, rose 60 per cent over the decade from 1954–55 to 1964–65.[110] It is likely that the real cost of cars fell in Australia over a long period of time, and the number of hours needed to be worked to buy a car also fell.

It was the larger corporations that led the way in product and process innovation. Many of the corporate leaders identified in earlier chapters gained and sustained their competitive advantage through innovation, a process that widened consumer choice as a stream of new and improved products came to market. Valve radios gave way to transistors, black and white televisions were superseded by colour and so on. A more competitive set of markets may have speeded up the process, but innovatory activity went on nevertheless.

James Hardie, the building supply firm, continuously upgraded the pipe-making machines employed in its eight factories between 1926 and 1968. It used three different types, and new models of both the 'Magnani' and 'Mazza' machines, each technically superior to its predecessor. This frequent process of replacing machines factory by factory enhanced the firm's technological base.[111] A similar upgrading of technology across a broad front of industries, that in all probability took place more slowly than in other advanced industrial economies, led to improvements in dynamic efficiency. Insofar as big business, and corporate leaders in particular, were in the vanguard of innovation, it contributed in an important way to the secular improvement in Australian standards of living.

In sum, the three principal beneficiaries of the presence of large business enterprises in the Australian economy over the past 100 years have been their employees, owners and customers. A significant share of the civilian workforce was employed by large corporations, both public and private. Up until the 1980s, workers in these firms had greater job security, the greater prospect of a career ladder, on-the-job training, and the greater likelihood of non-wage benefits than workers in smaller firms. Those owning shares in large firms listed on stock exchanges, appear to have been well rewarded for risking their capital. Over the long term, dividend payments and rising equity prices provided higher returns than investments in alternative financial assets. Consumers enjoyed a wider choice of both goods and services as firms competed by lowering prices and improving quality.

Conclusion

The contention of this chapter has been that large corporations, exemplified by corporate leaders, played a central role in the transformation of the Australian economy in much the same manner as has been described for many other countries.[112] In the main, new sources of energy and advances in manufacturing and communications technology provided the wellspring for new types of industrial organisation in the late nineteenth and early twentieth centuries. Giant industrial enterprises sprang forth, integrating mass production with mass distribution. The exploitation of scale and scope brought dominant market positions and further diversification in products and geographic scope. It is a story of industrialisation and increasingly of competition for international markets.

Australian experience differed at the margins from that of other countries. Its industrialisation came later and was unusually reliant on government assistance. Trade barriers designed to protect the marginal firms in product markets worked against the consolidating tendencies of competition experienced in the United States or Germany, in particular. In its full flowering in the 1960s, Australia's industrial sector had a smaller share of GDP than in the major industrial economies. Moreover, it was weighted more towards consumer than producer goods. In many respects, until mid-century, Australian big business was closer to the British model of 'personal capitalism' than to the United States' 'competitive managerial capitalism' or Germany's 'cooperative managerial capitalism'. The argument made above is that Australian large corporations converged towards an Anglo-Saxon form of shareholder capitalism during the end of the twentieth century. However, the largest firms remained small by international standards and were less international in their orientation than their foreign peers.

Big business and corporate leaders did make a positive contribution to raising Australian living standards. This claim is in sharp contrast to a long tradition of condemnation of market power by radicals dating back to World War One,[113] and a growing chorus of academic critics from the 1960s who calculated seller concentration and market power industry by industry.[114] This identification of static inefficiencies arising from concentrated markets was confirmed by reports of the federal government's Industries Assistance Commission, and its successors, the Industry and the Productivity Commissions.

Again and again, their inquiries highlighted a lack of international competitiveness on the part of Australian firms. Furthermore, long-standing anti-competitive agreements among firms in many industries demonstrated an abuse of market power. While such strictures hold true, the counterview that corporations developed superior organisational capabilities, that they applied new technologies to create new products or cheapen and improve old ones, should be seen to carry equal weight.

Australian Standard Industrial Classification, 1969

A   **Agriculture, Forestry, Fishing and Hunting**
1   Agriculture
2   Services to Agriculture
3   Forestry and Logging
4   Fishing and Hunting

B   **Mining**
11   Metallic Minerals
12   Coal
13   Crude Petroleum (including Natural Gas)
14   Construction Materials
15   Other Non-Metallic Minerals
16   Services to Mining

C   **Manufacturing**
21–22   Food, Beverages and Tobacco
23   Textiles
24   Clothing and footwear (including Knitting Mills)
25   Wood, Wood Products and Furniture (except Sheet Metal)
26   Paper and Paper Products, Printing and Publishing
27   Chemical, Petroleum and Coal Products
28   Glass, Clay and other Non-metallic Mineral Products
29   Basic Metal Products
31   Fabricated Metal Products
32   Transport Equipment
33   Other Industrial Machinery and Equipment and Household Appliances
34   Leather, Rubber and Plastic Products and Manufacturing n.e.c.

D   **Electricity, Gas and Water**
36   Electricity and Gas
37   Water, Sewerage and Drainage

E   **Construction**
41   General Construction
42   Special-Trade Contracting

F	**Wholesale and Retail Trade**
46–7	Wholesale Trade
48	Retail Trade

G	**Transport and Storage**
51	Road Transport
52	Railway Transport
53	Water Transport
54	Air Transport
55	Other Transport and Storage

H	**Communication**
56	Communication

I	**Finance, Insurance, Real Estate and Business Services**
61	Finance and Investment
62	Insurance
63	Real Estate and Business Services

J	**Public Administration and Defence**
71	Public Administration
72	Defence

K	**Community Services**
81	Health
82	Education, Libraries, Museums and Art Galleries
83	Welfare and Charitable Services and Religious Institutions
84	Other Community Service

L	**Entertainment, Recreation, Restaurants, Hotels and Personal Services**
91	Entertainment and Recreational Services
92	Restaurants, Hotels and Clubs
93	Personal Services
94	Private Households Employing Staff
99	Non-Classifiable Establishments

Abbreviations

Most Australian company names have been produced in full in the text, except for three, which are particularly well known by their acronym, notably:

AMP (Australian Mutual Provident Society)
BHP (Broken Hill Proprietary Ltd)
CSR (Colonial Sugar Refining Company Ltd)

For simplicity, the prefix 'Australia' has been omitted from the name in the text of many local subsidiaries of foreign multinationals where it is clear that the reference is not to the parent. The following is a list of company abbreviations used in tables:

Name	Abbreviation
Non-Australian	
ABB Group	ABB
ABN-Amro Holding	ABN
Aegon Insurance Group	Aegon
Ahold	Ahold
Akzo Nobel Group	Akzo Nob.
Alusuisse-Lonza Holding	Al-Lo.
American Sugar Refining	AmSR
American Tobacco	AmTob
Anheuser-Busch	An-Bus
Baloise Group	Baloise
Bank of Montreal	BM
Bank of Nova Scotia	BNS
Bell Canada Enterprises	BCE
Bombardier	Bombard.
British Motor Corporation	BMC
Canadian Imperial Bank of Commerce	CIBC
Canadian Pacific	Can Pac
Ciba-Geigy Group	Ciba

Cie Financière Richmont	Cie F R
Credit Suisse Holding Group	CSH
DSM	DSM
Electrolux Group	Electr.
Fortis Group	Fortis
George Weston	G. Weston
Holderbank Financière Glarus	Holderb.
Imperial Oil	Imp Oil
ING Group	ING
International Paper & Power	IPP
International Paper Company	IP
KNP-BT	KNP-BT
Pittsburgh Plate Glass Company	Pitts
Reed Elsevier	Reed
Royal Bank of Canada	RBC
Royal Hoogovens	R. Hoog
SCA-Svenska Cellulosa	SCA-S
Schlumberger	Schlumb.
Skandia Insurance	Skandia
Skandinaviska Enskilda Bank	SkEnB
Skanska	Skanska
SKF Group	SKF
Stora Group	Stora
Svenska Handelsbanken	Svenska
Swiss Bank Corporation	Swiss
Swiss Re Group	Swiss Re
Thomson Corporation	Thomson
Toronto-Dominion Bank	TDB
TransCanada PipeLines	TC PL
Union Bank of Switzerland	UBS
Vendex International Group	Vendex
Winterthur Group	W'thur
Zurich Insurance Group	Zurich

Australian government enterprises

Commonwealth Railways	Clth Rail
Electricity Commission of New South Wales	ECNSW
Electricity Trust South Australia	ETSA
Gas and Fuel Victoria	Gas&FuelVic
Hydro Electricity Commission of Tasmania	HECTas

Metropolitan Transport Victoria	MetroTrsVic
New South Wales Railways	NSWR
Overseas Telecommunications Commission	OTC
Postmaster-General	PMG
Public Transport Victoria	PubTrsVic
Queensland Power Trading	QPowerT
Queensland Railways	Q Rail
South Australian Railways	SA Rail
South East Queensland Electricity Board	SEQEB
State Electricity Commission of Queensland	SECQ
State Electricity Commission of Victoria	SECV
State Electricity Commission of West Australia	SECWA
Trans-Australia Airways	TAA
Victorian Railways	VRail
West Australian Railways	WA Rail

Australian private enterprises

Adelaide Steamship Company	Adsteam
Amalgamated Wireless Australasia	AWA
Australasian Temperance & General	
Mutual Life Assurance Company	Aust Temp & Gen
Australian & New Zealand Bank	ANZ
Australian Bank of Commerce	Aust Bank Com
Australian Consolidated Industries	ACI
Australian Gas Light Company	AGL
Australian Glass Manufacturers	AGM
Australian Industrial Development Corporation	AIDC
Australian Mercantile Loan & Finance Company	AMLF
Australian Metropolitan Life Assurance	Aln Metropolitan
Australian Newsprint	ANwsprnt
Australian Paper Manufacturers	APM
Australian Provincial Assurance Association	Aln Provincial
Australian United Corporation	AUC
Bank of New South Wales	BNSW
British Tobacco Australia	Br Tob
Broken Hill South	BHS
Carlton & United Breweries	CUB
Commercial & General Acceptance	CGA
Commercial Bank of Australia	CBA
Commercial Banking Company of Sydney	CBCS

Commonwealth Bank of Australia	Cwealth
Commonwealth Industrial Gases	CIG
Commonwealth Savings Bank	Com Savings Bank
Consolidated Zinc Corporation	CZC
Conzinc Riotinto Australia	CRA
Dalgety	Dlgty
English, Scottish & Australian Bank	ES&A
General Motors Acceptance Corporation	GMAC
General Motors-Holden's	GM-H
Goldsbrough Mort	GMort
Herald &Weekly Times	HWT
Imperial Chemical Industries of Australia and New Zealand	ICIANZ
Industrial Acceptance Corporation Holdings	IAC Holdings
Mount Isa Mines	MIM
Mutual Life & Citizens' Assurance	MLC
National Australia Bank	NAB
National Mutual Life	NML
New Zealand & Australian Land Co	NZAL
New Zealand Loan & Mercantile Agency	NZLMA
North Broken Hill	NBH
Petersville	Peters
Publishing and Broadcasting Limited	PBL
Queensland Government Insurance Office	Qld Govt IO
RESI-Statewide Building Society	RESI-Statewide
Rural & Industries Bank of Western Australia	R&I Bank WA
South Australian Gas Company	SAGASCO
Union Bank of Australia	UBA
Western Mining Corporation	WMC
Westpac	Wpac

Appendix A: Government-owned business enterprises ranked by assets, 1910–97

	1910 $m	1930 $m	1952 $m	1964 $m	1986 $bn	1997 $bn
PMG	27.8[1]	107.0	436.0	1289.2	0.717	2.736
Telecom					14.466	
Telstra						26.470
OTC					0.885	
Clth Rail				75.0		0.862[2]
Vic Rail	92.0	163.0	165.6	390.9	1.291[3]	
PubTrsVic						4.390
MetroTrsVic					1.492	
NSW Rail		265.8		668.5	4.220	4.623
Qld Rail				229.6	1.899	6.487
SA Rail		74.6	89.0	133.3		
WA Rail				140.7	0.587	1.244[4]
TAA				43.4	1.351	
Qantas				113.8	2.025	[5]
SECV		39.6	294.2	771.7	8.288	0.835
ECNSW				502.1	6.569	
ETSA			63.2	214.8	2.174	3.166
SECQ				142.0	4.299	
SEQEB					1.395	
QTPower						6.272
SECWA				88.0	3.655	
Gas&FuelVic			26.0	102.0	0.860	2.465
HECTas					2.032	

Notes: [1] PMG's first accounts 1913; [2] Includes National Rail; [3] Includes State Transport Vic; [4] Includes Westrail; ANA became Australian Airlines; [5] Qantas was privatised in 1996.

Sources: 1910–52: Auditor-General's Reports for state and Commonwealth governments; 1964: *Delfin Digest*; 1986 and 1997: *Business Review Weekly*.

Appendix B: Top 25 financial firms ranked by assets, 1910–97

Rank 1910	Firm	Assets £m	Industry/ownership
1	Bank New South Wales	41	Trading bank
2	Union Bank of Australia	26	Trading bank
3	AMP	26	Life office
4	Commerc Banking Co. Syd.	23	Trading bank
5	Bank of Australasia	22	Trading bank
6	State Savings Bank Vic.	16	Savings bank/government
7	Govt. Savings Bank NSW	15	Savings bank/government
8	National Bank Australasia	14	Trading bank
9	Queensland National Bank	9	Trading bank
10	Bank of Victoria	9	Trading bank
11	Commonwealth Bank Aust	9	Trading bank
12	Eng, Scottish & Australian	8	Trading bank
13	Savings Bank NSW	8	Savings bank/government
14	State Savings Bank SA	7	Savings bank/government
15	Bank Adelaide	6	Trading bank
16	London Bank Aust.	6	Trading bank
17	Qld Govt Savings Bank	6	Savings bank/government
18	National Mutual Life	6	Life office
19	Mutual Life Citizens Ass.	5	Life office
20	Colonial Bank Australia	5	Trading bank
21	Colonial Mutual Life Ass.	3	Life office
22	Royal Bank Aust	3	Trading bank
23	Commercial Bank Tasmania	2	Trading bank
24	Royal Bank Queensland	2	Trading bank
25	Bank North Queensland	1	Trading bank

Rank 1930	Firm	Assets £m	Industry/ownership
1	Bank NSW	90.8	Trading bank
2	AMP	83.2	Life office
3	State Savings Bk Vic	81.2	Savings/government
4	Govt SBNSW	72.9	Savings/government
5	CBCS	60.3	Trading bank
6	Commonwealth	52.4	Trading/government
7	Com Savings Bank	52.1	Savings/government
8	Bank Australasia*	49.3	Trading bank
9	National Bank Australasia	47.1	Trading bank
10	Union Bank of Australia*	46.8	Trading bank
11	English Scottish & Aust*	45.2	Trading bank
12	National Mutual Life	34.1	Life office
13	Commonwealth Bank Aust.	31.0	Trading bank
14	Savings Bank SA	23.0	Savings/government
15	MLC	20.1	Life office
16	Aust Bank Com	18.4	Trading bank
17	Aust Temp & Gen	16.1	Life office
18	Queensland National Bank	14.7	Trading bank
19	Colonial Mutual Life	13.1	Life office
20	Bank Adelaide	9.3	Trading bank
21	City Mutual	6.4	Life office
22	Qld Govt IO	3.2	Life/government
23	Australian Provincial	2.9	Life office
24	Queensland Insurance Co.	1.7	Insurer
25	United	1.1	Insurer

Notes: * Foreign owned. Seven of the banks listed in 1910 had been acquired by banks listed in 1930. The CBCS acquired the Bank of Victoria in 1927; the ES&A acquired the London Bank of Victoria and the Commercial Bank of Tasmania in 1921, and the Royal Bank of Australia in 1927; the Bank of New South Wales acquired the Western Australian Bank in 1927; the National Bank of Australasia acquired the Colonial Bank of Australia in 1918 and the Royal Bank of Queensland in 1922. The Commonwealth Savings Bank became a separate institution from the Commonwealth Bank of Australia in 1928.

Rank 1952	Firm	Assets £m	Industry/ownership
1	Com Savings Bank	595.2	Savings/government
2	Bank NSW	395.6	Trading bank
3	ANZ Bank*	348.7	Trading bank
4	AMP	255.6	Life office
5	State Savings Bk Vic	239.5	Savings/government
6	National Bank	210.9	Trading bank
7	CBCS	202.0	Trading bank
8	Commonwealth Bank Aust	159.3	Trading bank
9	English Scottish & Australian*	152.9	Trading bank
10	Commonwealth†	148.1	Trading/government
11	National Mutual Life	94.7	Life office
12	Mutual Life & Citizens	89.1	Life office
13	Savings Bank SA	86.6	Savings/government
14	Aust T&G	84.0	Life office
15	Colonial Mutual Life	78.9	Life office
16	Rural Bank NSW	56.7	Trading/government
17	Bank Adelaide	33.1	Trading bank
18	City Mutual Life	23.5	Life office
19	R&I Bank WA	13.5	Trading/government
20	Hobart Savings	10.4	Savings
21	State Bank SA	9.6	Trading/government
22	Launceston Savings Bk	9.0	Savings
23	Aln Metropolitan	4.6	Life office
24	Aln Provincial	4.1	Life office
25	Provident Life	3.6	Life office

Note: * Foreign owned. † General Banking Division of the Commonwealth Bank of Australia. A number of banks that were in the 1930 list were acquired by other banks before 1952. The Bank of New South Wales took over the Australian Bank of Commerce in 1931. ANZ Bank was an amalgamation of the Bank of Australasia and the Union Bank of Australia in 1951. The National Bank absorbed the Queensland National Bank in 1948. The Commonwealth Savings Bank absorbed the Government Savings Bank of New South Wales in 1931. New banks were forged from the divestment of existing government banks. The State Bank of South Australia, formerly the mortgage department of the Savings Bank of South Australia, was established in 1926. The Rural Bank of New South Wales, established in 1933, was formerly the Rural Bank Department and Advances for Homes Department of the Government Savings Bank of New South Wales.

Rank 1964	Firm	Assets £m	Industry/ownership
1	Commonwealth Bank Corp	3237.6	Bank/government
2	Bank NSW	2137.8	Bank
3	ANZ Bank*	1572.0	Bank
4	AMP	1446.3	Life office
5	National Bank	977.8	Bank
6	State Savings Bank Victoria	846.4	Savings/government
7	CBCS	747.6	Bank
8	Commercial	667.8	Bank
9	Colonial Mutual Life	597.0	Life office
10	English Scottish & Australian*	593.6	Bank
11	National Mutual	585.4	Life office
12	MLC	581.4	Life office
13	Aust T&G	434.0	Life office
14	Rural Bank NSW	266.6	Bank/government
15	IAC Holdings	210.6	Finance company
16	AGC	181.1	Finance company
17	City Mutual Life	159.1	Life office
18	Custom Credit	153.6	Finance company
19	Bank Adelaide	119.3	Bank
20	GIO NSW	99.1	Insurer/government
21	GMAC*	96.1	Finance company
22	R&I Bank WA	95.8	Bank/government
23	CGA	90.0	Finance company
24	State Bank SA	86.7	Bank/government
25	AUC	83.3	Money market

Notes: * Foreign owned. The Commonwealth Savings Bank was now part of the Commonwealth Banking Corporation. With the exception of the General Motors Acceptance Corporation, the other finance companies were affiliated with private trading banks. A number became wholly-owned subsidiaries: AGC of the Bank of New South Wales; Custom Credit of the National; CGA of the Commercial Banking Company of Sydney. IAC Holdings was associated with ANZ Bank prior to that bank's merger with ES&A in 1969. IAC was sold to Citibank, while ESANDA, ES&A's finance company, became the vehicle for ANZ.

Rank 1986	Firm	Assets $bn	Industry/ownership
1	Westpac	60.7	Bank
2	ANZ Bank	56.6	Bank
3	Commonwealth	43.9	Bank/government
4	NAB	42.4	Bank
5	AMP	22.3	Life office
6	State Bank Victoria	16.3	Bank/government
7	National Mutual Life	10.4	Life office
8	State Bank NSW	10.2	Bank/government
9	State Bank SA	7.9	Bank/government
10	AGC	7.8	Finance company
11	R&I Bank WA	5.2	Bank/government
12	State Super NSW	5.1	Super/government
13	Colonial Mutual	4.8	Life office
14	Citibank*	4.3	Bank
15	Elders Finance	4.1	Merchant bank
16	St George Building Society	3.7	Building society
17	Advance Bank	3.5	Bank
18	Custom Credit	2.9	Finance company
19	AIDC	2.5	Bank/government
20	Natwest Aust Bank*	2.4	Bank
21	FAI Insurance	2.2	Insurer
22	RESI-Statewide	2.1	Building society
23	Suncorp Insurance & Finance	2.0	Insurer & finance
24	Challenge Bank	1.9	Bank
25	National Mutual Royal	1.9	Bank

Notes: * Foreign owned. There were a number of significant mergers among trading banks and life offices. The Bank of New South Wales and the Commercial Bank of Australia merged to become Westpac in 1982, the same year as the National Bank of Australasia merged with the Commercial Banking Company of Sydney to become NAB. ANZ Bank merged with the ES&A in 1969 and took over the Bank of Adelaide in 1979. Transfer of domicile to Australia in 1976 meant that ANZ was no longer foreign-owned. National Mutual Life took over Australian T & G, now known as T & G Mutual Life, in 1983.

Rank 1997	Firm	Assets $bn	Industry/ownership
1	NAB	202.0	Bank
2	ANZ Bank	138.2	Bank
3	Commonwealth	130.5	Bank
4	Westpac	119.0	Bank
5	AMP	60.1	Life office
6	St George	45.1	Bank
7	Colonial Life	34.3	Life office
8	SA State Trustee	20.9	Pension fund/government
9	MLC	19.0	Life office
10	Colonial State Bank†	18.1	Bank
11	NML*	17.8	Life office
12	Bank West* ‡	14.0	Bank
13	Esanda	9.6	Finance
14	Bankers Trust*	8.4	Merchant bank
15	Société Generale*	8.4	Bank
16	Mercantile Mutual Life*	8.2	Life office
17	Commonwealth Life	8.2	Life office
18	Macquarie Bank	7.9	Bank
19	GIO Australia	7.7	Insurer
20	NRMA Insurance	7.6	Insurer
21	Citibank*	7.3	Bank
22	AGC	7.1	Finance
23	Deutsche Australia*	7.0	Bank
24	Brierley Investment*	6.9	Investor
25	ABN-Ambro*	6.5	Bank

Note: * Foreign owned. NML was sold to the French insurance group, AXA in 1995. Mercantile Mutual Life became part of what was to be the ING group in 1982.
† Colonial State Bank was formerly SBNSW.
‡ Bank West was formerly R&IBWA. It was sold to the Bank of Scotland shortly after the name change in 1994. The Commonwealth Bank acquired the State Bank of Victoria in 1991 and was itself progressively privatised in the late 1990s. GIO Australia, now privatised, was previously GIO NSW.

Sources: *Australasian Insurance & Banking Record*; Butlin, *Australian Monetary System*; Gray, *Life Insurance*; Butlin, Hall & White, *Australian Banking and Monetary Statistics*, pp. 98–101 & Tables 54(ii), 56(ii), 57(ii), 58(ii) & 59(ii); *Australian Banking and Monetary Statistics*, Table 70, p. 503; Block (ed.), *Delfin Digest 1964*, pp. 102–5 & 108–111; *Business Review Weekly*, 20 November, 1987; *Business Review Weekly*, 16 November, 1998.

Notes

1 Introduction

1 A few important examples among many include N. G. Butlin, *Investment in Australian Economic Development, 1861–1900* (Cambridge University Press, 1964); C. Forster (ed.), *Australian Economic Development in the Twentieth Century* (London: Allen & Unwin, 1970); C. B. Schedvin, *Australia and the Great Depression: a Study of Economic Development and Policy in the 1920s and 1930s* (Sydney University Press, 1970); E. A. Boehm, *Twentieth-Century Economic Development in Australia* (Melbourne, 1971); N. G. Butlin, A. Barnard & J. J. Pincus, *Government and Capitalism: Public and Private Choice in Twentieth Century Australia* (St Leonards: Allen & Unwin, 1982); B. Head (ed.), *State and Economy in Australia* (Melbourne: Oxford University Press, 1983); R. Maddock & I. W. McLean (eds), *The Australian Economy in the Long Run* (Cambridge University Press, 1987); B. Pinkstone, *Global Connections: A History of Exports and the Australian Economy* (Canberra: Australian Government Publishing Service, 1992).

2 For example, see D. Merrett (ed.), *Business Institutions and Behaviour in Australia* (London: Frank Cass, 2000).

3 A. D. Chandler Jr, *Scale and Scope: The Dynamics of Industrial Capitalism* (Cambridge, MA and London: Belknap Press of Harvard University Press, 1990).

4 Cf W. G. Roy, *Socializing Capital* (Princeton University Press, 1997); M. C. Jensen, 'Eclipse of the public corporation', *Harvard Business Review*, 67, 5, 1989.

5 Chandler, *Scale and Scope*.

6 A. D. Chandler Jr, F. Amatori & T. Hikino (eds), *Big Business and the Wealth of Nations* (Cambridge University Press, 1997); W. M. Fruin, *The Japanese Enterprise System. Competitive Strategies and Cooperative Structures* (Oxford: Clarendon Press, 1992).

7 Chandler, Amatori & Hikino, *Big Business*; G. Jones & M. B. Rose (eds), 'Family capitalism', special issue of *Business History*, 35, 4, 1993.

8 Chandler, Amatori and Hikino, *Big Business*; G. D. Taylor & P. A. Baskerville, *A Concise History of Business in Canada* (Toronto: Oxford University Press, 1994).

9 L. Hannah, *The Rise of the Corporate Economy* (London and New York: Methuen, 1983), for example, analyses only manufacturing firms. More recent changes in attitude are reflected in Mary Rose's observation that, 'there can be no doubting the necessity to move beyond the Chandlerian school's preoccupation with manufacturing industry'. M. W. Kirby & M. B. Rose, 'Introduction', in M. W. Kirby & M. B. Rose (eds), *Business Enterprise in Modern Britain* (London: Routledge,

1994), p. 24. For an example of a wider perspective see G. Jones, 'Great Britain: big business, management and competitiveness in twentieth-century Britain', in A. D. Chandler Jr, F. Amatori & T. Hikino (eds), *Big Business and the Wealth of Nations* (Cambridge University Press, 1997).

10 M. E. Porter, *The Competitive Advantage of Nations* (London: Macmillan, 1990).

11 F. J. Contractor & P. Lorange (eds), *Cooperative Strategies in International Business* (Lexington MA: Lexington Books, 1989); G. H. Boyce, *Information, Mediation and Institutional Development. The Rise of Large-Scale Enterprise in British Shipping 1870–1919* (Manchester University Press, 1995); M. L. Gerlach, *Alliance Capitalism. The Social Organization of Japanese Business* (Berkeley: University of California Press, 1992).

12 M. Levy-Léboyer, 'The large corporation in modern France', in A. D. Chandler Jr & H. Daems (eds), *Managerial Hierarchies*, (Cambridge, MA 1980), p. 155 draws attention to different depreciation practices by French firms.

13 C. J. Schmitz, 'The world's largest industrial companies of 1912', *Business History* 37, 4, 1995, p. 94 shows a close correlation between the two for a selection of leading United States firms in 1912 until the highly capitalised US Steel is removed. However, the discrepancies can be greater when comparing workforce and capitalisation methods of measurement. See L. Johnman, 'The large manufacturing companies of 1935', *Business History*, 28, 1986, p. 228.

14 Hannah, *Corporate Economy*; P. Wardley, 'The anatomy of big business: Aspects of corporate development in the twentieth century', *Business History* 33, 2, 1991.

15 Schmitz, 'The world's largest industrial companies'.

16 Fruin, *Japanese Enterprise System*.

17 For a discussion of the range of multinational enterprise forms see G. Jones, *The Evolution of International Business: An Introduction* (London: Routledge, 1996), pp. 32–5.

18 *Shell in Australia: The story of a great achievement* (Melbourne: Shell Company of Australia, 1928), p. 33; D. K. Fieldhouse, *Unilever Overseas: The Anatomy of a Multinational 1895–1965* (London: Croom Helm, 1978), Table 3.1, p. 71. We owe the point that the assets of these two companies would exceed the amount of capital employed, so pushing them both further up the list, to Mira Wilkins.

19 M. Stichtenoth, 'The 100 largest Australian domiciled companies, 1920–52: Evidence and conjectures' (Honours thesis, Department of Economic History, Monash University, 1986).

20 The industry classification approach fails to identify links between firms that are vertically related in the supply chain or through serving the same or similar markets.

21 P. Dawkins, M. Harris & S. King (eds), *How Big Business Performs: Private Performance and Public Policy* (St Leonards, NSW: Allen and Unwin in conjunction with the Melbourne Institute of Applied Economic and Social Research, 1999).

22 See P. J. Buckley & M. C. Casson, 'Models of the multinational enterprise', *Journal of International Business Studies*, 29/1, 1998, pp. 23–25 for a succinct discussion of models versus frameworks for analysing business strategy.

23 G. Boyce & S. Ville, *The Development of Modern Business* (Houndmills: Palgrave, 2002), pp. 1–2, 232–44 for a brief explanation of these terms.

24 For example, W. Vamplew (ed.), *Australians: Historical Statistics* (Broadway, NSW: Fairfax, Syme and Weldon Associates, 1987); A. Maddison, *Dynamic Forces in Capitalist Development: A Long-run Comparative View* (Oxford University Press, 1991).

25 H. L. Wilkinson, *The Trust Movement in Australia* (Sydney: Critchley Parker Pty Ltd, 1914); J. N. Rawlings, *Who Owns Australia?* (Sydney: Modern Publishers Pty Ltd, 1939, 4th edn); B. Fitzpatrick, *The Rich Get Richer: Facts of the Growth of Monopoly in the Economic Structure of Australia Before and During the War* (Melbourne: Rawson's Book Shop, 1944); E. W. Campbell, *The 60 Rich Families Who Own Australia* (Sydney: Current Book Distributors, 1963).

26 E. L. Wheelwright, *Ownership and Control of Australian Companies: A Study of 102 of the Largest Public Companies Incorporated in Australia* (Sydney: Law Book Company of Australasia, 1957); E. L. Wheelwright & J. Miskelly, *Anatomy of Australian Manufacturing Industry: The Ownership and Control of 300 of the Largest Manufacturing Companies in Australia* (Sydney: Law Book Co., 1967); H. Rolfe, *The Controllers: Interlocking Directories in Large Australian Companies* (Melbourne: F. W. Cheshire, 1967).

27 P. H. Karmel and M. Brunt, *The Structure of the Australian Economy* (Melbourne: F. W. Cheshire, 1962).

28 K. Sheridan, *The Firm in Australia: A Theoretical and Empirical Study of Size, Growth and Profitability* (Melbourne: Nelson. 1974).

29 For example, Department of Trade and Industry, *Directory of Overseas Investment In Australian Manufacturing Industry* (Canberra: Department of Trade and Industry, 1966) and *Directory of Overseas Investment in Australian Manufacturing Industry 1971* (Canberra: Department of Trade and Industry, 1971).

30 *Australian Investment Digest*, vol. 1, no. 1, January 1920, p. 3.

31 These include Nash, *Australasian Joint Stock Companies Year Book*, which was published between 1896 and 1914; Jobson & Pooley, *Digest Year Book of Public Companies of Australia and New Zealand*, published between 1928 and 1966; H. Y. Braddon, *Business Principles and Practice (Australia)* (Sydney: W. Brookes & Co., 1921); A. R. Hall, *The London Capital Market and Australia, 1870–1914* (Canberra: Australian National University, 1963); Wilkinson, *Trust Movement in Australia*; Wheelwright and Miskelly, *Anatomy of Australian Manufacturing Industry*. Information on share prices can be found in *The 'Wild Cat' Monthly* published by the *Bulletin* magazine. Sporadic information on workforce sizes can be found in a number of publications including *Jobson's, J. B. Were's Statistical Service* (Melbourne), and A. Pratt, *The National Handbook of Australian Industries* (Melbourne: Specialty Press, 1934).

32 For estimates of entry by foreign firms see: G. Blainey, 'The history of multinational factories in Australia', in A. Okochi & T. Inoue (eds), *Overseas Business Activities* (Tokyo: University of Tokyo Press, 1984), appendix III, pp. 230–2; D. T. Brash, *American Investment in Australian Industry* (Canberra: Australian National University Press, 1966), appendix A, 'Survey of American-affiliated companies known to be manufacturing in Australia at 30 June 1962', pp. 289–327. The Australian government did not collect or disseminate data on the operations of foreign firms before the 1960s. See, for example, the Department of Trade and Industry, *Directory of Overseas Investment in Australian Manufacturing Industry 1966* (Canberra, 1966), and Commonwealth Treasury, Treasury Economic Paper No. 1, *Overseas Investment in Australia* (Canberra, 1972).

33 Stichtenoth, 'Australian domiciled companies', pp. 46–9 discusses these problems.

2 The Development of Large-scale Enterprise in Australia

1 A. D. H. Kaplan, *Big Enterprise in a Competitive System* (Washington DC: Brookings Institution, 1964, rev. edn); A. D. Chandler, *Scale and Scope. The Dynamics of Industrial Capitalism* (Cambridge MA: Belknap Press of Harvard University Press, 1990); W. M. Fruin, *The Japanese Enterprise System. Competitive Strategies and Cooperative Structures* (Oxford: Clarendon Press Oxford, 1992); L. Johnman, 'The large manufacturing companies of 1935', *Business History*, 28 (1986), pp. 226–45; P. L. Payne, 'The emergence of the large-scale company in Great Britain, 1870–1914', *Economic History Review*, 2nd Ser., XX (1967), pp. 519–42; C. J. Schmitz, *The Growth of Big Business in the United States and Western Europe, 1850–1939* (Basingstoke: Macmillan, 1993); C. J. Schmitz, 'The world's largest industrial companies of 1912', *Business History* 37, 4 (1995), pp. 85–96; P. Wardley, 'The anatomy of big business: aspects of corporate development in the twentieth century', *Business History* 33, 2 (1991), pp. 268–96; P. Wardley, 'The emergence of big business: the largest corporate employers of labour in the United Kingdom, Germany and the United States, c. 1907', *Business History*, 41, 4 (1999), pp. 88–116; L. Hannah, *The Rise of the Corporate Economy* (London & New York: Methuen, 1983, 2nd edn); M. Levy-Léboyer, 'The large corporation in modern France', in A. Chandler and H. Daems (eds), *Managerial Hierarchies. Comparative Perspectives on the Rise of the Modern Industrial Enterprise* (Cambridge MA: Harvard University Press, 1980), pp. 117–60; H. Pohl (ed.), *The Concentration Process in the Entrepreneurial Economy since the Late Nineteenth Century* (Stuttgart: German Society for Business History, 1988); A. D. Chandler, Jr, F. Amatori & T. Hikino (eds), *Big Business and the Wealth of Nations* (Cambridge: Cambridge University Press, 1997).

2 Chandler, *Scale and Scope*.

3 World Bank Group, *World Development Indicators 2001* (http://www.worldbank.org/data/wdi2001/Index.html).

4 Austria, Belgium, Denmark, Finland, Netherlands, Norway, Sweden and Switzerland. A. Maddison, *Phases of Capitalist Development* (Oxford: Oxford University Press, 1982).

5 B. Pinkstone, *Global Connections: A History of Exports and the Australian Economy* (Canberra: Australian Government Publishing Service, 1992), Table 63, p. 393.

6 E. A. Boehm, *Twentieth Century Economic Development In Australia* (Melbourne: Longman Cheshire, 1993, 3rd edn), Table 4.2, p. 97.

7 R. A. Foster, *Australian Economic Statistics 1949–50 to 1994–95* (Sydney: Reserve Bank of Australia, 1996), Table 1.20c, p. 55; *World Investment Report 1997: Transnational Corporations, Market Structure and Competition Policy* (New York & Geneva: United Nations, 1997), Annex table B.6, p. 340.

8 D. T. Merrett, 'Australian firms abroad before 1970: Why so few, why those and why there?', *Business History*, 44, 2 (2002), pp. 65–87.

9 D. T. Merrett, 'Australia's emergent multinationals: The legacy of having a natural resource intensive, small and closed economy as home', *International Studies in Management and Organization*, 32, 1, Spring (2002), pp. 109–35.

10 I. McLean, 'Australian savings since 1861', in P. J. Stemp (ed.), *Saving and Policy* (Canberra: Centre for Economic Policy Research, Australian National University, 1991), pp. 7–10.

11 D. T. Merrett, 'Capital markets and capital formation in Australia, 1945–1990', *Australian Economic History Review*, 38, 2 (1998), pp. 136–47.

12 K. F. Walker, *Industrial Relations in Australia* (Cambridge MA: Harvard University Press, 1956); S. F. Macintyre, 'Labour, capital and arbitration, 1890–1920', in B. Head (ed.), *State and Economy in Australia* (Melbourne: Oxford University Press, 1983), pp. 98–114.

13 M. MacKinnon, 'Schooling: Examining some myths', in D. Pope & L. Alston (eds), *Australia's Greatest Asset: Human Resources in the Nineteenth and Twentieth Centuries* (Annandale: The Federation Press, 1989), pp. 102–29; T. J. Hatton & B. J. Chapman, 'Apprenticeship and technical training', in D. Pope & L. Alston (eds), *Australia's Greatest Asset: Human Resources in the Nineteenth and Twentieth Centuries* (Annandale, NSW: The Federation Press, 1989), pp. 130–58; M. Edelstein, 'Professional engineers and the Australian economy, 1866–1980', in D. Pope & L. Alston (eds), *Australia's Greatest Asset: Human Resources in the Nineteenth and Twentieth Centuries* (Annandale, NSW: The Federation Press, 1989), pp. 276–301.

14 R. Lattimore, 'Research and development: hidden investment in Australian Industry', in C. Hamilton (ed.), *The Economic Dynamics of Australian Industry* (St Leonards NSW: Allen & Unwin, 1991), pp. 173–95; P. Stubbs, *Innovation and Research: A Study in Australian Industry* (Melbourne: F. W. Cheshire for the Institute of Applied Economic Research, University of Melbourne, 1968); A. Eleck, A. Camilleri & M. Lester, 'Innovation and technological change in Australia: problems and prospects', in B. Chapman (ed.), *Australian Economic Growth* (Canberra: Centre for Economic Policy Research, Australian National University, 1989), pp. 190–209; L. Dwyer, 'Government policy to promote industrial research and development: 1983–90', in G. Mahony (ed.), *The Australian Economy under Labor* (St Leonards NSW: Allen & Unwin, 1993), pp. 121–38; D. P. Mellor, *The Role of Science and Industry* (Canberra: Australian War Memorial, 1958); C. B. Schedvin, *Shaping Science and Industry: A History of Australia's Council for Scientific and Industrial Research, 1926–49* (St Leonards NSW: Allen & Unwin, 1987).

15 H. P. Schapper, 'The farm workforce', in D. B. Williams (ed.), *Agriculture in the Australian Economy* (Sydney University Press, 1982, 2nd edn), pp. 244, 248.

16 There is a large literature on this issue. The leading account is N. G. Butlin, A. Barnard & J. J. Pincus, *Government and Capitalism: Public and Private Choice in Twentieth Century Australia* (St Leonards NSW: Allen & Unwin, 1982). For accounts of the rise and withdrawal of state intervention and regulation see P. Kelly, *The End of Certainty: The Story of the 1980s* (St Leonards NSW: Allen & Unwin, 1992); S. Bell & B. Head (eds), *State, Economy and Public Policy* (Oxford University Press, 1994); G. Bailey, *Mythologies of Change and Certainty in late-20th Century Australia* (Melbourne: Australian Scholarly Publishing, 2000); S. Bell, *Ungoverning the Economy: The Political Economy of Australian Economic Policy* (Melbourne: Oxford University Press, 1997); B. Walker & B. C. Walker, *Privatisation: Sell Off or Sell Out? The Australian Experience* (Sydney: ABC Books, 2000); J. Quiggin, *Great Expectations: Microeconomic Reform and Australia* (St Leonards NSW: Allen & Unwin, 1996).

17 Reserve Bank of Australia, 'Privatisation in Australia', *Reserve Bank of Australia Bulletin*, December (Sydney, 1997), pp. 7–16.

18 F. W. Eggleston, *State Socialism in Victoria* (London: P. S. King & Son, 1932); R. R. Hirst, 'The transport industry', in A. Hunter (ed.), *The Economics of Australian Industry: Studies in Environment and Structure* (Melbourne University Press,

1963); N. G. Butlin, A. Barnard & J. J. Pincus, *Government and Capitalism: Public and Private Choice in Twentieth Century Australia* (St Leonards, NSW: Allen and Unwin, 1982), chapters 9–11; P. Forsyth, 'Achieving reform in transport: Land transport and the transport sector in general', in P. Forsyth (ed.), *Microeconomic Reform in Australia* (St Leonards NSW: Allen & Unwin, 1992), pp. 179–203; R. Maddock, 'Microeconomic reform of telecommunications: The long march from duolopy to duopoly', in Forsyth, *Microeconomic Reform*, pp. 243–62.

19   G. N. Blainey, *White Gold: The Story of Alcoa in Australia* (St Leonards NSW: Allen & Unwin, 1997), pp. 205–08.

20   Supporting and related industries form one point in the diamond schema developed by Michael Porter to explain the domestic sources of international competitiveness. M. E. Porter, *The Competitive Advantage of Nations* (London: Macmillan, 1990).

21   G. Blainey, 'The history of foreign factories in Australia', in A. Okochi & T. Inoue (eds), *Overseas Business Activities: Proceedings of the Fuji Conference* (Tokyo: University of Tokyo Press, 1984), pp. 183–210; C. Forster, *Industrial Development in Australia 1920–1930* (Canberra: Australian National University, 1964), Appendix III, pp. 230–2.

22   D. T. Brash, *American Investment in Australian Industry* (Canberra: Australian National University Press, 1966), p. 24.

23   Department of Trade and Industry, *Directory of Overseas Investment in Australian Manufacturing Industry* (Canberra: Department of Trade and Industry, 1966) and *Directory of Overseas Investment in Australian Manufacturing Industry 1971* (Canberra: Department of Trade and Industry, 1971), Table 2, p. 6.

24   Boehm, *Economic Development*, Tables 5.11 and 5.12, pp. 164, 167. Foreign firms operating through joint ventures and 'naturalising' by running down their equity stake are included as part of foreign 'control'.

25   H. W. Arndt & D. R. Sherk, 'Export franchises of Australian companies with overseas affiliations', *Economic Record* 35 (1959), pp. 239–42; W. P. Hogan, 'British manufacturing subsidiaries in Australia and export franchises', *Economic Papers* 22 (1966), pp. 10–25; Industry Commission, *Commercial Restrictions on Exporting (Including Franchising)* (Canberra: Australian Government Publishing Service, 1992), Report No. 23.

26   W. Prest, 'The electricity supply industry', in A. Hunter (ed.), *Economics of Australian Industry: Studies in Environment and Structure* (Melbourne University Press), pp. 129–33.

27   P. H. Karmel & M. Brunt, *The Structure of the Australian Economy* (Melbourne: F. W. Cheshire, 1962), p. 106. R. Proudley, *Circle of Influence: A History of the Gas Industry in Victoria* (North Melbourne: Hargreen Publishing Company in association with Gas and Fuel Corporation of Victoria, 1987).

28   I. McLean, 'Australian savings since 1861', in P. J. Stemp (ed.), *Saving and Policy* (Canberra: Centre for Economic Policy Research, Australian National University, 1991), Table 1, p. 5.

29   W. Vamplew (ed.), *Australians: Historical Statistics* (Broadway NSW: Fairfax, Syme & Weldon Associates, 1987), Tables PF 19–27 & 28–46, pp. 242–3; PF 57–63, pp. 247–8; ANA 28–36, p. 131, ANA 50–64, p. 133 & ANA 119–29, p. 139.

30 R. E. Caves, 'Scale, openness and productivity in manufacturing industries', in R. E. Caves & L. B. Krause (eds), *The Australian Economy: The View from the North* (Sydney: George Allen & Unwin Australia, 1984), pp. 313–47.

31 P. Wardley, 'The anatomy of big business: Aspects of corporate development in the twentieth century', *Business History* 33, 2 (1991), Table 6, p. 281; W. M. Fruin, *Japanese Enterprise System*, Appendix.

32 D. T. Merrett, 'Business institutions and behaviour in Australia: a new perspective', in D. T. Merrett (ed.), *Business Institutions and Behaviour in Australia* (London: Frank Cass, 2000), pp. 1–2.

33 For example, A. G. Lowndes (ed.), *South Pacific Enterprise. The Colonial Sugar Refining Company Limited* (Sydney: Angus and Robertson, 1956), p. 25; K. Dunstan, *The Amber Nectar. A Celebration of Beer and Brewing in Australia* (Melbourne: Viking O'Neil, 1987), pp. 7–39; A. Barnard, *The Australian Wool Market* (Melbourne: Melbourne University Press on behalf of the Australian National University, 1958), p. 72.

34 Karmel & Brunt, *Structure*, pp. 59–60.

35 Karmel & Brunt, *Structure*, pp. 54–92.

36 See Boehm, *Economic Development*, pp. 197, 200–1.

37 Our data are in Australian currency. The number of British pounds required to buy an Australian pound were 0.992, 0.943, 0.797 and 0.797 in 1910, 1930, 1952 and 1964 respectively. The comparable data for United States dollars are 4.833, 4.586, 2.226 and 2.225. David Pope, 'Private Finance', in Wray Vamplew (ed.), *Historical Statistics*, Table PF 47–56, pp. 244–45.

38 Schmitz, 'Companies of 1912', pp. 87–90; Schmitz, *Big Business*, pp. 32–3.

39 'The International 500', *Fortune International*, 19 August (New York, 1985), pp. 156–65; 'Fortune 500', *Fortune International*, 29 April (New York: 1985), pp. 154–5.

40 This and the following paragraph are taken from Merrett, 'Emergent multinationals', pp. 123–6.

41 J. T. Davis (ed.), *Forbes Top Companies* (New York: John Wiley & Sons, Inc., 1997).

42 Holst, *Australia's Top 300 Listed Companies Handbook 1993* (Melbourne: F. W. Holst & Co. Pty Ltd, nd.), p. 258.

43 *World Investment Report 2000: Cross-border Mergers and Acquisitions and Development* (New York & Geneva: United Nations, 2000), Table III.1, pp. 72–4.

44 F. M. Scherer & David Ross, *Industrial Market Structure and Economic Performance* (Boston: Houghton Mifflin Company, 1990, 3rd edn), Table 3.4, p. 71.

45 Scherer & Ross, *Industrial Market Structure*, pp. 68–70.

3 Identifying the Corporate Leaders

1 R. M. Grant, *Contemporary Strategy Analysis* (Oxford: Blackwell, 1998, 3rd edn), p. 184.

2 M. B. Leiberman & D. B. Montgomery, 'First mover (dis)advantages: retrospective and link with the resource-based view', *Strategic Management Journal* 19, 1998, p. 1113.

3 See M. Porter, *Competitive Advantage of Nations* (London: Macmillan, 1990), pp. 33–53 for a full explanation of these strategies.

4 D. C. Mueller, 'First mover advantages and path dependence', *International Journal of Industrial Organisation* 15, 1997, pp. 831–40. 'Path dependency' refers to the idea that, once set upon an initial course of action, it is difficult to change. P. A. David, 'Clio and the economics of QWERTY', *American Economic Review* (Papers & Proceedings), 75, 2, 1985.

5 For example, see D. Gabel, 'Competition in a network industry: The telephone industry, 1894–1910', *Journal of Economic History* 54, 3, 1994.

6 A. D. Chandler Jr, *Scale and Scope: The Dynamics of Industrial Capitalism* (Cambridge, MA and London: Belknap Press of Harvard University Press, 1990), p. 599.

7 M. B. Leiberman & D. B. Montgomery, 'First-mover advantages', *Strategic Management Journal* summer special issue 9, 1988, p. 52.

8 Chandler, *Scale and Scope*, ch. 3.

9 R. S. Tedlow, 'The struggle for dominance in the automobile market: the early years of Ford and General Motors', *Business and Economic History*, 18, 1988.

10 D. Gabel, 'Competition in a network industry: the telephone industry, 1894–1910', *Journal of Economic History*, 54, 3, 1994.

11 P. N. Golder & G. J. Tellis, 'Pioneer advantage: marketing logic or marketing legend?' *Journal of Marketing Research* 30, 2, 1993, p. 169.

12 The term 'distinctive competences' is also used to describe those activities that a firm does well relative to others. P. Selznick, *Leadership in Administration: A Sociological Interpretation* (New York: Harper & Row, 1957).

13 Grant, *Contemporary Strategy Analysis*, pp. 129–30.

14 We are grateful to Professor Paul Robertson for this analogy.

15 R. Nelson & D. Mowery (eds) *Sources of Industrial Leadership. Studies of Seven Industries* (Cambridge University Press, 1999).

16 Golder & Tellis, 'Pioneer advantage', pp. 162–3.

17 A. D. Chandler, F. Amatori & T. Hikino (eds) *Big Business and the Wealth of Nations* (Cambridge University Press, 1997).

18 Chandler, *Scale and Scope*, p. 91.

19 We saw in Chapter 2 that our calculation of the top 100 series was also more inclusive than Chandler's top 100, which had concentrated upon the manufacturing and related sectors.

20 S. Ville & G. Fleming, 'Locating Australian Corporate Memory', *Business History Review* 73, 2, 1999, pp. 256–64.

21 It should be noted that in a few instances these *corporate leaders* are enterprises that have gone through name or partial ownership changes, but it has been judged appropriate to treat them as a single entity for the more detailed and textured story that endures over the next few chapters.

22 Also see Bureau of Industry Economics, *Mergers and Acquisitions*, Research Report 36 (Canberra: Australian Government Publishing Service, 1990), pp. 34–6.

23 K. Sheridan, 'An estimate of the business concentration of Australian manufacturing industries', *Economic Record* 44, 1968, p. 105; P. H. Karmel & M. Brunt, *The Structure of the Australian Economy* (Melbourne: Cheshire, 1963).

24 D. Hutchinson, 'Australian manufacturing business: entrepreneurship or missed opportunities?', *Australian Economic History Review* 41, 2, 2001, p. 109.

25 M. A. Alemson, 'Advertising and the nature of competition in oligopoly over time: a case study', *Economic Journal*, 80, 1970, pp. 282–306; A. Morkel, 'AMATIL Ltd', in Lewis et al., *Cases* (New York: Prentice Hall, 1991), Table 19.4, p. 343.

26 H. McQueen, 'Pop goes the bottler! The Australian soft drink industry, 1945–65: a study in management, marketing and monopolisers', *Journal of Australian Political Economy* 46, 2000.

27 Nestlé Alimentana Company, *This is Your Company, Nestlé and Anglo-Swiss Holding Company* (Vevey, Switzerland: Nestlé and Anglo-Swiss Holding Co, 1946), pp. 103–6; G. Jones, 'Multinational chocolate: Cadbury overseas, 1918–39', *Business History*, 26, 1984.

28 S. Sargent, *The Foodmakers* (Ringwood, Vic: Penguin, 1985), p. 268.

29 D. K. Fieldhouse, *Unilever Overseas: The Anatomy of a Multinational 1895–1965* (London: Croom Helm, 1978), Table 3.2, pp. 72 and 81; L. Brown, *Competitive Marketing Strategy: Developing, Maintaining and Defending Competitive Position* (South Melbourne: Thomas Nelson, 1990), pp. 206–7 and 210–27.

30 H. Fountain, 'Technology acquisition, firm capability, and sustainable competitive advantage: A study of Australian Glass Manufacturers Ltd, 1915–39', in D. Merrett (ed.) *Business Institutions and Behaviour In Australia* (London, 2000), p. 92; T. Barker, 'Pilkington: the reluctant multinational', in G. Jones (ed.) *British Multi-nationals: Origins, Management and Performance* (Aldershot, 1986), pp. 185–6.

31 *Wild Cat*, 1964, entry 31.

32 G. Maxcy, 'The motor industry', in A. Hunter (ed.) *The Economics of Australian Indus-try: Studies in Environment and Structure* (Melbourne University Press, 1963), p. 508.

33 *Australian*, 7 June 2002.

34 Hutchinson, 'Australian manufacturing', pp. 112–14.

35 M. Goot, 'Newspaper circulation 1932–1977', in P. Spearritt & D. Walker (eds) *Australian Popular Culture* (Sydney: Allen & Unwin, 1979), Table 2, p. 214; J. Henningham, 'The press', in S. Cunningham & G. Turner (eds), *The Media in Australia: Industries, Texts, Audiences* (St Leonards, NSW: Allen & Unwin, 1993), Fig. 2.9, p. 63.

36 D. H. Briggs & R. L. Smyth, *Distribution of Groceries: Economic Aspects of the Distribution of Groceries with Special Reference to Western Australia* (Perth: University of Western Australia Press, 1967), pp. 16, 21; *Fair Market or Market Failure? A Review of Australia's Retailing Sector* (Canberra: Australian Government Publishing Service, 1999) Table 4.1.

37 S. J. Butlin, J. R. Hall & R. C. White, *Australian Banking and Monetary Statistics, 1817–1945* (Sydney: Reserve Bank of Australia, 1971), Table 7(ii), p. 133; R. C. White, *Australian Banking and Monetary Statistics, 1945–70* (Sydney: Reserve Bank of Australia, 1973), Table 42, pp. 314–15; Reserve Bank of Australia, *Statistical Bulletin*, September 1997.

38 A. C. Gray, *Life Insurance in Australia: An Historical and Descriptive Account* (Melbourne : McCarron Bird, 1977), Table 4.1, p. 46, Table 9.1, p. 127, Table 10.2, p. 133 and Table 15.7, p. 264.

39 S. Ville, *Rural Entrepreneurs. A History of the Stock and Station Agent Industry in Australia and New Zealand* (Cambridge University Press, 2000), ch. 2.

40 G. Lewis, A. Morkel & G. Hubbard, *Australian Strategic Management. Concepts, Contexts and Cases* (New York: Prentice Hall, 1993), p. 791.

41 Lewis, Morkel & Hubbard, *Australian Strategic Management*, pp. 789–92.

42 Virgin Blue is currently the principal domestic competitor for Qantas.

43 R. R. Hirst, 'The transport industry' in Hunter (ed.) *The Economics of Australian Industry*, p. 76.

44 H. Hughes, *The Australian Iron and Steel Industry* (Melbourne University Press, 1964).

45 R. Broomham, *First Light: 150 Years of Gas* (Sydney: Hale and Iremonger, 1987), pp. 99–130.

46 See *Shell in Australia: The Story of a Great Achievement* (Melbourne: Shell Company of Australia, 1928).

47 Gray, *Life Insurance*, Table 5.1, p. 54.

48 D. Merrett, 'Paradise lost?: British banks in Australia', in G. Jones (ed.), *Banks as Multinationals* (London: Routledge, 1990); *Report of the Royal Commission into Monetary and Banking Systems in Australia* (Canberra: Commonwealth Government Printer, 1937), paras 277–88.

49 Ville, *Rural Entrepreneurs*, p. 43.

50 J. B. Were, *The Transport Industry in Australia* (Melbourne: J. B. Were, 1964), p. 22.

51 Broomham, *First Light*, pp. 193, 208.

52 K. Buckley & K. Klugman, *The Australian Presence in the Pacific: Burns Philp, 1914–1946* (Sydney: George Allen and Unwin, 1983).

53 *Delfin Digest of the Top Companies in Australia, New Zealand and South East Asia* (Sydney: Development Finance Corporation Limited), p. 198.

54 R. O. Block (ed.), *Delfin Digest 1965: The Top Companies in Australia, New Zealand and South East Asia* (Sydney: Development Finance Corporation Limited, 1965), p. 247.

55 *This is Your Company*, pp. 102–7.

56 Fieldhouse, *Unilever Overseas*, pp. 64–9, 78–93.

57 Brown, B., *I Excel! The Life and Times of Sir Henry Jones* (Hobart: Libra Books, 1991), pp. 66–7 & 78–9, 132.

58 *Delfin Digest 1965*; I. Potter and Co., *Australian Company Reviews* (Melbourne: Ian Potter and Co., 1972), p. 23.

59 Maxcy, 'Motor industry', p. 513.

60 D. M. Hocking, 'Research – the Economic Implications', *Journal of the Australian Institute of Metals* 3, 1958, pp. 28–9; Bureau of Industry Economics (BIE), *Multinationals and Governments. Issues and Implications for Australia*, Research Report (Canberra: Australian Government Publishing Service, 1993), p. 122.

61 T. G. Parry & J. F. Watson, 'Technology flows and foreign investment in Australian manufacturing', *Australian Economic Papers*, June, 1979, pp. 107–9.

62 A. G. Lowndes, *South Pacific Enterprise: The Colonial Sugar Refining Company Limited* (Sydney: Angus and Robertson, 1956).

63 M. F. Page, *Fitted for the Voyage: The Adelaide Steamship Company 1875–1975* (Adelaide: Rigby, 1975), p. 314.

64 Broomham, *First Light*, pp. 81–3, 120, 127, 188.

65 G. Boyce & S. Ville, *Development of Modern Business* (Basingstoke, 2002), pp. 33–4, 38–40.

66 See R. Tomasic, J. Jackson & R. Woellner, *Corporations Law: Principles, Policy and Process* (Sydney: Butterworths, 1996), pp. 92–5.

67 P. Chadwick, *Media Mates: Carving Up Australia's Media* (South Melbourne, Vic.: Macmillan, 1989), pp. xix–xlvii.

68 G. Blainey, *The Steel Master: A Life of Essington Lewis* (Melbourne: Macmillan, 1971).

69 Ville, *Rural Entrepreneurs*, pp. 24, 43, 169.

70 M. Hartwell & J. Lane, *Champions of Enterprise. Australian Entrepreneurship, 1788–1990* (Sydney: Focus Books, 1991).

71 E. K. Sinclair, *The Spreading Tree: A History of APM and AMCOR 1844–1989* (North Sydney: Allen and Unwin,1990).

72 G. Blainey, *A History of the AMP, 1848–1998* (St Leonards, NSW: Allen & Unwin, 1999), pp. 118–19, 173.

4 Paths of Corporate Development: Directions of Growth

1 A. D. Chandler Jr, *Scale and Scope: The Dynamics of Industrial Capitalism* (Cambridge, MA and London: Belknap Press of Harvard University Press, 1990), chs 3–6.

2 J. Kay, *Foundations of Corporate Success. How Business Strategies Add Value* (New York: Oxford University Press, 1993), pp. 116–17; R. M. Grant, *Contemporary Strategy Analysis: Concepts, Techniques, Applications* (Oxford: Blackwell, 1998, 3rd edn), p. 127.

3 For a broader discussion of the 'cost leadership' firm see M. Porter, *Competitive Advantage. Creating and Sustaining Superior Performance* (New York: Free Press, 1985), ch. 3.

4 Upstream and downstream refer respectively to earlier or later functions in the production process.

5 Where a firm, for example, 'makes' rather than 'buys' components and other semi-finished products.

6 In particular, see L. S. Welch & R. Luostarien, 'Internationalisation: Evolution of a concept', *Journal of General Management* 14, 2 (1988); A. Rugman & A. Verbeke, *Global Corporate Strategy and Trade Policy* (London: Routledge, 1990); J. H. Dunning, *Multinational Enterprises and the Global Economy* (Wokingham: Addison-Wesley, 1993).

7 See Kay, *Corporate Success*, ch. 8 for a discussion of strategic assets.

8 G. L. Clark, *Built on Gold: Recollections of Western Mining* (Melbourne: Hill of Content Publishing, 1983), pp. 120, 151–4.

9 P. Donovan & N. Kirkman, *The Unquenchable Flame. South Australian Gas Company, 1861–1986* (Netley, SA: Wakefield Press, 1986), pp. 107–11.

10 Donovan & Kirkman, *Unquenchable Flame*, pp. 221–3.

11 H. Fysh, *Qantas Rising: The Autobiography of the Flying Fysh* (Sydney: Angus and Robertson, 1965), pp. 142–3, 223–4.

12 Fysh, *Qantas Rising*, p. 279.

13 S. Brimson, *Ansett – the Story of an Airline* (Sydney: Dreamweaver Books, 1987), p. 77.

14 Under the two-airline policy that evolved in the 1950s, the trunk routes were reserved for two selected airlines.

15 D. T. Merrett & G. Whitwell, 'The empire strikes back: Marketing Australian beer and wine in the United Kingdom', in G. Jones & N. Morgan (eds) *Adding Value: Marketing and Brands in the Food and Drink Industries* (London: Routledge, 1994).

16 B. Brown, *I Excel! the Life and Times of Sir Henry Jones* (Hobart: Libra Books, 1991).

17 *Keith Murdoch, Journalist* (Melbourne: Herald & Weekly Times, 1952), p. 11.

18 M. F. Page, *Fitted for the Voyage: The Adelaide Steamship Company 1875–1975* (Adelaide: Rigby, 1975), p. 186.

19 *Finance Bulletin, Part 1, Public and Private Finance* (Canberra: Commonwealth Bureau of Census and Statistics), various.

20 http://www.ljhooker.com.au/Contacts.php?directive=AboutUs&navpage=corporate. Accessed 6.3.2003.

21 This section is largely taken from S. Ville, *The Rural Entrepreneurs. A History of the Stock and Station Agent Industry in Australia and New Zealand* (Cambridge University Press, 2000), ch. 2.

22 G. Boyce & S. Ville, *The Development of Modern Business* (Basingstoke: Palgrave, 2002), pp. 183-4.

23 K. Tsokhas, *Beyond Dependence: Companies, Labour Processes and Australian Mining* (Melbourne: Oxford University Press, 1986), pp. 37-8.

24 In 1973-4. Tsokhas, *Beyond Dependence*, p. 135.

25 K. Buckley & K. Klugman, *The Australian Presence in the Pacific: Burns Philp, 1914-1946* (Sydney: George Allen & Unwin, 1983), pp. 268-73.

26 Buckley & Klugman, *Australian Presence*, pp. 240-2, 326-7; *Wild Cat* 1/10/60, pp. 308-9.

27 Buckley & Klugman, *Australian Presence*, pp. 364-5.

28 Brown, *Sir Henry Jones*, pp. 67-72.

29 D. T. Merrett, 'The Victorian Licensing Court 1906-68: A study of its role and impact', *Australian Economic History Review*, 29, 2 (1979), pp. 123-50.

30 L. Clark, *Finding a Common Interest. The Story of Dick Dusseldorp and Lend Lease* (Cambridge University Press, 2002), pp. 28-31.

31 M. Murphy, *Challenges of Change: The Lend Lease Story* (Sydney: Lend Lease Corporation, 1984), pp. 55, 67.

32 Frank Lowy's Westfield, by contrast, owes its success to separating the property ownership and management businesses as two public companies in order to attract low and high risk investors accordingly.

33 R. Conlon & J. Perkins, *Wheels and Deals. The Automobile Industry in Twentieth-Century Australia* (Aldershot: Ashgate, 2001), pp. 115-16.

34 G. Maxcy, 'The motor industry', in A. Hunter (ed.) *The Economics of Australian Industry* (Melbourne University Press, 1963), p. 509.

35 Maxcy, 'Motor industry', p. 521.

36 Conlon & Perkins, *Wheels and Deals*, pp. 115-23.

37 J. McB. Grant, 'The petroleum industry', in Hunter (ed.), *Economics of Australian Industry*, pp. 249-52.

38 Grant, 'The petroleum industry', p. 253.

39 A. Moyal, *Clear Across Australia. A History of Telecommunications* (Melbourne: Thomas Nelson, 1984), pp. 131-43.

40 H. Fountain, 'Technology acquisition, firm capability and sustainable competitive advantage: A case study of Australian Glass Manufacturers Ltd, 1915-39, in D. Merrett (ed.), *Business Institutions and Behaviour in Australia* (London: Cass, 2000), pp. 92, 95-8.

41 Stages of the value chain that cannot easily be separated for technical reasons.

42 R. Broomham, *First Light: 150 Years of Gas* (Sydney: Hale & Iremonger, 1987), p. 120; Donovan & Kirkman, *Unquenchable Flame*, pp. 98-9.

43 Chandler, *Scale and Scope*, chs 5, 6.

44 N. Capon, C. Christodoulou, J. U. Farley & J. M. Hulbert, 'A comparative analysis of the strategy and structure of United States and Australian corporations', *Journal of International Business Studies* (Spring 1987), p. 54.

45 K. R. Harrigan & M. E. Porter, 'End game strategies for declining industries', in *Harvard Business Review* 1987, reprinted in *Michael E. Porter on Competition and Strategy* (Boston, MA: Harvard Business School Press, 1991), pp. 57–68, identify 'leadership', 'niche', and 'harvest' as alternative corporate strategies in a declining industry.

46 *Wild Cat*, 6 February 1960, p. 40.

47 *Wild Cat*, 5 March 1960, pp. 82–3.

48 Clark, *Built on Gold*, pp. 170–1.

49 Tsokhas, *Beyond Dependence*, p. 135.

50 Tsokhas, *Beyond Dependence*, pp. 42–4, 49.

51 W. A. McNair, *Radio Advertising in Australia* (Sydney: Angus and Robertson, 1937), pp. 127–31.

52 B. Bonney & H. Wilson, *Australia's Commercial Media* (South Melbourne: Macmillan, 1983).

53 See Boyce & Ville, *Development*, pp. 192–3.

54 Paul Chadwick, *Media Mates: Carving Up Australia's Media* (South Melbourne: Macmillan, 1989).

55 Bureau of Transport and Communications, *Economic Aspects of Broadcasting Regulation*, Report 71 (Canberra: AGPS, 1991), tables 5.3 and 5.4.

56 Chadwick, *Media Mates*, pp. 41, 117–19. Rupert Murdoch's United States citizenship additionally barred him from ownership of an Australian radio or television licence.

57 Brimson, *Ansett*, p. 148.

58 G. Blainey, *A History of the Australian Mutual Provident, 1848–1998* (St Leonards: Allen & Unwin, 1999), pp. 244–5.

59 Page, *Fitted for the Voyage*, pp. 238–9.

60 Ville, *Rural Entrepreneurs*, pp. 50–1.

61 Ville, *Rural Entrepreneurs*, pp. 51–4.

62 D. T. Brash, *American Investment in Australian Industry* (Canberra: Australian National University Press, 1966), p. 319; Linden Brown, *Competitive Marketing Strategy: Developing, Maintaining and Defending Competitive Position* (South Melbourne: Thomas Nelson, 1990), pp. 206–7, 210–27.

63 *Wild Cat*, 4/2/61, pp. 51–2.

64 D. Hutchinson, 'The transformation of Boral: From dependent, specialist bitumen refiner to major building products manufacturer', in Merrett (ed.), *Business Institutions*.

65 King, S. *From the Ground Up – Boral's First 50 Years* (Sydney: State Library of NSW Press, 2000), pp. 23–87; Hutchinson, 'Transformation', pp. 119–20.

66 Hutchinson, 'Transformation', p. 121.

67 H. W. Arndt & D. R. Sherk, 'Export franchises of Australian companies with overseas affiliations', *Economic Record*, 35, 71 (1959); W. P. Hogan, 'British investment in Australian manufacturing: The technical connections', *Manchester School of Economics and Social Studies*, 35 (1967).

68 D. Merrett, 'Australian firms abroad: Why so few, why those, and why there?', *Business History*, 44, 2 April (2002), pp. 65–87.

69 R. Emerson-Elliot, 'The Hume Pipe Company. Early internationalization by an Australian company', http://www.uow.edu.au/commerce/econ/modbusiness/Hume %20Pipe%20Company.pdf, p. 1.

70 For a more extensive discussion of this issue see D. T. Merrett, 'Australia's emergent multinationals: The legacy of having a natural resource intensive, small and closed

economy as home', *International Studies in Management and Organization*, 32,1, Spring (2002), pp. 109–35.

71 http://www.lendlease.com.au/llweb/llc/main.nsf/all/all_whooverview, accessed 25.2.2003.

72 Hutchinson, 'Transformation', p. 127; King, *From the Ground Up*, pp. 87–100.

73 King, *From the Ground Up*, pp. 52, 98–100.

74 As a result of its regional expansion, the company's name was changed to Pacific Dunlop in 1986.

75 Tsokhas, *Beyond Dependence*, p. 88.

76 D. Merrett, 'Global reach by Australian banks: Correspondent banking networks, 1830–1960', *Business History* 37, 3 (1995).

77 D. Merrett, 'The internationalization of Australian banks', *Journal of International Financial Markets, Institutions and Money* (2002).

78 T. da Silva Lopes, 'Brands and the evolution of multinationals in alcoholic beverages', *Business History* 44, 3 (2002), pp. 7–9.

79 N. R. Wills, 'The basic iron and steel industry', in Hunter (ed.), *The Economics of Australian Industry*, p. 224.

80 H. Hughes, *The Australian Iron and Steel Industry* (Melbourne University Press, 1964), p. 128.

81 A. Trengove, *What's Good for Australia: The Story of BHP* (Stanmore, NSW: Cassell, 1975), pp. 206–15.

82 D. Hutchinson, 'Australian manufacturing business: Entrepreneurship or missed opportunities?' *Australian Economic History Review* 41, 2 (2001), pp. 109–10.

83 R. C. White, *Australian Banking and Monetary Statistics, 1945–70* (Sydney: Reserve Bank of Australia, 1973), Table 11.5 p. 198 (for 1983); Holst, (n.d.), *Australia's Top 300 Listed Companies Handbook 1993* (Melbourne: F. W. Holst and Co. Pty Ltd), p. 107.

84 *The Australian*, 11.2.2003, p. 17.

85 A. G. Lowndes (ed.), *South Pacific Enterprise: The Colonial Sugar Refining Company Limited* (Sydney: Angus and Robertson, 1956), p. 155; G. Lewis, A. Morkel & G. Hubbard (eds), *Cases in Australian Strategic Management* (New York: Prentice Hall, 1991), p. 214.

86 http://www.newscorp.com/investor/index.html, accessed 25.02.2003.

87 J. F Norton & L. Willcocks, 'The News Corporation', in G. Johnson & K. Scholes (eds), *Exploring Corporate Strategy: Text and Cases* (New York: Prentice Hall, 1993, 3rd edn), p. 627.

5 Paths of Corporate Development: Methods of Growth

1 The term 'organic' is sometimes used in place of 'internal'. Internal should not be confused with 'internalisation', the term often used in transaction cost economics to distinguish the 'make' from the 'buy' decision in the value chain.

2 A. D. Chandler, *Scale and Scope: The Dynamics of Industrial Capitalism* (Cambridge: Belknap Press of Harvard University Press, 1990), chs 10–14; W. M. Fruin, *The Japanese Enterprise System: Competitive Strategies and Cooperative Structures* (Oxford: Clarendon Press, 1992); G. H. Boyce, *Cooperative Structures in Global Business. Communicating, Transferring Knowledge and Learning across the Corporate Frontier* (London: Routledge, 2001).

3 J. Nieuwenhuysen, *The Effects of Mergers on Australian Industry: A First Stage Report* (Canberra: DITAC, 1982), p. 27 has suggested that this process is particularly time-consuming in a stagnant or declining industry where rationalisation of the activities of merged firms is necessary. In rapidly growing industries, the opportunities for the firms to pursue new joint paths makes for more smooth and rapid integration.

4 G. Boyce & S. Ville, *The Development of Modern Business* (Basingstoke: Palgrave, 2002), p. 263. Ch. 9 discusses a wide range of interorganisational structures in detail. Also see Bureau of Industry Economics, *Beyond the Firm. An Assessment of Business Linkages and Networks in Australia* (Canberra: Australian Government Publishing Service, 1995), p. 10.

5 R. Broomham, *First Light: 150 Years of Gas* (Sydney: Hale & Iremonger, 1987), p. 102.

6 Broomham, *First Light*, pp. 123, 183, 193.

7 For example, B. Carroll, *A Very Good Business. One Hundred Years of James Hardie Industries Ltd, 1888–1988* (Sydney: James Hardie Industries Ltd, 1987), pp. 129–34, 155–9.

8 J. Wright, *Heart of the Lion: The 50 Year History of Australia's Holden* (St Leonards: Allen & Unwin, 1998), pp. 78–9, 87, 101, 107.

9 *Report of the Royal Commission into Monetary and Banking Systems in Australia* (Canberra: Commonwealth Government Printer, 1937), paras 277–88.

10 J. A. Bushnell, *Australian Company Mergers, 1946–59* (Melbourne University Press, 1961); I. C. Stewart, 'Australian company mergers: 1960–70, *Economic Record*, March, 1975, pp. 1–29; S. Bishop, P. Dodd & R. R. Officer, *Australian Takeovers: the Evidence 1972–85* (Sydney: Centre for Independent Studies, Policy Monograph 12, 1987); Treasury, *Some Economic Implications of Takeovers* (Canberra: Australian Government Publishing Service, Economic Paper 12, 1986); Bureau of Industry Economics, *Mergers and Acquisitions* (Canberra: Australian Government Publishing Service, Research Report 36, 1990).

11 Bureau, *Mergers and Acquisitions*, pp. 20–1. The data source is Huntley's Delisted Companies Report, which is updated to the present on a regular basis.

12 These particularly included a merger boom in 1898–1900, 1919–20 and 1926–30. L. Hannah, *The Rise of the Corporate Economy* (London: Methuen, 1983, 2nd edn), pp. 175–6; Ralph L. Nelson, *Merger Movements in American Industry 1895–1956* (Princeton University Press, 1959); N. Lamoreaux, *The Great Merger Movement in American Business, 1895–1904* (Cambridge University Press, 1985).

13 S. Ville, *The Rural Entrepreneurs. A History of the Stock and Station Agent Industry in Australia and New Zealand* (Cambridge University Press, 2000), pp. 47–8.

14 K. Buckley & K. Klugman, *The History of Burns Philp: The Australian Company in the South Pacific* (Sydney: Burns Philp & Co Ltd, 1981), for example, pp. 46, 55–6, 112.

15 K. Tsokhas, *Beyond Dependence. Companies. Labour Processes and Australian Mining* (Melbourne: Oxford University Press, 1986), pp. 13–14.

16 Bushnell, *Australian Company Mergers*, pp. 118–19.

17 Stewart, 'Mergers' pp. 25–6.

18 *Wild Cat* 3/12/1960, pp. 386–7.

19 *Wild Cat* 3/12/1960.

20 Stewart, 'Mergers', pp. 12–14.
21 These acquisitions are detailed in S. King, *From the Ground Up – Boral's First 50 Years* (Sydney: State Library of NSW Press, 2000).
22 For example, see T. da Silva Lopes, 'Brands and the evolution of multinationals in alcoholic beverages', *Business History* 44, 3 (2002), pp. 7–14.
23 *Wild Cat* 6/2/1960, pp 33–4.
24 Bureau, 'Mergers and acquisitions', pp. 20–1.
25 Seven raiders are normally identified, Alan Bond, Ron Brierley, John Elliott, John Spalvins, Robert Holmes à Court, Lawrence Adler, Lee Ming Tee.
26 Under corporate law of the 1980s, the subsidiary's accounts could be consolidated into the parent's where the latter's ownership was less than 50 per cent. T. Sykes, *The Bold Riders. Behind Australia's Corporate Collapses* (St Leonard's NSW: Allen & Unwin 1996, 2nd edn), p. 408.
27 R. Casey, P. Dodd & P. Dolan, 'Takeovers and corporate raiders: Empirical evidence from extended event studies', *Australian Journal of Management* 12 (1987), p. 211.
28 P. H. Eddey, 'Corporate raiders and takeover targets', *Journal of Business Finance and Accounting* 18, 2 (1991).
29 Bushnell, *Australian Company Mergers*, pp. 164–5.
30 Stewart, 'Mergers', p. 28.
31 Stewart, 'Mergers', pp. 4, 7, 9.
32 Stewart, 'Mergers', pp. 9, 26–7.
33 Stewart, 'Mergers', pp. 26–7.
34 D. T. Merrett & G. Whitwell, 'The empire strikes back: Marketing Australian beer and wine in the United Kingdom', in G. Jones & N. Morgan (eds), *Adding Value: Marketing and Brands in the Food and Drink Industries* (London: Routledge, 1994). Although the company also used licensing arrangements in Britain 1981–85 and since 1995.
35 Tsokhas, *Beyond Dependence*, pp. 127–8.
36 H. L. Wilkinson, *The Trust Movement in Australia* (Melbourne: Critchley Parker, 1914).
37 Bureau, *Beyond the Firm*.
38 J. Kay, *Foundations of Corporate Success. How Business Strategies Add Value* (New York: Oxford University Press, 1993), pp. 80–2. Many examples in the 1990s are listed on the current BHP-Billiton website at: http://www.bhpbilliton.com/ accessed February 2003.
39 Companies in clothing and footwear, engineering, information technology and telecommunications, scientific and medical equipment, and processed food and beverages. The proportion involved rises to two-thirds if marginal areas of co-operation are counted, notably feedback, forward planning, and forecasting. Bureau, *Beyond the Firm*, pp. 10–12, 39–53.
40 Bureau, *Beyond the Firm*, pp. 82–3.
41 Ville, *Rural Entrepreneurs*, pp. 159–60.
42 R. Parsons, *The Adelaide Line: A Centenary History of the Adelaide Steamship Company Ltd., 1875–1975* (Magill, SA: R. H. Parsons, 1975), pp. 94–5, 100.
43 P. L. Richardson, 'The origins and development of the Collins House Group 1915–1951', *Australian Economic History Review*, 27, 1 (1987), pp. 3–29.

44 Richardson, 'Collins House Group', p. 8.

45 F. A. Green, *The Port Pirie Smelters* (Melbourne: Broken Hill Associated Smelters, 1977), pp. 1–6.

46 This is also known as the conditional cooperation resulting from repeated 'games' among the parties. See G. H. Boyce, *Cooperative Structures in Global Business. Communicating, Transferring Knowledge and Learning across the Corporate Frontier* (London: Routledge, 2001), p. 8.

47 P. Burn, 'Opportunism and long term contracting: Transactions in Broken Hill zinc concentrates in the 1930s', in D. Merrett (ed.), *Business Institutions and Behaviour in Australia* (London: Cass, 2000), pp. 71–88.

48 G. Boyce, 'A joint exploration venture. Western Mining Corporation and Hanna/Homestake, 1960–72', *Australian Economic History Review* 37, 3 (1997), pp. 202–21.

49 Tsokhas, *Beyond Dependence*, p. 40.

50 Information in this paragraph is taken from J. McB. Grant, 'The petroleum industry' in A. Hunter (ed.) *The Economics of Australian Industry* (Melbourne University Press, 1963), pp. 247–88.

51 A. Hunter & L. R. Webb, 'The chemical industry' in Hunter, *The Economics of Australian Industry*, pp. 300–1, 311.

52 M. F. Page, *Fitted for the Voyage: The Adelaide Steamship Company 1875–1975* (Adelaide: Rigby, 1975), pp. 308–15.

53 H. Fountain, 'Technology acquisition, firm capability and sustainable advantage: a case study of Australian Glass Manufacturers Ltd, 1915–39', in Merrett (ed.), *Business Institutions*, pp. 92, 99–102; *Wild Cat* 9/1/1960, pp. 14–15.

54 J. Gunn, *The Defeat of Distance – Qantas 1919–1939* (St Lucia: University of Queensland Press, 1985), pp. 167–92, 226.

55 G. Lewis, A. Morkel & G. Hubbard, *Australian Strategic Management. Concepts, Contexts and Cases* (New York: Prentice Hall, 1993), pp. 797–800; A. Sampson, *Empires of the Skies: The Politics, Contests and Cartels of World Airlines* (London: Hodder and Stoughton, 1984).

56 Kay, *Corporate Success*, pp. 120–4.

57 Wilkinson, *Trust Movement*.

58 G. Fleming & D. Terwiel, 'How successful was early Australian antitrust legislation? Lessons from the Associated Northern Collieries, 1906–11', *Australian Business Law Review*, 27, 1 (1999).

59 N. G. Butlin, A. Barnard & J. J. Pincus, *Government and Capitalism. Public and Private Choice in Twentieth Century Australia* (Sydney: Allen & Unwin, 1982), p. 125.

60 J. P. Nieuwenhuysen, 'Recent light on trade practices in Australia', in J. P. Nieuwenhuysen (ed.), *Australian Trade Practices: Readings* (Melbourne: F. W. Cheshire, 1970), pp. 38–42.

61 Nieuwenhuysen, 'Recent light', p. 43.

62 The nature of inter-firm relations in this industry remains controversial today with a long-run investigation by the Australian Competition and Consumer Commission into price-fixing breaking down in 2003.

63 R. D. Freeman, 'Trade associations in the Australian economy', in C. A. Hughes (ed.), *Readings in Australian Government* (St Lucia: University of Queensland Press, 1968).

64 M. Olson, *Logic of Collective Action: Public Goods and the Theory of Groups* (Cambridge MA: Harvard University Press, 1971).

65 Butlin, Barnard & Pincus, *Government and Capitalism*, p. 146; S. Bell, *Australian Manufacturing and the State. The Politics of Industry Policy in the Post-War Era* (Cambridge University Press, 1993), ch. 2.

66 Bell, *Australian Manufacturing*, p. 32.

67 Bell, *Australian Manufacturing*, pp. 20–1, 103.

68 K. Tsokhas, *A Class Apart. Businessmen and Australian Politics, 1960–80* (Oxford University Press, 1984), p. 103.

69 Bell, *Australian Manufacturing*, p. 104

70 Australian National University, Noel Butlin Archives Centre, Goldsbrough Mort 2/174/296, correspondence.

71 Goldsbrough Mort, 2/174/587a, correspondence.

72 Tsokhas, *Class Apart*.

6 Financing Corporate Strategies

1 W. W. Powell, 'Neither market nor hierarchy: network forms of organisation', *Research in Organisational Behaviour*, 12 (1990), pp. 303–5.

2 A specific form of network finance is the establishment and operation of an internal capital market by a conglomerate firm. As first expounded by transaction cost theorists such as Williamson, internal capital markets can be more efficient than external markets in allocating finance due to information advantages that derive from internalisation. See O. Williamson, *Corporate Control and Business Behavior* (New Jersey: Prentice Hall, 1970). For a recent review of the evidence on internal capital markets see P. Bolton & D. Scharfstein, 'Corporate finance, the theory of the firm, and organizations', *Journal of Economic Perspectives*, 12, 4 (1998), pp. 106–11.

3 J. B. Baskin & P. J. Miranti, *A History of Corporate Finance* (Cambridge University Press, 1997) attribute the growth of broad, impersonal stock markets during the first half of the century in the United States to the improvements in confidence in equity. Shareholders were increasingly able to judge the quality of firms through greater disclosure of financial structure, and the provision of constant dividends and a consistent payout record that signalled financial soundness. In Australia, the regulation and relative smallness of the stock market means that we may find that equity looked like debt for much longer than in the United States, and that dividend yields were maintained at high levels.

4 D. T. Merrett, 'Capital markets and capital formation in Australia, 1890–1945', *Australian Economic History Review*, 37, 3 (1997), and D. T. Merrett, 'Capital markets and capital formation in Australia, 1945–1990', *Australian Economic History Review*, 38, 2 (1998).

5 C. Forster, *Industrial Development in Australia 1920–1930* (Canberra: Australian National University, 1964), p. 207.

6 The series, drawing upon data from *Jobson's Digest*, Commonwealth Bank of Australia, and Reserve Bank of Australia, will be published in a forthcoming paper by the current authors.

7 A. R. Hall, *Australian Company Finance: Sources and Uses of Funds of Public Companies, 1946–1955* (Canberra: Australian National University, 1956); R. L. Mathews and G. Harcourt, 'Company finance', in R. R. Hirst & R. H. Wallace (eds)

Studies in the Australian Capital Market (Melbourne: F. W. Cheshire, 1964); R. Ma and R. L. Mathews, 'Company finance', in R. R. Hirst & R. H. Wallace (eds) *The Australian Capital Market* (Melbourne: Cheshire, 1974), pp. 50–95.

8 Mathews & Harcourt and Ma & Mathews argued that high concentration levels in Australian industries allowed those firms to adopt pricing policies that generated a high level of undistributed profits. We would concur. See Mathews & Harcourt, 'Company finance', p. 412; Ma & Mathews, 'Company finance', p. 60. On the concentration levels of Australia industry, see P. H. Karmel & M. Brunt, *The Structure of the Australian Economy* (Melbourne: F. W. Cheshire, 1962).

9 K. Buckley & K. Klugman, *The History of Burns Philp: The Australian Company in the South Pacific* (Sydney: Burns Philp and Co Ltd, 1981), pp. 117, 119–20.

10 K. Buckley & K. Klugman, *The Australian Presence in the Pacific: Burns Philp, 1914–1946* (Sydney: George Allen & Unwin, 1983), pp. 216–20.

11 R. F. Holder, *Bank of New South Wales: A History* (Sydney: Angus and Robertson, 1970), 2 volumes, pp. 520, 588.

12 H. Hughes, *The Australian Iron and Steel Industry* (Melbourne University Press, 1964), p. 118.

13 J. B. Were, *The Transport Industry in Australia* (Melbourne: J. B. Were, 1964), pp. 18; S. Brimson, *Ansett – the Story of an Airline* (Sydney: Dreamweaver Books, 1987), pp. 81–2.

14 *Wild Cat Monthly*, 3 September 1960, pp. 278–9.

15 S. King, *From the Ground Up – Boral's First 50 Years* (Sydney: State Library of NSW Press, 2000), pp. 21, 28, 46, 77.

16 J. Wright, *Heart of the Lion: The 50 Year History of Australia's Holden* (St Leonards: Allen & Unwin, 1998), pp. 20–1, 121.

17 Wright, *Heart of the Lion*, pp. 9, 20–1, 26.

18 M. Schneider, 'Trade credit', in R. R. Hirst & R. H. Wallace (eds), *Australian Capital Market* (1974), pp. 96–128.

19 S. Ville, *The Rural Entrepreneurs. A History of the Stock and Station Agent Industry in Australia and New Zealand* (Cambridge University Press, 2000), chs 3 and 4.

20 R. Mathews & G. Harcourt, 'Company finance', p. 388; Ma & Mathews, 'Company finance', p. 58.

21 M. F. Page, *Fitted for the Voyage: The Adelaide Steamship Company 1875–1975* (Adelaide: Rigby, 1975), pp. 18–19.

22 Brimson, *Ansett*, pp. 81–2.

23 K. Tsokhas, *Beyond Dependence. Companies. Labour Processes and Australian Mining* (Melbourne: Oxford University Press, 1986), pp. 96–110.

24 Boyce, G. 'The Western Mining Corporation-Hanna/Homestake joint venture: Game theory and inter-organisational cooperation', *Australian Economic History Review*, vol. 37, 3 (1997), pp. 202–21.

25 N. G. Butlin, A. Barnard & J. J. Pincus, *Government and Capitalism: Public and Private Choice in Twentieth Century Australia* (St Leonards, NSW: Allen & Unwin, 1982).

26 H. Fysh, *Qantas Rising: The Autobiography of the Flying Fysh* (Sydney: Angus and Robertson, 1965), p. 279.

27 J. Gunn, *The Defeat of Distance – Qantas 1919–1939* (St Lucia: University of Queensland Press, 1985), pp. 281–2.

28 Ma and Mathews, 'Company finance', pp. 81–2; G. L. Clark, *Built on Gold: Recollections of Western Mining* (Melbourne: Hill of Content Publishing, 1983), p. 220.

29 Holder, *Bank of New South Wales*, pp. 520, 588.

30 Page, *Fitted for the Voyage*, pp. 44, 52, 190.

31 Page, *Fitted for the Voyage*, pp. 238–9.

32 Bureau of Industry Economics, *Mergers and Acquisitions*, Research report 36 (Canberra: Australian Government Publishing Service, 1990), p. 29.

33 *Wild Cat Monthly*, 4 February 1961, pp. 51–2.

34 Forster, *Industrial Development*, p. 197.

35 E. K. Sinclair, *The Spreading Tree: A History of APM and AMCOR 1844–1989* (North Sydney: Allen & Unwin, 1990), pp. 55–6, 64, 66–7, 93, 95.

36 Clark, *Built on Gold*, pp. 13, 26, 242–7.

37 P. J. Drake & D. W. Stammer, 'The stock exchange', in M. K. Lewis & R. H. Wallace, *The Australian Financial System* (Melbourne: Longman Cheshire, 1993), pp. 313–17, 293–4.

38 K. T. Davis, 'Corporate debt markets', in M. K. Lewis & R. H. Wallace, *The Australian Financial System* (Melbourne: Longman Cheshire, 1993), p. 262.

39 B. Barry, S. Easton & S. Pinder, 'The globalisation of capital markets: An empirical examination of the impact of foreign listing on the returns and systematic risk of equity securities', manuscript, 2001.

40 S. Myers & N. Majluf, 'Corporate financing and investment decisions when firms have information that investors do not have', *Journal of Financial Economics*, 13, 1984, pp. 187–221.

41 The pecking order theory implies that: (1) managers have a preference for internal over external sources of finance; (2) dividend payout by managers are 'sticky' so that changes in the earnings of the firm dictate the demand for external finance; and (3) if external finance is required, managers will issue the safest security first. Firms will finance growth with debt and only use equity when other sources are exhausted. See S. Myers, 'Capital structure', *Journal of Economic Perspectives*, 15, 2 (2001), p. 91.

42 Myers, 'Capital structure', pp. 91–3; Myers & Majluf 'Corporate financing', pp. 219–20.

43 Total assets in the electricity industry grew threefold from £4.97 million in 1920 to £14.95 million in 1929. Assets in the gas industry grew twofold from £11.73 million in 1920 to £21.21 million in 1929 (Forster, *Industrial Development*, pp. 204–5).

44 P. Donovan & N. Kirkman, *The Unquenchable Flame. South Australian Gas Company, 1861–1986* (Netley, SA: Wakefield Press, 1986), pp. 105–11.

45 See, for example, Hall, *Company Finance*, pp. 41, 42; Mathews & Harcourt 'Company finance', pp. 405–7.

46 R. Broomham, *First Light: 150 years of Gas* (Sydney: Hale and Iremonger, 1987), pp. 172, 174–5.

47 D. Hutchinson, 'The transformation of Boral: From dependent, specialist bitumen refiner to major building products manufacturer', in D. Merrett (ed.), *Business Institutions and Behaviour in Australia* (London: Frank Cass, 2000), p. 113.

48 M. Murphy, *Challenges of Change: The Lend Lease Story* (Sydney: Lend Lease Corporation, 1984), p. 34.

49 Similar increases have been noted by P. Lowe & G. Shuetrim, *The Evolution of Corporate Financial Structure 1973–1990*, Reserve Bank of Australia Research Discussion Paper No. 9216, December (Sydney, 1992), pp. 7–16; and Davis, 'Corporate debt markets', p. 255, Table 7.5.

50 See Myers, 'Capital structure'.

51 G. Hubbard, A. Morkel, S. Davenport & P. Beamish, *Cases in Strategic Management* (Frenchs Forest: Prentice Hall, 2000), pp. 377–85.

52 F. L. Clarke, G. W. Deane & K. G. Oliver, *Corporate Collapse: Regulatory, Accounting and Ethical Failure* (Cambridge University Press, 1997), p. 157.

53 T. Sykes, *The Bold Riders: Behind Australia's Corporate Collapses* (St Leonards, NSW: Allen & Unwin, 1994), 2nd edn (1996), p. 429.

54 R. H. Wallace, 'The business financiers: Merchant banks and finance companies', in M. K. Lewis & R. H. Wallace, *The Australian Financial System* (Melbourne: Longman Cheshire, 1993), pp. 214–48.

55 Wallace, 'Business financiers', p. 219.

56 Davis, 'Corporate debt markets', p. 259.

57 Davis, 'Corporate debt markets', pp. 275–77.

58 M. Lincoln & G. Burrows, *Australian Case Studies in Business Finance* (Sydney: McGraw Hill, 1975), pp. 73–80.

59 G. Blainey, *Jumping Over the Wheel* (St Leonards: Allen & Unwin 1993), pp. 229–45.

60 BHP Directors' Report 1967, quoted in Lincoln & Burrows, *Australian Case Studies*, p. 82.

7 Organisational Configuration and Corporate Governance

1 The literature is too voluminous to mention here. Reviews of organisational structures and configurations are available in standard texts such as G. Johnson & K. Scholes, *Exploring Corporate Strategy* (Harlow: Financial Times and Prentice Hall, 2002).

2 A. D. Chandler, *Scale and Scope: The Dynamics of Industrial Capitalism* (Cambridge: Belknap Press of Harvard University Press, 1990), p. 15.

3 K. Tsokhas, *Beyond Dependence. Companies. Labour Processes and Australian Mining* (Melbourne: Oxford University Press, 1986), p. 121.

4 G. L. Clark, *Built on Gold: Recollections of Western Mining* (Melbourne: Hill of Content Publishing, 1983), pp. 120, 151–4.

5 N. R. Wills, 'The basic iron and steel industry', in A. Hunter (ed.) *The Economics of Australian Industry: Studies in Environment and Structure* (Melbourne University Press, 1963), pp. 237–44.

6 Clark, *Built on Gold*, pp. 151–4.

7 Tsokas, *Beyond Dependence*.

8 R. Broomham, *First Light: 150 Years of Gas* (Sydney: Hale and Iremonger, 1987), p. 121.

9 S. P. Ville & G. A. Fleming, 'Financial intermediaries and the design of loan contracts in the Australasian pastoral sector' *Financial History Review*, 7 (2000), pp. 201–18.

10 S. Ville, *The Rural Entrepreneurs. A History of the Stock and Station Agent Industry in Australia and New Zealand* (Cambridge University Press, 2000), pp. 178–9.

11 On organisational configurations in the pastoral industry, see S. Ville, *Rural Entrepreneurs*, ch. 8.

12 A. Seltzer & D. T. Merrett, 'Human resource management practices at the Union Bank of Australia: panel evidence from the 1887–1893 entry cohorts', *Journal of Labor Economics*, 18, 4, October (2000).

13 A. C. Gray, *Life Insurance in Australia: An Historical and Descriptive Account* (Melbourne: McCarron Bird, 1977), pp. 197–9.

14 K. Buckley & K. Klugman, *The Australian Presence in the Pacific: Burns Philp, 1914–1946* (Sydney: George Allen & Unwin, 1983), p. 326.

15 K. Buckley & K. Klugman, *The History of Burns Philp: The Australian Company in the South Pacific* (Sydney: Burns Philp and Co Ltd, 1981), pp. 214, 300–5.

16 L. Clark, *Finding a Common Interest: The Story of Dick Dusseldorp and Lend Lease* (Cambridge University Press, 2002).

17 G. D. Snooks, 'Innovation and the growth of the firm: Hume enterprises, 1910–40', *Australian Economic History Review*, 13, 1 (1973); R. Emerson-Elliot, 'The Hume Pipe Company. Early internationalization by an Australian company', http://www.uow.edu.au/commerce/econ/modbusiness/Hume%20Pipe%20Company. pdf..

18 J. Todd, 'Cars, paint, and chemicals: Industry linkages and the capture of overseas technology between the wars', *Australian Economic History Review*, 38, 2 (1998); G. Maxcy, 'The motor industry', in A. Hunter (ed.) *The Economics of Australian Industry: Studies in Environment and Structure* (Melbourne University Press, 1963), pp. 526–8. D. T. Brash, *American Investment in Australian Industry* (Canberra: Australian National University Press, 1966).

19 Maxcy, 'Motor industry', p. 518; J. Wright, *Heart of the Lion*.

20 J. Wright, *Heart of the Lion: The 50 Year History of Australia's Holden* (St Leonards: Allen & Unwin, 1998), pp. 346, 222–3, 257.

21 J. Rich, *Hartnett: Portrait of a Technocratic Brigand* (Sydney: Turton and Armstrong 1996), ch. 16.

22 D. Hutchinson, 'The transformation of Boral: From dependent, specialist bitumen refiner to major building products manufacturer', in D. Merrett (ed.), *Business Institutions and Behaviour in Australia* (London: Frank Cass, 2000).

23 A. Birch & J. F. Blaxland (1956), 'The historical background', in A. G. Lowndes (ed.) *South Pacific Enterprise: The Colonial Sugar Refining Company* (Sydney: Angus and Robertson), pp. 36–7.

24 R. W. Harman (1956), 'Men and organization', in A. G. Lowndes (ed.), *South Pacific Enterprise: the Colonial Sugar Refining Company* (Sydney: Angus and Robertson) pp. 245–8.

25 H. L. Wilkinson, *The Trust Movement in Australia* (Melbourne: Critchley Parker, 1914), pp. 35–49.

26 E. K. Sinclair, *The Spreading Tree: a History of APM and AMCOR 1844–1989* (North Sydney: Allen & Unwin, 1990), pp. 30, 45.

27 H. Fountain, 'Technology acquisition, firm capability and sustainable advantage: a case study of Australian Glass Manufacturers Ltd, 1915–39', in D. Merrett (ed.), *Business Institutions and Behaviour in Australia* (London: Frank Cass, 2000), pp. 96–7.

28 J. E. Norton & L. Willcocks (1993), 'The News Corporation', in G. Johnson & K. Scholes (eds), *Exploring Corporate Strategy* (Harlow: Financial Times and Prentice Hall), pp. 628–9.

29 E. Carew, *Westpac. The Bank that Broke the Bank* (Sydney: Doubleday, 1997).

30 Wills, 'The basic iron and steel industry'.
31 Broomham, *First Light*, p. 174.
32 See Appendices 10.2 and 10.3, Broomham, *First Light*.
33 D. Stace, *Reaching Out from Down Under: Building Competence for Global Markets* (Sydney: McGraw-Hill Companies, Inc., 1997).
34 Sinclair, *Spreading Tree*, pp. 178, 246-7.
35 *Wild Cat* 9 June 1960, 3 December 1960.
36 B. Carroll, *A Very Good Business. One Hundred Years of James Hardie Industries Ltd, 1888-1988* (Sydney: James Hardie Industries Ltd, 1988), pp. 82-3.
37 Carroll, *James Hardie*, pp. 223-5, 249-52.
38 P. G. Berger & E. Ofek, 'Diversification's effect on firm value', *Journal of Financial Economics*, 37 (1995), pp. 39-65; J. Campa & S. Kedia, 'Explaining the diversification discount', *Journal of Finance*, vol. 57, 2 (2002), pp. 1731-62; G. A. Fleming, B. R. Oliver & S. Skourakis, 'The valuation discount of multi-segment firms in Australia', *Accounting and Finance*, 43, 2 (2003).
39 L. Fauver, J. Houston & A. Naranjo, 'Capital market development, integration, legal systems, and the value of corporate diversification: a cross-country analysis', Paper to the Tuck-JFQA Contemporary Corporate Governance Issues II Conference, 2002.
40 G. Blainey, *Jumping Over the Wheel* (St Leonards: Allen & Unwin, 1993), pp. 68-86, 150-68.
41 F. L. Clarke, G. W. Deane & K. G. Oliver, *Corporate Collapse: Regulatory, Accounting and Ethical Failure* (Cambridge University Press, 1997), p. 154.
42 Blainey, *Jumping Over the Wheel*, p. 212.
43 Blainey, *Jumping Over the Wheel*, p. 220.
44 This section draws from Clarke, Dean & Oliver, *Corporate Collapse*, ch. 12 and T. Sykes, *The Bold Riders: Behind Australia's Corporate Collapses* (St Leonards, NSW: Allen and Unwin, 1994), ch. 13.
45 Clarke, Dean & Oliver, *Corporate Collapse*, pp. 154, 156.
46 Sykes, *Bold Riders*, p. 428.
47 Sykes, *Bold Riders*, pp. 429-30.
48 Ville, *Rural Entrepreneurs*, p. 52.
49 Ville, *Rural Entrepreneurs*, p. 54; T. Hewat, *The Elders Explosion. One Hundred and Fifty Years of Progress from Elder to Elliott* (Sydney: Bay Books, 1998).
50 On the market for corporate control in Australia see P. Dodd, 'Company takeovers and the Australian equity market', *Australian Journal of Management* 15, 1976; T. Walter, 'Australian takeovers: Capital market efficiency and shareholder risk and return' *Australian Journal of Management* 63, 1984; P. Brown & A. Horin, 'Assessing competition in the market for corporate control: Australian evidence' *Australian Journal of Management* 23 (1986); S. Bishop, P. Dodd & R. Officer, *Australian Takeovers: The Evidence 1972-1985* (Centre for Independent Studies Policy Monograph 12, 1987).
51 Chandler, *Scale and Scope*, pp. 232-3 noted an increase in executive directors on company boards as firms moved towards multidivisional structures (as size and organisational divisions increased the number and complexity of managerial decisions). Empirical evidence on the relationship between board size and company size is provided by Denis & Sarin (for the United States) and Lawrence &

Stapledon (for Australia). See D. J. Denis & A. Sarin, 'Ownership and board structures in publicly traded corporations', *Journal of Financial Economics*, 52 (1999), pp. 187–223; J. Lawrence & G. Stapledon, 'Is board composition important? A study of listed Australian companies', manuscript 1999.

52 M. C. Jensen, 'The modern Industrial Revolution, exit, and the failure of internal control systems', *Journal of Finance*, 48, 3 (1993), p. 865; M. Lipton & J. W. Lorsch, 'A modest proposal for improved corporate governance', *The Business Lawyer*, 48, 1 (1992), p. 65. Debate over the costs and benefits of larger boards has led to suggestions that there is an optimal board size. For example, Lipton and Lorsch recommend 'that the size of a board should be limited to a maximum of ten directors (indeed we would favor boards of eight or nine)' (p. 67). Jensen argues that when 'boards go beyond seven or eight people they are less likely to function effectively and are easier for the CEO to control' (p. 865).

53 S. N. Kaplan & D. Reishus, 'Outside directorships and corporate performance', *Journal of Financial Economics*, 27 (1990).

54 See E. F. Fama & M. C. Jensen, 'Separation of ownership and control', *Journal of Law and Economics* 26 (1983), pp. 301–25; Hampel Report 1998, p. 26.

55 See, for example, J. E. Core, R. W. Holthausen & D. F. Larcker, 'Corporate governance, Chief Executive Officer compensation and firm performance', *Journal of Financial Economics*, 51 (1999), pp. 343–70; S. Rosenstein & J. G. Wyatt, 'Outside directors, Board independence, and shareholder wealth', *Journal of Financial Economics* 26, 1990.

56 See C. G. Holderness & D. P. Sheehan, 'The role of majority shareholders in publicly held corporations: an exploratory study', *Journal of Financial Economics*, 20 (1988), pp. 317–46; D. K. Shome & S. Singh, 'Firm value and external blockholdings', *Financial Management* 24 (1995), pp. 3–14; and J. E. Bethel, J. Liebeskind & T. Opler, 'Block share purchases and corporate performance', *Journal of Finance*, 53 (1998), pp. 605–34.

57 On the proxy voting behaviour of Australian institutions see G. Stapledon, S. Easterbrook, P. Bennett & I. Ramsey, *Proxy Voting in Australia's Largest Companies* (Centre for Corporate Law and Securities Regulation, and Corporate Governance International Pty Limited, 2000).

8 Corporate Leaders, Big Business and the Economy

1 A. D. Chandler, Jr, *Scale and Scope: The Dynamics of Industrial Capitalism* (Cambridge, MA & London: Belknap Press of Harvard University Press, 1990).

2 A. D. Chandler, Jr, F. Amatori & T. Hikino (eds), *Big Business and the Wealth of Nations* (Cambridge University Press, 1997); W. Mark Fruin, *The Japanese Enterprise System: Competitive Strategies and Cooperative Structures* (Oxford: Clarendon Press, 1992); T. McCraw (ed.), *Creating Modern Capitalism* (Cambridge, MA and London: Harvard University Press, 1995).

3 R. T. Madigan, *Technology in Australia, 1788–1988: A Condensed History of Australian Technological Innovation and Adaptation During the First Two Hundred Years* (Melbourne: Australian Academy of Technological Sciences and Engineering, 1988); G. B. Magee, *Knowledge Generation: Technological Change and Economic Growth in Colonial Australia* (Melbourne: Australian Scholarly Publishing, 2000).

4 G. Bindon & D. P. Miller, '"Sweetness and light": Industrial research in the Colonial Sugar Refining Company, 1855–1900', in R. W. Home (ed.), *Australian Science in the Making* (Cambridge University Press in association with the Australian Academy of Science, 1988), pp. 170–94; A. G. Lowndes (ed.), *South Pacific Enterprise:The Colonial Sugar Refining Company* (Sydney: Angus and Robertson, 1956), appendix 27, pp. 459–62.

5 *The B.H.P. Review Jubilee Number*, June (1935), p. 86.

6 D. Hutchinson, 'Australian manufacturing business: entrepreneurship or missed opportunities?', *Australian Economic History Review*, 41, 2, 2001, pp. 103–34; H. Fountain, 'Technology acquisition, firm capability and sustainable competitive advantage: A study of Australian Glass Manufacturers Ltd, 1915–39', *Business History*, 42, 3 (2000), pp. 89–108; J. Todd, 'Cars, paint, and chemicals: industry linkages and the capture of overseas technology between the wars', *Australian Economic History Review*, 38, 2 (1998), pp. 176–93.

7 'Secondary Industries Testing and Research – Extension of Activities of Council for Scientific and Industrial Research', Report (1937), *Commonwealth of Australia Papers Presented to Parliament*, 1937–38, IV.

8 D. C. Mowery & N. Rosenberg, *Paths of Innovation: Technological Change in 20th-Century America* (Cambridge University Press, 1998); D. C. Mowery & R. R. Nelson (eds), *Sources of Industrial Leadership: Studies of Seven Industries* (Cambridge University Press, 1999).

9 G. N. Blainey, 'The history of multinational factories in Australia', in A. Okochi & T. Inoue (eds), *Overseas Business Activities: Proceedings of the Fuji Conference* (Tokyo: University of Tokyo Press, 1984), pp. 183–210; C. Forster, *Industrial Development in Australia 1920–1930* (Canberra: Australian National University, 1964); D. T. Brash, *American Investment in Australian Manufacturing* (Canberra: Australian National University Press, 1966).

10 J. Stanton, 'Protection, market structure and firm behaviour: inefficiency in the early Australian tyre industry', *Australian Economic History Review*, 24, 2 (1984), pp. 91–114.

11 For information on the extent of foreign ownership and control in Australian manufacturing industry see: Department of Trade and Industry, *Directory of Overseas Investment in Australian Manufacturing Industry 1966* (Canberra, 1966); *Idem, Directory of Overseas Investment in Australian Manufacturing Industry 1971* (Canberra, 1971); Commonwealth Treasury, *Overseas Investment in Australia*, Treasury Economic Paper No. 1 (Canberra: Australian Government Publishing Service, 1972).

12 *Financial Review*, 18 November 1963, quoted in B. Fitzpatrick & E. L. Wheelwright, *The Highest Bidder: A Citizen's Guide to Problems of Foreign Investment in Australia* (Melbourne: Lansdowne, 1965), pp. 87–9.

13 They were acquired by W. R. Grace (1966), Unilever (1914), Vesteys (1955) and Cadbury Fry Pascall (1967), respectively. T. Wilson, *Years of Grace: The First Fifty Years in Australia* (Melbourne: T. Wilson Publishing Company, 1986), pp. 92–3; D. K. Fieldhouse, *Unilever Overseas: The Anatomy of a Multinational 1895–1965* (London: Croom Helm, 1978), pp. 67–9; P. d'Abbs, *The Vestey Story* (Melbourne: Australasian Meat Industry Employees' Union (Victorian Branch), n.d.), p. 19; Ian Potter & Co. *Australian Company Reviews 1972* (Melbourne: Ian Potter & Co., n.d.), p. 59.

14 G. Jones, *The Evolution of International Business: An Introduction* (London and New York: Routledge, 1996), Figs 2.1, 2.2, 2.4, 2.5, pp. 30, 31, 42, 43.

15 Chandler, *Scale and Scope*, p. 597.

16 Chandler, *Scale and Scope*, p. 36. Emphasis in the original.

17 See, for example: J. R. Williams, 'Strategy and the search for rents: the evolution of diversity amongst firms', in Richard P. Rumelt, Dan E. Schendel & David J. Teece (eds), *Fundamental Issues in Strategy: A Research Agenda* (Boston, MA: Harvard Business School, 1994), pp. 229–46; R. R. Nelson, 'Why do firms differ, and how does it matter?' in *idem*, pp. 247–69; C. K. Prahalad & G. Hamel, 'The core competencies of the corporation', *Harvard Business Review* May–June, 1990, pp. 79–91; G. Stalk, P. Evans & L. E Shulman, 'Competing on capabilities: The new rules of corporate strategy', *Harvard Business Review*, March–April (1992), pp. 57–69; J. B. Barney, 'Firm resources and sustained competitive advantage', *Journal of Management*, 17, 1 (1991), pp. 99–120.

18 R. M. Grant, *Contemporary Strategy Analysis: Concepts, Techniques, Applications* (Oxford: Blackwell, 1998, 3rd edn), pp. 125–38.

19 Sir H. Gepp, 'The scientist in industrial administration', in H. Gepp, *Democracy's Danger: Addresses on Various Occasions* (Sydney & London: Angus & Robertson Limited, 1939), pp. 200–21.

20 *B.H.P. Review Jubilee Number*, June (1935), pp. 151–66; R. W. Harman, 'Men and organization', in Lowndes (ed.), *South Pacific Enterprise*, pp. 231–55.

21 A. D. Chandler, Jr, *The Visible Hand: The Managerial Revolution in American Business* (Cambridge, MA and London: Belknap Press of Harvard University Press, 1977); and *idem, Strategy and Structure: Chapters in the History of the American Industrial Enterprise* (Cambridge, MA and London: MIT Press, 1962).

22 Chandler, *Scale and Scope*, pp. 235–7.

23 Madigan, *Technology in Australia 1788–1988*; See D. P. Mellor, *The Role of Science and Industry* (Canberra: Australian War Memorial, 1958), Volume 5, for a detailed account of the state of manufacturing technology during the war. For more popular accounts see B. Carroll, *Australian Made: Success Stories in Australian Manufacturing since 1937* (Parkville: Institution of Production Engineers Australian Council, 1987); R. Renew, *Making It: Innovation and Success in Australia's Industries* (Sydney: Power House Museum, 1993).

24 P. Stubbs, *Innovation and Research: A Study in Australian Industry* (Melbourne: F. W. Cheshire, 1968), pp. 32–8.

25 See J. C. Timms, *Australian and New Zealand Advertising* (Melbourne: Sir Isaac Pitman & Sons, 1940); W. A. McNair, *Radio Advertising in Australia* (Sydney: Angus & Robertson, 1937); B. Carroll, *The Australian Advertising Album* (South Melbourne: Macmillan, 1975), *Idem, The Australian Poster Album* (South Melbourne: Macmillan, 1974); J. Bryden-Brown, *Ads That Made Australia* (Lane Cove, NSW: Doubleday, 1981).

26 W. Hamish Fraser, *The Coming of the Mass Market 1850–1914* (London: Macmillan, 1981); S. Strasser, *Satisfaction Guaranteed: The Making of the American Mass Market* (New York: Pantheon Books, 1989); P. Walker Laird, *Advertising Progress: American Business and the Rise of Consumer Marketing* (Baltimore & London: Johns Hopkins University Press, 1998).

27 N. Shoebridge, *Great Australian Advertising Campaigns* (Sydney: McGraw-Hill Book Company, 1992), p. 2.

28 R. Hambleton, *The Branding of America* (Camden, ME: Yankee Books, 1987).

29 J. P. Nieuwenhuysen, 'Recent light on trade practices in Australia', in J. Nieuwenhuysen (ed.), *Australian Trade Practices: Readings* (Melbourne: F. W. Cheshire, 1970); R. D. Freeman, 'Trade associations in the Australian economy', in C. A. Hughes (ed.), *Readings in Australian Government* (St Lucia: University of Queensland Press, 1968), pp. 443–58.

30 J. Kay, *Foundations of Corporate Success: How Business Strategies Add Value* (Oxford and New York: Oxford University Press, 1993).

31 F. A. Green, *The Port Pirie Smelters* (Melbourne: Broken Hill Associated Smelters, 1977); P. Richardson, 'The origins and development of the Collins House Group 1915–1951', *Australian Economic History Review*, 27, 1 (1987), pp. 3–29.

32 Richardson, 'Collins House Group'; Department of National Development, *The Structure and Capacity of Australian Manufacturing Industries* (Melbourne: Department of National Development, 1952), pp. 172–7.

33 J. McB. Grant, 'The petroleum industry', in A. Hunter (ed.), *The Economics of Australian Industry: Studies in Environment and Structure* (Melbourne University Press, 1963), p. 263; A. Hunter & L. R. Webb, 'The chemical industry' in A. Hunter (ed.), *The Economics of Australian Industry*, pp. 300–01; Madigan, *Technology in Australia 1788–1988*, pp. 709–14.

34 Madigan, *Technology in Australia*, pp. 671–75.

35 R. B. McKern, *Multinational Enterprise and Natural Resources* (Sydney: McGraw-Hill Book Company, 1976); G, Boyce, 'Multilateral contracting in Australian mining: the development of Hamersley Iron, 1961–1966', *Enterprise & Society*, 2 (2001), pp. 543–75; *idem*, 'The Western Mining Corporation-Hanna/Homestake joint venture: Game theory and inter-organizational cooperation', *Australian Economic History Review*, 37, 3 (1997), pp. 202–21.

36 Kay, *Corporate Success*, ch. 5.

37 Chandler, *Visible Hand*, pp. 484–90.

38 F. R. E. Mauldon, *Mechanisation in Australian Industries* (Hobart: University of Tasmania Department of Economics and Commerce, 1938), pp. 33–65.

39 See Department of National Development, *Structure and Capacity*, pp. 168–77; Richardson, 'Collins House Group'.

40 Sir N. Young, *Figuratively Speaking: The Reminiscences, Experiences & Observations of Sir Norman Young* (Adelaide: published by the author, 1991), pp. 42–4; D. H. Briggs & R. L. Smith, *Distribution of Groceries: Economic Aspects of the Distribution of Groceries with Special Reference to Western Australia* (Perth: University of Western Australia Press, 1967); M. Hast, *100 Years of Power: The Lawrence & Hanson Story* (South Melbourne: Lawrence & Hanson, 1986).

41 Lowndes (ed.), *South Pacific Enterprise*, pp. 207–30, 474–5.

42 Potter, *Australian Company Reviews*, p. 87.

43 D. T. Merrett, 'Australian firms abroad before 1970: Why so few, why those, and why there?', *Business History*, 44, 2 (2002), pp. 77–80.

44 Chandler, *Scale and Scope*, pp. 599–601.

45 See Mellor, *Science and Industry*.

46 D. T. Merrett & C. B. Schedvin, 'Australia: Dependence at the periphery', in Benjamin Franklin Cooling (ed.), *War, Business and World Military-Industrial Complexes* (Port Washington, NY & London: Kennikat Press, 1981), pp. 106–19.

47 Details of entry and exit can be found in Appendix C.

48 C. D. Kemp, *Big Businessmen: Four Biographical Essays* (Melbourne: Institute of Public Affairs, 1964), 'Introduction'.

49 Joint Industry Commission and Department of Industry, Science and Tourism, *A Portrait of Australian Business: Results of the 1995 Business Longitudinal Survey* (Canberra: Australian Government Publishing Service, 1997), pp. 27-8, Tables 3.226-237, pp. 167-76 and Table 3.96-3.101, pp. 87-90. J. Mathews, *Catching the Wave: Workplace Reform in Australia* (St Leonards, NSW: Allen & Unwin, 1994).

50 Australian Manufacturing Council, *Leading the Way: A Study of Best Manufacturing Practices in Australia and New Zealand* (Melbourne: Australian Manufacturing Council, 1994).

51 P. Stubbs, *Technology and Australia's Future: Industry and International Competitiveness* (Melbourne: Australian Industry Development Association Research Centre Publication, 1980); P. J. Sheehan, N. Pappas, G. Tikhomirova & P. Sinclair, *Australia and the Knowledge Economy: An Assessment of the Enhanced Economic Growth through Science and Technology* (Melbourne: Victoria University, Centre for Strategic Economic Studies, 1995).

52 R. O. Block, *Delfin Digest 1965: The Top Companies in Australia, New Zealand and South-East Asia* (Sydney: Development Finance Corporation Limited, 1965), pp. 27-54; 'The top 1000', *Business Review Weekly*, 27 October (1997).

53 R. H. Chenhall, 'Some elements of organisational control in Australian divisionalised firms', *Australian Journal of Management*, 4, 1 (1979), Supplement, Table 6, p. 22.

54 Chenhall, 'Organisational control', p. 6 and Table 8, p. 24.

55 Block, *Delfin Digest 1967*, pp. 186-263.

56 J. A. Bushnell, *Australian Company Mergers 1946-1959* (Melbourne University Press, 1961).

57 T. Sykes, *The Bold Riders: Behind Australia's Corporate Collapses* (St Leonards: Allen & Unwin, 1994).

58 W. Lazonick & M. O'Sullivan (eds), *Corporate Governance and Sustainable Prosperity* (Basingstoke: Palgrave, 2002).

59 D. T. Merrett, 'Corporate governance, incentives and the internationalization of Australian business', unpublished paper delivered to the Business History Conference, Hagley Museum and Library, Wilmington, DE, 19-21 April (2002c).

60 Lazonick & O'Sullivan, *Corporate Governance* (2002).

61 'The top 1000', *Business Review Weekly*, 27 October (1997).

62 Merrett, 'Corporate governance'; D. T. Merrett & K. A. Houghton, 'Takeovers and corporate governance: whose interests do directors serve?', *ABACUS*, 35, 2 (1999), pp. 223-40.

63 Life and pension funds owned 24 per cent of equities in Australian stock exchanges in 1995. P. Davies & D. Peacock, 'The role of the stock exchange and financial characteristics of Australian companies', in R. Bruce, B. McKern & M. Skully (eds), *Handbook of Australian Corporate Finance* (Sydney: Butterworths, 1997, 5th edn).

64 N. G. Butlin, A. Barnard & J. J. Pincus, *Government and Capitalism: Public and Private Choice in Twentieth Century Australia* (Sydney: George Allen & Unwin, 1982).

65 For a sample of the large literature on this transformation see: H. V. Emy, *Remaking Australia: The State, The Market and Australia's Future* (St Leonards, NSW: Allen & Unwin, 1993); M. Pusey, *Economic Rationalism in Canberra: A Nation Building*

State Changes Its Mind (Cambridge University Press, 1991); A. Capling & B. Galligan, *Beyond The Protective State: The Political Economy of Australia's Manufacturing Industry Policy* (Cambridge University Press, 1992); S. Bell, *Ungoverning the Economy: The Political Economy of Australian Economic Policy* (Melbourne: Oxford University Press, 1997); P. Kelly, *The End of Certainty: The Story of the 1980s* (St Leonards, NSW: Allen & Unwin, 1992).

66 B. Walker & B. C. Walker, *Privatization: Sell Off or Sell Out? The Australian Experience* (Sydney: ABC Books, 2000), Table 2.1, pp. 20–4.

67 Reserve Bank of Australia, *Statistical Bulletin*, Table HO3 Exports and Imports of Goods and Services, HO3hist.xls.

68 'Top exporters are going north', *Business Review Weekly*, 27 January (1997), pp. 48–68.

69 Changes in the definition of foreign direct investment post-1985, including lowering the threshold of equity holdings that qualify as being foreign direct investment from 25 to 10 per cent and valuing equity at market rather than book values, make comparisons before and after 1985 problematic. Australia Bureau of Statistics, *International Investment Position 1985–86*, Catalogue No. 5305.0 (Canberra: Australian Government Publishing Service, 1987).

70 The data come from a variety of sources including P. Yetton, J. Davis & P. Swan, *Going International: Export Myths and Strategic Realities*, Report to the Australian Manufacturing Council (North Ryde, NSW: Australian Graduate School of Management, 1992), Table 2.1, p. 13; 'Where our top 50 multinationals are investing', *Business Review Weekly*, 17 July (1995), pp. 20–4; G. Korporaal, *Yankee Dollars: Australian Investment in America* (Sydney: Allen & Unwin, 1986); D. Stace, *Reaching Out from Down Under: Building Competence for Global Markets* (Sydney: McGraw-Hill Companies, Inc., 1997); J. V. Langdale, *Internationalisation of Australia's Service Industries* (Canberra: Department of Industry, Technology and Commerce, Australian Government Publishing Service, 1991).

71 'Top 50 multinationals', *Business Review Weekly*, 17 July (1995), pp. 20–4; Appendix C.

72 Merrett, 'Australian firms abroad before 1970'; *idem*, 'Australia's emergent multinationals: The legacy of having a natural resource intensive, small and closed economy as home', *International Studies in Management and Organization*, 32, 1, Spring (2002b), pp. 109–35; *idem*, 'The internationalization of Australian banks', *Journal of International Financial Markets, Institutions and Money*, 12, 4–5, October/December (2002), pp. 377–97.

73 C. Wright, 'From shop floor to boardroom: The historical evolution of Australian management consulting, 1940s to 1980s', *Business History*, 42, 1 (2000), pp. 85–106.

74 J. Sinclair, 'Advertising' in S. Cunningham & G. Turner (eds), *The Media in Australia: Industries, Texts, Audiences* (St Leonards, NSW: Allen & Unwin, 1993), pp. 90–9.

75 Chandler, *Scale and Scope*; Chandler, Amatori & Hikino, *Big Business and the Wealth of Nations*.

76 W. A. Sinclair, *The Process of Economic Development in Australia* (Melbourne: Cheshire Publishing, 1976); I. W. McLean & A. Taylor, 'Australian growth: A Californian perspective', *NBER Working Paper Series*, Working Paper 8408, August (2001).

77 R. Maddock & I. W. McLean, 'The Australian economy in the very long run', in R. Maddock & I. W. McLean (eds), *The Australian Economy in the Long Run* (Cambridge University Press, 1987), pp. 5–29; A. Maddison, *Phases of Capitalist Development* (Oxford University Press, 1982).

78 N. G. Butlin, 'Some perspectives of Australian economic development, 1890–1965', in C. Forster (ed.), *Australian Economic Development in the Twentieth Century* (London: George Allen & Unwin, 1970), pp. 266–327; I. W. McLean & J. J. Pincus, 'Did Australian living standards stagnate between 1890 and 1940?', *Journal of Economic History*, 43, 1 (1983), pp. 193–202.

79 S. Dowrick & T. Nguyen, 'Measurement and international comparisons', in B. Chapman (ed.), *Australian Economic Growth: Essays in Honour of Fred H. Gruen* (South Melbourne: Macmillan, 1989), Table 2.1, pp. 36–7.

80 McLean and Taylor, 'Australian growth', p. 5.

81 Chandler, *Visible Hand*.

82 See O. E. Williamson, 'Strategizing, economizing, and economic organization', in R. P. Rumelt, D. E. Schendel & D. J. Teece (eds), *Fundamental Issues in Strategy: A Research Agenda* (Boston, MA: Harvard Business School, 1994), pp. 361–401.

83 Chandler, *Visible Hand*.

84 Madigan, *Technology in Australia 1788–1988, passim*; K. H. T. Farrer, *A Settlement Amply Supplied: Food Technology in Nineteenth Century Australia* (Melbourne University Press, 1980).

85 P. Gilmour (ed.), *Physical Distribution in Australia* (Melbourne: Cheshire, 1974); *idem*, (ed.), *Logistics Management in Australia* (Melbourne: Longman Cheshire, 1987); D. J. Bloomberg, A. Murray & J. B. Hanna, *The Management of Integrated Logistics: a Pacific Rim Perspective* (Sydney: Prentice Hall-Sprint Print, 1998, 2nd edn).

86 C. B. Schedvin, *Shaping Science and Industry: A History of Australia's Council for Scientific and Industrial Research* (Sydney: Allen & Unwin, 1987); T. G. Parry & J. F. Watson, 'Technology flows and foreign investment in the Australian manufacturing sector', *Australian Economic Papers*, 18, 32 (1979), pp. 103–18; T. G. Parry, 'Plant size, capacity utilisation and economic efficiency: foreign investment in the Australian chemical industry', *Economic Record*, 50 (1974), pp. 218–44.

87 D. C. North, *Institutions, Institutional Change and Economic Performance* (Cambridge University Press, 1990); T. Eggertsson, *Economic Behavior and Institutions* (Cambridge University Press, 1990).

88 S. M. Jacoby, *Employing Bureaucracy: Managers, Unions, and the Transformation of Work in Amercian Industry, 1900–1945* (New York: Columbia University Press, 1985).

89 F. R. E. Mauldon, 'Cooperation and welfare in industry', *The Annals of the American Academy of Political and Social Science*, 158 (1931), pp. 183–92.

90 A. Seltzer & D. T. Merrett, 'Human resource management practices at the Union Bank of Australia: panel evidence from the 1887–1893 entry cohorts', *Journal of Labor Economics*, 18, 4 (2000), pp. 573–61.

91 C. Wright, *The Management of Labour: A History of Australian Employers* (Melbourne: Oxford University Press, 1995).

92 *Commonwealth Year Book of Australia* (Canberra: Australian Government Printer, 1931).

93 *Three Decades: The Story of the State Electricity Commission of Victoria from its Inception to December 1948* (Melbourne: Hutchinson, 1949).

94 A. Pratt, *The National Handbook of Australian Industries* (Melbourne: Specialty Press, 1934); J. B. Were, *Were's Statistical Service 1933* (Melbourne); General Motors-Holden's annual report 1936; D. C. Cameron, *Hardie Investments Pty Ltd and Associated Companies 1888–1938* (Sydney: privately published); *B.H.P. Review Jubilee Number*, June (1935); Richardson, 'Collins House Group'.

95 M Keating, *The Australian Workforce 1910–11 to 1960–61* (Canberra: Australian National University, 1973), Table 3.14, p. 70.

96 Block, *The Delfin Digest 1967*, p. 1.

97 R. A. Foster, *Australian Economic Statistics, 1949–50 to 1994–95* (Sydney; Reserve Bank of Australia, 1996), Table 4.10c, p. 194.

98 E. L. Wheelwright, *Ownership and Control of Australian Companies: A Study of 102 of the Largest Public Companies Incorporated in Australia* (Sydney: Law Book Company of Australasia Pty Ltd, 1957), Table IIIC, p. 46; Davies & Peacock, 'The role of the stock exchange', Table 4.11, p. 110.

99 Davies & Peacock, 'The role of the stock exchange', Tables, 4.10–12, pp. 109–13.

100 M. Edey & J. Simon, 'Australia's retirement income system: implications for savings and capital markets', *Research Discussion Paper 9603* (Sydney: Reserve Bank of Australia, 1996).

101 See, for example, T. Sykes, *Two Centuries of Panic; idem, The Bold Riders; idem, Operation Dynasty: How Warwick Took John Fairfax Ltd* (Elwood, Vic: Greenhouse Publications, 1989); F. L. Clarke & G. W. Dean, *Corporate Collapse: Regulatory, Accounting and Ethical Failure* (Melbourne: Cambridge University Press, 1997); P. Barry, *The Rise and Fall of Alan Bond* (Sydney: Bantam Books, 1990); B. Ross, *The Ariadne Story: The Rise and Fall of a Business Empire* (Elwood, Vic: Greenhouse Publications, 1988); D. Janetzki, *The Gollin Years* (Burleigh Heads, Qld: privately published, 1989).

102 P. H. Karmel & M. Brunt, *The Structure of the Australian Economy* (Melbourne: F. W. Cheshire, 1962), pp. 54–102; R. Caves, I. Ward, P. Williams & C. Wright, *Australian Industry: Structure, Conduct, Performance* (Sydney: Prentice-Hall of Australia, 1981).

103 Nieuwenhuysen, 'Recent light on trade practices in Australia; A. Hunter, 'Restrictive practices and monopolies in Australia', in Nieuwenhuysen (ed.), *Australian Trade Practices*, pp. 169–201.

104 Briggs & Smyth, *Distribution of Groceries*, 20–3.

105 D. T. Merrett, 'Stability and change in the Australian brewing industry, 1920–1994', in R. G. Wilson & T. R. Gourvish (eds), *The Dynamics of the International Brewing Industry Since 1800* (London and New York: Routledge, 1998), pp. 229–46.

106 Karmel & Brunt, *Australian Economy*, p. 81.

107 Bushnell, *Australian Company Mergers*, chs 5, 8.

108 R. Dixon, 'The cost of monopoly in Australia', in P. Dawkins, M. Harris & S. King (eds), *How Big Business Performs: Private Performance and Public Policy* (St Leonards, NSW: Allen & Unwin in conjunction with the Melbourne Institute of Applied Economic and Social Research, 1999), p. 135.

109 N. Darwin, *The History of the Holden Since 1917* (Newstead, Vic.: E. L. Ford Publications P/L, 1983).

110 P. Stubbs, *The Motor Industry in Australia: A Study in Protection and Growth* (Melbourne: Cheshire for the Institute of Applied Economic and Social Research, University of Melbourne, 1972), Table 2.6, pp. 38–9.

111 C. D. Cameron, *History of James Hardie & Coy. Pty. Limited 1888–1966* (Sydney: Privately published), Appendix D.

112 Chandler, *Scale and Scope*; Chandler, Amatori & Hikino (eds), *Big Business and the Wealth of Nations*.

113 See, for example, H. L. Wilkinson, *The Trust Movement in Australia* (Sydney: Critchley Parker Pty Ltd, 1914); J. N. Rawlings, *Who Owns Australia?* (Sydney: Modern Publishers Pty Ltd, 1939, 4th edn); Research Department of the Left Book Club, *Monopoly* (Sydney, 1940); B. Fitzpatrick, *The Rich Get Richer: Facts of the Growth of Monopoly in the Economic Structure of Australia Before and During the War* (Melbourne: Rawson's Book Shop, 1944); E. W. Campbell, *The 60 Rich Families Who Own Australia* (Sydney: Current Book Distributors, 1963).

114 Karmel & Brunt, *Australian Economy*.

Bibliography

Alemson, M. A. (1970), 'Advertising and the nature of competition in oligopoly over time: a case study', *Economic Journal*, 80.

Arndt, H. W. & Sherk, D. R. (1959), 'Export franchises of Australian companies with overseas affiliations', *Economic Record*, 35.

Australia Bureau of Statistics (1987), *International Investment Position 1985–86*, Catalogue No. 5305.0 (Canberra: Australian Government Publishing Service).

Australian Manufacturing Council (1994), *Leading the Way: A Study of Best Manufacturing Practices in Australia and New Zealand* (Melbourne: Australian Manufacturing Council).

Bailey, G. (2000), *Mythologies of Change and Certainty in late-20th Century Australia* (Melbourne: Australian Scholarly Publishing).

Barker, T. (1986), 'Pilkington: The reluctant multinational', in G. Jones (ed.) *British Multinationals*.

Barnard, A. (1958), *The Australian Wool Market* (Melbourne University Press on behalf of the Australian National University).

Barney, J. B. (1991), 'Firm resources and sustained competitive advantage', *Journal of Management*, 17, 1.

Barry, B., Easton, S. & Pinder, S. (2001), 'The globalisation of capital markets: An empirical examination of the impact of foreign listing on the returns and systematic risk of equity securities', manuscript.

Barry, P. (1990), *The Rise and Fall of Alan Bond* (Sydney: Bantam Books).

Baskin, J. B & Miranti, P. J. (1997), *A History of Corporate Finance* (Cambridge University Press).

Bell, S. (1997), *Ungoverning the Economy: The Political Economy of Australian Economic Policy* (Melbourne: Oxford University Press).

Bell, S. (1993), *Australian Manufacturing and the State. The Politics of Industry Policy in the Post-War Era* (Cambridge University Press).

Bell, S. & Head, B. (eds) (1994), *State, Economy and Public Policy* (Melbourne: Oxford University Press).

Berger, P. G. & Ofek, E. (1995), 'Diversification's effect on firm value', *Journal of Financial Economics*, 37.

Bethel, J. E., Liebeskind, J. & Opler, T. (1998), 'Block share purchases and corporate performance', *Journal of Finance*, April, 53.

Bindon, G. & Miller, D. P. (1988), '"Sweetness and light": Industrial research in the Colonial Sugar Refining Company, 1855–1900', in R. W. Home (ed.), *Australian Science in the Making*.

Birch, A. & Blaxland, J. F. (1956), 'The historical background', in A. G. Lowndes (ed.) *South Pacific Enterprise.*

Bishop, S., Dodd, P. & Officer, R. R. (1987), *Australian Takeovers: the Evidence 1972–85,* Policy Monograph 12 (Sydney: Centre for Independent Studies).

Blainey, G. N. (1999), *A History of the Australian Mutual Provident, 1848–1998* (St Leonards, NSW: Allen & Unwin).

Blainey, G. N. (1997), *White Gold: The Story of Alcoa in Australia* (St Leonards, NSW: Allen & Unwin).

Blainey, G. N. (1993), *Jumping Over the Wheel* (St Leonards: Allen & Unwin).

Blainey, G. N. (1984), 'The history of multinational factories in Australia', in A. Okochi & T. Inoue (eds), *Overseas Business Activities* (Tokyo: University of Tokyo Press).

Blainey, G. N. (1971), *The Steel Master: A Life of Essington Lewis* (Melbourne: Macmillan).

Block, R. O. (ed.) (1967), *Delfin Digest 1967: The Top Companies in Australia, New Zealand and South East Asia* (Sydney: Development Finance Corporation Limited).

Block, R. O. (ed.) (1965), *Delfin Digest 1965: The Top Companies in Australia, New Zealand and South East Asia* (Sydney: Development Finance Corporation Limited).

Bloomberg, D. J., Murray, A. & Hanna, J. B. (1998), *The Management of Integrated Logistics: A Pacific Rim Perspective* (Sydney: Prentice Hall-Sprint Print), 2nd edn.

Boehm, E. A. (1971), *Twentieth-Century Economic Development in Australia* (Melbourne), 3rd edn (1993) (Melbourne: Longman Cheshire).

Bolton, P. & Scharfstein, D. (1998), 'Corporate finance, the theory of the firm, and organizations', *Journal of Economic Perspectives,* 12, 4.

Bonney, B. & Wilson, H. (1983), *Australia's Commercial Media* (South Melbourne: Macmillan).

Boyce, G. H. (2001), *Cooperative Structures in Global Business. Communicating, Transferring Knowledge and Learning across the Corporate Frontier* (London: Routledge).

Boyce, G. H. (2001), 'Multilateral contracting in Australian mining: the development of Hamersley Iron, 1961–1966', *Enterprise and Society,* 2.

Boyce, G. H. (1997), 'A joint exploration venture. Western Mining Corporation and Hanna/Homestake, 1960–72', *Australian Economic History Review,* 37, 3.

Boyce, G. H. (1997), 'The Western Mining Corporation-Hanna/Homestake joint venture: Game theory and inter-organisational cooperation', *Australian Economic History Review,* 37, 3.

Boyce, G. H. (1995), *Information, Mediation and Institutional Development. The Rise of Large-Scale Enterprise in British Shipping 1870–1919* (Manchester University Press).

Boyce, G. & Ville, S. (2002), *The Development of Modern Business* (Basingstoke: Palgrave).

Braddon, H. Y. (1921), *Business Principles and Practice (Australia)* (Sydney: W. Brookes and Co.)

Brash, D. T. (1966), *American Investment in Australian Industry* (Canberra: Australian National University Press).

Briggs, D. H. & Smyth, R. L. (1967), *Distribution of Groceries: Economic Aspects of the Distribution of Groceries with Special Reference to Western Australia* (Perth: University of Western Australia Press).

Brimson, S. (1987), *Ansett – the Story of an Airline* (Sydney: Dreamweaver Books).

Broomham, R. (1987), *First Light: 150 Years of Gas* (Sydney: Hale and Iremonger).

Brown, B. (1991), *I Excel! the Life and Times of Sir Henry Jones* (Hobart: Libra Books).

Brown, L. (1990), *Competitive Marketing Strategy: Developing, Maintaining and Defending Competitive Position* (South Melbourne: Thomas Nelson).

Brown, P. & Horin, A. (1986), 'Assessing competition in the market for corporate control: Australian evidence', *Australian Journal of Management*, 23.

Bruce, R., McKern, B. & Skully, M. (eds), *Handbook of Australian Corporate Finance* (Sydney: Butterworths), 5th edn.

Bryden-Brown, J. (1981), *Ads That Made Australia* (Lane Cove, NSW: Doubleday).

Buckley, K. & Klugman, K. (1983), *The Australian Presence in the Pacific: Burns Philp, 1914–1946* (Sydney: George Allen & Unwin).

Buckley, K. & Klugman, K. (1981), *The History of Burns Philp: The Australian Company in the South Pacific* (Sydney: Burns, Philp and Co Ltd).

Buckley, P. J. & Casson, M. C. (1998), 'Models of the multinational enterprise', *Journal of International Business Studies*, 29, 1.

Bureau of Industry Economics (1995), *Beyond the Firm. An Assessment of Business Linkages and Networks in Australia* (Canberra: Australian Government Publishing Service).

Bureau of Industry Economics (1993), *Multinationals and Governments. Issues and Implications for Australia* (Canberra: Australian Government Publishing Service).

Bureau of Industry Economics (1990), *Mergers and Acquisitions* (Canberra: Australian Government Publishing Service).

Bureau of Transport and Communications (1991), *Economic Aspects of Broadcasting Regulation* (Canberra: Australian Government Publishing Service).

Burn, P. (2000), 'Opportunism and long term contracting: transactions in Broken Hill zinc concentrates in the 1930s', in D. T. Merrett (ed.) *Business Institutions and Behaviour*.

Bushnell, J. A (1961), *Australian Company Mergers, 1946–59* (Melbourne University Press).

Butlin, N. G. (1970), 'Some perspectives of Australian economic development, 1890–1965', in C. Forster (ed.) *Australian Economic Development in the Twentieth Century*.

Butlin, N. G. (1964), *Investment in Australian Economic Development, 1861–1900* (Cambridge University Press).

Butlin, N. G., Barnard, A. & Pincus, J. J. (1982), *Government and Capitalism: Public and Private Choice in Twentieth Century Australia* (St Leonards, NSW: Allen & Unwin).

Butlin, S. J. (1986), *The Australian Monetary System 1851–1914* (Sydney: privately published).

Butlin, S. J., Hall, A. R. & White, R. C. (1971), *Australian Banking and Monetary Statistics 1817–1945* (Sydney: Reserve Bank of Australia).

Cameron, D. C. (n.d.), *Hardie Investments Pty. Ltd. and Associated Companies 1888–1938* (Sydney: privately published).

Cameron, D. C. (n.d.), *History of James Hardie and Coy. Pty. Limited 1888–1966* (Sydney: privately published).

Campa, J. & Kedia, S. (2002), 'Explaining the diversification discount', *Journal of Finance*, 57, 2.

Campbell, E. W. (1963), *The 60 Rich Families Who Own Australia* (Sydney: Current Book Distributors).

Capling, A. & Galligan, B. (1992), *Beyond The Protective State: The Political Economy of Australia's Manufacturing Industry Policy* (Cambridge University Press).

Capon, N., Christodoulou, C., Farley, J. U. & Hulbert, J. M. (1987), 'A comparative analysis of the strategy and structure of United States and Australian corporations', *Journal of International Business Studies*, Spring.

Carew, E. (1997), *Westpac. The Bank that Broke the Bank* (Sydney: Doubleday).

Carroll, B. (1988), *A Very Good Business. One Hundred Years of James Hardie Industries Ltd, 1888–1988* (Sydney: James Hardie Industries Ltd).

Carroll, B. (1987), *Australian Made: Success Stories in Australian Manufacturing since 1937* (Parkville: Institution of Production Engineers Australian Council).

Carroll, B. (1975), *The Australian Advertising Album* (South Melbourne: Macmillan).

Carroll, B. (1974), *The Australian Poster Album* (South Melbourne: Macmillan).

Casey, R., Dodd, P. & Dolan, P. (1987), 'Takeovers and corporate raiders: empirical evidence from extended event studies', *Australian Journal of Management*, 12.

Caves, R. E. (1984), 'Scale, openness and productivity in manufacturing industries', in R. E. Caves & L. B. Krause (eds), *The Australian Economy*.

Caves, R. E. & Krause, L. B. (eds) (1984), *The Australian Economy: The View from the North* (Sydney: Allen & Unwin).

Caves, R. E., Ward, I., Williams, P. & Wright, C. (1981), *Australian Industry: Structure, Conduct, Performance* (Sydney: Prentice-Hall of Australia).

Chadwick, P. (1989), *Media Mates: Carving Up Australia's Media* (South Melbourne: Macmillan).

Chandler, A. D. Jr (1990), *Scale and Scope: The Dynamics of Industrial Capitalism* (Cambridge, MA and London: Belknap Press of Harvard University Press).

Chandler, A. D. Jr (1977), *The Visible Hand: The Managerial Revolution in American Business* (Cambridge, MA and London: Belknap Press of Harvard University Press).

Chandler, A. D. Jr (1962), *Strategy and Structure: Chapters in the History of the American Industrial Enterprise* (Cambridge, MA and London: MIT Press).

Chandler, A. D. Jr, Amatori, F. & Hikino, T. (eds) (1997), *Big Business and the Wealth of Nations* (Cambridge University Press).

Chandler, A. D. Jr & Daems, H. (eds) (1980), *Managerial Hierarchies: Comparative Perspectives on the Rise of the Modern Industrial Enterprise* (Cambridge, MA: Harvard University Press).

Chandler, A. D. Jr & Hikino, T. (1997), 'The large industrial enterprise and the dynamics of modern economic growth', in A. D. Chandler, F. Amatori & T. Hikino (eds), *Big Business and the Wealth of Nations* (Cambridge University Press).

Chapman, B. (ed.) (1989), *Australian Economic Growth: Essays in Honour of Fred H. Gruen* (South Melbourne: Macmillan).

Chenhall, R. H. (1979), 'Some elements of organisational control in Australian divisionalised firms', *Australian Journal of Management*, 4, 1, Supplement.

Clark, G. L. (1983), *Built on Gold: Recollections of Western Mining* (Melbourne: Hill of Content Publishing).

Clark, L. (2002), *Finding a Common Interest: The Story of Dick Dusseldorp and Lend Lease* (Cambridge University Press).

Clarke, F. L., Deane, G. W. & Oliver, K. G. (1997), *Corporate Collapse: Regulatory, Accounting and Ethical Failure* (Melbourne: Cambridge University Press).

Commonwealth Treasury (1972), *Overseas Investment in Australia*, Treasury Economic Paper No. 1 (Canberra: Australian Government Publishing Service).

Conlon, R. & Perkins, J. (2001), *Wheels and Deals. The Automobile Industry in Twentieth-Century Australia* (Aldershot: Ashgate).

Contractor, F. J. & Lorange, P. (eds) (1989), *Cooperative Strategies in International Business* (Lexington MA: Lexington Books).

Cooling, B. F. (ed.) (1981), *War, Business and World Military-Industrial Complexes* (Port Washington, NY and London: Kennikat Press).

Core, J. E., Holthausen, R. W. & Larcker, D. F. (1999), 'Corporate governance, Chief Executive Officer compensation and firm performance', *Journal of Financial Economics*, 51.

Cunningham, S. & Turner, G. (eds) (1993), *The Media in Australia: Industries, Texts, Audiences* (St Leonards, NSW: Allen & Unwin).

d'Abbs, P. (n.d.), *The Vestey Story* (Melbourne: Australasian Meat Industry Employees' Union [Victorian Branch]).

da Silva Lopes, T. (2002), 'Brands and the evolution of multinationals in alcoholic beverages', *Business History*, 44, 3.

Darwin, N. (1983), *The History of the Holden Since 1917* (Newstead, Vic.: E. L. Ford Publications P/L).

David, P. A. (1985), 'Clio and the economics of QWERTY', *American Economic Review* (Papers and Proceedings), 75, 2.

Davies, P. & Peacock, D. (1997), 'The role of the stock exchange and financial characteristics of Australian companies', in R. Bruce, B. McKern & M. Skully (eds), *Handbook of Australian Corporate Finance*.

Davis, J. T. (ed.) (1997), *Forbes Top Companies* (New York: John Wiley and Sons, Inc.).

Davis, K. T. (1993), 'Corporate debt markets', in M. K. Lewis & R. H. Wallace, *The Australian Financial System* (Melbourne: Longman).

Dawkins, P., Harris, M. & King, S. (eds) (1999), *How Big Business Performs: Private Performance and Public Policy* (St Leonards, NSW: Allen & Unwin in conjunction with the Melbourne Institute of Applied Economic and Social Research).

Denis, D. J. & Sarin, A. (1999), 'Ownership and board structures in publicly traded corporations', *Journal of Financial Economics*, 52.

Department of National Development (1952), *The Structure and Capacity of Australian Manufacturing Industries* (Melbourne: Department of National Development).

Department of Trade and Industry (1971), *Directory of Overseas Investment in Australian Manufacturing Industry* (Canberra: Australian Government Publishing Service).

Department of Trade and Industry (1966), *Directory of Overseas Investment In Australian Manufacturing Industry* (Canberra: Australian Government Publishing Service).

Dixon, R. (1999), 'The cost of monopoly in Australia', in P. Dawkins, M. Harris & S. King (eds), *How Big Business Performs*.

Dodd, P. (1976), 'Company takeovers and the Australian equity market', *Australian Journal of Management*, 15.

Donovan, P. & Kirkman, N. (1986), *The Unquenchable Flame. South Australian Gas Company, 1861–1986* (Netley, SA: Wakefield Press).

Dowrick, S. & Nguyen, T. (1989), 'Measurement and international comparisons', in B. Chapman (ed.), *Australian Economic Growth*.

Drake, P. J. & Stammer, D. W. (1993), 'The stock exchange', in M. K. Lewis & R. H. Wallace, *The Australian Financial System* (Melbourne: Longman).

Dunning, J. H. (1993), *Multinational Enterprises and the Global Economy* (Wokingham: Addison-Wesley).

Dunstan, K. (1987), *The Amber Nectar. A Celebration of Beer and Brewing in Australia* (Melbourne: Viking O'Neil).

Dwyer, L. (1993), 'Government policy to promote industrial research and development: 1983–90', in G. Mahony (ed.), *The Australian Economy under Labor*.

Eddey, P. H. (1991), 'Corporate raiders and takeover targets', *Journal of Business Finance and Accounting* 18, 2.

Edelstein, M. (1989), 'Professional engineers and the Australian economy, 1866–1980', in Pope and Alston (eds), *Australia's Greatest Asset*.

Edey, M. & Simon, J. (1996), 'Australia's retirement income system: implications for savings and capital markets', *Research Discussion Paper 9603* (Sydney: Reserve Bank of Australia).

Eggertsson, T. (1990), *Economic Behavior and Institutions* (Cambridge University Press).

Eggleston, F. W. (1932), *State Socialism in Victoria* (London: P. S. King and Son).

Eleck, A., Camilleri, A. & Lester, M. (1989), 'Innovation and technological change in Australia: problems and prospects', in B. Chapman (ed.), *Australian Economic Growth*.

Emerson-Elliot, R., 'The Hume Pipe Company. Early internationalization by an Australian company', http://www.uow.edu.au/commerce/econ/modbusiness/Hume%20Pipe%20Company.pdf.

Emy, H. V. (1993), *Remaking Australia: The State, The Market and Australia's Future* (St Leonards, NSW: Allen & Unwin).

Fair Market or Market Failure? A Review of Australia's Retailing Sector (1999) (Canberra: Australian Government Publishing Service).

Fama, E. F. & Jensen, M. C. (1983), 'Separation of ownership and control', *Journal of Law and Economics*, 26.

Farrer, K. T. H. (1980), *A Settlement Amply Supplied: Food Technology in Nineteenth Century Australia* (Melbourne University Press).

Fauver, L., Houston, J. & Naranjo, A. (2002), 'Capital market development, integration, legal systems, and the value of corporate diversification: a cross-country analysis'. Paper to the Tuck-JFQA Contemporary Corporate Governance Issues II Conference.

Fieldhouse, D. K. (1978), *Unilever Overseas: The Anatomy of a Multinational 1895–1965* (London: Croom Helm).

Fitzpatrick, B. (1944), *The Rich Get Richer: Facts of the Growth of Monopoly in the Economic Structure of Australia Before and During the War* (Melbourne: Rawson's Book Shop).

Fitzpatrick, B. & Wheelwright, E. L. (1965), *The Highest Bidder: A Citizen's Guide to Problems of Foreign Investment in Australia* (Melbourne: Lansdowne).

Fleming, G. & Terwiel, D. (1999), 'How successful was early Australian antitrust legislation? Lessons from the Associated Northern Collieries, 1906–11', *Australian Business Law Review*, 27, 1.

Fleming, G. A., Oliver, B. R. & Skourakis, S. (2003), 'The valuation discount of multi-segment firms in Australia', *Accounting and Finance*, 43, 2.

Forster, C. (ed.) (1970), *Australian Economic Development in the Twentieth Century* (London: Allen & Unwin).

Forster, C. (1964), *Industrial Development in Australia 1920–1930* (Canberra: Australian National University).

Forsyth, P. (1992), 'Achieving reform in transport: land transport and the transport sector in general', in P. Forsyth (ed.), *Microeconomic Reform in Australia*.

Forsyth, P. (ed.) (1992), *Microeconomic Reform in Australia* (St Leonards, NSW: Allen & Unwin).

Foster, R. A. (1996), *Australian Economic Statistics 1949–50 to 1994–95* (Sydney: Reserve Bank of Australia).

Fountain, H. (2000), 'Technology acquisition, firm capability and sustainable competitive advantage: A case study of Australian Glass Manufacturers Ltd, 1915–39', in D. T. Merrett (ed.) *Business Institutions and Behaviour*.

Fraser, W. Hamish (1981), *The Coming of the Mass Market 1850–1914* (London: Macmillan).

Freeman, R. D. (1968), 'Trade associations in the Australian economy', in C. A. Hughes (ed.), *Readings in Australian Government*.

Fruin, W. M. (1992), *The Japanese Enterprise System. Competitive Strategies and Cooperative Structures* (Oxford: Clarendon Press).

Fysh, H. (1965), *Qantas Rising: the Autobiography of the Flying Fysh* (Sydney: Angus and Robertson).

Gabel, D. (1994), 'Competition in a network industry: The telephone industry, 1894–1910', *Journal of Economic History*, 54, 3.

Gepp, Sir H. (1939), 'The scientist in industrial administration', in H. Gepp, *Democracy's Danger* (Sydney and London: Angus and Robertson Limited).

Gerlach, M. L. (1992), *Alliance Capitalism. The Social Organization of Japanese Business* (Berkeley: University of California Press).

Gilmour, P. (ed.) (1987), *Logistics Management in Australia* (Melbourne: Longman Cheshire).

Gilmour, P. (ed.) (1974), *Physical Distribution in Australia* (Melbourne: Cheshire).

Golder, P. N. & Tellis, G. J. (1993), 'Pioneer advantage: marketing logic or marketing legend?', *Journal of Marketing Research*, 30, 2.

Goot, M. (1979), 'Newspaper circulation 1932–1977', in P. Spearritt & D. Walker (eds), *Australian Popular Culture* (Sydney: Allen & Unwin).

Grant, J. McB. (1963), 'The petroleum industry', in A. Hunter (ed.), *The Economics of Australian Industry*.

Grant, R. M. (1998), *Contemporary Strategy Analysis: Concepts, Techniques, Applications* (Oxford: Blackwell), 3rd edn.

Graubard, S. R. (ed.) (1985), *Australia: The Daedalus Symposium* (North Ryde, NSW: Angus and Robertson).

Gray, A. C. (1977), *Life Insurance in Australia: An Historical and Descriptive Account* (Melbourne: McCarron Bird).

Green, F. A. (1977), *The Port Pirie Smelters* (Melbourne: Broken Hill Associated Smelters).

Gunn, J. (1985), *The Defeat of Distance – Qantas 1919–1939* (St Lucia: University of Queensland Press).

Hall, A. R. (1956), *Australian Company Finance: Sources and Uses of Funds of Public Companies, 1946–1955* (Canberra: Australian National University).

Hall, A. R. (1963), *The London Capital Market and Australia, 1870–1914* (Canberra: Australian National University).

Hall, A. R. & White, R. C. (1971), *Australian Banking and Monetary Statistics 1917–1945* (Sydney, Reserve Bank of Australia).

Hambleton, R. (1987), *The Branding of America* (Camden, ME: Yankee Books).

Hamilton, C. (ed.) (1991), *The Economic Dynamics of Australian Industry* (St Leonards, NSW: Allen & Unwin).

Hannah, L. (1983), *The Rise of the Corporate Economy* (London and New York: Methuen), 2nd edn.

Harman, R. W. (1956), 'Men and organization', in A. G. Lowndes (ed.), *South Pacific Enterprise*.

Harrigan, K. R. & Porter, M. E. (1991), 'End game strategies for declining industries', in *Harvard Business Review* (1987), reprinted in *M. E. Porter on Competition and Strategy* (Boston, MA: Harvard Business School Press).

Hartwell, M. & Lane, J. (1991), *Champions of Enterprise. Australian Entrepreneurship, 1788–1990* (Sydney: Focus Books).

Hast, M. (1986), *100 Years of Power: The Lawrence and Hanson Story* (South Melbourne: Lawrence and Hanson).

Hatton, T. J. & Chapman, B. J. (1989), 'Apprenticeship and technical training', in Pope and Alston (eds), *Australia's Greatest Asset*.

Head, B. (ed.) (1983), *State and Economy in Australia* (Melbourne: Oxford University Press).

Henningham, J. (1993), 'The press', in Cunningham & Turner (eds), *The Media in Australia*.

Hewat, T. (1998), *The Elders Explosion. One Hundred and Fifty Years of Progress from Elder to Elliott* (Sydney: Bay Books).

Hirst, R. R. (1963), 'The transport industry', in A. Hunter (ed.), *Economics of Australian Industry*.

Hirst, R. R. & Wallace, R. H. (eds) (1964, revised edn 1974), *The Australian Capital Market* (Melbourne: Cheshire).

Hocking, D. M. (1958), 'Research – the economic implications', *Journal of the Australian Institute of Metals*, 3.

Holder, R. F. (1970), *Bank of New South Wales: A History* (Sydney: Angus and Robertson), 2 volumes.

Hogan, W. P. (1967), 'British investment in Australian manufacturing: The technical connections', *Manchester School of Economics and Social Studies*, 35.

Hogan, W. P. (1966), 'British manufacturing subsidiaries in Australia and export franchises', *Economic Papers*, 22.

Holderness, C. G. & Sheehan, D. P. (1988), 'The role of majority shareholders in publicly held corporations: An exploratory study', *Journal of Financial Economics*, 20.

Holst, (n.d.), *Australia's Top 300 Listed Companies Handbook 1993* (Melbourne: F. W. Holst and Co. Pty Ltd).

Home, R. W. (ed.) (1988), *Australian Science in the Making* (Cambridge: Cambridge University Press in association with the Australian Academy of Science).

Hubbard, G., Morkel, A., Davenport, S. & Beamish, P. (2000), *Cases in Strategic Management* (Frenchs Forest: Prentice Hall).

Hughes, C. A. (ed.) (1968), *Readings in Australian Government* (St Lucia: University of Queensland Press).

Hughes, H. (1964), *The Australian Iron and Steel Industry* (Melbourne University Press).

Hunter, A. (1970), 'Restrictive practices and monopolies in Australia', in J. Nieuwenhuysen (ed.) *Australian Trade Practices*.

Hunter, A. (ed.) (1963), *The Economics of Australian Industry: Studies in Environment and Structure* (Melbourne University Press).

Hunter, A. & Webb, L. R. (1963), 'The chemical industry', in A. Hunter (ed.), *Economics of Australian Industry*.

Hutchinson, D. (2001), 'Australian manufacturing business: entrepreneurship or missed opportunities?', *Australian Economic History Review*, 41, 2.

Hutchinson, D. (2000), 'The transformation of Boral: from dependent, specialist bitumen refiner to major building products manufacturer', in D. T. Merrett (ed.), *Business Institutions and Behaviour*.

Industry Commission (1992), *Commercial Restrictions on Exporting (Including Franchising)*, Report No. 23 (Canberra: Australian Government Publishing Service).

Jacoby, S. M. (1985), *Employing Bureaucracy: Managers, Unions, and the Transformation of Work in American Industry, 1900–1945* (New York: Columbia University Press).

Janetzki, D. (1989), *The Gollin Years* (Burleigh Heads, Qld: privately published).

Jensen, M. C. (1989), 'Eclipse of the public corporation', *Harvard Business Review*, 67, 5.

Jensen, M. C. (1993), 'The modern Industrial Revolution, exit, and the failure of internal control systems', *Journal of Finance*, 48, 3.

Johnman, L. (1986), 'The large manufacturing companies of 1935', *Business History*, 28.

Johnson, G. & Scholes, K. (2002) *Exploring Corporate Strategy* (Harlow: Financial Times and Prentice Hall)

Johnson, G. & Scholes, K. (eds) (1993), *Exploring Corporate Strategy: Text and Cases* (New York: Prentice Hall), 3rd edn.

Joint Industry Commission and Department of Industry, Science and Tourism (1997), *A Portrait of Australian Business: Results of the 1995 Business Longitudinal Survey* (Canberra: Australian Government Publishing Service).

Jones, G. (1997), 'Great Britain: big business, management and competitiveness in twentieth-century Britain', in A. D. Chandler, F. Amatori & T. Hikino (eds), *Business and the Wealth of Nations*.

Jones, G. (1996), *The Evolution of International Business: An Introduction* (London: Routledge).

Jones, G. (ed.) (1990), *Banks as Multinationals* (London: Routledge).

Jones, G. (ed.) (1986), *British Multinationals: Origins, Management and Performance* (Aldershot: Gower).

Jones, G. (1984), 'Multinational chocolate: Cadbury overseas, 1918–39', *Business History*, 26.

Jones, G. & Morgan, N. (eds) (1994), *Adding Value: Marketing and Brands in the Food and Drink Industries* (London: Routledge).

Jones, G. & Rose, M. B. (eds) (1993), *Family Capitalism*, special issue of *Business History*, 35, 4.

Kaplan, D. H. (1964), *Big Enterprise in a Competitive System*, revised edn (Washington, DC: Brookings Institution).

Kaplan, S. N. & Reishus, D. (1990), 'Outside directorships and corporate performance', *Journal of Financial Economics*, 27.

Karmel, P. H. & Brunt, M. (1962), *The Structure of the Australian Economy* (Melbourne: F. W. Cheshire).

Kay, J. (1993), *Foundations of Corporate Success. How Business Strategies Add Value* (New York: Oxford University Press).

Keating, M. (1973), *The Australian Workforce 1910–11 to 1960–61* (Canberra: Australian National University).

Keith Murdoch, Journalist (1952) (Melbourne: Herald & Weekly Times).

Kelly, P. (1992), *The End of Certainty: The Story of the 1980s* (St Leonards, NSW: Allen & Unwin).

Kemp, C. D. (1964), *Big Businessmen: Four Biographical Essays* (Melbourne: Institute of Public Affairs).

King, S. (2000), *From the Ground Up – Boral's First 50 Years* (Sydney: State Library of NSW Press).

Kirby, M. W. & Rose, M. B. (1994), 'Introduction', in M. W. Kirby & M. B. Rose (eds), *Business Enterprise in Modern Britain* (London: Routledge).

Korporaal, G. (1986), *Yankee Dollars: Australian Investment in America* (Sydney: Allen & Unwin).

Laird, P. W. (1998), *Advertising Progress: American Business and the Rise of Consumer Marketing* (Baltimore and London: Johns Hopkins University Press).

Lamoreaux, N. (1985), *The Great Merger Movement in American Business, 1895–1904* (Cambridge University Press).

Langdale, J. V. (1991), *Internationalisation of Australia's Service Industries* (Canberra: Department of Industry, Technology and Commerce, Australian Government Publishing Service).

Langfield-Smith, K. (1991), 'Carlton and United Breweries (A): The Australian brewing industry', in G. Lewis, A. Morkel & G. Hubbard (eds), *Cases in Australian Strategic Management*.

Lattimore, R. (1991), 'Research and development: Hidden investment in Australian Industry', in C. Hamilton (ed.), *The Economic Dynamics of Australian Industry*.

Lawrence, J. & Stapledon, G. (1999), 'Is board composition important? A study of listed Australian companies', manuscript.

Lawriwsky, M. L. (1978), *Ownership and control of Australian corporations* (Sydney: Transnational Corporations Research Project, University of Sydney).

Lazonick, W. & O'Sullivan, M. (eds) (2002), *Corporate Governance and Sustainable Prosperity* (Basingstoke: Palgrave).

Leiberman, M. B. and Montgomery, D. B. (1998), 'First mover (dis)advantages: retrospective and link with the resource-based view', *Strategic Management Journal*, 19.

Levy-Léboyer, M. (1980), 'The large corporation in modern France', in A. D. Chandler & H. Daems (eds), *Managerial Hierarchies*.

Lewis, G., Morkel, A. & Hubbard, G. (1993), *Australian Strategic Management. Concepts, Contexts and Cases* (New York, Prentice Hall).

Lewis, G., Morkel, A. and Hubbard, G. (eds) (1991), *Cases in Australian Strategic Management* (New York: Prentice Hall).

Lewis, M. K. & Wallace, R. H. (1993), *The Australian Financial System* (Melbourne: Longman).

Lincoln, M. & Burrows, G. (1975), *Australian Case Studies in Business Finance* (Sydney: McGraw Hill).

Lipton, M. & Lorsch, J. W. (1992), 'A modest proposal for improved corporate governance', *The Business Lawyer*, 48, 1.

Lowe, P. & Shuetrim, G. (1992), *The Evolution of Corporate Financial Structure 1973–1990*, Reserve Bank of Australia Research Discussion Paper No. 9216, December (Sydney).

Lowndes A. G. (ed.) (1956), *South Pacific Enterprise: The Colonial Sugar Refining Company* (Sydney: Angus and Robertson).

Ma, R. & Mathews R. L. (1974), 'Company finance', in R. R. Hirst & R. H. Wallace (eds), *The Australian Capital Market*.

Macintyre, S. F. (1983), 'Labour, capital and arbitration, 1890–1920', in B. Head (ed.), *State and Economy in Australia*.

MacKinnon, M. (1989), 'Schooling: examining some myths', in D. Pope & L. Alston (eds), *Australia's Greatest Asset*.

Maddison, A. (1991), *Dynamic Forces in Capitalist Development: A long-run comparative view* (Oxford University Press).

Maddison, A. (1982), *Phases of Capitalist Development* (Oxford University Press).

Maddock, R. (1992), 'Microeconomic reform of telecommunications: the long march from duolopy to duopoly', in P. Forsyth (ed.), *Microeconomic Reform*.

Maddock, R. & McLean, I. W. (eds) (1987), *The Australian Economy in the Long Run* (Cambridge University Press).

Maddock, R. & McLean, I. W. (1987), 'The Australian economy in the very long run', in R. Maddock & I. W. McLean (eds), *The Australian Economy in the Long Run*.

Madigan R. T. (1988), *Technology in Australia, 1788–1988: A Condensed History of Australian Technological Innovation and Adaptation During the First Two Hundred Years* (Melbourne: Australian Academy of Technological Sciences and Engineering).

Mahony, G. (ed.) (1993), *The Australian Economy under Labor* (St Leonards, NSW: Allen & Unwin).

Magee, G. B. (2000), *Knowledge Generation: Technological Change and Economic Growth in Colonial Australia* (Melbourne: Australian Scholarly Publishing).

Mathews, J. (1994), *Catching the Wave: Workplace Reform in Australia* (St Leonards, NSW: Allen & Unwin).

Mathews, R. & Harcourt, G. (1964) 'Company finance', in R. R. Hirst & R. H. Wallace (eds), *Studies in the Australian Capital Market*.

Mauldon, F. R. E. (1938), *Mechanisation in Australian Industries* (Hobart: University of Tasmania Department of Economics and Commerce).

Mauldon, F. R. E. (1931), 'Cooperation and welfare in industry', *The Annals of the American Academy of Political and Social Science*, 158, November.

Maxcy, G. (1963) 'The motor industry', in A. Hunter (ed.) *Economics of Australian Industry*.

McCraw, T. (ed.) (1995), *Creating Modern Capitalism* (Cambridge, MA and London: Harvard University Press).

McKern, R. B. (1976), *Multinational Enterprise and Natural Resources* (Sydney: McGraw-Hill Book Company).

McLean, I. (1991), 'Australian savings since 1861', in P. J. Stemp (ed.), *Saving and Policy* (Canberra: Centre for Economic Policy Research, Australian National University).

McLean, I. W. & Pincus, J. J. (1983), 'Did Australian living standards stagnate between 1890 and 1940?', *Journal of Economic History*, 43, 1.

McLean, I. W. & Taylor, A. M. (2001), 'Australian growth: A Californian perspective', *NBER Working Paper Series*, Working Paper 8408.

McNair, W. A. (1937), *Radio Advertising in Australia* (Sydney: Angus and Robertson).

McQueen, H. (2000), 'Pop goes the bottler! The Australian soft drink industry, 1945–65: a study in management, marketing and monopolisers', *Journal of Australian Political Economy*, 46.

Mellor, D. P. (1958), *The Role of Science and Industry* (Canberra: Australian War Memorial).

Merrett, D. T. (2002), 'Australian firms abroad before 1970: Why so few, why those and why there?', *Business History*, 44, 2.

Merrett, D. T. (2002), 'Australia's emergent multinationals: The legacy of having a natural resource intensive, small and closed economy as home', *International Studies in Management and Organization*, 32, 1.

Merrett, D. T. (2002), 'Corporate governance, incentives and the internationalization of Australian business', unpublished paper delivered to the Business History Conference, Hagley Museum and Library, Wilmington, DE, 19–21 April.

Merrett, D. T. (2002), 'The internationalization of Australian banks', *Journal of International Financial Markets, Institutions and Money*, 12, 4–5.

Merrett, D. T. (ed.) (2000), *Business Institutions and Behaviour in Australia* (London: Frank Cass).

Merrett, D. T. (2000), 'Business institutions and behaviour in Australia: A new perspective', in D. T. Merrett (ed.), *Business Institutions and Behaviour in Australia* (London: Frank Cass).

Merrett, D. T. (1998), 'Capital markets and capital formation in Australia, 1945–1990', *Australian Economic History Review*, 38, 2.

Merrett, D. T. (1998), 'Stability and change in the Australian brewing industry, 1920–1994', in R. G. Wilson & T. R. Gourvish (eds), *The Dynamics of the International Brewing Industry Since 1800*.

Merrett, D. T. (1997), 'Capital markets and capital formation in Australia, 1890–1945', *Australian Economic History Review*, 37, 3.

Merrett, D. T. (1995), 'Global reach by Australian banks: Correspondent banking networks, 1830–1960', *Business History* 37, 3.

Merrett, D. T. (1990), 'Paradise lost? British banks in Australia', in G. Jones (ed.), *Banks as Multinationals*.

Merrett, D. T. (1979), 'The Victorian Licensing Court 1906–68: A study of its role and impact', *Australian Economic History Review*, 29, 2.

Merrett, D. T. & Houghton, K. A. (1999), 'Takeovers and corporate governance: whose interests do directors serve?', *ABACUS*, 35, 2.

Merrett, D. T. & Schedvin, C. B. (1981), 'Australia: dependence at the periphery', in B. F. Cooling (ed.) *War, Business and World Military-Industrial Complexes*.

Merrett, D. T. & Whitwell, G. (1994), 'The empire strikes back: marketing Australian beer and wine in the United Kingdom', in Jones & Morgan (eds), *Adding Value*.

Morkel, A. (1991), 'AMATIL Ltd', in G. Lewis, A. Morkel & G. L. Hubbard, (eds), *Cases in Australian Strategic Management*.

Mowery, D. C. & Nelson, R. R. (eds) (1999), *Sources of Industrial Leadership: Studies of Seven Industries* (Cambridge University Press).

Mowery, D. C. & Rosenberg, N. (1998), *Paths of Innovation: Technological Change in 20th-Century America* (Cambridge University Press).

Moyal, A. (1984), *Clear Across Australia. A History of Telecommunications* (Melbourne: Thomas Nelson).

Mueller, D. C. (1997), 'First mover advantages and path dependence', *International Journal of Industrial Organisation*, 15.

Murphy, M. (1984), *Challenges of Change: The Lend Lease Story* (Sydney: Lend Lease Corporation).

Myers, S. (2001), 'Capital structure', *Journal of Economic Perspectives*, 15, 2.

Myers, S. & Majluf, N. (1984), 'Corporate financing and investment decisions when firms have information that investors do not have', *Journal of Financial Economics*, 13.

Nelson, R. L. (1959), *Merger Movements in American Industry 1895–1956* (Princeton University Press).

Nelson, R. R. (1994), 'Why do firms differ, and how does it matter?', in R. P. Rumelt, D. E. Schendel & D. J. Teece (eds), *Fundamental Issues in Strategy*.

Nelson, R. & Mowery, D. (eds) (1999), *Sources of Industrial Leadership. Studies of Seven Industries* (Cambridge University Press).

Nestlé Alimentana Company (1946), *This is Your Company, Nestlé and Anglo-Swiss Holding Company* (Vevey, Switzerland: Nestlé and Anglo-Swiss Holding Co).

Nieuwenhuysen, J. (1982), *The Effects of Mergers on Australian Industry: a First Stage Report* (Canberra: DITAC).

Nieuwenhuysen, J. P. (ed.) (1970), *Australian Trade Practices: Readings* (Melbourne: F. W. Cheshire).

Nieuwenhuysen, J. P. (1970), 'Recent light on trade practices in Australia', in J. Nieuwenhuysen (ed.), *Australian Trade Practices*.

North, D. C. (1990), *Institutions, Institutional Change and Economic Performance* (Cambridge University Press).

Norton, J. E. & Willcocks, L. (1993), 'The News Corporation', in G. Johnson and K. Scholes (eds), *Exploring Corporate Strategy*.

Olson, M. (1971), *Logic of Collective Action: Public Goods and the Theory of Groups* (Cambridge MA: Harvard University Press).

Okochi, A. & Inoue, T. (eds) (1984), *Overseas Business Activities: Proceedings of the Fiji Conference* (University of Tokyo Press).

Page, M. F. (1975), *Fitted for the Voyage: The Adelaide Steamship Company 1875–1975* (Adelaide: Rigby).

Parry, T. G. (1974), 'Plant size, capacity utilisation and economic efficiency: foreign investment in the Australian chemical industry', *Economic Record*, 50, June.

Parry, T. G. & Watson, J. F. (1979), 'Technology flows and foreign investment in the Australian manufacturing sector', *Australian Economic Papers*, 18, 32.

Parsons, R. (1975), *The Adelaide Line: a Centenary History of the Adelaide Steamship Company Ltd., 1875–1975* (Magill, SA: R. H. Parsons).

Payne, P. L. (1967), 'The emergence of the large-scale company in Great Britain, 1870–1914', *Economic History Review*, 2nd Ser., 20.

Pinkstone, B. (1992), *Global Connections: A History of Exports and the Australian Economy* (Canberra: Australian Government Publishing Service).

Pohl, H. (ed.) (1988), *The Concentration Process in the Entrepreneurial Economy since the Late Nineteenth Century* (Stuttgart: German Society for Business History).

Pope, D. (1987), 'Private Finance', in W. Vamplew (ed.), *Australians. Historical Statistics*.

Pope, D. & Alston, L. (eds) (1989), *Australia's Greatest Asset: Human Resources in the Nineteenth and Twentieth Centuries* (Annandale, NSW: The Federation Press).

Porter, M. E. (1990), *The Competitive Advantage of Nations* (London: Macmillan).

Porter, M. (1985), *Competitive Advantage. Creating and Sustaining Superior Performance* (New York: Free Press).

Potter, I. and Co. (1972), *Australian Company Reviews* (Melbourne: Ian Potter and Co).

Powell, W. W. (1990) 'Neither market nor hierarchy: network forms of organisation', *Research in Organisational Behaviour*, 12.

Prahalad, C. K. & Hamel, G. (1990), 'The core competencies of the corporation', *Harvard Business Review*, May–June.

Pratt, A. (1934), *The National Handbook of Australian Industries* (Melbourne: Specialty Press).

Prest, W. (1963), 'The electricity supply industry', in A. Hunter (ed.), *Economics of Australian Industry*.

Proudley, R. (1987), *Circle of Influence: A History of the Gas Industry in Victoria* (North Melbourne: Hargreen Publishing Company in association with Gas and Fuel Corporation of Victoria).

Pusey, M. (1991), *Economic Rationalism in Canberra: A Nation Building State Changes Its Mind* (Cambridge University Press).

Quiggin, J. (1996), *Great Expectations: Microeconomic Reform and Australia* (St Leonards: Allen & Unwin).

Rawlings, J. N. (1939), *Who Owns Australia?* (Sydney: Modern Publishers Pty Ltd), 4th edn.

Renew, R. (1993), *Making It: Innovation and Success in Australia's Industries* (Sydney: Power House Museum).

Research Department of the Left Book Club (1940), *Monopoly* (Sydney).

Reserve Bank of Australia (1997), 'Privatisation in Australia', *Reserve Bank of Australia Bulletin*, December.

Rich, J. (1996), *Hartnett: Portrait of a Technocratic Brigand* (Sydney: Turton and Armstrong).

Richardson, P. (1987), 'The origins and development of the Collins House Group 1915–1951', *Australian Economic History Review*, 27, 1.

Rolfe, H. (1967), *The Controllers: Interlocking Directories in Large Australian Companies* (Melbourne: F. W. Cheshire).

Rosenstein, S. & Wyatt, J. G. (1990), 'Outside directors, board independence, and shareholder wealth', *Journal of Financial Economics*, 26.

Ross, B. (1988), *The Ariadne Story: The Rise and Fall of a Business Empire* (Elwood, Vic: Greenhouse Publications).

Roy, W. G. (1997), *Socializing Capital* (Princeton University Press).

Rugman, A. & Verbeke, A. (1990), *Global Corporate Strategy and Trade Policy* (London: Routledge).

Rumelt, R. P., Schendel, D. E. & Teece, D. J. (eds) (1994), *Fundamental Issues in Strategy: A Research Agenda* (Boston, MA: Harvard Business School).

Sampson, A. (1984), *Empires of the Skies: the Politics, Contests and Cartels of World Airlines* (London: Hodder and Stoughton).

Sargent, S. (1985), *The Foodmakers* (Ringwood, Vic: Penguin).

Schapper, H. P. (1982), 'The farm workforce', in D. B. Williams (ed.) *Agriculture in the Australian Economy*.

Schedvin, C. B. (1987), *Shaping Science and Industry: A History of Australia's Council for Scientific and Industrial Research, 1926–49* (St Leonards, NSW: Allen & Unwin).

Schedvin, C. B. (1970), *Australia and the Great Depression: A Study of Economic Development and Policy in the 1920s and 1930s* (Sydney University Press).

Scherer, F. M. & Ross, D. (1990), *Industrial Market Structure and Economic Performance* (Boston: Houghton Mifflin Company).

Schmitz, C. J. (1993), *The Growth of Big Business in the United States, and Western Europe, 1850–1939* (Basingstoke: Macmillan).

Schmitz, C. J. (1995), 'The world's largest industrial companies of 1912', *Business History* 37, 4.

Schneider, M. (1974), 'Trade credit', in R. R. Hirst & R. H. Wallace (eds), *Australian Capital Market*.

'Secondary Industries Testing and Research – Extension of Activities of Council for Scientific and Industrial Research', Report (1937), *Commonwealth of Australia. Papers presented to Parliament*, 1937–38, IV.

Seltzer, A. & Merrett, D. T. (2000), 'Human resource management practices at the Union Bank of Australia: panel evidence from the 1887–1893 entry cohorts', *Journal of Labor Economics*, 18, 4, October.

Selznick, P. (1957), *Leadership in Administration: A Sociological Interpretation* (New York: Harper and Row).

Sheehan, P. J., Pappas, N., Tikhomirova, G. & Sinclair, P. (1995), *Australia and the Knowledge Economy: An Assessment of the Enhanced Economic Growth through Science and Technology* (Melbourne: Victoria University, Centre for Strategic Economic Studies).

Shell in Australia: the Story of a Great Achievement (1928) (Melbourne: Shell Company of Australia).

Sheridan, K. (1968), 'An estimate of the business concentration of Australian manufacturing industries', *Economic Record* 44, 105.

Sheridan, K. (1974), *The Firm in Australia: A Theoretical and Empirical Study of Size, Growth and Profitability* (Melbourne: Nelson).

Shoebridge, N. (1992), *Great Australian Advertising Campaigns* (Sydney: McGraw-Hill Book Company).

Shome, D. K. & Singh, S. (1995), 'Firm value and external blockholdings', *Financial Management*, 24.

Sinclair, E. K. (1990), *The Spreading Tree: A History of APM and AMCOR 1844–1989* (North Sydney: Allen & Unwin).

Sinclair, J. (1993), 'Advertising', in Cunningham & Turner (eds), *The Media in Australia*.

Sinclair, W. A. (1976), *The Process of Economic Development in Australia* (Melbourne: Cheshire).

Snooks, G. D. (1973), 'Innovation and the growth of the firm: Hume enterprises, 1910–40', *Australian Economic History Review*, 13, 1.

Spearritt, P. & Walker, D. (eds) (1979), *Australian Popular Culture* (Sydney: Allen & Unwin).

Stace, D. (1997), *Reaching Out from Down Under: Building Competence for Global Markets* (Sydney: McGraw-Hill Companies, Inc.).

Stalk, G., Evans, P. & Shulman, L. E. (1992), 'Competing on capabilities: The new rules of corporate strategy', *Harvard Business Review*, March–April.

Stanton, J. (1984), 'Protection, market structure and firm behaviour: inefficiency in the early Australian tyre industry', *Australian Economic History Review*, 24, 2.

Stapledon, G., Easterbrook, S., Bennett, P. & Ramsey, I. (2000), *Proxy Voting in Australia's Largest Companies* (Centre for Corporate Law and Securities Regulation, and Corporate Governance International Pty Limited).

Stemp, P. J. (ed.) (1991), *Saving and Policy* (Canberra: Centre for Economic Policy Research, Australian National University).

Stewart, I. C. (1975), 'Australian company mergers: 1960–70', *Economic Record*, March.

Stichtenoth, M. (1986), 'The 100 Largest Australian domiciled companies, 1920–52: evidence and conjectures' (Honours thesis, Department of Economic History, Monash University).

Strasser, S. (1989), *Satisfaction Guaranteed: The Making of the American Mass Market* (New York: Pantheon Books).

Streeten, H. (1985), 'The quality of leading Australians', in S. Graubard (ed.), *Australia*.

Stubbs, P. (1980), *Technology and Australia's Future: Industry and International Competitiveness* (Melbourne: Australian Industry Development Association Research Centre Publication).

Stubbs, P. (1972), *The Motor Industry in Australia: A Study in Protection and Growth* (F. W. Cheshire for the Institute of Applied Economic and Social Research, University of Melbourne).

Stubbs, P. (1968), *Innovation and Research: A Study in Australian Industry* (F. W. Cheshire for the Institute of Applied Economic Research University of Melbourne).

Sykes, T. (1994), *The Bold Riders: Behind Australia's Corporate Collapses* (St Leonards, NSW: Allen & Unwin), 2nd edn (1996).

Sykes, T. (1989), *Operation Dynasty: How Warwick Took John Fairfax Ltd* (Elwood, Vic: Greenhouse Publications).

Sykes, T. (1988), *Two Centuries of Panic: A History of Corporate Collapses in Australia* (Sydney: Allen & Unwin).

Taylor, G. D. & Baskerville, P. A. (1994), *A Concise History of Business in Canada* (Toronto: Oxford University Press).

Tedlow, R. S. (1988), 'The struggle for dominance in the automobile market: the early years of Ford and General Motors', *Business and Economic History*, 18.

Three Decades: The Story of the State Electricity Commission of Victoria from its Inception to December 1948 (1949) (Melbourne: Hutchinson).

Timms, J. C. (1940), *Australian and New Zealand Advertising* (Melbourne: Sir Isaac Pitman and Sons).

Todd, J. (1998), 'Cars, paint, and chemicals: industry linkages and the capture of overseas technology between the wars', *Australian Economic History Review*, 38, 2.

Tomasic, R., Jackson, J. & Woellner, R. (1996), *Corporations Law: Principles, Policy and Process* (Sydney: Butterworths).

Treasury (1986), *Some Economic Implications of Takeovers*, Economic Paper 12 (Canberra: Australian Government Publishing Service).

Trengove, A. (1975), *What's Good for Australia: The Story of BHP* (Stanmore, NSW: Cassell).

Tsokhas, K. (1984), *A Class Apart. Businessmen and Australian Politics, 1960–80* (Oxford University Press).

Tsokhas, K. (1986), *Beyond Dependence. Companies. Labour Processes and Australian Mining* (Melbourne: Oxford University Press).

Vamplew, W. (ed.) (1987), *Australians: Historical Statistics* (Broadway, NSW: Fairfax, Syme and Weldon Associates).

Ville, S. (2000), *The Rural Entrepreneurs. A History of the Stock and Station Agent Industry in Australia and New Zealand* (Cambridge University Press).

Ville, S. P. & Fleming, G. A. (2000), 'Financial intermediaries and the design of loan contracts in the Australasian pastoral sector', *Financial History Review*, 7.

Ville, S. & Fleming, G. (1999), 'Locating Australian corporate memory', *Business History Review* 73, 2.

Ville, S. & Merrett, D. T. (2000), 'The development of large scale enterprise in Australia, 1910–64', *Business History*, 42, 3.

Walker, K. F. (1956), *Industrial Relations in Australia* (Cambridge, MA: Harvard University Press).

Walker, B. & Walker, B. C. (2000), *Privatisation: Sell Off or Sell Out? The Australian Experience* (Sydney: ABC Books).

Wallace, R. H. (1993), 'The business financiers: merchant banks and finance companies', in M. K. Lewis & R. H. Wallace, *The Australian Financial System* (Melbourne: Longman).

Walter, T. (1984), 'Australian takeovers: capital market efficiency and shareholder risk and return', *Australian Journal of Management*, 9, 63.

Wardley, P. (1999), 'The emergence of big business: the largest corporate employers of labour in the United Kingdom, Germany and the United States, c.1907', *Business History*, 41, 4.

Wardley, P. (1991), 'The anatomy of big business: aspects of corporate development in the twentieth century', *Business History*, 33, 2.

Welch, L. S. & Luostarien, R. (1988), 'Internationalisation: evolution of a concept', *Journal of General Management*, 14, 2.

Were, J. B. (1964), *The Transport Industry in Australia* (Melbourne: J. B. Were).

Wheelwright, E. L. (1957), *Ownership and Control of Australian Companies: A Study of 102 of the Largest Public Companies Incorporated in Australia* (Sydney: Law Book Company of Australasia).

Wheelwright, E. L. & Miskelly, J. (1967), *Anatomy of Australian Manufacturing Industry: The Ownership and Control of 300 of the Largest Manufacturing Companies in Australia* (Sydney: Law Book Co.).

White, R. C. (1973), *Australian Banking and Monetary Statistics, 1945–70* (Sydney: Reserve Bank of Australia).

Wilkinson, H. L. (1914), *The Trust Movement in Australia* (Sydney: Critchley Parker Pty Ltd).

Williams, D. B. (ed.) (1982), *Agriculture in the Australian Economy* (Sydney University Press), 2nd edn.

Williams, J. (1994), 'Strategy and the search for rents: The evolution of diversity amongst firms', in R. P. Rumelt, D. E. Schendel & D. J. Teece (eds), *Fundamental Issues in Strategy*.

Williamson, O. (1970), *Corporate Control and Business Behavior* (New Jersey: Prentice Hall).

Williamson, O. E. (1994), 'Strategizing, economizing, and economic organization', in R. P. Rumelt, D. E. Schendel & D. J. Teece (eds), *Fundamental Issues in Strategy*.

Wills, N. R. (1963), 'The basic iron and steel industry', in A. Hunter (ed.) *The Economics of Australian Industry*.

Wilson, R. G. & Gourvish, T. R. (eds) (1998), *The Dynamics of the International Brewing Industry Since 1800* (London: Routledge).

Wilson, T. (1986), *Years of Grace: The First Fifty Years in Australia* (South Yarra, Vic: T. Wilson Publishing Company).

World Investment Report 1997: Transnational Corporations, Market Structure and Competition Policy (New York: United Nations).

World Investment Report 2000: Cross-border Mergers and Acquisitions and Development (2000) (New York: United Nations).

Wright, C. (2000), 'From shop floor to boardroom: The historical evolution of Australian management consulting, 1940s to 1980s', *Business History*, 42, 1.

Wright, C. (1995), *The Management of Labour: A History of Australian Employers* (Melbourne: Oxford University Press).

Wright, J. (1998), *Heart of the Lion: The 50 Year History of Australia's Holden* (St. Leonards: Allen & Unwin).

Yetton, P., Davis, J. & Swan, P. (1992), *Going International: Export Myths and Strategic Realities*. Report to the Australian Council (North Ryde, NSW: Australian Graduate School of Management).

Young, Sir N. (1991), *Figuratively Speaking: The Reminiscences, Experiences and Observations of Sir Norman Young* (Adelaide: published by the author).

Tables and Figures

Index

An index of the names of principal companies and individuals follows the Subjects index.